Dictionary of Sexual Slang

Dictionary of Sexual Slang

Words, Phrases, and Idioms
from AC/DC to Zig-zig

Alan Richter, Ph.D.

John Wiley & Sons, Inc.
New York • Chichester • Brisbane • Toronto • Singapore

Maps by Ted Dawson

Quotation from "my sweet old etcetera" by e.e. cummings
on page 74:

> Reprinted from IS 5 poems by E.E. Cummings, edited by George James Firmage,
> by permission of Liveright Publishing Corporation, Copyright © 1985 by E.E.
> Cummings Trust. Copyright 1926 by Horace Liveright. Copyright 1954 by E.E.
> Cummings. Copyright © 1985 by George James Firmage. British Commonwealth
> excluding Canada, © HarperCollins Publishers Limited.

In recognition of the importance of preserving what has been written, it is a policy of
John Wiley & Sons, Inc., to have books of enduring value printed on acid-free paper,
and we exert our best efforts to that end.

Library of Congress Cataloging-in-Publication Data:

Richter, Alan
   Dictionary of sexual slang: words, phrases, and idioms
  from AC/DC to zig-zig / Alan Richter.
     p. cm.
  Includes bibliographical references.
  ISBN 0-471-54057-9
    1. Sex—Terminology. 2. Sex—Slang—Dictionaries. I. Title.
HQ9.R53 1992
306.7'03—dc20   92-6316

Printed in the United States of America

10 9 8 7 6 5 4 3 2 1

For Meredith

Preface

My fascination with sexual language began in an indirect way. I finished a doctorate in philosophy at Birkbeck College, London University, in the late 1970s, and became instantly unemployed. After some wider exploration, beyond the handful of unattainable philosophy teaching posts, I ended up as a neophyte lexicographer on an English dictionary project.

Besides learning much about language and lexicography, I was struck with the realization that about every third word in the English language has, or has had, a sexual meaning or connotation, or so it seemed. As a quick test, here's the complete list of core words for the letter K from a dictionary of English for "second language" learners that uses approximately 1,500 core words to define the rest of the entries (words with sexual meaning are in bold type):

keen, keep, key, kick, kill, kilo, **king, kiss, kitchen, knee, kneel,** knife, **knock, knot,** and **know**. Of the fifteen words in this list, eleven, or over 70 percent, have sexual meanings. Of course, the percentage will vary with the letters of the alphabet, but the notion that every third word has a sexual meaning is not farfetched if we focus on basic English.

My interest in the language of sexuality led to my first book on the subject, *The Language of Sexuality* (McFarland, 1987), which primarily dealt with the philosophy, sociology, and metaphor underlying sexual terminology. Included at the back of the book was a glossary of over a thousand terms and phrases. It was this glossary that caught the eye of Steve Ross, my editor at Wiley, by way of Lee Gelber and Kim Hendrickson. Steve shared my vision of taking the glossary and turning it into a fuller dictionary with quotations to enliven the definitions.

This has been an enjoyable project; I have sought to include quotes ranging from Chaucer to Madonna, all with the aim of both illustrating word usage and entertaining the reader. I hope I have done so—at least with every third word.

Acknowledgments

I wish to thank the following people for their generous help in providing me with sources for quotations in this book: Jonathan Bass, Martin and Virginia Davis, Merryl Futerman, Lee Gelber, Richard, Elaine and Alex Kahn, Jonathan Katz, Beth Krieger, Pat and Nef Martinez, Steve Pred, Annie Robinson, Kenny and Barbara Sachar, and Elliott Shapiro.

My thanks also to Margaret Harter, head of Information Services at the Kinsey Institute for Research in Sex, Gender and Reproduction at Indiana University, Bloomington, Indiana; Bill Schurk, at the Music Library and Sound Recordings Archives, Bowling Green State University, Bowling Green, Ohio; and Penny Silva, editor and executive director of the *Dictionary of South African English*, Rhodes University, Grahamstown, South Africa.

I also wish to thank Post-It™ notes from 3M for making a write-on sticker that greatly helped me locate material in the myriad books I surveyed, and the New York City Public Library simply for having so many books available.

Contents

Introduction

Language and sexuality are central features of our lives. This book is concerned with their point of intersection. In a broad sense the language of sexuality includes body language, gestures, and all other forms of communication, in addition to words and expressions. But this book focuses exclusively on the words and phrases that have come to have sexual meanings in English over the past 500 years or so. Throughout, I have striven to provide their origins and meanings, and the metaphors expressed through them. This book, then, is a catalogue of the wonderfully varied English language as it has evolved and been applied to sexuality.

Many languages could probably support a whole book about their sexual terms and phrases. But no other language can rival the variety, color, or sheer number of sexual terms to be found in English. Not only is the history of the English language long (almost a thousand years) and complex, but English has successfully assimilated many other languages (Anglo-Saxon, Celtic, Latin, Scandinavian, French) and continues to borrow widely. Furthermore, English has been spoken in vastly spread-out geographic locations over long periods of time, making its dialects extraordinarily rich.

In any perusal of the rich language of sexuality, two notions quickly become evident. The first is how blatantly male-centered much of sexual language is. Karl Marx said that the ideas of the ruling class are the ruling ideas. That is true also of language: the language of the ruling class is the ruling language. Think of the connotations of the pair of terms *master* and *mistress*—these terms, purportedly opposites, are far from being equal or balanced with regard to positive associations and power. While recognizing this imbalance, I have, as a rule, tried to be descriptive of the language and its use, rather than prescriptive, that is, informing how it ought to be. At times the prescriptive pull might have gotten the better of me. In addition to being male-centered, English sexual terminology reflects a heterosexual-dominant perspective. Again, I have tried to be descriptive.

The second notion that becomes evident is the pervasiveness, range, and creativity of metaphor. Metaphor provides us with ways in which to understand the world, ourselves, and our thoughts and feelings. A metaphor allows us to understand and experience one thing in terms of another thing that is clear or basic. For example, through our experience of the animal world, food and eating, sports, etc., we can sometimes better understand sexuality (and other areas of human life) in those terms. Animality, for example, is a common and pervasive metaphor in the expression of sexual concepts. To **goose**, to **tup**, the **beast with two backs**, and **dog's rig** are all expressions that, at one time or another, were used to describe sexual intercourse. Similarly, **cat, civet**, and **periwinkle** are terms for the female genitals, while **donkey, python**, and **rooster** are terms for the penis. The Sexual Metaphor Matrix that follows provides a fuller picture. All of the metaphoric terms in the matrix can be found in this dictionary.

The first five metaphoric themes are from the natural world, in which sexuality itself is firmly rooted. The body, animality, nature, death, and food and eating form the basis for much of our lives. That is not to say that food and eating, for example, have not become enculturated. Perhaps aggression and war are natural, too, although some might consider war cultural. Religion, sport, music, and names are all cultural themes that provide a rich supply of sexual metaphor. For a review of place names with sexual meanings, see the maps on pages xvi and xvii.

So sexuality encompasses both nature and culture. On the cultural side, the theme of religion raises the issue of morality, which is closely entwined with our understanding of sexuality. But regardless of how cultures and religions have varied with respect to sexuality, the notion of the acceptable and the taboo, or the sacred and the profane, has always been present in all human societies. And just as sexual practices are either acceptable or not, so too is sexual language. In general, since sexuality is in so many ways a taboo subject, much of sexual language has been vulgar or taboo, that is, regarded as dirty. Mary Douglas, in a different context, defined dirt as "matter out of place." That definition captures much of what sexual language is about.

There is nothing inherently "dirty," say, about the term **grind**; it has a long history, and at bottom is simply five letters strung together with a set of meanings and connotations, some sexual, some not. In some contexts using this term in its sexual sense is "in place," but in many contexts (in business, with children, etc.) it is regarded as "out of place" and hence "dirty." The point is that such words are not inherently dirty; only their context makes them so.

Sexual language in English ranges from formal and standard terms through euphemistic, colloquial, and informal terms to slang, vulgar, and taboo terms and expressions. Together they make up the rich language of sexuality and the wealth of sexual synonyms. Because of the ways in which English-speaking societies have treated sexuality over the centuries, a large body of

Sexual Metaphor Matrix

Theme	Metaphor	Metaphoric Term For Sexual Intercourse	For Female Genitals	For Penis	For Other Sexual Concepts
Body	Sex is embodied	ear, foot, leg business	eye, hot lips, dimple	bone, best leg of three, nose	lungs, bent wrist, tongue
Animality	Sexuality is animality	dog's rig, goose and duck, rabbit	cat, cockles, oyster	cock, donkey, lizard	bitch, wolf, zoo
Nature	Sex is part of nature	nature's duty, exchange DNA, root	rose, star, garden	stem, stalk, tree of life	petal, stones, mountains
Death	Sex is ultimate; sex is an end	sweet death, bury the bone, lie in state	box, undertaker, everlasting wound	devil, stiff, life preserver	die, infanticide, little death
Food/Eating	Sex is consuming; sex is appetite	fork, bit of cauliflower, spoon	bread, cabbage, cake	banana, baloney, cucumber	fruit, melons, vegetable
Aggression and War	Sex is conquest; sex is attack/ being attacked	impale, charge, screw	arsenal, fort, target	club, weapon, bayonet	bullets, barbettes, break and enter
Religion	Sex is sacred/ profane	knowledge, religious observances, pray with the knees upward	pulpit, hell, limbo	idol, bishop, rector of the females	church, abbess, angel
Sport	Sex is play/ sex is contest	hole in one, tilting, couch rugby	target, saddle, wicket	putter, stick, bat	the game, pocket pool, catcher's mitt
Music	Sex is making music	strum, play the trombone, jazz	lute, fiddle, organ grinder	bugle, flute, lullaby	orchestra, kettledrums, blow some tunes
Names	Sex is communication/ personifica- tion	Colonel Puck, in Cupid's alley, take Nebuchadnezzar out to grass	Fanny, Lady Jane, Miss Horner	Jack, Abraham, Dick	Mae West, Mata Hari, Jodrell Bank

slang, colloquial, and euphemistic—that is, at least moderately taboo—sexual terms has evolved.

Slang has been traced back to the underworld or to criminal
dialects and can be seen as a (lower) class cant used to commu-

Place Names with Sexual Meaning: The World

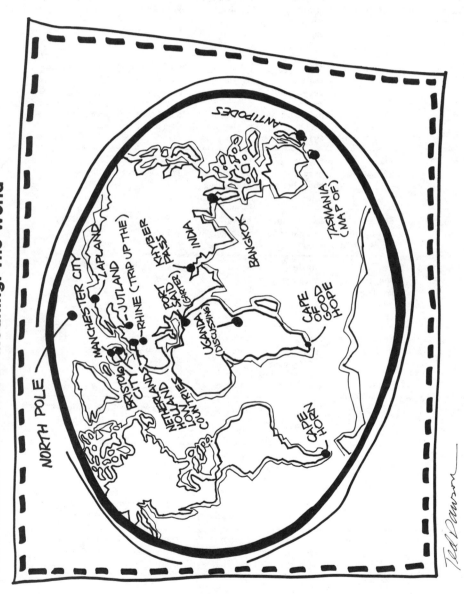

Place Names With Sexual Meaning: The United States of America

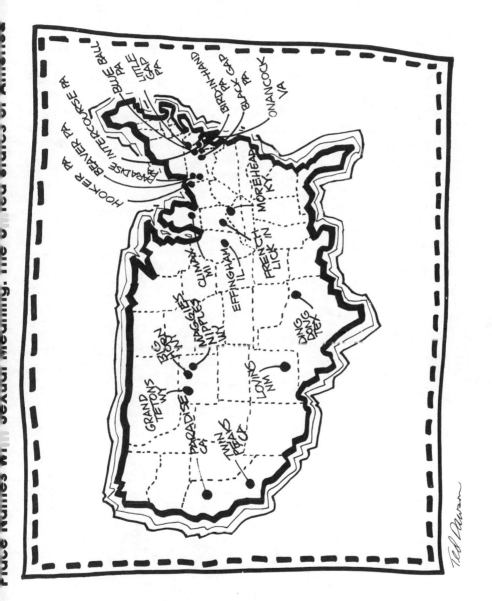

xvii

nicate secretly. Much of slang is simply euphemism or a substitution of a mild or neutral term or expression for taboo or vulgar terms. A variety of slang that uses substitution in a special way is rhyming slang, often called Cockney rhyming slang. Originating with the Cockney eastenders of London before spreading around the English-speaking world, rhyming slang deliberately misleads by dropping the original rhyming term. For example, **Khyber Pass** rhymes with **arse** (in Cockney dialect), so **khyber** alone stands for anus or buttocks.

Slang has always started as the *outsider*—unwelcome by polite society. Eventually, with acceptance, much of slang becomes colloquial or informal and spreads to society at large. Over the centuries, slang has added color, humor, and grit to our language. The process continues today.

Note on the Dictionary Entries

All words and phrases are listed alphabetically by headword or main entry, with sub-entries following alphabetically, unless their meanings forced groupings of sub-entries in a nonalphabetic way. Within entries, boldfaced type indicates both variant spellings and cross-references.

I have attempted to capture the broadest range of terms—across centuries, continents, and metaphors—and have tried to provide the etymology, if known; the nature of the term (standard, slang, euphemism, etc.); the century or period of use, however vague; and, where appropriate, the metaphor(s) employed. Also included are many nonce words and phrases—pithy or poetic coinages from English literature that are too colorful to omit.

Since slang is the predominant linguistic form in this dictionary, it is to be assumed that all words are slang unless stated otherwise, as, for example, standard, colloquial, euphemistic, formal, etc.

Furthermore, I have focused on the central aspects of sexuality, particularly sexual actions and sexual organs, and to some extent on sexual roles (e.g., bisexual, prostitute, etc.). Other aspects of sexuality, such as menstruation and pregnancy, and sexual terms in anatomy, medicine, and law, for example, have therefore received some but not full attention.

Finally, even within this focus, I am sure that I have missed slang, colloquial, and euphemistic terms that are recent, or from a circumscribed location. For any terms, expressions, or quotations that you would like to see included in the next edition, please write to me, Alan Richter, c/o PJ Dempsey, John Wiley & Sons, Inc., 605 Third Avenue, New York, NY 10158-0012.

Dictionary of
Sexual Slang

A

abbess n

the madam of a brothel. This usage can be traced back to the 18th century in England. In standard English an abbess is the female superior of a convent or nunnery. See also **bishop** and **nun** (under **nunnery**).

- "So an old Abbess, for the rattling rakes,
  A tempting dish of human nature makes,
  And dresses up a luscious maid."
  (John Wolcot, *Odes to the Pope*, 1782)

Abraham n

penis. This jocular 19th-century term is now obsolete, unlike **dick, peter**, etc., which remain in use. It exemplifies a biblical or religious metaphor; Abraham was the father of the Hebrew people. Derived from Hebrew *av*, meaning "father," and *raham*, meaning "a multitude," "Abraham" means "father of a multitude." Furthermore, in the Bible, God commands Abraham to "go forth and multiply," thus referencing the penis's reproductive function.

Abraham's bosom, a 19th-century euphemism for vagina, is now obsolete. Its original meaning was "heaven," as expressed in the Bible by Luke (16:22): "And it came to pass that [Lazarus] died and was carried away by an angel into Abraham's bosom." It is to Abraham's bosom, or heaven, that the righteous go after death. See also **die** and **heaven**.

academy n British

brothel. This obsolete euphemism plays off on the pun in the word **knowledge**, meaning both learning in the strict academic sense and in the biblical sense of **carnal knowledge,** or sexual intercourse. The term was used as early as the 17th century. A collection of lewd poems titled *Academie des Pays-Bas; Ou L'École des Voluptueux* (Academy of the Low Countries; or the School of Pleasure) was published in 1709 (see **low countries**); and in 1739 an *Academie de ces Dames et de ces Messieurs* (Academy for Ladies and Gentlemen) was founded in France and dedicated to erotic literature.

academician meaning prostitute, plays on the same pun, and contrasts book learning with actual experience.

accommodate v

copulate. This colloquial and literary term is usually used of a woman in the sense of serving a man sexually, and dates back to the 19th century. Since the act of sexual intercourse can be seen in physical terms as a kind of accommodation, it is not surprising to find this verb being used to describe intercourse.

accommodation is the noun form, meaning copulation. Accommodation helps to explain the sexual sense of **hotel**, meaning vagina, which is, after all, a place that provides accommodation. See also **Cupid's arms** and **Cupid's hotel**.

accommodation house is a colloquial term for a brothel, forming one of a large family of sexual terms that end in "house," meaning a brothel (e.g., **bawdy house, coupling-house, parlor-house**).

- "The truth of it is, of all the bawds I know, she merits most, having an house fit for the accommodation of the best."
  (Richard Head, *The English Rogue*, 1665)

AC/DC adj, n

bisexual. This modern jocular term derives from "alternating current/direct current," the way in which electrical current is supplied to equipment. Electricity is the juice that makes machines work, and it can be supplied in different forms. The metaphor can be explained as follows: current stands for sexual desire, while alternating means male/female and direct means same sex. Direct can also mean straight heterosexuality, while alternate can mean the alternative to heterosexuality, namely, homosexuality. This electrical metaphor for sexuality also brings to mind the male/female classification of coupling hardware items—objects with sockets are termed "female," while objects with prongs, etc., are called "male."

acey-deucey is a variant of AC/DC, but is also tangentially related to another sexual term, **ace**. The second part of the term, "deucey," also suggests **juicy**, which has the sexual meaning of lusty. Deucey also suggests deuce, the tennis term describing a 40–40 score, implying equal weighting.

ace n British

female genitals. This 19th-century term is based on a number of associations, including excellence, singularity, and winning as in tennis. However, the term probably derives from **ace of spades**, meaning female pubic hair, from both the color and shape of pubic hair.

acorn n

head of the penis. This is a contemporary gay term for the glans. The Latin term *glans* means "acorn." Furthermore, acorn suggests reproduction, since acorns grow into oaks.
acorn picker is a gay term for **fellator**. Picker is used, instead of, say, gatherer, possibly because of its closeness to **pecker**.

• "He rammed his soft acorn against my pudendum." (Gore Vidal, *Myra Breckenridge*, 1968)

act, the act, action n

sexual intercourse. The central importance of sexuality is highlighted in calling it *the* act. Action refers to any sexual activity, while act and the act refer specifically to copulation.
act of darkness is found in Shakespeare's *King Lear*: "A servingman ... that ... served the lust of my mistress's heart, and did the act of darkness with her."
act of shame and **act of sport** can both be found in Shakespeare's *Othello*: "Iago knows / That she with Cassio hath the act of shame / A thousand times committed," and "When the blood is made dull with the act of sport, there should be—again to inflame it, and to give satiety a fresh appetite—loveliness in favour."
act of generation, an obsolete British euphemism, specifies a possible reproductive outcome of the act.
More recent euphemisms include the British phrases **act of kind** and **act of love**.

addition n

sexual intercourse. This obsolete euphemism is derived from the arithmetic property of sexual reproduction. It does, however, tie in with the etymology of sexuality itself, since sex comes from the Latin *sexus*, related to *secare*, meaning "to cut" or "to divide." This brings to mind the ancient creation myth in which God created people who were all hermaphrodites; then God cut people in two, creating males and females. Leonard Levinson, in *Webster's New World Dictionary of Quotable Definitions*, 1988, defined sex as "a formula by which one and one makes three." *See also* **multiplication**.

adult *adj*

relating to sexual matters or sexual explicitness. This adjective can be applied to a number of nouns to form terms such as adult concerns, adult entertainment, adult movies, and adult themes. Adult is derived from the Old English *eald*, meaning "old." Adult, meaning sexually explicit, has been in use since the 1960s.

- "Officials of a few cities, including Las Vegas . . . have proposed location of specific adult business districts." (*The New York Times*, November 28, 1976)

adultery *n*

sexual intercourse by a married person with someone other than his or her spouse. This standard term derives from the Latin *ad* and *alter*, meaning "from" and "other."

affair *n*

1. genitals. Like the neutral **it** and **thing**, "affair" goes back in English to a time probably earlier than Shakespeare's. Affair is derived from the Middle French *a faire*, meaning "to do."

2. female genitals. Shakespeare used the term in this sense in the plural in *Sonnet 151*: ". . . Proud of this pride, / He is contented thy poor drudge to be, / To stand in thy affairs, fall by thy side."

3. male genitals.

- ". . . the young fellow . . . draws out his affair, so shrunk and diminish'd, that I could not but remember the difference . . ." (John Cleland, *Fanny Hill: Memoirs of a Woman of Pleasure*, 1749)

having an affair, a common euphemism meaning having a sexual relationship with someone, possibly derives from the genital meaning of affair.

afghan *n*

elderly male homosexual. This 20th-century gay term derives from the shawl, or afghan, that older people wear to keep warm. This term reflects the clothing sense of the standard term rather than the national sense. As such it is not a slur on foreigners in the way that, say, **French disease** or **French pox** is.

agility *n*

female genitals. Farmer and Henley, in their *Dictionary of Slang and Its Analogues*, 1890, refer to agility as a common noun for "the female privity." Quickness and nimbleness in action or performance is probably implied: In Peter Fryer's *Mrs Grundy: Studies in English Prudery*, 1963, we read, "A young lady was out riding . . . (and) fell off her horse and in so doing displayed some of her charms; but jumped up very quickly and said to the groom: 'Did you see my agility, John?' 'Yes, miss' said he, 'but I never heard it called by that name before!' Another version has the groom reply, 'Yes, miss, but we calls it a cunt in the kitchen.' " *See also* **regulator**.

AIDS *n*

acquired immune deficiency syndrome. This lethal infectious virus destroys a person's ability to fight infections. The U.S. Center for Disease Control first used the acronym AIDS in 1982.

- "This is everything I am afraid of: cholesterol, nitrates, AIDS, vagina dentata, . . . large penises, small penises, AIDS, . . . AIDS, cancer, pneumonia, . . . AIDS, AIDS, AIDS . . ." (David Feinberg, *Eighty-Sixed*, 1989)

alchemy *n*

sexual intercourse. This obsolete literary term draws its meaning from alchemy's search for the elixir of life. If love is a matter of the right chemistry, sex is perceived as an elixir of timelessness and perhaps as a search for immortality.

• "I'll show you why he haunts to Henley oft . . . there to spend the night in alchemy."
(Robert Greene, *The Honorable Historie of Frier Bacon and Frier Bongay*, 1594)

alley n

vagina. As a common term for a passage, or narrow path, this serves as a fitting euphemism. It is usually qualified, as in **Cupid's alley** (under **Cupid**) or **cock alley**. An alley is also a lane, so **cock alley** and **cock lane** are interchangeable.

alley cat is early 20th-century American slang for a prostitute. *See also* **cat**.

all forlorn n phrase British

erect penis. This 20th-century Cockney rhyming slang term is based on the rhyme with **horn**; it suggests the pain of unrequited sexual desire.

almond n British

penis. This usage derives from the rhyme of almond rock with **cock**. Almond rock cakes (cookies) were common in the early part of the 20th century. The choice of almond may have been influenced by **nuts**, a common slang term for testicles.

alpha and omega n phrase

female genitals. This obsolete euphemism refers to the first and last letters of the Greek alphabet. The phrase means, in standard English, "the most important thing." In Revelations 1:8 it refers to God's eternity. Both notions, importance and eternity, apply here.

alternating flame n

mutual oral sex. **Flame** has long been used to refer to sexual passion and to a mistress or lover. In addition, flames have the quality of flickering, or licking, and it is this sense that is employed in this 20th-century euphemistic coinage. Alternating explains the mutual aspects of oral sex.

all the way adv

sexual intercourse as opposed to sexual activity that does not culminate in intercourse. This informal expression, often **go all the way**, positions intercourse as the final action in the gamut of sexual activity. The term is frequently used by adolescents who, in experimenting with sexual activity, define intercourse as a sexual end point. *See also* **the limit**.

• "Then there's another great classification—the promiscuous virgin: 'I don't go all the way. That's all—I don't go all the way.' And these chicks better be careful. Because when they're gonna go, that may not be the way anymore."
(Lenny Bruce, John Cohen, editor, *The Essential Lenny Bruce*, 1967)

ambidextrous adj

bisexual. This 20th-century jocular term draws its humor from its standard meaning of both left- and right-handed. A recent flippant version is **ambisextrous**.

amorous adj

pertaining to sexual love. This well established term is derived from the Latin *amor*, meaning "love." It has been in use since the time of Middle English. Amorous is synonymous with sexually aroused.

amorous rites is a Shakespearean term for sexual intercourse.

• "Lovers can see to do their
amorous rites by their own
beauties."
(William Shakespeare, *Romeo and Juliet*, 1596)
amorous congress is another euphemism for sexual intercourse, **congress** itself being an old euphemism.

ampersand n

buttocks. Children's nursery books in the 19th century ended with the & after the Z, hence the character acquired the meaning of the end, or behind. Variants include **and-pussy-and, am-passy-and**, and **ampus-end**. A number of other alphabetic terms are used similarly in a sexual context, suggesting a connection between language and sex. *See also* **alpha and omega, linguist**, and **O**.

angel n

1. male homosexual. Dating back to the early 20th century, this term is far kinder than **fairy**, since angel in common usage means a dear, kind person. Significantly, angels are supernatural creatures of indeterminate sex; this usage perhaps reflects a heterosexual view of homosexuals. However, angel originally referred to a female, and has only recently been desexualized. Applied to a homosexual, angel can refer to either active or passive partners. Because of the pictorial representation of angels as having wings, angel also brings with it the connotation of flying, which can have sexual overtones.
• "I heard you asking questions of each: Who killed the pork chops? What price bananas? Are you my Angel?"
(Allen Ginsberg, "A Supermarket in California," 1955)
2. *British* prostitute. This 19th-century usage stems from the Angel district in London where prostitutes worked.

angle n *British*

penis. This 19th-century term may refer to the appearance of an erect penis or perhaps to fishing imagery, in which the penis is likened to an angler who uses a **rod** to catch **fish**. Angling is also slang for cheating or stealing, a theme behind such sexual terms as **diddle, screw**, and **trick**.

anilingus n

oral stimulation of the anus. This standard English term derives from the Latin *anus*, meaning "ring," and *lingere*, meaning "lick."

antipodes n

female genitals. The literal meaning is "the opposite foot"; significantly, the sexual meaning of **foot** is to copulate. "The opposite sex" is a common phrase used by each sex to refer to the other. However, as a 19th-century euphemism, antipodes clearly reflects the male point of view, in that the female genitals are seen as the opposite of the male genitals. The Antipodes are actually a group of islands in the South Pacific close to New Zealand. From a British point of view, these islands are on the other, or opposite, side of Earth.

anus n

excretory opening at the end of the rectum. This standard term is derived from the Latin, meaning "ring," and dates back to the 15th century.
• "The whole alimentary Duct, quite down to the Anus."
(David Hartley, *Observations on Man*, 1749)
anal is the adjective that characterizes standard sexual terms relating to the anus, as in **anal intercourse, anal retentive** (referring to a person who is tense, overorderly, and unable to let go), **anal virgin** (referring to someone who has not had anal intercourse), etc.

appetite n

lascivious desire or lust. The Latin root *appetere* means "ardently desire." Since desire can be separated from the object of desire, the word can be applied to food, sex, etc., even though in modern English the usual application is to food. In terms of both survival and child development, eating and food precede sex as a need. Consequently, sexual appetite is often understood or represented in terms of an appetite for food, rather than vice versa. The metaphor has given rise to a smorgasbord of sexual terms, including **banana, beef, bread, cabbage, cake, cauliflower, cucumber, eat, fish, fork, fruit, gravy, meat,** and **tomato.**

apples n pl

1. breasts. The sexual meaning derives from the shape of an apple, and from it being a food. Apple also has sexual overtones because of the biblical story of Adam and Eve in the Garden of Eden in which the fruit of carnal knowledge is often portrayed as an apple. Farmer and Henley, in their *Dictionary of Slang and Its Analogues*, 1890, quote Thomas Carew's *A Rapture*, 1638: "The warm firm apples, tipp'd with coral berries." A more recent anonymous ribald verse goes:
A woman has bosoms, a bust or a breast,
Those lily-white swellings that bulge 'neath her vest;
They are towers of ivory, sheaves of new wheat;
In a moment of passion, ripe apples to eat.
2. testicles. This is 19th-century usage. Like definition 1, it also refers to spherical objects that come in pairs. *See also* **chestnuts.**

arborvitae n

penis. This obsolete literary term is Latin for "tree of life." In "tree" the erect penis is implied, while "life" refers to its reproductive quality. Martial, the Roman poet, described Priapus, the phallic god, as follows: "I am not hewn out of fragile elm, nor is the erect pillar fashioned of just any wood, but born of living cypress." *See also* **Cyprus sap** and **tree of life.**

ardor n

lust. This word that dates back to Middle English derives from the Latin *ardere*, meaning "to burn." Sexual activity results in the body heating up, hence the poetic use of fires and flames of passion. *See also* **fire** and **flame.**
• ". . . the compulsive ardour gives the charge."
(William Shakespeare, *Hamlet*, 1600)

armor n

condom. This euphemism dates back to the 17th century. Since armor is used for protection, the sexual sense applies when a condom is used for protection against venereal disease. Armor, of course, was used in fighting, thus extending the metaphor to terms of war and aggression in connection with sexual intercourse (e.g., **fire, impale, screw**) and terms for the penis (e.g., **club, sword, weapon**). James Boswell, in his *London Journal*, covering the years 1762–1763, wrote: "I picked up a girl in the Strand; went into a court with intention to enjoy her in armour." *See also* **fight in armor.**

around the world, round the world v phrase

lick one's partner all over the body. This recent expression implies going or traveling everywhere, covering all erogenous zones. A further meaning is a sexual encounter that includes penetration of the vagina, mouth, and anus. In the 1970s, at British colleges, a number of "round the world" clubs flourished briefly. Variants include **take a trip around the world, go around the world in eighty ways**, and **do the grand tour**.

arrow n

penis. This colloquial term coheres with a group of sexual terms that uses the metaphor of archery. **Target, bull's-eye**, and **quiver** all mean vagina. An arrow is aimed at the target or bull's-eye, and arrows are kept in a container called a quiver. Further metaphorical congruence comes with the act of shooting arrows (that is, ejaculating). This group of terms is typical of the "sex as war" metaphor, though Cupid shoots arrows of love.
- "Howbeit one time disposed to sport and play
  Thus to his wife he pleasantly did say,
  'Since strangers lodge their arrows in thy quiver,
  Dear dame, I pray you yet the cause deliver,
  If you can tell the cause and not dissemble,
  How all our children me so much resemble?' "
  (Sir John Harington, 1561?–1612, "Of an Heroical Answer of a Great Roman Lady to her Husband")

arse n British

1. buttocks. This usage can be traced back to Old English. Arse was a standard English term till the 17th century; it then became a vulgar term that was rarely printed (at least in full and uncensored) until the second half of the 20th century. "Tha's got a proper, woman's arse, proud of itself" Mellors says to Connie in D.H. Lawrence's *Lady Chatterley's Lover*, 1928. Chaucer used a variation of the term, in a comic context, in "The Miller's Tale" part of *The Canterbury Tales*,

1387: ". . . with his mouth he kiste hir naked ers." Ers is derived from Indo-European, meaning "to be wet."
2. anus. The common usage is in derogatory phrases such as "stick it up your arse."
3. sexual intercourse. Common slang phrases include "get a little arse" and "have some arse."

For American usage, *see also* **ass**.

arsenal n

female genitals. This obsolete 19th-century term is perhaps an unusual one in that arsenal exemplifies the theme of aggression, more commonly seen in terms for male genitals. It conforms, however, to the metaphor of a container for the female genitals, since an arsenal stores weapons. The word can be viewed as a direct response to the 16th-century term for penis, **weapon**, since weapons are stored in an arsenal. As such, arsenal relates to **bayonet, bilbo, dirk, sword**, and other words that are weaponlike terms for the penis. The term arsenal is also a pun on the first syllable—**arse**—which in addition to meaning buttocks also means sexual intercourse. The etymology of the word arsenal points to both an Italian word for dockyard and an Arabic word for workshop. *See also* **dock** and **workshop**.
Adam's arsenal is a British euphemism for the male genitals. Adam serves as an adjective meaning male since, according to the biblical story, he was the first male, he was naked, and he was the first male to encounter sex.

art, art of pleasure n
British

sexual intercourse or techniques of copulation. These euphemistic terms are obsolete.
- "Oh fie! they scarce extend a virgin's span.

Art should exceed what Nature gave to man."
(John Wilmot, the earl of Rochester, *Sodom; or, The Quintessence of Debauchery*, 1680)
Sex involves both art and nature, or culture and nature; that sex is natural is self-evident. But for evidence that sex also involves art and culture, think simply of the changing sexual mores over periods of time, and in different geographic locations, and how differently sex has been portrayed by different cultures. It has been proposed that sexuality can be approached through both art and science. The perception of sex as an art has traditionally been an Eastern one, while the West, over the past century, has put sex under the magnifying glass and into the laboratory, and turned it into a science. Foucault, in *The History of Sexuality*, 1978, calls these approaches "ars erotica" and "scientia sexualis," respectively. The plethora of slang, metaphorical, and literary terms for sex, through the ages, however, is proof of the strength of "ars erotica" in the West.

artichoke n
vagina. This 20th-century term is based on both appearance (the leaves imply the labia) and edibility.
Jerusalem artichoke is a mainly American term for the vagina of a Jewish woman.

article n British
girl or woman as a **sex object** and, by extension, a vagina. This 19th-century derogatory term is not unlike **thing**, because of its generic nature. Article is also similar to **ware** in its sexual objectification. Grose's *Dictionary of the Vulgar Tongue*, 1811, defined an article as "a wench . . . a hell of a goer."
article of virtue is an obsolete euphemism for a virgin. It incorporates

a pun on virtue, meaning both goodness and righteousness, and virtu (French *vertu*), meaning connoisseurship or the love of fine, rare objects of beauty or art.

ass n
1. buttocks or anus. This term dates back to the 17th century. In the United States it was derived from British dialects of **arse**. Ass in its standard English sense, meaning a donkey, dates back to Middle English *asse*. Much of the derogatory sense of the word can be attributed to the fact that donkeys are regarded as stupid and stubborn.
Derivative sexual terms include **ass-fuck(er), ass-kiss(er), ass-lick(er),** and **ass-blow(er)**, the meanings of which are evident. But many terms and phrases that include "ass" are nonsexual, such as "kick ass," "pain in the ass," and "haul ass."
asshole means anus. However, this is another term that more often than not means a stupid person, referring back to the donkey as well as the anatomical sense. Yet another slang sense of asshole, meaning friend or buddy, is not pejorative and exists in mainly military usage.
2. woman as a sex object, the female genitals, or copulation. This often derogatory usage can be seen especially in the expression **piece of ass** [under **piece**].
assman, meaning a lecher, Don Juan, or very sexually active man, derives from this sense of ass.
ass peddler is a 20th-century expression for a pimp or a prostitute.

aunt n
1. madam of a brothel or prostitute. This term has been in use since the 16th century. Shakespeare, in *The Winter's Tale*, wrote: "Summer songs for me and my aunts / While we lie tumbling in the hay." As a common

relative, aunt serves as a convenient euphemism. Grose's *Dictionary of the Vulgar Tongue*, 1811, defined aunt as: ". . . a bawd or procuress: a title of eminence for the senior dells . . . ," and then defined dells as "young buxom wenches."

2. older or aging male homosexual. In this context, the term is commonly rendered as **auntie.** *See also* **uncle.**

- "Quentin Crisp, perfect gentleman, and minor legend, was 82 on Christmas Day. . . . Like a benign elderly auntie, his blue rinse is fading, his mottled skin is powdered rather more unevenly than in younger years and his mascara seems rather unconvincing."
(Jim Shelly, *The Manchester Guardian*, January 1991)

3. *British* menstruation. Phrases such as to **see one's aunt** and **have one's aunt with one** are common expressions. To **have** or **see an aunt from Reading** is based on the pun of Reading, an English town outside London, and red-ding, the color of blood. Variations include "her relations have come," "have a friend to stay," and "have a visitor."

B

baby n

1. mate. This old, established term of endearment is usually said of a girlfriend or woman. **Babe** is a variation. The terms reflect a transfer of love for a child or baby to an adult. In the song index of *Blues' Who's Who*, there are over forty song titles that start with the word "baby." Many more songs contain the word "baby" somewhere in their title.

2. male homosexual sweetheart. This meaning dates back to the early 20th century and clearly derives from the first sense. It is used in the same way, as in "You're my baby."

3. *British* prostitute's client or **john.** This sense, which dates back to the early 20th century, carries with it connotations of endearment, and contrasts with the negative terms for a prostitute's client, such as **trick**.

baby maker is a 19th-century term for penis that reflects its reproductive attributes. The term has also been applied to the female genitals.

baby juice and **baby paste** are 19th-century euphemistic terms for semen; both derive from the reproductive sense of the word.

baby pillows is an informal term for breasts, since a baby can rest on a breast. Pillows suggest the soft tactile sense of the breasts.

back v

copulate. This obsolete term is usually used of animals. The *Oxford English Dictionary* quotes John Rowland's *History of Four-footed Beasts,* 1658: ". . . when as the female or she Asse would be backt."

back, backside n

buttocks. Since the orientation of the face and eyes determines the front side, the buttocks are on the back side. "Backside" can be traced to the 16th century. Its usage was standard English until it became a vulgarism late in the 19th century.

- "With an arrowe so broad, He shott him into the back-syde." (J. Ritson, editor, *Robin Hood: from A Collection of Ancient Poems, Songs and Ballads Now Extant Relative to that Celebrated Outlaw,* 1795)

back door refers to the anus, in contrast to **front door**, which refers to the vagina. This 20th-century colloquialism also serves as a qualifier in **back-door work**, meaning anal copulation.

backgammon player is an 18th-century British term for a sodomite. Gammon means game, hence a backgammon player is a player of the back game.

back scuttle is a British term describing copulation from behind, or anal intercourse. See also **scuttle**.

back way is a euphemism for the anus, akin to back door.

badger n British

prostitute. This 19th-century derogatory term may derive from the sense of badger meaning pester. The other sense is that of a furry animal, thus contributing to the menagerie of furry animals that refer either to women as sex objects or to the female genitals (e.g., **beaver**, **cunny**, and **pussy**).

bag n

1. breast. This oldest meaning of the term is used more commonly in the plural, **bags**, which can also mean udders. The reference was usually to animals.

- "The cow is sacrificed to her bag."
  (Ralph Waldo Emerson, *English Traits*, 1856)

2. scrotum. The plural, **bags**, can refer to testicles, consistent with the singular meaning scrotum. See also **tool bag** [under **tool**].

bag of tricks is an expression in which bag refers to the scrotum while tricks suggests **tool**. Tricks may also suggest **trick**, meaning a prostitute's customer.

- "... be it concluded,
  No barricado for a belly; know't;
  It will let in and out the enemy
  With bag and baggage."
  (William Shakespeare, *The Winter's Tale*, 1611)

3. *American* female genitals.

4. old prostitute. This usage probably derives from the same source as that for woman in "old bag," or from **bagnio**. The term is also short for the derogatory "douche bag," which can be applied to both males and females.

baggage is primarily a British term for prostitute that dates back to the 17th century.

- "I believe the baggage loves me."
  (William Congreve, *The Old Batchelor*, 1693)

5. condom. American expressions incorporating this usage include **baggie** and **jo-bag**. See also **joy-bag**.

bag v

copulate. This sense is based on the hunting meaning of shoot or catch an animal. See also **venery**.

bagnio n

brothel. This colloquial literary term derives from the Italian word meaning "bathing house"; it dates back to the 16th century. Public baths served as places for sexual contact, hence the derivation of the sexual meaning of the term.

- "They were soon used to such an extent for illicit intrigues, that the name of a hothouse or bagnio became equivalent to that of a brothel."
  (Thomas Wright, *Domestic Manners in England during the Middle Ages*, 1862)

bagpipe v

1. perform oral sex on a man. This term makes logical use of both parts of the word—**bag** meaning scrotum and **pipe** meaning penis—in addition to which, one can **blow** a bagpipe. The term dates back to the late 16th century. In Farmer and Henley's *Dictionary of Slang and Its Analogues*, 1890, the word is defined as follows: "*Verb* (old). A lascivious practice; too

indecent for explanation." The second sense of bagpipe, below, could also be implied. *See also* **flute**.

2. copulate in the armpit. This recent, but rare, male homosexual term derives from the way a bagpipe is held, under the armpit. *See also* **pit job**.

bagpipes *n pl*

male genitals. The term derives from the shape of bagpipes, and from the terms **bag** and **pipe** taken separately.

• "A father is bending over arranging presents under the Christmas tree in his nightshirt. A little boy's voice: 'Hey, Pop, who gets the bagpipes?'"
(Gershon Legman, *Rationale of the Dirty Joke*, 1968)

bald-headed hermit *n*

penis or glans of the penis. This expression refers to the fact that the glans has no hair and hence the penis can be said to be bald-headed. Like the hermit, the penis is single; furthermore, hermits sometimes live in caves (*see also* **cave**). **Bald-headed mouse** is a variation. *See also* **mouse**.

ball *n*

testicle. The derivation here is obvious from the spherical shape of the testicle. The term is most commonly found in the plural. **Balls** derives from the Old English standard term "ballocks," meaning small balls. Over time, **ballocks** changed from standard English to slang. Interestingly, both ballocks (and its variations—**bollocks**, **bollix**, etc.) and balls can mean nonsense, and probably derive their forcefulness from the sexually charged nature of these terms.

• "I inserted my prick, and almost instantly spent the semen in her, which had been boiling in my ballocks."
(Anonymous, *My Secret Life*, 1890)

• "Do your balls hang low? Do they wiggle to and fro?
Can you tie 'em in a knot? Can you tie 'em in a bow?"
(Anonymous ribald song)

ball *v*

copulate. This 20th-century, originally African American usage clearly derives its meaning from the dance (the ball), together with the obvious association with the noun ball, meaning testicle. **Have a ball** is a colloquial phrase meaning have a pleasurable time.

• "Do you want me to ... well, to ball you?"
(Gore Vidal, *Myra Breckenridge*, 1968)

balling the jack refers to copulation from the male point of view, in light of the term **jack**, meaning penis.

ball off means masturbate. It joins the ranks of many other English phrasal verbs for masturbation ending with the preposition "off," such as **beat off**, **jack off**, **whack off**, etc. The preposition "off" implies completion or conclusion—in this instance that ejaculation or orgasm was reached.

buff ball and **ballum rancum**, defined euphemistically as a naked dance by Grose in the *Dictionary of the Vulgar Tongue*, 1811, refer to orgiastic copulation. *See also* **buttock ball**.

ballocks

See **ball**.

balloon *n*

1. breast. Dating back to the early 20th century, this term is usually found in the plural, **balloons**. It is based on the shape of the breasts.

2. condom. This 20th-century euphemism is also based on shape. A rolled-out condom looks like an uninflated balloon.

baloney n American

penis. This 20th-century term brings together both food and shape metaphors. Baloney is a kind of processed **meat** in tubular form, or **sausage**. Furthermore, like **balls**, baloney can mean nonsense.

banana n

1. penis, particularly an erect one. This usage, based on shape, dates back to the 19th century. It is most often found in the more recent phrase **have one's banana peeled**, meaning copulate.
2. male homosexual, especially a fellator.

band n

1. *British* prostitute. This term could derive from a number of sources, including the group sense of band, as in a band of musicians, implying togetherness and/or entertainment. It also could derive from the flat strip sense of band, as in rubber band or waistband, something that binds. In this connection, *see* **flatcock**.
2. *Australian* brothel.

band in the box n phrase
American

syphilis. This expression is based on **box** rhyming with **pox**, the most widespread slang term for syphilis. It is significant that box is the rhyming term since it is sexual slang itself—meaning the vagina.

B and T

See **T and A**.

bang v

copulate. This common 20th-century term derives from the knocking sense of bang, as in banging on a door. This usage reflects the male point of view and the theme of aggression that runs through a fair amount of sexual terminology. Recently, the "Big Bang" theory in astronomy has given rise to sexual allusions, connecting the creation of the universe with human procreation.

banger n British

penis. This 20th-century term derives from another sense of banger, meaning **sausage**.
bangers refers to the testicles. This British term, dating back to the 19th century, is part of billiards jargon in which **stick and bangers** does double duty both for cue and balls and for penis and testicles.
bangster is British terminology for prostitute, dating from the 19th century. The suffix "-ster" in English has a lengthy history of referring to someone engaging in a specified activity; unlike the common suffix "-er", however, "-ster" often has pejorative overtones, as in "gangster," "mobster," and "prankster."

bank n British

female genitals. This 19th-century term derives its connotation from **deposit**, meaning ejaculate. Bank is one of many container terms for the female genitals; **money** is an even older British euphemism with the same meaning.
bank and biff is a rhyming slang term for **syphilis**, where biff rhymes with **syph**, a common abbreviation for syphilis. The juxtaposition of bank (female genitals) with syphilis reflects the male perspective on venereal disease.
Barclay's bank is 20th-century Cockney rhyming slang for mastur-

bation: bank rhymes with **wank**, the most common British term for masturbation. Bank also puns on semen bank and monetary bank. *See also* **deposit** and **spend**.

barbettes *n pl*

breasts. This obsolete term may derive from the standard sense of barbette, meaning a cylinder that covers a gun or turret on a warship, itself derived from barb, meaning something pointed. This derivation, if correct, would exemplify an aggressive term for a part of the female anatomy. While there are some aggressive terms for the vagina, such as **bite**, reflecting a male castration fantasy, aggressive terms for the breasts are rare. *See also* **Berthas**.

basher *n British*

lecherous person. This is an early 20th-century term.

bash the bishop *v phrase*

masturbate. In this recent expression, the bishop refers to the glans of the penis, which is said to resemble a bishop's miter in shape. It may be more than coincidence that a religious term is used in a phrase meaning masturbate, given that many religions condemn masturbation. *See also* **bishop** *and* **beat the bishop**.

basket *n American*

1. male genitals. This mid-20th-century euphemism refers to the bulging shape of the male genitals when clothed in a jockstrap or athletic supporter. This meaning is mainly a homosexual usage.
2. scrotum. This 20th-century usage implies a container, like **bag**.
3. female genitals. This sense is primarily 20th-century usage.

basket making *n phrase*
British

copulation. In Grose's *Dictionary of the Vulgar Tongue*, 1811, basket making is defined as "The good old trade ... copulation, or making feet for children's stockings."

bat *n*

1. prostitute. This obsolete 19th-century derogatory term derives from the animal that is a creature of the night. The fact that bats are often regarded as vampires and seen as ghoulish creatures may have influenced the pejorative sexual meaning of the term. Interestingly, "bats" and "batty" both mean crazy. The linguistic connection between sex and craziness does not occur in the English language, although the linguistic connection between love and craziness is strong. The metaphor of love as craziness can be seen in such phrases as "to be crazy about someone," "to flip over someone," "to be head over heels in love," etc.
2. penis. This 20th-century usage derives from **club**, the hitting instrument. The sports metaphor is evident, especially since bat goes with **ball**, a common colloquialism for testicle.
coupling bat is an older, but now obsolete, term for penis.
bat and balls refers to the male genitals. This phrase applies to the penis and the testicles respectively.

bat *v*

masturbate. This usage may derive from an abbreviation of bachelor, and is probably related to the second meaning of bat, above, namely the penis.

baths, bathhouse *n*

Turkish baths where male homosexuals meet for sex. This mid-20th-century colloquialism is related to

bagnio, which in Italian means "bath," and is slang for brothel.

- "A county health department worker tells of going to a bathhouse to conduct syphilis testing and catching sight of the priest who had given prenuptial counseling to him and his fiancée."
(Katie Leishman, "Heterosexuals and AIDS," *The Atlantic*, February 1987)

bauble n

penis. Since bauble in standard English means plaything or toy, this connotation is not surprising. Shakespeare wrote in *Romeo and Juliet*: ". . . this drivelling love is like a great natural, that runs lolling up and down to hide his bauble in a hole." Bauble as a sexual term is now obsolete, but see **play**, **thing**, and **toy** for evidence that the metaphor is very much alive.

- "The Elizabethan fool held a bauble or 'plaything'; in contemporary comedy, the phallic anarchy is symbolized by Chaplin's cane, Harpo's horn, Groucho's cigar, Monsieur Hulot's umbrella."
(John Lahr, *Prick Up Your Ears*, 1978)

bawd n

one who panders to sexual debauchery. The application of this standard term ranges from a lecherous person to a pimp or procuress to a prostitute. The word derives from the Old French *baude* and is probably related to "bold." Bawd dates back to Middle English. The abstract nouns from bawd are **bawdry** and **bawdiness**. Bawdry often refers to lascivious language or writing.

bawdy adj

lecherous. Shakespeare wrote in *Romeo and Juliet*: ". . . for the bawdy hand of the dial is now upon the prick of noon." Shakespeare also referred to "bawdy talk" in *Measure for Measure*.

bawdy house n

brothel. This is colloquial usage.

- "I perceived . . . by the naked queans that I was come into a bawdy-house."
(Robert Burton, *The Anatomy of Melancholy*, 1621)

bayonet n British

penis, especially an erect one. The bayonet, which is a blade attached to a firearm, is named after Bayonne, the town in France where the weapon originated. This obsolete usage joins a multitude of terms representing piercing objects that are euphemisms for the penis, including **blade**, **needle**, **prick**, and **sword**.

bazaar n

female genitals. This obsolete term stresses the marketplace sense of bazaar, and also puns on "bizarre," or something strange or weird; both senses strongly reflect a male perspective. For more on the marketplace sense, in which a female can be bought for sex, compare **commodity**, **merchandise**, and **ware**.

bazoo n American

female genitals. This 20th-century term may derive from **bazaar**, though it could simply be a nonce word used as a euphemism. *See also* **kazoo** *and* **wazoo**.

bazooms n pl

breasts. This mid-20th-century term is probably a variation on **bosom**. The suffix "-zooms" suggests an object that one can "zoom in on" or ogle, hinting that the word is one used mainly by males. **Bazoongas** and **bazongas** are 20th-century variations.

beak n British

penis. This 18th-century usage probably derives from the protruding shape of a beak. Beak is also a term for the nose. Wilhelm Fliess, one of Freud's colleagues, made a psycho-analytical connection between the nose and the penis. Both have discharges and both jut out from the body. Fliess's hypothesis was that ailments of the nose are sexual in nature. Beak brings to mind the many bird-related terms that have a sexual connotation, such as **canary**, **cock**, **cuckoo**, **feathers**, and **pecker**. See also **strop one's beak**.

bean n British

1. penis. This early 20th-century term probably derives from the shape of a green bean. Beans are also a food and therefore join a number of food-related penis terms such as **banana**, **carrot**, and **sausage**.
beanshooter and **beantosser** are variants. See also **shoot** and **toss off**.
• "A small boy is sitting on the curb with an erection, using it to snap pebbles into the air. A woman observes him from the window, invites him upstairs, and seduces him. An hour later, seeing him in the street, she invites him to come up again. 'Aw, go to hell, you busted my bean shooter!' "
(Gershon Legman, *Rationale of the Dirty Joke*, 1968)
2. *American* hymen. This early 20th-century usage is akin to that of **cherry**, and may derive from the old sense of bean as money, as in "I don't have a bean." A modern Italian slang term for the female genitals is *fava*, which means "bean."
beanfeast in standard English refers to an annual feast given by employers for their workers, while the British slang meaning is sexual intercourse. The latter meaning probably derives

from both meanings of bean, above, as well as the eating metaphor for sexual activity.

bear v

copulate. This polite informal term, said of women, derives its meaning from the **missionary position**, in which the woman is below the man, bearing his weight during intercourse. There is also the pun on the possible consequences of intercourse, namely, bearing a child or giving birth.

beard n

female pubic hair. Dating back to the 17th century, this term reflects both a bodily and a gender displacement. In the first case, the standard meaning of beard applies to the face; therefore, the displacement is from the face to the genitals. Since the beard is a masculine sexual trait, the second displacement is a gender change from male to female.
beard-splitter means penis. By extension, it can also mean a lecherous male. See also **split**.

bearskin n British

female pubic hair. This 19th-century colloquialism derives from the furriness of a bear. It also puns on being bare.

beast n

1. prostitute. This 20th-century derogatory term derives from the lowly animal nature of a beast.
2. *British* sex offender. This is a 20th-century prison term.

beast with two backs n
phrase
figurative appearance assumed by a copulating couple. This old literary phrase emphasizes the animal nature of sexuality.

• "... your daughter and the Moor are now making the beast with two backs."
(William Shakespeare, *Othello*, 1605)

beat *v*

masturbate. Beat is used in a number of expressions that mean masturbate.

beat off joins the many expressions with the preposition "off," such as **jack off**, **jerk off**, and **whack off**.

beat the bishop refers to the glans of the penis, which is shaped somewhat like a bishop's miter. *See also* **bishop** and **bash the bishop**.

beat the dummy refers to the fact that the penis is dumb.

beat the meat includes **meat**, a term for the genitals, male or female, though beat the meat always refers to male masturbation.

beauty parlor *n*

brothel. This 20th-century euphemism may be based on the attractiveness of prostitutes, a gathering place for women, or the meaning of **beauty spot**. *See also* **parlor-house**.

beauty spot *n*

female genitals. In standard English it can mean a birthmark or a place of outstanding beauty. Both meanings could be the rationale for the sexual meaning.

beaver *n American*

female genitals. Since a beaver is a furry animal, this sexual sense, dating back to the early 20th century, is not surprising. It joins the menagerie of **bunny**, **pussy**, **squirrel**, etc. But there are two other reasons for beaver's sexual sense. First, the beaver has a flat tail, and **flat-cock** is slang for a woman considered sexually. Second, beaver also means **hat**, which itself connotes the female genitals. Just as the meaning of pussy has extended from the genitals to woman as a sex object, so has the meaning of beaver.

• "The expression was first used by news photographers who often got to see up women's skirts at accidents ... They needed a code word to yell to other newsmen ... to let them know what could be seen in case they wanted to see it. The word was this: beaver!"
(Kurt Vonnegut, *Breakfast of Champions*, 1973)

beaver shots are sexually explicit photographs of women with their pubic hair showing. The term dates back to the late 1950s. Its usage became widespread in the late 1960s when it became permissible for pornographic magazines to show pubic hair in nude photographs.

bed, take to bed *v, v phrase*

copulate. This old euphemism demonstrates the classic transfer of meaning from the place of sex to the sex act itself. The term can be traced back to Middle English. *See also* **blanket** and **sheets**.

• "O, then we'll wed, and then we'll bed—
But not in our alley!"
(Henry Carey, "Sally in our Alley," 1729)

• "No Boy Scout's fleapit dreams of bedding Brigitte Bardot could ever better these."
(Tony Harrison, "The Songs of the PWD Man," in John Whitworth, editor, *The Faber Book of Blue Verse*, 1990)

bed sports is a colloquialism for sexual intercourse. *See also* **sport**.

bed bunny is used for a woman who "goes to bed" frequently, since bunnies are said to copulate often.

bed-hop is a recent British colloquialism meaning to be sexually promiscuous.

- "I would have had to read 'Goldilocks' under the bed-covers if they'd realised it was a story about 'A little girl who goes bed-hopping and gets her oats.'" (*The Observer*, January 19, 1986, quoted in Simon Mort, editor, *Longman/Guardian New Words*, 1986)

bed rite is another euphemism for sexual intercourse that Shakespeare used in *The Tempest*: "No bed-rite shall be paid / Till Hymen's torch be lighted." Hymen is the Greek and Roman god of marriage, and the hymen (membrane) is named after this god. Shakespeare also used the expressions **bed-fellow** (sexual mate), **bed-presser** (a lecherous male), and **bed-swerver** (a woman who swerves from her sexual duty in bed).

bedtime story is a quaint modern euphemism for sex.

Beecham's pills *n pl British*

testicles. This 19th-century Cockney rhyming slang term is commonly used to mean nonsense, and as such is like **balls** and **cobblers**, other rhyming slang terms for testicles that mean nonsense. The choice of "pills" may not be arbitrary, as they are usually round.

beef *n*

genitals. Like the generic **meat** and **flesh**, this is an old term that is applied to both sexes. It is sexually clarified in the following phrases.

beefcake is a mid-20th-century colloquialism meaning a nude or semi-nude picture of a male. Beefcake contrasts with the feminine version, **cheesecake** (under **cheese**).

beef gravy means semen. *See also* **gravy**.

beefsteak is an early 20th-century British term for a prostitute. Beefsteak joins many food terms for women as sex objects and for the female genitals (e.g., **cabbage**, **fish**, and **mutton**).

do a bit of beef means copulate; it is said of men.

take in beef also means copulate; it is said of women.

behind *n*

buttocks. The *Oxford English Dictionary* gives the first usage in 1786, and identifies the term as both colloquial and vulgar. The vulgar identification has recently disappeared. The term is simply derived from the relative position of the buttocks to the face, namely, behind one.

- "When you see me comin' mama,
     hang yo' draws on the line,
  When you see me comin' mama,
     hang yo' draws on the line.
  All I want is yo' behind."
  (Anonymous blues lyrics quoted in Thomas Kochman, *Black and White Styles in Conflict*, 1981)

be into *v phrase*

copulate. This 19th-century expression is used in reference to men.

bell *n*

clitoris. This term has been used among African Americans since the 1940s. "Ring My Bell" is the title of a song by Anita Ward.

bell end *n British*

penis. This 20th-century euphemism is based on the similarity of the shape of a bell to the glans of the penis.

bell-rope *n American*

penis. The term is based on both the shape of a bell (similar to that of the glans) and the similarity of the pulling of a bell-rope to masturbation.

This is a 20th-century usage. *See also*
pull wire.

belle *n*

1. attractive girl or woman. The
term comes from the French, the feminine of *beau*, and dates back to the
17th century.
belle chose, literally "pretty thing,"
is a euphemism for the female genitals. Geoffrey Chaucer wrote in *The
Canterbury Tales*: "Is it for ye wolde
have my queinte alone. . . . For if I
wolde sell my belle chose, I could
walke as freshe as is a rose." (For
queinte, *see also* **cunt** and **quaint**.)
2. male homosexual. This is a
20th-century gay term.

belly *n*

female genitals. The meaning has
evolved from "stomach" and
"womb." The word is a cognate of
"bellows," and as such is related to
bag.
There are many sexual phrases
that incorporate the word belly.
Phrases for copulation include **belly
work**, **play at belly to belly**, **belly
warmer**, **belly ride**, and **belly bump**.
These terms can all refer to males or
females. **Lay one's belly** is another
phrase for copulation, but it is said of
women only. *See also* **lay**.
belly bumper and **belly buster** refer
to a lecherous male and date back to
the 17th century.
belly whiskers and **belly bristles** are
19th-century British colloquialisms
for female pubic hair.
itch in the belly is an old term for
female lasciviousness. Farmer and
Henley's *Dictionary of Slang and Its
Analogues*, 1890, quotes Thomas
D'Urfey in *Wit and Mirth*, 1719: "Each
has an itch in her belly, / To play
with the scarlet hue."

belt *v British*

copulate. This 19th-century term
derives from the meaning to **hit** or
punch, adding to the long list of aggressive verbs for sexual intercourse.

belter *n British*

prostitute. This is a 19th-century
term.

bend over, bend down, bend someone over *v*
phrase

perform anal intercourse. These
complementary terms date back to
the early 20th century.
bender is the male homosexual who
is the receiver.

bent *adj British*

pertaining to a male homosexual.
This derogatory term may derive
from bending over or bending down
to receive anal intercourse, or it
could be linked to another meaning
of bent, namely, crooked in the criminal sense. Bent is also the opposite
of **straight**, a term for heterosexual.
See also **kinky** and **twisty**.

- "No one cares if you're boy, or
  girl, or bent, or versatile, or what
  you are."
  (Colin MacInnes, *Absolute
  Beginners*, 1959)

bent wrist stands for an effeminate
male homosexual. It is derived from
bent, as well as from the limpness of
the wrist that is associated with effeminate males.

berk *n British*

vagina. This term, rarely used in
the sexual sense, is a Cockney rhyming slang term for **cunt**, since berk is
a contraction of **Berkshire hunt** (another variation points to **Berkeley
hunt**). Typically, the word is used euphemistically, as in "Peter, you are a
berk!" meaning Peter is a silly fool.
Significantly, the rhyming part for
cunt is hunt, which itself is ambig-
uous as to the sport of hunting and

that of sex. A similar ambiguity exists with the word **venery**.

berries n pl American

testicles. This 20th-century euphemism is derived from the way berries hang on a bush. Berries are also a food item, joining **eggs**, **nuts**, and **gooseberries** of which berries may be a contraction. See also **twig and berries**.

Berthas n pl British

breasts, especially large or prominent ones. The term derives from Bertha, the name of an antitank gun used by the Germans in World War I. The gun was named after Bertha Krupp, then owner of the Krupp steelworks in Germany. See also **barbettes**.

best, best part n

vagina. "Best in Christendom" was an 18th-century toast, from which the sexual use of best may stem. Best, meaning finest, is similar to **alpha and omega**, another euphemism for the vagina derived from the meaning "the most important thing."
best and plenty of it is a 19th-century British phrase for sexual intercourse, said of women. The **it** here refers to the penis, while best is a pun on the vagina and the standard meaning of best, namely, most enjoyable or finest.

bestiality n

sexual activity between a human and an animal. This standard term dates back to the 14th century, as does the adjective **bestial**. Both terms derive from the Latin *bestialis*, meaning "beast."

best leg of three n phrase
British

penis. This jocular term dates back to the 19th century. The reference is to the two anatomical legs, with the erect penis making up the third.

between the sheets phrase

copulation. Sheets refer to the **bed**. As Shakespeare wrote in *King Lear*: "Let copulation thrive; for Gloster's bastard son / Was kinder to his father than my daughters / Got 'tween the lawful sheets." See also **dance the sheets**.

bicycle n British

prostitute. This usage stems from the fact that one rides a bicycle. See also **ride**.
bike as a term for prostitute, probably derived from bicycle, is predominantly Australian. See also **town bike**.

bicycle adj

bisexual. This recent coinage is probably based on similarity of sound, and is certainly based on the common prefix "bi-," which alone is an abbreviation for bisexual.

big brother n

penis. This 19th-century term suggests family membership. See also **little brother**.

big brown eyes n pl
American

breasts and nipples. The "brown" specifically refers to the coloration of nipples in this early 20th-century euphemism.

big time n

copulation. This is a mid-20th-century adolescent colloquialism. See also **all the way**.

bike n

See **bicycle**.

bilbo n

penis. In standard English a bilbo is a sword or blade that was made in Bilboa, Spain, hence the weapon's name. This obsolete term is one of the many warlike terms for the penis such as **bayonet**, **blade**, **sword**, and the generic **weapon**.

bim n American

woman of loose morals or a prostitute. This early 20th-century term could derive from **bum**, meaning buttocks (see also **ass** and **tail**). However, it is more likely an abbreviation of **bimbo**.
bimmy, a 20th-century term for a prostitute, derives from bim.

bimbo n

woman of loose morals or a prostitute. The *Oxford English Dictionary* gives its first quote for bimbo in this sense in 1929. The derivation of bimbo is probably from the Italian *bambino*, meaning "baby," though another possible derivation is from the Italian *bombo*, a child's word for "drink." A 19th-century punch with cognac was called a bimbo. More recently, the term has evolved to mean a woman who is both sexy and stupid.

- ". . . the bimbo exists on the fringes of pornography, and some cynics might say she has the mental capacity of a minor kitchen appliance."
  (*Independent*, July 23, 1988, quoted in Sara Tulloch, compiler, *The Oxford Dictionary of New Words*, 1991).

bint n British

woman regarded as a sex object. First used in the late 19th century, this derogatory term was in widespread use among servicemen in the Middle East during World Wars I and II. Bint, meaning "daughter," comes from the Arabic, with *saida bint* meaning "good-day girl."

bird n

1. woman. This usage can be traced back to Middle English. Perhaps woman is associated with bird because of the connection of a bird's feathers with a woman's finery. See also **chick**.
2. penis. This usage dates back to the 19th century. See also **cock**.
3. female genitals. Because of the first meaning of bird, and because **cock** also has the meaning female genitals, this usage appears logical.
birds and bees is a euphemism for the sexual facts of life. Children are said to be taught about the birds and the bees, meaning the nature of sexual intercourse. Birds and bees is euphemistic since it literally refers to nonmammalian reproduction and the pollination of plants.
bird's nest is a colloquialism for the female genitals. The nest may suggest both pubic hair and a place for eggs, that is, the womb. Shakespeare wrote in *Romeo and Juliet*: "I must another way, / To fetch a ladder, by the which your love / Must climb a bird's nest soon when it is dark."

birthday party n

orgy. This 1960s euphemism derives from the standard meaning of **party** and the term **birthday suit**, meaning naked, dating back to the late 16th century.

biscuit n American

woman considered as a sex object. This mid-20th-century food term joins **bun**, **cake**, and **muffins**.

bisexual n, adj

1. person who is attracted to, or is sexually involved with, people of both sexes. The term is standard English and dates back to the early 19th

century. Bisexual is also a standard adjective. **Bi** is an informal abbreviation. The abstract noun is **bisexuality**.

● "I'm a practicing heterosexual . . . but bisexuality immediately doubles your chances for a date on Saturday night."
(Woody Allen)

2. homosexual. This is 20th-century usage.

● ". . . the distinctive clientele [of Paresis Hall in New York City] were bitterly hated, and finally scattered by the police, merely because of their congenital bisexuality. The sexually full-fledged were crying for blood. . . . Bisexuals must be crushed—right or wrong!"
(Earl Lind, *Autobiography of an Androgyne*, 1918)

bishop n

1. large condom. Grose, in *Dictionary of the Vulgar Tongue*, 1811, defined bishop as ". . . one of the largest of Mrs. Philips's purses, used to contain the others." The Mrs. Philips referred to had a shop in London near Leicester Square that stocked sexual aids.

2. glans of the penis. This usage derives from the shape of a bishop's miter. *See also* **bash the bishop**.

bit n

1. *British* female genitals. This meaning dates back to the 19th century. Since genitals are part of a woman, bit is somewhat like **piece**. It also means **money**.

2. sexual intercourse. This usage stems from the episodic aspect of copulation.

3. woman considered sexually. This definition is by extension from the genital sense. A recent version of this meaning is found in the African American variant **bitty**.

● "Are there going to be a lot of bitties at the party?"
(David Toop, *The Rap Attack*, 1984)

The phrases that follow present multiple sexual meanings.

bit of brown means anal intercourse. *See also* **brown**.

bit of cauliflower is British usage for copulation (*see also* **cauliflower**). So is **bit of fish** and **bit of flat** (*see also* **fish** and **flat-cock**). Other phrases for copulation include **bit of front door work**, said of males (*see also* **front door** [under **front attic**] and **work**); **bit of fun**, a colloquialism; **bit of hair**, which is British (*see also* **hair**); **bit of hard (for a bit of soft)**, based on the presumption of a hard penis and a soft vagina; **bit of snug (for a bit of stiff)**, which is British and the reverse of "bit of hard (for a bit of soft)"; **bit of jam**, which is British and covers the female genitals, copulation, and a woman considered sexually (*see also* **jam**); and **bit of the other**, also British, in which "other" implies the opposite sex or sex organs (*see also* **antipodes**).

bit of meat is British for copulation and for prostitute. *See also* **meat**.

bit of pork is British for both copulation and the female genitals (*see also* **pork** and **meat**), as is **bit on a fork** (*see also* **fork**).

bit of rough is British usage for aggressive copulation, or for a lover of either sex who enjoys aggression with sex. *See also* **rough trade**.

bit of skin is British coinage both for copulation and for a woman considered sexually. So is a **bit of fluff**, **bit of skirt**, and **bit of stuff**. *See also* **fluff**, **skin**, **skirt**, and **stuff**.

bitch n

1. female. This derogatory term dates as far back as Middle English. Farmer and Henley, in their *Dictionary of Slang and Its Analogues*, 1890, quote a line from 1400: "Whom callest thou queine skabde biche?"

Shakespeare, in *King Lear*, was one of the first to use the phrase "son of a bitch." In standard English the term "bitch" simply means a female dog, though other slang meanings include a vicious or rude person of either sex, or a thing that is very difficult.

- "Tha'rt real, even a bit of a bitch."
  (D.H. Lawrence, *Lady Chatterley's Lover*, 1928)

2. prostitute. This 19th-century usage gave rise to **bitchery**, a colloquial term for prostitution.

3. blatant homosexual, especially one who is the passive partner. This usage is more recent, dating only to the mid-20th century.

bitch *v British*

copulate, especially with prostitutes. This sense of the word dates back to the 17th century.

bite *n British*

vagina. This usage is obsolete. The word "bite," however, can be traced back to the Indo-European, with the meaning to **split** or **fork**. The identification of vagina with mouth is evident in related terms for the vagina, such as **nether mouth** and **mouth thankless**. Farmer and Henley, in their *Dictionary of Slang and Its Analogues*, 1890, quote the *Dictionary of the Canting Crew*, 1690, which illustrates "bite" as follows: "The Cull wapt the Morts bite, [meaning] the Fellow enjoyed the Whore briskly." *See also* **mouth that cannot bite** and **vagina dentata**.

blackness *n*

female genitals. This euphemism may have come about because the female genitals are largely hidden and therefore dark, or because pubic hair is commonly dark. Shakespeare wrote in *Othello*: "She'll find a white that shall her blackness hit."

black hole, black joke, black meat, and **black ring** are all terms for the vagina, playing on the sense of blackness described above. All except black hole are British usage. Additionally, **hole**, **meat**, and **ring** signify the vagina. **Black joke** is a British term apparently derived from a popular song in the 19th century; black humor may also be at play here. **Black hole** has an astronomical meaning today that adds a twist to the sexual meaning—a black hole is a collapsed star in which the gravitational force is so great that nothing, including light, can escape it.

black jack and **black snake** are both terms for the penis of a black man (*see also* **jack** and **snake**). Black jack is a British term.

blade *n British*

1. penis. This metaphor dates to earlier than the 19th century. Blade is one of many warlike terms, such as **sword**, for the penis. An obsolete meaning of blade is a gallant man.

2. male homosexual. This is a 20th-century gay usage.

blanket *n*

This word has a general sexual connotation, as do **bed** and **sheets**:

blanket drill is an early 20th-century British euphemism signifying copulation and masturbation, that is, sexual activity in bed.

blanket hornpipe is an 18th-century British term for copulation (*see also* **horn** and **pipe**). Grose's *Dictionary of the Vulgar Tongue*, 1811, defines blanket hornpipe as "The amorous congress."

bless *v*

perform anal intercourse. This 20th-century gay term also has an antithetical meaning of curse, which may explain the derivation of the sexual meaning. Bless joins a number of religious terms such as **kneel at the altar** and **religious observances**.

blind n

uncircumcised penis. This is a recent gay term attributed to the fact that the foreskin hides the opening of the penis. **Blinds** refers to the foreskin itself. The notion of being hidden from view, or the idea of not being able to be seen, explains the following sexual terms.

blind alley is a British euphemism referring to the vagina. See also **alley**.

blind cheeks is an old euphemism for the buttocks. Farmer and Henley, in their *Dictionary of Slang and Its Analogues*, 1890, quote Thomas Dekker and John Webster in *Northward Hoe*, 1607: "I'll make him know how to kiss your blind cheeks sooner." The obvious bodily displacement is from the face to the buttocks. See also **cheeks**.

blind entrance is much like blind alley, a British euphemism for the vagina.

blind eye is an 18th-century British euphemism for either the anus or the vagina, based on shape. See also **eye**.

blister n

prostitute. This obsolete term gave rise to the synonym **blisterine**, possibly derived from Listerine, a trademarked antiseptic. Blister is derogatory and implies disease, hence the pun in blisterine.

block v British

copulate. This usage dates back to the 19th century. In standard English to block is to fill up or occupy; hence, the term is used of men.

blood n

lust or sexual passion. This old literary term often refers to hot blood. Shakespeare wrote in *Love's Labour's Lost*: "The blood of youth burns not

with such excess / As gravity's revolt to wantonness." Blood, through menstruation, also connects sexuality to reproduction.

blot n Australian

anus or buttocks. This is a 20th-century term. See also **dot**.

blow v

perform oral sex. This appears to be surprisingly a modern slang term; the verb does not appear in the *Oxford English Dictionary Supplement* of 1972, even though that supplement makes up for many of the sexual lexical omissions over the past century. Blow is probably a euphemism for **suck**, since suck is simply the converse of blow—both being oral actions. Blow could be a shortened version of **blow off**, with "off" implying that orgasm was reached. However, blow off can also mean ejaculate or masturbate, said of males. Blow could also be derived from **whore-pipe**, an 18th-century term for the penis, or from the noun blow, defined below.

blow job (also **blowjob**) means an act of oral sex, either cunnilingus or fellatio (see also **job**). *Blow Job* is the title of an Andy Warhol movie made in 1964.

• "Her manner of speaking veers wildly, from tentative and shy to disarmingly blunt: 'I love hearing the word *blowjob* in an English accent.' "
(Doug Simmons, "Harder They Come," *The Village Voice*, December 17, 1991)

blow some tunes is an African American expression meaning perform cunnilingus.

blowtorch is an early 20th-century American term for the penis, possibly derived from **Cupid's torch** (under **Cupid**).

blow, blowen n

prostitute or mistress. This is an 18th-century term. Grose's *Dictionary of the Vulgar Tongue, 1811, provides the following use of the term: "The blowen kidded the swell into a snoozing ken, and shook him of his dummee and thimble; [meaning] the girl inveigled the gentleman into a brothel and robbed him of his pocket book and watch." Blow and blowen may derive from the term "blossom," which is a flower.

blubber(s) n, n pl

breasts, especially large ones. This derogatory term dates back to the 19th century. Blubber is etymologically connected to both "blob" and "bubble." In standard English it means fat, especially whale fat.
sport blubber means show or expose one's breasts, said of females.

blue adj

relating to pornographic or smutty material. Some authors have traced blue back to the French *Bibliotheque Bleue*, a series of pornographic books published in the 17th century. *The Slang of Venery*, 1916, suggests that the blue dresses that prostitutes wore in Elizabethan times (perhaps as prison dress—see **blue gown** below) explains the sexual use of the term. The blues, a form of American folk music, derives from the "blue notes" that characterize the blues scale, a term that may have sexual connotation. It is interesting that jazz and blues are closely related, at least through the early formative years of jazz, since **jazz** has a decidedly sexual sense including the meaning to copulate. Whatever the antecedent, we now have **blue movies**, advertised by blue neon lights, that show pornography. *Blue Movie* is the title of an Andy Warhol and Paul Morrissey movie from 1969; it is also titled *Fuck*.

To illustrate that much of sexuality is cultural, consider that in French and Turkish, the color green has the sexual connotations that the color blue has in English.

blue balls is a recent term for pain in the testicles brought on by prolonged arousal. The term may derive from the blue color of the veins in the scrotum.

bluebeard is a British term signifying a lascivious male, a **whoremonger**. The word derives from blue and **beard**, meaning female pubic hair. Consequently, **bluebeard's closet** means female genitals.

blue gown means a prostitute. The customary color of Elizabethan prostitutes' gowns may have led to the sexual connotations of blue. Thomas Dekker, in *The Honest Whore*, 1604, wrote: "Your puritanical honest whore sits in a blue gown—Where!—do you know the brick house of castigation?"

blue steeler is a recent term for an exceptionally hard erection, derived from the hardness of steel and the connotation of blue seen in **blue balls**, above.

bluff n American

lesbian. This mid-20th-century derogatory term may derive from the combination of **bitch** and **fluff**. Bluff also means hoodwink, adding to the derogation.

blunt end n British

penis. This is a 20th-century military term that may stem from the fact that the glans or end of the penis is rounded (see also **bell end**). Blunt may also be employed because of its rhyme with **cunt**.

board v

copulate. This old euphemism is said of the male role in copulation; typically, one boards a boat. Shakespeare, in *Much Ado About Nothing*, has Beatrice say: "I would he had boarded me." See also **boat**.

boat n

vulva. The archetypal shape for a boat is two arcs that join at both ends, much like the vulva, hence the sexual meaning. Shakespeare wrote in *King Lear*: ". . . her boat hath a leak." This alludes to the urethral opening in the vulva. Another part of the vulva is the clitoris, sometimes referred to as the **boy in the boat**.

boating or **go boating** are recent terms for mutual cunnilingus.

boat and oar is an early 20th-century rhyming slang term for prostitute, based on the rhyme with **whore**.

bobbers n pl British

breasts. This 20th-century euphemism derives from the bouncing of breasts in movement. Bobbers is close to, and possibly derived from, **bubbies** or **boobs**.

bobbles n British

testicles. In dialect, this 19th-century term means **stones**. *See also* **bauble**.

bodkin n British

penis. The standard archaic meaning of this obsolete 19th-century term is dagger, while its current standard meaning is large needle. In both cases, the connection with penis is obvious; however, bodkin's sexual derivation may be linked to **bodikin**, a 19th-century word meaning a brothel, itself derived from both **bawdy** and ken, a cant term for **house**.

boff v

copulate or masturbate. This 20th-century term is said of males. It may derive from a contraction of **bang** with "off" or even of **bring off**.

- "But surely you aren't shy with all those girls you've . . . 'boffed'?"
  (Gore Vidal, *Myra Breckenridge*, 1968)

bog(s) n

anus. This usage derives from another meaning of bog(s), namely, a latrine or toilet. Shakespeare wrote in *A Comedy of Errors*: "In what part of her body stands Ireland? / Marry, sir, in the buttocks: I found it out by the bogs." Ireland is well known for its wet climate and its bogs.

bollocks, bollix n

See **ball**.

bone n

erect penis. This colloquialism, dating back to the early 20th century, is based on hardness. This is another bodily displacement term, since the penis does not actually contain a bone.

bone-ache and **bone-ague** are old terms for syphilis. Farmer and Henley, in their *Dictionary of Slang and Its Analogues*, 1890, quote Thomas Nashe, in *Pierce Penilesse*, 1592: ". . . 'tis not their newe bonnets will keepe them from this old boan-ack."

bone-on also means erection. Interestingly, the suffix "-on", meaning sexually aroused, leads to terms with the suffix "-off," such as **blow off**, **bring off**, and **rub off**, implying that orgasm was reached.

bone queen is a gay term for a fellator. *See also* **queen**.

boner is a term for erection or an erect penis and dates back to the mid-20th century.

bone v American

copulate. This current term is used in Spike Lee's film *She's Gotta Have It* (1986).

bonfire n British

penis. This obsolete 19th-century term may derive from the sexual sense of **fire**. *See also* **blowtorch**.

bonk *v British*

copulate. This recent term is used especially by adolescents. Bonk originally meant hit; this connotation could have been applied to the genitals and thus acquired sexual meaning (*see also* **bang**). However, its derivation could be back slang from **knob**, meaning penis. The British tabloid *Sport*, during the 1991 Gulf War, claimed that prostitutes were playing their part by donating their wages to a Gulf charity. This was reported under the headline: "Call Girls Bonk for Britain."

bonk-on meaning erection has been in use since the 1950s.

boobs *n pl*

breasts. This 20th-century colloquial term probably derives from **bubs**. Boob also has a slang meaning of mistake, making boobs similar in derogation to the term **balls**, meaning both testicles and nonsense.

• "The only gal who came near to me in the sex appeal department was pretty little Marilyn Monroe. All the others had were big boobs."
(Mae West)

book, two leav'd book *n*

female genitals. These obsolete literary terms date back to the Renaissance.

• "A handsome Maid did undertake,
And into bed she leap'd;
She open'd wide her Conjuring book,
And lay'd the leaves at large."
(Thomas D'Urfey, *Wit and Mirth*, 1719)

bookbinder's wife is an obsolete jocular British term for female genitals, because both work between the **sheets**. The pun here is on sheets, meaning those of books and those on a bed.

bordel, bordello *n*

brothel. This very old term derives from the Italian. Farmer and Henley, in their *Dictionary of Slang and Its Analogues*, 1890, provide the first quote for bordel in 1402. The *Dictionary of the Canting Crew*, 1690, defines bordello as "a bawdy-house."

bore *v British*

copulate. This 19th-century term is said of men. The word derives from the action of the penis, which can be seen as boring, that is, making a hole. Similar verbs include **prick**, **puncture**, and **scuttle**. Bore is also the past tense of **bear**, which in standard English means carry a child in pregnancy, the result of copulation.

bore *n British*

female genitals. This usage is based on the verb defined above.

bosom *n*

female breasts. Originally, this very old term applied to the breasts of males. The *Oxford English Dictionary* first quotes the word in Old English in 1000. It was a standard term for breasts, and then became a polite euphemism in Victorian times. The etymology of bosom can be traced back to a Sanskrit word meaning "bellows." *See also* **lungs**, another euphemism for breasts.

• "Let not his hand within your bosom stray,
And rudely with your pretty bubbies play."
(Ovid, "To His Mistress," translated by John Dryden, 1693)

bottle *n*

prostitution. This usage derives from a Cockney expression in which **bottle and glass** rhymes with **arse**. In England **on the bottle** means engaged in male prostitution, while in the box 27

United States, bottle refers to prostitution in general.

bottle opener is British terminology for a male homosexual, especially the **insertor**.

bottle v

perform anal intercourse. This is a derivation of the noun bottle, defined above.

bottom n British

buttocks. This colloquial term derives from the location of the buttocks at the bottom part of the body or torso. The first quote for this meaning in the *Oxford English Dictionary* is from Erasmus Darwin's *Zoonomia*, 1794: "So as to have his head and shoulders much lower than his bottom."

bottomless pit is a British derogatory term for vagina. In the Bible (Revelations) the bottomless pit is hell. *See also* **hell** and **pit**.

bottom's up refers to anal intercourse or vaginal intercourse with entry from the rear. The phrase in standard English is an informal drinking toast.

• "I say bottom's up both to women and to glasses!"
(Lewis Nkosi, *The Rhythm of Violence*, 1964)

boulders n pl American

breasts, especially large, firm ones. This is a 20th-century jocular term. The brassiere has been jokingly defined as an **over the shoulder boulder holder**.

bounce v

copulate. This 19th-century term stems from the movement of copulation, especially on a bed. **Bouncy** is an informal variant, sometimes extended to **bouncy-bouncy**.

bow n

penis. This 19th-century term derives from the musical sense of playing a **fiddle**, a euphemism for the female genitals. **Fiddle bow** is a fuller variant. Bow joins **bugle**, **drumstick**, **flute**, and **trombone** as musical terms for the penis.

box n American

1. vagina. This usage derives from box as a container and dates back to the early 20th century. Perhaps significant is the fact that box is also a colloquialism for coffin, and sex and death have some terminological overlap in that orgasm is a "little death" of sorts. Sexual intercourse has also been viewed as a burying of the penis in the vagina. *See also* **be buried alive** (under **bury**).

• "Darling, you've got no tits and a tight box." "Herbie, get off my back."
(Joke told by Bette Midler)

box lunch means cunnilingus, based on the pun of a transportable meal and an edible box.

box unseen is a variant on box, adding the hidden element of the female genitals. Shakespeare wrote in *All's Well That Ends Well*: "He wears his honour in a box unseen."

in the box stands for copulation and is said of males. It also suggests death.

2. male genitals, especially when the crotch is bulging and highly visible. *See also* **basket**.

box v

copulate. This term is usually used of men. It partly derives from the noun sense of box meaning female genitals, though it may also derive from the standard English verbal meanings of box, namely, punch and enclose.

box the Jesuit (and get cockroaches) is a British phrase for masturbation, said of males. Grose's *Dic-*

tionary of the Vulgar Tongue, 1811, suggests it is a naval term for masturbation. This phrase reflects a derogatory attitude toward Jesuits, a monastic order whose practices were regarded as leading to masturbation and sodomy. "Get cockroaches" implies ejaculation, though it is a highly unusual expression except for the prefix "cock-," and the association of cockroaches with dirt.

boy n

male homosexual, especially an effeminate one. An implication is that a boy has not yet matured to a heterosexual male. *Boys in the Band*, a 1970 movie based on the play by Matt Crowley, deals with male homosexuality.

boy in the boat n phrase

clitoris. Since the clitoris is in some ways analogous to the penis, it may not be surprising that the male gender is used and that the word is boy, not man, because of its size relative to the penis. **Boat** represents the vulva. Variants are **little boy in the boat, little man in the boat,** and **man in the boat**.

brace and bits n pl

American

breasts. This 20th-century rhyming slang term is based on the rhyme with **tits**. Significantly, bits is the rhyming term. See also **bit** for a host of sexual meanings.

brakes n

female pubic hair. In standard English, brakes are thickets. This old literary term is a pun on **break**, meaning deflower. See also **bush**.

brass, brass nail n British

prostitute. This Cockney rhyming slang term is based on the rhyme of

nail with **tail**, which is common British usage for prostitute, and brass with **arse**, meaning sexual intercourse. Brass is also a term for **money**, which is associated with prostitution.

bread n

female genitals. In *The Canterbury Tales*, Chaucer has the Wife of Bath say: "... we wives are called barley bread." Other related food terms include **biscuit, bun,** and **muffin**. Bread also has the meaning of **money**.
breadwinner is a 19th-century British term used mainly by prostitutes for the female genitals. It derives from the standard meaning of provider of a living.

break v

deflower. This usage stems from the fact that the hymen is broken in defloration. Farmer and Henley, in their *Dictionary of Slang and Its Analogues*, 1890, quote Thomas Harman's *Caveat*, 1567: "A dell is a yonge wenche, able for generation, and not yet knowen or broken by the upright man."
break and enter is a male homosexual expression for anal rape.
break her leg above the knee means deflower. This analogy between the hymen and the "leg above the knee"—farfetched as it may be—exemplifies the many sexual euphemisms that employ displacement from the genitals to other body parts.

breasts n pl

female mammary glands. In the singular, breast can apply to males as well, referring simply to the front part of the upper body. In the Victorian era, prudery temporarily turned breasts into a taboo word. However, the term returned to its standard use in the 20th century. Etymologically, breast derives from the Old English *breost*, which itself can be traced back to the Indo-European *bhreus,* meaning "to swell." *See also* **bosom.**

breeder *n*

heterosexual. This is a 20th-century homosexual term that identifies heterosexuals by their reproductive propensity.

brim *n*

prostitute. This term derives from "brimstone," an archaic term for a virago or scolding woman. The *Dictionary of the Canting Crew,* 1690, defines brim as ". . . a very Impudent, Lew'd Woman."

brim *v*

copulate. This usage derives from the noun, defined above. The *Dictionary of the Canting Crew,* 1690, defines brimming as ". . . a Boor's copulating with a Sow, also now us'd for a Man's with a Brim."

bring off *v phrase*

induce orgasm or ejaculation. The phrase contrasts with **bring on,** meaning sexually arouse someone.
• "It's much more thrilling bringing someone else off."
(A.S. Byatt, *Possession,* 1990)

Bristol City *n British*

breast. This British rhyming slang term is based on the rhyme with **titty** (under **tit**). Bristol City is the name of a football team, ample proof that the word is for male use. The significance of the choice of Bristol may be that "Bristol milk" was a slang term for sherry. (Bristol has imported sherry since the 17th century.) **Bristols** is a British term for breasts.
• "The main point (or should it be points?) of this programme is Miss Barbara Windsor's bristols which are . . . well-developed."
(*The Observer,* February 2, 1969)

broad *n*

woman. The *Oxford English Dictionary's* first quote, from L. E. Jackson and C. R. Hellyer's *Vocabulary of Criminal Slang,* 1914, defines a broad as ". . . a female confederate, a female companion, a woman of loose morals." Broad may derive from women being broad in the hips. There may also be some suggestion of **bawd** since it is close in sound to broad. *A Feminist Dictionary,* 1985, by Cheris Kramarae and Paula Treichler, defines broad as ". . . a woman who is liberal, tolerant, unconfined and not limited or narrow in scope."

broaden one's outlook *v phrase*

perform anal intercourse. This 20th-century gay jocular expression centers on "outlook," implying **eye,** which is slang for anus.

broken *adj*

deflowered. *See also* **break.**
broken oar is a variant of **boat and oar;** both are American rhyming slang terms for prostitute based on the rhyme with **whore.**

bronco *n American*

male homosexual. This early 20th-century term derives from the Spanish word for wild horse. The passive homosexual is usually referred to as the bronco, while the active homosexual is called a **broncobuster.** Bronco is one of a number of equine terms used sexually. *See also* **ass, horse,** and **stallion.**

broom *n British*

female genitals. This 19th-century usage probably derives from the brush on a broom resembling **hair** and from a pairing with **broomstick** (see below). It is also possible that the sexual meaning of this term was influenced by the Italian word *scopare*, which means "to sweep" and is a common euphemism for copulation. **broomhandle** and **broomstick** are both British terms for penis, based on **broom** and **stick**. Broomstick also means **dildo**.

brothel n

house of prostitution. This standard English term applied in the 14th century to a person, not a place, and meant a worthless fellow. By the 15th century a gender switch had occurred and a brothel referred to a female prostitute. By the 16th century **brothel house** had been shortened to brothel, which then applied to a house of prostitution only, and no longer to a person. Shakespeare made use of the term on a number of occasions, referring to a place and not a person, as in *King Lear*: "... epicurism and lust / Make it more like a tavern or a brothel / Than a grac'd palace." The etymology of brothel points to the Middle English word *breothan*, meaning "go to ruin."

brown n

anus. This is probably a shortening of brown ass or brown asshole, derived from the color of feces, and dating back to the 19th century.
brown berry is a term for a virginal anus, berry being analogous to **cherry**.
brown family is American gay terminology for the male homosexual community. **Browning family** is a variant.
brown wings is a humorous award given to Hell's Angels who perform anilingus. *See also* **red wings**.

brown v

perform anal intercourse. This verb derives from the noun defined above. Variations include **brown hole** and **do a brown (job)**.

brown madam n

female genitals. This term is a variant on **Miss Brown**. There are three plausible threads to the derivation of this term: first, Miss Brown (and consequently Brown madam) is a common name, at least in Great Britain; second, brown is a common color of pubic hair; third, since brown has a sense of propriety, as opposed to **blue**, which implies lewdness, it could be that brown is being used with irony—or in reaction formation, according to Freudian theory (that is, saying the exact opposite of what is meant). This phenomenon is not uncommon in slang.

brush n

1. *British* pubic hair. This 19th-century term is not surprising since one brushes hair and a brush can be made from hair. Brush is also a hunting term for the fox's tail, which is considered a trophy. *See also* **scut**.
• "While the penis betrayed him by visibly shrinking into the safety of the brush."
(Gore Vidal, *Myra Breckenridge*, 1968)
2. *Australian* woman considered as a sex object. This meaning derives from the fact that women are distinguished from men both by their head of hair and by their pubic hair.

brush v British

copulate. The verb form stems from the noun, defined above, and perhaps from the movement implied in the standard sense of the verb. Grose's *Dictionary of the Vulgar Tongue*, 1811, defines to brush as "... to lie with her [a woman]."

bubble-gum machine n

condom vending machine. This mid-20th-century euphemism is based on the fact that bubble gum, like condoms, is commonly sold in vending machines. Of all vending machine items, the condom is probably the most similar to gum in that it can be stretched.

bubs n pl

breasts. The term probably derives from the obsolete slang term "bub," meaning a drink. The more common and more recent **boobs** probably derives from bubs.
bubbies is a variation implying the diminutive. Farmer and Henley, in their *Dictionary of Slang and Its Analogues*, 1890, provided the first quote from Thomas D'Urfey's *New Poems*, 1686: "The Ladies here may without Scandal shew, / Face or white bubbies, to each ogling Beau."

buck v

copulate. This 18th-century usage derives from the noun buck, meaning the male of a number of animal species, and the verb buck, meaning move jerkily. Buck may also be a euphemism for **fuck**, with which it rhymes.

bucket n

1. *British* female genitals. This 19th-century derogatory term alludes to a bucket as a container. This sense may also have been influenced by **buck**.
2. *American* buttocks or anus. This term dates back to the late 19th century.

buckets n pl

breasts. This usage is probably based on the milk pail sense of bucket, in which a cow's milk is collected.

bud n American

1. virginity or virgin. This 19th-century usage stems from the standard sense of bud as a flower that has not yet opened.

2. clitoris. This recent usage is also rendered as **love bud**. *See also* **button**.
* "Her little bud was so deeply embedded that it was hardly involved in the play ..."
(Edmud Wilson, *Memoirs of Hecate County*, 1959)

budget n British

female genitals. In the 15th century, a budget meant a leather pouch or purse, that is, a container. As such, budget relates to **bag**. Additionally, budget conjures up the notion of **money**, another term for female genitals.

buds of beauty n phrase

nipples. This obsolete euphemism is based on shape. *See also* **rosebuds**.

buff-ball n

orgy. Based on "buff," meaning naked, and **ball**, this term is now obsolete.
* "The most favourite entertainment at this place is known as buff-ball, in which both sexes—innocent of clothing—madly join."
(James Greenwood, *In Strange Company*, 1873).

buffers n pl British

breasts. This 19th-century term is similar to **bumpers**, but derives from the term "buff," meaning naked, which dates back to the early 17th century.

bugger v

perform anal intercourse. Dating back to the 16th century, this term derives from the Latin *Bulgaris*, meaning "Bulgars," people who allegedly practiced anal intercourse. This is a classic case of foisting sexual practices regarded as in any way perverse onto foreigners. In addition to

the sexual meaning of bugger, the word also serves as a generally derogatory term, found in such phrases as "bugger off," "bugger you," and "bugger it." Dylan Thomas, in his play *Under Milk Wood*, wrote of a fictional Welsh town called Llareggub, which is "bugger all," which means "nothing," spelled backwards. The BBC broadcast the play in the dark days of television censorship (1954) without realizing Thomas's satire.
buggery is a formal or legal term that refers to both anal and bestial intercourse.

- "There was a young monk of
    Siberia,
  Who of frigging grew weary and
    wearier.
      At last with a yell,
      He burst from his cell,
  And buggered the Father
    Superior."
  (Anonymous, quoted in Gershon Legman, editor, *The Limerick*, 1964)

bugger n

one who performs anal intercourse. Recently the term has been used as a derogatory word for a person, as in "You silly bugger," and as a colloquial but nonderogatory term, as in "He's a cute little bugger." The term is less acceptable in Great Britain than in the United States.

bugle n British

penis. This obsolete term derives its force from the fact that a bugle is a **horn**. It adds to the list of musical instruments with sexual meanings, such as **flute** and **trombone**. A bugle or horn is also the instrument of the hunt, which can always be interpreted in the venereal sense (*see also* **venery**).

- "That a woman conceived me, I thank her . . . but that I will . . . hang my bugle in an invisible

baldrick, all women shall pardon me."
(William Shakespeare, *Much Ado About Nothing*, 1599)

bulb n

glans of the penis. This gay term is based on shape.

bulbs n pl

breasts. This mid-20th-century term takes its meaning from shape, particularly the round shapes of certain flower bulbs, or perhaps even light bulbs.

bull v

copulate. The term, said of men, dates back to the 17th century, when it was the standard verb for a bull's copulation with a cow. This is one of many terms for copulation that uses the animal world as a metaphor for human sexuality.

bull dike (dyke) n

masculine woman, usually a lesbian. The first appearance of this expression, in the *Oxford English Dictionary Supplement*, was in 1926. See also **molly dike** (under **moll**).

bull's-eye n British

vagina. This 19th-century usage reflects the male view of the vagina as the object that the penis is aiming for. *See also* **target** and **arrow**.

bullets n pl

1. testicles. In 1598, William Shakespeare wrote in *Henry IV: Part II*: "I will discharge upon her . . . with two bullets." Bullet, quite appropriately, derives from the French *boulette*, meaning "small ball," the diminutive of *boule*, meaning "ball."
2. semen. This usage is based on the fact that one shoots bullets. Aggression is clearly implied in this

term; it is consistent with other terms, such as **gun**, that link the penis with weapons. *See also* **shoot blank bullets**.

bully n

pimp. The *Dictionary of the Canting Crew*, 1690, defines bully as ". . . a supposed Husband to a Bawd, or Whore." The meaning probably stems from the standard meaning of bully, as well as from **bull**. A variation is **bully back**, which Grose's *Dictionary of the Vulgar Tongue*, 1811, defines as "A bully to a bawdy-house; one who is kept in pay, to oblige the frequenters of the house to submit to the impositions of the mother abbess, or bawd; and who also sometimes pretends to be the husband of one of the ladies, and under that pretence extorts money from greenhorns, or ignorant young men, whom he finds her with."

bum n

buttocks. This old colloquial term derives from Middle English and the Dutch *bom*. Shakespeare wrote in *A Midsummer Night's Dream*: "The wisest aunt, telling the saddest tale, / Sometimes for three-foot stool mistaketh me; / Then slip I from her bum, down topples she." The *Oxford English Dictionary* provides the first quote for bum in 1387, but cautions that the word is "not in polite use"—referring to the late 19th century. Though today more colloquial than slang, the term still carries with it a negative connotation, perhaps because of another sense meaning a hobo, dating back to the 16th century.

• "Then Sarah raised her own petticoats to her knees, to let the warmth of the fire reach her bum, as the most modest woman will do if by herself, or with her female friends, or husband, present."
(Anonymous, *My Secret Life*, 1890)

bum boy is a 19th-century derogatory expression for a passive male homosexual, derived from **bum**, above, and boy, meaning servant.

bumkin and **bumpkin** are variations of bum. Farmer and Henley, in their *Dictionary of Slang and Its Analogues*, 1890, provide a quote from 1658: "And so I take my leave; prithee sweet Thumkin, / Hold up thy coats, that I may kisse thy bumkin."

bum-tickler is British for penis, suggesting what the penis can do.

bump v

copulate. Bumping can be considered a movement of sexual intercourse.

• "Faith it odd is. For mortal to bump goddess. . . . Yeh. . . . I'll try if I can't get a stroke [and make] the light-heeled gipsy grin."
(Thomas Bridges, *A Burlesque Translation of Homer*, 1770)

bumper to bumper is an American phrase meaning lesbian sexual activity. This recent term references **bump** meaning copulate, but, from the automobile metaphor, implies rubbing, not penetration.

bumps and grinds are the pelvic thrusts and rotations in a striptease act, notable for the way they simulate the movements of copulation.

bumpers n pl

breasts. This usage derives from shape, and perhaps from the adjectival use of bumper, meaning exceptional, as in "bumper crop."

bun n British

1. female genitals. This usage, which dates back to the 17th century, may derive from other related food terms for the female genitals such as **bread**, or it may stem from a shortening of **bunny**. *See also* **buttered bun** and **touch bun for luck**.

2. prostitute. This meaning could derive from the first meaning above.

bung, bunghole n

anus. This term derives from the standard sense of bunghole, which is a hole in a cask into which a stopper can be placed, and dates back to the 17th century.

bun in the oven phrase

pregnancy. This euphemism derives from the metaphor of womb as oven. See also **oven**.

bunny n

1. female genitals. This term may refer to the fur of the four-legged bunny or the rabbit's proclivity for mating. Farmer and Henley, in their *Dictionary of Slang and Its Analogues*, 1890, quote Thomas D'Urfey's *Old Song*, 1720: "Old musty Maids that have Money / ... May have a bit for their Bunny, / To pleasure them in their Beds."

2. woman considered sexually. Playboy clubs in the 1960s had their waitresses, called Bunny Girls, dressed in bunny or rabbit costumes. The clubs closed in the 1980s.

buns n

buttocks. This usage, dating back to the 1950's, may stem from the fact that some buns have a furrow in them; however, the closeness to **bun**, meaning female genitals, may not be coincidental. *A Woman Looks at Men's Buns*, 1980, is the title of a book of nude photographs by Christie Jenkins.

burgle v

perform anal intercourse, especially forced. This 20th-century usage derives from the standard sense of burgle, meaning **break and enter**. The choice of burgle may also have been influenced by its closeness in sound to **bugger**.

burlap n

copulation. This obsolete 19th-century term may stem from the standard meaning of coarse cloth (see also **cloth**, meaning female pubic hair, and **muslin**, meaning female genitals). It may have been influenced by **lap**, meaning female genitals.
burlap sister is an obsolete term for prostitute. See also **sister**.

burning shame n

female genitals. Since the genitals metaphorically burn when aroused with lust, and shame often accompanies sexuality (**pudenda**, meaning the genitals, is derived from the Latin *pudere*, "to be ashamed"), this obsolete phrase comes as no surprise. It may also derive from the burning sensation that accompanies veneral disease.

bury v

Though the verb on its own is not used in sexual slang, it does form the basis of a number of sexual phrases:
be buried alive is 19th-century British terminology for copulate, said of men. This jocular phrase relates being buried in intercourse to being buried in death, and suggests the **sweet agony** or **sweet death** of orgasm. **Bury the bone** is a variation. See also **bone**.
bury one's wick is also 19th-century British terminology for copulate, said of a man. See also **wick**.
bury the hatchet where it won't rust is a jocular 20th-century phrase that means "make love, not war." Bury the hatchet is an idiom meaning to end strife; in this extended phrase, hatchet means the penis. The whole phrase means copulate, and is said of men.

bush n

female pubic hair or female genitals. The sexual sense of this 20th-century term obviously derives from the association of bush with **hair**.
bush beater and the variant **bush whacker** are both British terms for the penis, based on the meaning of bush and the aggressive beating or whacking task that the penis supposedly performs in intercourse.
bushy and **Bushy Park** are both British terms for female pubic hair. Park has the added connotation of parking in the vagina. To **take a turn in Bushy Park** means to copulate, and is said of men.

business n

sexual intercourse. This very old euphemism can be found in Shakespeare's *Antony and Cleopatra*: "... the business you have broached here cannot be without you; especially that of Cleopatra's, which wholly depends on your abode." "Wholly" is a pun on **hole**-y. Since business in its standard sense means any kind of busy-ness, it is a natural euphemism for sexual intercourse. In addition, the idea of **money** is present; See also **commerce**.

bust n

breasts. This old euphemism derives from the Italian *busto*, meaning "sculpture," a standard sense of bust. In the late 19th century women wore bust bodices, precursors of the modern brassiere.

butch n

1. an active or masculine lesbian. This 20th-century usage may stem from the male name or from the word "butcher." See also **femme**.
• "Then some of the girls began wearing mannish clothing. They called themselves 'Butches.'" (San Francisco *News*, September 10, 1954)

2. an active male homosexual, especially an aggressive one.

butch adj

1. pertaining to an active or masculine lesbian.
2. pertaining to an active male homosexual, especially an aggressive one.

butt n

buttocks. This term was standard from the 15th through the 17th century, but thereafter became vulgar usage. More recently the term has become colloquial. Butt originally meant the thicker end of something. *See also* **buttock**.
butt bang is a 20th-century expression meaning perform anal intercourse. *See also* **bang**. **Butt fuck** is a variant. *See also* **fuck**.

butter n British

semen. This usage dates back to the 18th century. It probably derives from **melted butter**, another term for semen, and is likely based on similarity of appearance. Yet another variation is **buttermilk**, which like **milk** itself can be compared in appearance with semen. *See also* **cream**.
buttered bun is defined thus in Grose's *Dictionary of the Vulgar Tongue*, 1811: "One lying with a woman that has just lain with another man, is said to have a buttered bun." *See also* **bun** and **sloppy seconds**.

buttock(s) n

1. musculature that forms the human rump or posterior. The term derives from the Old English *buttuc*, which essentially is **butt** plus the diminutive "-uc," which in Modern English became the suffix "-ock." The singular form refers to one of the two cheeks. The term dates back to 13th-

century Middle English, and has been standard ever since.

- "It is like a barber's chair, that fits all buttocks—the pin-buttock, the quatch-buttock, the brawn-buttock, or any buttock." (William Shakespeare, *All's Well That Ends Well*, 1604)
- "Yes, this was love, this ridiculous bouncing of the buttocks, and the wilting of the poor insignificant, moist penis." (D. H. Lawrence, *Lady Chatterley's Lover*, 1928)

buttock ball is a British term for copulation, or as Grose's *Dictionary of the Vulgar Tongue*, 1811, defines it: "The amorous congress." **Buttock stirring** is a variation.

2. *British* prostitute. This 17th-century usage is obsolete. This sense of buttock is reminiscent of other terms for the posterior that double as a reference to a prostitute or woman as a sexual object, such as **ass** and **tail**.

buttock broker means pimp or madam.

buttocking shop stands for brothel.

button n

clitoris. One possible derivation of this 19th-century colloquial term is the connection of button to sewing (*see* **buttonhole** below) and sewing's connection to sowing, as in **sow one's wild oats**. Another possible derivation is from the effect of pressing a button, that is, turning something on. A further source may be similarity of shape. The *Oxford English Dictionary* provides a medical definition from 1876: ". . . any small rounded elevation."

buttonhole, a 19th-century British term for vagina, probably derives from the sewing analogy in which the penis is a **needle**. Related penis terms are **pin** and **prick**. The **hole** in buttonhole further explains the meaning of vagina.

buttonhole factory is a British term for brothel, based on all the **work**, that is, copulation, that is done in this kind of factory.

buttonhole worker is a British euphemism for penis, based on who or what is working the buttonhole.

buttons n

nipples. This association is based on shape. The notion of turning something on by pressing buttons is implied, pointing to a similarity between clitoris and nipple, both regarded as "hot buttons."

- ". . . the thing you'll like best about going to bed with men is the featherbrush of hands like spanners on anxious buttons . . ." (Zoë Fairbairns, "the thing you'll like best," in John Whitworth, editor, *The Faber Book of Blue Verse*, 1990)

C

cab n

brothel. This term is obsolete. Grose's *Dictionary of the Vulgar Tongue*, 1811, provides the following definition: "Cab. A brothel. Mother: how many tails have you in your cab? how many girls have you in your bawdy house?"

cab-moll is an obsolete term for prostitute. *See also* **moll**.

cabbage n

vulva. This 19th-century euphemism derives from the resemblance of the vulva to a cut cabbage. The lyrics for Jelly Roll Morton's "Lowdown Blues" include the following lines: "I got a sweet woman; / She lives right back of the jail. / She's got a sign on her window / Good cabbage for sale." *See also* **greens**.

cabbage field, cabbage garden, and **cabbage patch** all mean the female genitals. *See also* **garden** and **patch**.

caboose n American

1. buttocks. This late 19th-century term is based on the caboose being the last car at the back of a train.

2. last male in a series when a number of males copulate with the same female. The caboose is therefore the last turn in a **gang bang**.

Cadbury canal n British

anus. This is the equivalent of **Hershey highway**, and is a gay term from the 1960s. Cadbury, like Hershey, is a manufacturer of chocolate.

cake n

1. female genitals. This meaning probably derives from the food's connotations of sweetness and tastiness. It dates back to the early 20th century. *See also* **bread, bun**, and **muffin**.

2. buttock. Usually found in the plural, **cakes** probably derives from the round shape of cakes.

3. sexually desirable female. This usage may have derived from **tart**, or from the first meaning above.

4. *Australian* prostitute. This meaning may have come from the first or third meaning above.

calico n American

woman considered as a sex object. This is a mid-19th-century term. Calico is a coarse cotton fabric. As with **cloth** and **muslin**, a woman's clothing can stand for a woman herself, especially as a sexual being.

call girl n

prostitute. This term is based on the fact that a prostitute can be summoned by telephone. The *Oxford English Dictionary Supplement* provides a quote from 1940, "Call Girls Die Young," the title of an article in *American Speech*; however, the term may be somewhat older, but not by much since the telephone became commonplace only in the second quarter of the 20th century. **Callhouse** is a euphemism for brothel. *See also* **house of call** under **house**.

camp n American

1. brothel. This early 20th-century underworld term may derive from the standard meaning of to camp: to sleep or rest.

2. exaggerated homosexual behavior or gestures. The *Oxford English Dictionary* cites the first use in 1909 by J. R. Ware in *Passing English of the Victorian Era*. Susan Sontag wrote an essay titled "Notes on 'Camp' " in 1964 in which she says: "The hallmark of Camp is the spirit of extravagance." Bruce Rodgers, in *Gay Talk*, 1972, also defined the term: "Camp is burlesque, fun, an ability to poke a jocular finger at one's own frustrations and guffaw at the struggles of other pathetics, homosexuals or famous, influential people." Eric Partridge suggests the term derives from *kemp*, British dialect for rough. It may also derive from the theater use of "to camp something up," that is, to satirize something in an outrageous way. It is worth noting that men used to play women's roles in the theater, and this could have given rise to the homosexual sense of the word.

can n

1. *British* female genitals. This obsolete 19th-century term probably derives from the container sense of the word. Perhaps the association of the verb can, meaning able to, influenced the sexual use.

2. *American* buttocks. Often in the plural, **cans**, this term is based on shape.

3. *American* breasts. This term is always used in the plural.

canary n

1. penis. This obsolete term probably derives from another old sense, meaning a **codpiece**. Canary is similar to **cock**, since both terms relate to both a bird and the penis.

2. mistress. Also obsolete, this usage derives from the fact that a canary is a commonly kept or caged **bird** and has bright plumage, suggesting a mistress's smart dress.

candle n British

penis. This old coinage is based on a candle's shape and on the fact that it will **melt** when lit. *See also* **wick** and **burning shame**.

- ". . . didst thou Soul by Inch of
  Candle sell, /
  To gain the glorious Name of
  Pimp to Hell?"
  (John Wilmot, the earl of
  Rochester, "To the Author of a
  Play Call'd Sodom," in *Works*,
  1680)
- "You worthless son of a bitch—
  I'm about to polish your god
  damned candle and you hoch me
  about Cosmo . . ."
  (Howard Chaykin, *The
  Satisfaction of Black Mariah*, 1987)

candlestick is a British term for the female genitals, based on it being a container for a candle. *See also* **stick**.

candy n

sexual gratification. This 20th-century term also means penis, especially in the term **candy stick**. Terry Southern and Mason Hoffenberg wrote an erotic novel titled *Candy*, 1958, which has become a classic of sexual literature.

cane v British

copulate. Said of men, this 20th-century distinctly British usage may reflect the so-called **English vice**, namely, flagellation.

cane n British

penis. This obsolete 19th-century term stems from the fact that a cane is a **stick**, and that one can beat or **hit** with a cane.

canned fruit n

a homosexual who hides or denies his homosexuality. This 20th-century gay coinage stems from **fruit**, which is a slang term for homosexual.

cannibal n American

fellator. This obsolete 20th-century term is based on the standard sense of the term, meaning a person who eats another. *See also* **eat**.

canoodle v American

caress or fondle. This onomatopoeic term dates back to the 19th century. It may derive from "act as a noodle," meaning play the fool. *See also* **firkytoodle**.

cans n pl

See **can**, senses 2 and 3.

cap n

diaphragm used for contraception. This shortened version of **Dutch cap**, which dates back to the 17th century, is a 20th-century term.

Cape Horn n British

female genitals. This jocular geographic reference derives from the sexual sense of **horn**. In circumnavigating the world, ships passed Cape Horn at the southern tip of South America, hence this 19th-century naval usage, now obsolete.

Cape of Good Hope n

British

female genitals. Like **Cape Horn**, this is obsolete naval usage. There is a jocular wishfulness in the name, particularly since the Cape of Good Hope is the beautiful port at Cape Town, South Africa, where one can **dock**.

captain n *British*

menstruation. Colloquialisms using this term include **my captain has come** and **the captain is home**; they date back to the 18th century and are now obsolete. **The cardinal is home** is a variant, probably based on cardinal meaning a deep red color.

Captain Standish n *British*

erect penis. This obsolete term dates back to the 19th century. *See also* **stand**.

caress v

touch or fondle sexually. This standard English term dates back to the 12th century. It is derived from the Latin *carus*, meaning "dear." *See also* **whore**.

carnal knowledge n

sexual intercourse. This well-known euphemism refers to **knowledge** of the **flesh**. Carnal is derived from the Latin *carnus*, meaning "meat." Carnal knowledge is a legal term, used in courts of law. The term is also used in English translations of the Bible, and can be traced back to Middle English. It is one of a family of euphemistic phrases that include **carnal acquaintance**, **carnal connection**, **carnal enjoyment**, and **carnal intercourse**. *Carnal Knowledge*, 1971, by Jules Feiffer, is the title of a play and a movie.

carnal parts n pl

male or female genitals. **Carnal stump** (under **stump**) is a 17th-century colloquialism for penis, while **carnal trap** (under **trap**) is a 17th-century colloquialism for the vagina.

carrion n

prostitute. This obsolete derogatory term derives from the term's standard meaning of **meat** or **flesh**.

carrot n

penis. This term based on shape, was first used in the 17th century. *See also* **banana**.

Carvel's ring n *British*

female genitals. This obsolete jocular term is best explained by Grose in the *Dictionary of the Vulgar Tongue*, 1811: "Hans Carvel, a jealous old doctor, being in bed with his wife, dreamed that the Devil gave him a ring, which, so long as he had it on his finger, would prevent his being made a cuckold: waking he found he had got his finger the Lord knows where." *See also* **ring** and **Lord knows what**.

casanova n

successful seducer of many women. This colloquialism, used from the 19th century onward, is based on the life of Giovanni Jacopo Casanova de Seingalt (1725–1798). In twelve volumes of memoirs, he listed over a hundred mistresses and claimed many more seductions.
- "A resplendent Casanova in a royal blue sports jacket." (John Braine, *The Vodi*, 1959)

case n *British*

vagina. This obsolete term is based on the metaphor of a container (*see also* **bag** and **box**). **Caze** and **kaze** are variations. Shakespeare used the term in *The Merry Wives of Windsor*: "Vengeance on Jenny's case! fie on her!—never name her, child, if she be a whore."

case *v*

copulate. This 20th-century term is used of men.

cat *n*

1. prostitute. The *Dictionary of the Canting Crew*, 1690, defines cat as "a common whore." One might assume that the word is derived from the catching of mice, since **mouse** is a slang term for the penis; however, in the sexual sense, cat predates mouse by centuries. The association of cat with female sexuality is very old, and explains the derivation of the term. *See also* **alley cat**.

cathouse is a 20th-century term for brothel, based on **cat** and **house**. A variation is **catflat**.

2. *American* female genitals. This usage is derived by extension from cat meaning prostitute, and possibly from the French *chat*, which means both "cat" and "female genitals." The fur of a cat is also associated with the female pubic hair. *See also* **puss** and **pussy**.

cat and kitties is an American rhyming slang term for breasts, since kitties rhymes with **titties** (under **tit**). The choice of this rhyme is transparent because of the female sexual meaning of cat and the association of kitties being fed milk.

catheads is an obsolete British naval term for breasts, based on the standard meaning of cathead—namely, a beam on a ship. A cathead is also a kind of large apple. *See also* **apples**.

catmeat is a 19th-century British term for the female genitals. *See also* **meat**.

catskin is a 19th-century British term for pubic hair.

cat with its throat cut is a recent 20th-century British derogatory

expression for the female genitals. The term reflects aggression against women.

3. male homosexual, usually a passive one. This 20th-century term is probably an abbreviation of **catamite**.

catamite *n*

homosexual boy, usually the passive partner of a pederast. The term originated with a character from Greek mythology, *Ganymede*, who was a youth abducted by Zeus. The Latin name is Catamitus, from which catamite is derived. Catamite is a standard, formal term that has been used since the 16th century.

• "It was the afternoon of my eighty-first birthday, and I was in bed with my catamite when Ali announced that the archbishop had come to see me." (Anthony Burgess, *Earthly Powers*, 1980)

catch *n American*

homosexual boy. This variation on **catamite** is based on the baseball concepts of pitch and catch. *See also* **pitch**.

catch a buzz *v phrase*

stimulate oneself with an electric vibrator. This recent expression used by females plays on the pun in buzz, meaning both the noise of vibration and a good sensation. The phrase is also a 1960s term meaning to get high on drugs or whatever stimulates one.

catch an oyster *v phrase* *British*

copulate. This 19th-century phrase expresses the female point of view, since **oyster** refers to ejaculated semen.

catcher's mitt *n American*

cervical diaphragm used for contraception. This humorous term exploits a baseball metaphor in which the mitt catches or stops the ball. In addition, the mitt and the diaphragm have a similar shape, namely round and concave.

catso, catzo n British

penis. This obsolete 17th-century term is based on the Italian *cazzo*, meaning "penis."

cattle, cattle truck n

copulation. These early 20th-century rhyming slang terms are based on the actual and implied rhyme with **fuck**. See *also* **bull** and **cow**.

cauliflower n British

female genitals. This obsolete 19th-century term may derive from **flower** and from the fact that cauliflower as a vegetable is one of the **greens**. See *also* **cabbage**.

cave n

vagina, especially a large one. This 19th-century term alludes to cave temples, or *cunnus diaboli*, as the church called them, which were used for religious and sexual purposes. See *also* **den** and **grotto**.

cellar n British

female genitals. This obsolete usage stems from a cellar being dark, moist, and situated below or at the bottom of a building. See *also* **bottomless pit**.

center n

female genitals. The female genitals are located at the center of the body, and many of the euphemisms originated by men for this area employ this term. John Cleland's *Fanny Hill: Memoirs of a Woman of Pleasure*, 1749, makes use of the following terms for the female genitals: **center of desire**, **center of the senses**, and

center spot. Other terms include **center of attraction** and **center of bliss**, both of which are 18th-century euphemisms that pun on the central bodily location of the genitals and their attractiveness to males and source of bliss to both sexes.

central furrow and **central cut** are 19th-century British terms for the female genitals. See *also* **cut** and **furrow**.

central office, another 19th-century euphemism for the female genitals, attains its force from the **business** metaphor. See *also* **commerce** and **commodity**.

chain gang n

male homosexual orgy. This modern gay coinage jocularly suggests prisoners (of sex) chained together. See *also* **daisy chain**.

chamber n British

room, especially a bedroom that serves as the setting for sex. Sexual phrases with the word chamber include the Elizabethan **chamber combat**, meaning sexual intercourse, in which the metaphor of war is employed, and **chamber work**, in which labor is implied.

chamber of commerce is an American underworld expression for a brothel, punning on the business side of the operation. See *also* **commerce**.

charge v

copulate. This colloquial term dates back to the 16th century and is said of men. Charge derives its sexual meaning from the concept of battle, since a man charges with his **weapon**; however, the monetary sense of charge, as in charge a fee, may have influenced the use of this verb. Shakespeare has Pistol say in *Henry IV: Part II*: "Then to you, Mistress Dorothy; I will charge you."

charley, charlie n

1. *British* vagina. This 19th-century term is rhyming slang based on the rhyme of Charley/Charlie Hunt with **cunt**. (See also **berk**, where the rhyming term is also hunt.) Charley is simply a common male name, while hunt has both rhyming properties and the suggestion of a sexual chase. *See also* **venery**.

2. *Australian* a girl considered sexually. This rhyming slang term derives from Charlie Wheeler rhyming with **sheila**, the most common Australian slang term for a girl or woman. Charlie can also mean a prostitute.

charleys, charlies n pl

1. breasts. This 19th-century term may derive from the common name or from King Charles II, who had many mistresses.

2. *British* testicles. This meaning of the term has come into use during the 20th century.

charms n pl

breasts. This 17th-century colloquialism may stem from the male fascination with breasts. The term is commonly used in the phrase "flashing one's charms," and often implies more than breasts.

- "Naked she lay; clasped in my
  longing arms,
  I filled with love, and she all over
    charms."
  (John Wilmot, the earl of
  Rochester, Introduction to "The
  Imperfect Enjoyment," in *Works*,
  1680)

charver n British

sexual intercourse. This mid-19th-century term was used mainly in the underworld but is now obsolete. The term may derive from the Romany *charvo*, meaning "interfere with someone." The French *chauffer*,

meaning "to heat," is another etymological possibility.

chassis n

a woman's body, particularly viewed as a sex object. The automobile metaphor in this 20th-century term gives rise to the pun on **ride** and **drive**. The poet e.e. cummings made great use of the automobile metaphor in the poem "she being Brand." *See also* **convertible**.

chat n British

female genitals. This 19th-century term derives from the French *chat*, meaning **cat**.

cheater n

condom. This 20th-century colloquialism is now obsolete, since the advent of **AIDS** has changed perceptions of condom use. The term was probably coined by males, since males may have regarded themselves as being cheated of pleasure when wearing a condom.

cheaters n pl American

padding for the breasts or buttocks. *See also* **falsies**.

cheeks n pl

buttocks. This colloquialism has been prevalent since the 18th century. It alludes to the similar roundness of facial cheeks and buttocks.

cheese n American

attractive young woman. **Cheesecake** refers to photographs of seminude or nude women. Both of these 20th-century terms may derive from the expression "say cheese" to the camera. *See also* **cake** and **beefcake**.

cherries n pl

nipples. This term refers to the reddish color and probably can be traced to the older term **cherrilets** or **cher-rylets**, which was almost standard English in the 16th and 17th centuries.

cherry n

1. girl or young woman. This is a 19th-century colloquial term. Since the 16th century, however, cherry has been used as a term of endearment, probably deriving from the French *chérie*, meaning "beloved."
cherry pie is a recent term for a young girl, especially a virgin. *See also* **pie**, **cake**, and **tart**.
cherry-pipe is a 19th-century British rhyming slang term for a sexually aroused woman, based on the rhyme with ripe, meaning sexually ripe or mature. **Pipe** also means either male or female genitals, while the verb pipe means copulate.
2. hymen. This usage is based on red cherry juice being similar to the blood that may flow after deflowering. Though a current term, it has been used for centuries, as these anonymous 17th-century lines attest: "My tender youth thy waist shall clip, / And fix upon thy cherry lip; / And lay thee down on this green bed, / Where thou shalt lose thy maidenhead."
3. virgin. This extension from the second sense above can be applied to both females and males.
cherry-picker is a British term for a man who pursues either virgins or a **catamite** (a boy kept by a pederast).

chestnuts n pl

1. breasts. This colloquial 20th-century term is based on the shape of "nuts on the chest" as well as the food aspect.
2. testicles. This 20th-century usage is also based on shape and the fact that chestnuts are **nuts**.

chick n

young woman. This informal term was widely used in the 1960s. Dating back to the early part of the 20th century, chick has been used as jazz slang for a young, hip woman. *See also* **bird**.

chicken n

1. young woman. This usage is a variant of **chick**.
chicken ranch is a 20th-century slang term for a brothel, especially one in a rural area. The derivation may be linked to the notion that customers paid for services with chickens instead of cash, though the prostitutes themselves could be the chicks or chickens. A well-known chicken ranch in Gilbert, Texas, inspired the musical *The Best Little Whorehouse in Texas*.
2. boy with little or no homosexual experience, considered as a sexual object by a homosexual.
chicken fancier, **chicken queen**, and **chicken hawk** refer to a man in pursuit of a chicken.
3. penis. Since a **cock** is a chicken, this euphemism appears reasonable.

chimney n British

vagina. This 19th-century term alludes to a chimney as a passageway. Expressions such as **sweep out the chimney** and **make the chimney smoke** refer to copulation and extend the sexual use of the term. The chimney is also associated with **fire**.
chimney-stopper is a British term for penis.

chink n British

female genitals. This obsolete 19th-century term is based on the meaning of **crack** or **cleft**, but also puns on chink's other slang meanings of money and prison.

chitty n British

semen. This obsolete 18th-century term derives from the Middle English term *chithe*, meaning "seed."

chop-chop n South African

sexual molestation. This recent term is used especially by black street orphans.
- "They submit to . . . 'chop-chop,' sexual molestation by cruising pedophiles who give them unaccustomed affection and enough for a meal afterward." (The New York Times, December 10, 1991)

chopper n British

penis. This 20th-century term implies sexual brutality from the male's point of view. Tony Thorne, in his Bloomsbury Dictionary of Contemporary Slang, 1990, refers to chopper as "a working-class vulgarism." Once when Harold Wilson, the British Prime Minister, rearranged his cabinet, one of London's evening newspapers had to change its headline from "Wilson Gets His Chopper Out" to, in the later edition, "Wilson Gets His Axe Out."

chuck v

copulate. This usage dates back to the 19th century. Chuck a tread is an obsolete British phrase also meaning copulate. See also tread.

chuff n

1. British passive male homosexual. The etymology of this 20th-century term is obscure, but the verb form of chuff means to thrust.
2. Australian buttocks or anus. This meaning could be derived from chuffy, meaning chubby or having fat cheeks.
chuff box means vagina. See also box.

chuff v British

masturbate. This 19th-century term probably refers to the standard meaning to thrust. Additionally,

"chuffed" means happy or pleased. Chuffer is a variant, also meaning masturbate.

chuffer n British

active male homosexual. This obsolete term probably derives from chuff meaning thrust.

chum n British

1. female genitals. This 19th-century usage refers back to chum meaning friend. This term could be used by either sex, but is probably used mainly by males.
2. penis. Often jokingly called man's best friend, this 19th-century term is used mainly by males.

chunk n American

copulation. This early 20th-century coinage is similar in flavor to piece or bit.
chunk of meat is a derogatory expression meaning a female as a sex object. See also meat.

church n

bathhouse or Turkish bath, a place where male homosexuals meet for sex (see baths). This jocular gay usage stems from the regular, or religious, attendance at these venues by some gay men.

churn v

masturbate. This obsolete 19th-century term refers to the churning movement or agitation involved in the act.

churn n British

female genitals. This obsolete 19th-century usage derives from the conventional meaning of churn, that is, a container or receptacle in which a paddle is moved in order to make butter from milk.

circle n

vagina. This Elizabethan literary euphemism is based on shape. Shakespeare wrote in *Romeo and Juliet*: "... 'twould anger him / To raise a spirit in his mistress' circle...." *See also* **hole** and **ring**.

circus n

orgy or erotic performance or exhibition. This 20th-century expression is based on the standard sense of a varied and entertaining performance.

civet n British

female genitals. This usage is now obsolete. A civet is a type of wild cat known for its fur and for its secretions, which are the ingredients of some perfumes. The etymology of civet traces back to Arabic *zabad*, meaning "civet perfume." *See also* **cat** and **fur**.

clam diving n phrase

American, Australian

cunnilingus. In this 20th-century expression, clam suggests the female genitals. *See also* **dive**.

clangers n pl British

testicles. This term dates back to the 19th century. *See also* **clappers** and **ding-dongs**.

clap n

venereal disease, usually gonorrhea. This term was standard English from the 16th through the 19th century. Clap is derived from the Old French *clapoir*, meaning "venereal sore" and *clapier*, meaning "brothel." Perhaps that explains why the 16th-century term **malady of France** referred to venereal disease. The military's concern with clap was evident from George Farquhar's *The Recruiting Officer*, 1706: "Five hundred a year besides guineas for claps." From the 19th century onward, clap became a slang term. *See also* **pox**.

clappers n pl British

testicles. This 19th-century usage derives from the standard meaning of clapper, the part of a bell that hangs down and swings. The connection to **clap** may also have influenced the use of this term.

clean up the kitchen v

phrase

perform **anilingus**. This 20th-century expression is based on both cleaning up a mess and eating.

cleavage n American

the space between a woman's breasts, especially the crease created when the breasts are pushed together by clothing or a brassiere. This colloquial term dates back to the 19th century. It has also been applied to the crease at the top of the buttocks.
• "Kids have to learn not to copy the stars. I tell them, cleavage won't get you to the top. Sex is something different. It's not obvious."
(*The Spectator*, June 6, 1958)

cleave, cleaver n British

a woman considered to be sexually promiscuous. These obsolete 18th-century terms may derive from the standard clasping or splitting sense of the words.

cleft n

female genitals. This usage dates back to the 17th century. It is one of the many shape terms, including **cut**, **furrow**, and **slit**, that are used in a sexual sense.
• "... Fielding anointed her there with a million kisses, gentle,

lapping, and then bolder, the cleft itself. . . ."
(Morris Lurie, *Seven Books for Grossman*, 1983)

clicket *n*

sexual intercourse. This 17th-century term is obsolete. In standard English it applied to the copulation of foxes. Grose's *Dictionary of the Vulgar Tongue*, 1811, provided the following use of the term: "The cull and the mort are at clicket in the dyke; the man and the woman are copulating in the ditch."

cliff *n*

breasts. This Elizabethan literary term alludes to the breasts' outline against the body. Shakespeare, in *A Comedy of Errors*, refers geographically to breasts as follows: "Where England?—I look'd for the chalky cliffs, but I could find no whiteness in them."

climax *n*

orgasm. This standard English term was first used in the 17th century. It derives from the Greek *klimax*, meaning "ladder." *See also* **climb**.
• "First: breast-fondling. Then light n' lively kissing;
next: pet-to-climax (tongue and ear)."
(Lincoln Kirstein, "Double Date," in John Whitworth, editor, *The Faber Book of Blue Verse*, 1990)

climax *v*

reach orgasm. This is polite 20th-century usage.

climb *v*

copulate with a woman. This term, said of men, dates back to the 17th century. In his classic study on dreams and sexuality *The Interpretation of Dreams*, 1913, Freud refers to climbing stairs as an unconscious metaphor for sexual intercourse.

clipped in the ring *phrase*

deflowered. This Elizabethan pun is based on clipped meaning **hit** and **ring**, referring to the vagina while punning on the boxing ring.

clitoris *n*

female erectile organ located at the front of the vulva, regarded as homologous to the penis. This standard English term was first used in the 17th century. The word may derive from the Greek *kleitoris*, which in turn comes from the Greek *kleiein*, meaning "close." Conjecture has it that this derivation results from the clitoris being hidden from view by the labia and having no urethral opening, unlike the penis. Wayland Young, in *Eros Denied*, 1964, suggests that the word may derive from the Greek *kleitos*, meaning "renowned," "famous," or "excellent," or from *kleitor*, meaning "hill," hence clitoris, a "little hill." William Smellie's *Treatise on the Theory and Practice of Midwifery*, 1752, regarded by Peter Thicknesse as "the most bawdy, indecent and shameful Book which the Press ever brought into the world," is quoted in Peter Fryer's *Mrs Grundy: Studies in English Prudery*, 1963, as stating: "The Clitoris . . . is found between the Labia on the middle and forepart of the Pubis."
clit and **clitty** are colloquial variations, with clitty being the more affectionate term.
• "She began to draw on paper. 'Now this is a cunt, and here is something you probably don't know about—the clit. That's where the feeling is. The clit hides, you see, it comes out now and then, it's pink and very sensitive."
(Charles Bukowski, *Women*, 1979)

clithopper is 1970s terminology for a promiscuous lesbian.

clitorize is an obsolete 19th-century British colloquialism meaning masturbate, said of women.

closet case n

gay male who keeps his homosexuality a secret. Variations on this 20th-century gay slang term include **closet gay**, **closet queen**, and **closet queer**. See also **gay**, **queen**, and **queer**; and **come out of the closet**.

cloth n

female pubic hair. This is an obsolete 18th-century euphemism. See also **cotton**.

club n

penis. This 19th-century term is one of many warlike words such as **bayonet**, **poker**, **sword**, and **weapon** that signify the penis. Club additionally puns on the societal sense of the term, in which a club implies **members**.

club v British

copulate. This 19th-century term is used of males.

club sandwich n American

sexual intercourse between three people. This 20th-century colloquialism is based on the composition of a club sandwich (three slices of bread or toast with filling between them). See also **cluster fuck** and **sandwich**.

clucky adj Australian

pregnant. This 20th-century euphemism is based on the sound of a hen with her brood of chicks. See also **hen**.

cluster fuck n

sexual threesome. This 20th-century term is based on the physical in-timacy of a cluster. See also **club sandwich**.

cluster fuck party means an orgy. See also **party**.

coachman on the box n
phrase

venereal disease. This early 20th-century rhyming slang term is based on the rhyme with **pox**, meaning syphilis.

cobblers, cobblers' awls n pl British

testicles. These Cockney rhyming slang terms derive from the rhyme with **balls** (under **ball**). Significantly, an awl is a pointed instrument or tool for piercing holes. Also, **cobs** is a colloquial term for **stones** or **pebbles**, both of which also mean testicles. A variation is **cobbs**.

cock n

1. penis. From the 15th through the 18th century, this term was standard English; only from the 19th century onward did it become a vulgar term. This sexual usage most likely derives from the watercock, spout, or faucet sense of the term rather than from the male chicken sense.
* "O man, what art thou when thy cock is up?"
(Nathaniel Fields, *Amends for Ladies*, 1618)

cock alley is 18th-century British terminology for the female genitals. Variants include **cock hall**, an 18th-century term, and **cock inn**, a variation of cock hall, with inn punning on **hotel** and "in." "The Widow That Keeps the Cock Inn" was a popular street ballad of the 19th century. **Cock lane** is another variant. See also **alley**.

cockatrice is a term for prostitute dating back to the 16th century. The cockatrice was a legendary monster hatched by a serpent from a cock's egg.

cockchafer is a 19th-century British term for the female genitals, based on the action of the vagina during intercourse.

cockeater is a 20th-century term for a fellator, often a male homosexual (*see also* **eat**). **Cocklover** is a more endearing 20th-century reference to a fellator.

cock holder is another 19th-century British term for the vagina.

cock loft is a British term for the female genitals dating from the 18th-century. It is based on the standard meaning of a place where male chickens are kept.

cockpit is an older term for the female genitals, dating back to the 16th century. *See also* **pit** and **bottomless pit**.

- "Now all caution abandoned, he poured a long slow stream of fire into her cockpit."
  (Philip Jose Farmer, *The Henry Miller Dawn Patrol*, 1977)

Cockshire is a 19th-century British jocular term for the vagina, based on the punning phrase **member for Cockshire**.

cockstand is British usage for an erection; it dates back to the 18th century. *See also* **stand**.

- "He had a tremendous cockstand, and felt that if it was not allayed pretty quickly that he must burst."
  (Rosa Fielding, in Steven Marcus, *The Other Victorians*, 1966)

cocksucker is perhaps the most derogatory term for a fellator; it is also used as an insult among males. This term can be traced back to the 19th century. *See also* **sucker**.

cocktail is a 19th-century British term for prostitute. In the 20th century the term has also been used for male homosexual prostitute. The now standard English sense of cocktail—a mixed alcoholic drink usually

taken before a meal—could derive from the sexual sense of the term, though this has not been shown. *See also* **tail**.

cockteaser means a woman who leads a man on sexually but does not permit copulation. The term dates back to the 19th century. **Cocktease** is a variation and may also be used as a verb. Farmer and Henley's *Dictionary of Slang and Its Analogues*, 1890, defines cockteaser as: "A girl in the habit of permitting all familiarities but the last."

2. *American* female genitals. This southern dialectal usage may derive from **cockles**. Frederic Cassidy, editor of the *Dictionary of American Regional English* (Volume 1, 1985), explains: "At a point roughly the same as the Mason-Dixon Line, there is a division in meaning. In the North cock refers to the male genitals, but in the South its use is restricted to the female genitals. Missouri is a border state in which both meanings are used."

cockles n pl

female genitals, especially the labia. This obsolete 18th-century term is based on appearance.

cocoa butter n

semen of a black man. This 20th-century coinage is based on cocoa being dark brown and **butter** being a euphemism for semen.

coconuts n pl

1. breasts, especially large ones. This usage is based on both shape and the fact that coconuts contain milk.

2. testicles. This term is based on shape and the sexual meaning of **nuts**.

cod n

scrotum. This very old term was standard English from the 14th through the 18th century; it became a slang term from the 19th century onward. The word derives from the Old English meaning of shell or **bag**, dating back, according to the *Oxford English Dictionary*, to 1000.

codpiece is a bag or piece of a man's clothing that covers his genitals. Grose's *Dictionary of the Vulgar Tongue*, 1811, defines codpiece as: "The fore flap of a man's breeches." The flap was fashionable from the 14th through the 15th century. It was originally intended as protection in combat, but in Shakespeare's day it had already become the subject of bawdy jokes. Usually brightly decorated, the codpiece is regarded by some historians of dress as one of the most audacious pieces of clothing ever invented. By extension, codpiece also came to mean penis; this meaning survived from the 17th through the 19th century.

- "Nor do you think it worth your care
  How empty and how dull
  The heads of your admirers are,
  So that their cods be full."
  (John Wilmot, the earl of Rochester, *Works*, 1680)

cods has been a colloquial British term for testicles since the 16th century.

coffeehouse n

vagina. Dating back to the 18th century, this term is now obsolete. Grose, in his *Dictionary of the Vulgar Tongue*, 1811, provides usage of the term as follows: "To make a coffee house out of a woman's **** [sic]; to go in and out and spend nothing." **Coffee shop** is a variant.

coffee grinder is a 20th-century American term for prostitute. *See also* **grind**.

coffee stalls is 20th-century British rhyming slang for testicles, based on the rhyme with **balls**.

coinslot n

vagina. This recent term suggests a coinage influenced by prostitution because of the connection between sex and **money**. However, the "slot" part of the term may simply be a variation on **slit**.

coit v

copulate. Derived from the Latin *coire*, meaning "go together," this formal euphemism was first used in the 16th century.

coit n

1. copulation. This is an abbreviation of **coition** and **coitus**.

2. *Australian* buttocks. Possibly derived from a **quoit**, meaning a ring or round object in standard English, this is a 20th-century term.

coition, coitus n

copulation. In the 16th century, coition was also used to mean conjunction in the general, nonsexual, sense. The sexual connotation of coition eventually became the only sense of the word. Both coition and coitus are technical terms derived from the Latin *coire*, meaning "come together."

- "A little coitus never hoitus." (Anonymous)

coitus in axilla means sexual intercourse in the armpit.

coitus interruptus means sexual intercourse in which withdrawal occurs before ejaculation.

coitus per anum means anal intercourse.

coitus reservatus means sexual intercourse with the male delaying or avoiding ejaculation.

cojones n pl American

testicles. This 20th-century term derives from the Spanish slang term. Like **balls** (under **ball**), it can also mean guts, strength, or chutzpah.

- "The baseball field was mud up to your cojones."
(Truman Capote, *In Cold Blood*, 1965)

Colonel Puck n *American*

copulation. This usage is based on the rhyme with **fuck**. This early 20th-century term is now obsolete. A variation is **colonial puck**.

come v

reach or experience orgasm. This expression has been used since Shakespeare's time, and although originally euphemistic, it is less so today because of the slang use of the noun come, meaning semen. Whereas **die** and **spend** were the foremost terms used in centuries past to refer to the experiencing of orgasm, come has become the dominant euphemism of this century.
- "A notorious harlot named Hearst
In the pleasures of men is well-versed.
     Reads a sign o'er the head
     Of her well-rumpled bed:
'The Customer Always Comes First!' "
(Anonymous, quoted in Gershon Legman, editor, *The Limerick*, 1969)

come about is a British euphemism from the 19th century meaning copulate, said of men.

come aloft is a variant of come about, though an older, now obsolete 16th-century meaning was to get an erection.
- "I cannot come aloft to an old woman."
(John Dryden, *The Maiden Queen*, 1668)

come off is an old expression meaning ejaculate.
- "You come on, you come off—say, do what you please—
And the worst you can fear is but a disease."
(John Wilmot, the earl of Rochester, *Works*, 1680)

come one's cocoa is a 20th-century British expression meaning ejaculate. *See also* **cocoa butter**.

come n

semen. This meaning derives from the verb, defined above.

comefreak is a recent 20th-century term for a fellator, especially a male homosexual. It derives from "freak" and refers to any nonstandard sexual practice.

come out of the closet v *phrase*

reveal one's homosexuality. **Come out** is an abbreviated version.
- "Dudley had come out of the closet and announced he was a homosexual."
(Charles Bukowski, *Women*, 1979)

commerce n

sexual intercourse. This is a 16th-century euphemism. *See also* **business**, **commodity**, and **ware**.

commodity n

female genitals. This term is a 16th-century euphemism. A ballad titled "The Maid of Tottenham," from a collection of songs and sonnets called *Choyce Drollery* (edited in 1886, but containing much older material), offers the following lines:
She made to him low curtsies
And thankt him for his paine,
The young man is to High-gate gone,
The maid to London came
To sell off her commodity
She thought it for no shame.

Commodity joins a number of related terms such as **business**, **thing**, and **ware**.

common adj

describing a prostitute who is available to all. From this adjective comes

commoner, meaning prostitute. Shakespeare was referring to this meaning when he wrote in *All's Well That Ends Well*: "A commoner o' the camp."

common house is an Elizabethan term for brothel.

common sewer is a derogatory British term for a prostitute dating from the 19th century. *See also* **drain**.

conceive *v*

become pregnant. This standard English meaning dates back to the 13th century. It derives from the Latin *concipere*, meaning "take in." To conceive also means to have a conception of or to know, and thus relates to **knowledge**, which has both epistemological and sexual meaning.

concern *n British*

genitals of either sex. This obsolete 19th-century euphemism probably derives from the interest people generally have in the genitals. *See also* **affair**.

concubine *n*

mistress or secondary wife. This standard English term dates back to the 13th century and is found in translations of the Bible. It derives from the Latin *concubere*, meaning "lie down together," a biblical euphemism for sexual intercourse.

condom *n*

sheath worn over the erect penis during sexual intercourse to prevent pregnancy or venereal infection. This standard English term dates back to the 17th century. John Wilmot, the earl of Rochester, coauthored a pamphlet in 1667 titled "A Panegyric Upon Cundum," in which is written: "Happy the man who in his pocket keeps ... a well-made cundum." Early versions of the condom were made from the dried gut of a sheep;

a primary purpose of primitive condoms was probably to artificially increase the size of the penis. The term may derive from a certain Colonel Cundum, who is attributed with the condom's invention, though there are competing theories, including that Cundum was a doctor. Some hold that the device was named after the town of Condom in France, perhaps home of the invention. It is possible that condom is simply a made-up word combining the French *con*, meaning **cunt**, with the suffix "-dom," indicating domain. The variant **cundum** could be a combination of "cun-," as in **cunny**, with "-dum," as in dumb, meaning silent or stupid (*see also* **dumb**). Condomania is the name of a store in New York City that specializes in selling condoms.

congress *n*

sexual intercourse. This term is based on the coming together, meeting, or union of the sexes. The term has been used in this sense since the 16th century, and has slowly evolved from a euphemism into a formal, legalistic term. James Boswell wrote in his *London Journal*: "I picked up a fresh, agreeable young girl ... and we had a very agreeable congress." Besides its modern legal usage, it is also occasionally used in humorous fashion.

- "Nothing in our culture, not even home computers, is more overrated than the epidermal felicity of two featherless bipeds in desperate congress." (Quentin Crisp, quoted in Jon Winokur, editor, *The Portable Curmudgeon*, 1987)

conjugate *v*

copulate. This 18th-century jocular term derives from the Latin *conjugare*, meaning "join together." Conjugate joins the term **monosyllable** as a primarily linguistic term that has taken on sexual connotation.

constable n

female genitals. This obsolete jocular term dates back to the 16th century. Its humor derives from the pronunciation of the first syllable, namely, **cunt-**, together with the pun on the supposed policing activity of the female genitals. Shakespeare was probably punning on the word in both *Henry V* ("I tell thee, constable, my mistress wears her own hair.") and in *All's Well That Ends Well* ("From below your duke to beneath your constable . . .").

continental shots n pl
British

pornographic photographs of the female genitals. This mid-20th-century usage stems from the import of European pornography into Great Britain.

contrapunctum n British

female genitals. This obsolete 19th-century term derives from the Latin meaning "opposite of the point," in which **point** means penis. *See also* **antipodes**.

controlling part n

vagina. This obsolete 18th-century humorous term derives from the pun on how the vagina rules or regulates man's sexual desire. *See also* **regulator**.
- "There is a controlling part or queen-seat in us, that governs itself by its own maxims of state." (John Cleland, *Fanny Hill: Memoirs of a Woman of Pleasure*, 1749)

conundrum n British

female genitals. This 17th-century jocular term refers to the female genitals as a riddle or puzzle to the sexually inexperienced male. Conundrum also contains a pun in its first syllable, *con*, which is French for **cunt**.

convenient n British

mistress or prostitute. This 17th-century euphemism appears in Sir George Etherege's play *The Man of Mode*, 1676: "Dorimant's convenient, Madam Loveit."

converse v

copulate. This Elizabethan euphemism is based on the communication sense of the word. The term implies that sex is like speaking or talking together, and illustrates the metaphoric bond between sexuality and language. *See also* **discourse**.

convertible adj

bisexual. This 20th-century usage is based on the automobile metaphor. *See also* **chassis**.

convulsion of bliss n
phrase

orgasm. This 19th-century literary expression derives from the enjoyable spasms that characterize orgasm.

cony n British

female genitals. Dating from the 16th century, this usage is now obsolete. The term derived from the colloquial name for a rabbit, one of the furry animals, like **beaver** and **puss**, but no doubt was also influenced by the closeness of the term to **cunny** and **cunt**.

cooch n American

vagina. This 20th-century coinage may refer to the hootchy-kootchy, a sexy dance.

cookie n American

female genitals. This 20th-century term derives from the sweet food metaphor, much like **biscuit** and **cake**.

cool out v phrase American

copulate. This phrase probably relates to the "cool" period of jazz in the late 1950s and 1960s, and originated among blacks. Cool out reflects its opposite meaning, since copulation involves heating up.

coot n American

1. female genitals. This 20th-century coinage may derive from **cooch** or **cooze**.
2. woman regarded as a sex object. In standard English a coot is also both a **bird** and a foolish person.

cooze n American

1. female genitals. This is a mid-20th-century term typically found in pornographic writing. See also **case** and **cooch**.
2. women regarded as sex objects.

cop v

catch, grab, or steal. This usage derives from the Old French *caper*, meaning "seize." It is found in the sexual phrases **cop a bird**, **cop a doodle**, and **cop a joint**, all of which are 20th-century expressions for fellate based on **bird** (**cock**), **doodle**, and **joint** being terms for the penis. Originally, these terms were prostitutes' slang. **cop a feel** is a 20th-century expression meaning caress sexually.
- "Yes, Valerie . . . a legend in the neighborhood, there wasn't a boy who hadn't at least copped a feel . . ."
  (Morris Lurie, *Seven Books for Grossman*, 1983)

cop a cherry is a 20th-century phrase meaning deflower a virgin, based on **cherry** meaning hymen or virginity.

copperstick n British

penis. This obsolete 19th-century term derives from the police truncheon and the metaphors of both shape and aggression.

copulate v

have sexual intercourse. This standard English term derives from the Latin *copulare*, meaning "join together." The *Oxford English Dictionary* provides its first quote in 1632, though the noun **copulation** dates back to the 15th century: "Made one flesshe by carnal copulacyon" is attributed to William Caxton, 1483. The dictionary qualifies both words as "Now chiefly a term of Zoology." As with **coition**, copulation originally was applied to any conjunction; however, the sexual sense eventually dominated.

coral branch n

penis. This obsolete 17th-century literary term is found in translations of Rabelais. See also **arborvitae** and **stem**.

corner n

female genitals. This obsolete Elizabethan euphemism can be found in *Othello*. Shakespeare has Othello, doubting Desdemona's chastity, say: "I had rather be a toad . . . / Than keep a corner in the thing I love / For others' uses." See also **cranny** and **nooky**.

cornhole n American

anus. Based on **hole** and on the now extinct rural practice of wiping one's anus with dried corncobs, this term dates back to the early 20th century.

cornhole v American

perform anal intercourse.

cornholer means one who performs anal intercourse.

corral n American

group of prostitutes working for the same pimp or madam. This is a 20th-century underworld euphemism.

cottage n British

public lavatory used for male homosexual cruising. See also **cruise** and **teahouse**.

cotton n American

female pubic hair. This 20th-century term is based on appearance and texture. See also **cloth**.

couch v

copulate. Shakespeare, in The Merchant of Venice, has Gratiano say: "I should wish it dark, / That I were couching with the doctor's clerk." The term derives from the French coucher, meaning "lie down," and is well known from the phrase, "Voulez-vous coucher avec moi?" ("Will you sleep with me?").
couch rugby is a 20th-century British jocular term for sexual intercourse, based on the rough-and-tumble of rugby.

couple v

copulate. This informal term stems from the joining that occurs during copulation. It has been in use since the 14th century.
coupler is a British term for the vagina dating back to the 19th century. See also **joint**.
coupling bat is an 18th-century term for penis; now obsolete.
coupling-house is an 18th-century term for brothel; it is now obsolete. See also **house**.

course, courses n

menstruation. These usages, based on the menstrual cycle, were first seen in the 19th century. They may have influenced, or been influenced by, the term **curse**.

Covent Garden n British

area in London that teemed with brothels in the 18th century. The name is used in several sexual expressions.
Covent Garden abbess is the madam of a brothel, or a procuress. See also **abbess**.
Covent Garden ague stands for venereal disease.
Covent Garden nun means a prostitute. See also **nun** (under **nunnery**).

cover v

copulate. This colloquial term in use since the 16th century is usually said of males, and often of animals. In Othello Shakespeare wrote: "You'll have your daughter cover'd with a Barbary horse."

cover the waterfront v phrase Australian

work the docks (applied to prostitutes). This 20th-century term is also slang, meaning wear a sanitary pad.

covey n

group of prostitutes. This informal usage dates back to the 17th century. In standard English, covey is the collective noun for quail (a covey of quail), hence the sexual meaning, since **quail** denotes prostitute.

cow n

1. woman. This derogatory term has been used since the 18th century. See also **bitch**.
2. British prostitute, usually an old one. This usage dates back to the 19th century.

cowboy n American

male prostitute. This is a 20th-century term. Midnight Cowboy, 1969, is the title of a popular movie dealing with male prostitution.

coyote n British

female genitals. This obsolete 19th-century term may derive from associations with a wild, furry animal related to the wolf. See also **cat** and **civet**.

crabwalk n American

perineum, the area between the genitals and the anus in both sexes. This humorous 20th-century term stems from the locale of crabs or body lice.

crack n

1. female genitals. This term dates back to the 16th century and is based on appearance. A pun may also be intended on crack meaning excellent. **Crack of heaven** is a variant. See also **cleft, slit**, and **wound**.

• "Five and twenty virgins came
    Down from Inverness;
And when the ball was over
        There were five and twenty
    less.
First lady forward;
    Second lady back;
Third lady's finger
        Up fourth lady's crack"
(Anonymous ribald song, "The Ball at Kerremuir")

2. prostitute. This obsolete usage dates back to the 17th century.

• "You imagine I have got your whore, cousin, your crack."
(George Farquhar, *Love and a Bottle*, 1698)

3. *American* copulation. This is a 20th-century term.

4. *American* woman considered as a sex object. This is an early 20th-century term.

crack a judy (or **pitcher** or **teacup**) are all 19th-century British expressions for deflower, based on the pun on crack, meaning both the female genitals and break. **Judy** is a slang term for a woman or prostitute, while pitcher and teacup are both container terms.

cracked is a 19th-century term meaning deflowered, though its origins are found as early as Shakespeare's time. In *Hamlet*, Shakespeare used the expression **crack'd within the ring** to mean deflowered. See also **ring**.

• "A vaulting house [brothel] . . . where I used to spend my afternoons among superb she-gamesters . . . I have cracked a ring or two there."
(Philip Massinger, *Unnatural Combat*, 1639)

crack hunter is a 19th-century British expression meaning penis.

crackling is a 19th-century British colloquialism for a woman considered as a sex object, based on the connection with **pork** or **meat**, from which crackling, meaning roasted pork skin, is made.

crack salesman is a 20th-century American term for a male homosexual prostitute, probably derived from the crack between the buttocks rather than the female crack. The term has also been used in the American underworld for pimp; in this case the first meaning of crack, above, is referenced.

cradle n British

female genitals. This 19th-century term derives from the association of sex with reproduction.

cram v

copulate. This 19th-century term is said of men. It is also used to describe the entry of the penis into the vagina, as in "He crammed it up her." See also **shove** and **stuff**.

cranny n

female genitals. This coinage dates back to the 19th century. See also **cleft, corner, crack**, and **nooky**.

cranny hunter is a term for penis. *See also* **crack hunter**.

crapper n

anus. This 20th-century usage derives from crap, meaning excrement, which in turn derives from crapper, meaning toilet, invented by Thomas Crapper in 1882.

cream n

semen. This term, dating back to the 19th century, is based on the similarity in appearance between cream and semen. See also **dream whip** and **whipped cream**.
cream-catcher stands for vagina. *See also* **catch**.
cream jug is British terminology for vagina; jug is another container term. The plural, **cream jugs**, however, is a 19th-century British term for breasts, based on their milk-producing capability. *See also* **jugs**.
cream-stick signifies the penis. *See also* **stick**.

cream v

1. ejaculate. This meaning is based on the noun use of the term. A typical 20th-century colloquial usage is in the phrase "To cream one's jeans," meaning to ejaculate in one's pants, which is used metaphorically to describe extreme sexual excitation.
2. copulate and impregnate.

crease n American

female genitals. This 19th-century usage is based on shape. *See also* **cleft**, **crack**, **cranny**, and **slit**.
• "Give me, any day, a length of gleaming rail . . . or one electrified that I could slide my crease along."
(Paul West, *Zazie in the Metro*, 1990)

crevice n

female genitals. This is an obsolete 19th-century euphemistic term for **crack** or **cranny**.

crim con n

act of adultery. This is an abbreviation of the legal term criminal conversation, which was used from the 17th century until British divorce laws were changed in 1857. During that time *The Crim Con Gazette* chronicled the more famous cases. Conversation is a euphemism for fornication. *See also* **converse**.

crime against nature n
phrase

sodomy. In this 19th-century euphemism, nature refers to the natural order of things, which sodomy supposedly violates. Homosexual acts, bestiality, and heterosexual anal intercourse were all criminal offenses through the 19th century in Great Britain and the United States.

crook n

penis. This usage may be based on the shape of a shepherd's crook or an association with criminality.

crotch n

male and female genitals. This euphemism dates back to the 19th century. An obsolete meaning of the term was fork. The word derives from both the Middle English *croche*, meaning "shepherd's crook," and "crutch."
• "By mid 1974 the publication [*Playgirl*] was selling in excess of 2 million copies monthly—one of the most successful of the crotch publications."
(Wilson Bryan Key, *Media Sexploitation*, 1976)

crown n

glans or head of the penis. This 20th-century colloquialism is based on shape and position.

crown jewels is a 20th-century colloquialism for the male genitals, including the testicles, based on their perceived value to the owner. *See also* **family jewels**.

crown and feathers n

British

female genitals, including the pubic hair. This expression dates back to the 19th-century. *See also* **jewel** and **feathers**.

cruise v

walk or drive the streets looking for a homosexual with whom to have sex. **Cruising** is the noun form of this 20th-century expression. The term is also used by heterosexuals looking for sex.

• "The danger of the Strip is that
cruising may become a
neverending way of life."
(Andrew Gordon, "Sex in the *Star
Wars* Trilogy," in Donald
Palumbo, editor, *Eros in the
Mind's Eye*, 1986)

cruiser is a 20th-century term for a male homosexual who cruises, but it is also a 19th-century term for a prostitute, based on her search for a client.

crumpet n British

1. female genitals. A crumpet in standard English is a soft bread that resembles a **muffin**. Thus, this 19th-century term joins **bread**, **cake**, **biscuit**, and **buttered bun** as a food metaphor. The etymology of crumpet dates back to the Old English *crump*, meaning "bent" or "crooked."

2. sexual intercourse. The term is usually found in the phrase **have a bit of crumpet**, usually said of men. *See also* **bit**.

3. a woman regarded as a sex object. However, in the 1980s the term began to be used by women to refer to men as sex objects. This usage was reflected in a BBC television program titled "Double First," 1988: "It's Paul Newman—the older woman's crumpet."

cuckold n

man whose wife has committed adultery. This standard English term has been used for many centuries; the *Oxford English Dictionary* provides its first quote from 1250; Chaucer spelled it "cokewold." The term refers to the cuckoo, a bird that has the habit of laying its eggs in another bird's nest, and from the female cuckoo's habit of never staying long with the same male.

• "Two or three visits, and two or
three bows,
Two or three civil things, two or
three vows,
Two or three kisses, with two or
three sighs,
Two or three Jesus's—and let me
dies—
Two or three squeezes, and two
or three towses,
With two or three thousand
pound lost at their houses,
Can never fail cuckolding two or
three spouses."
(Alexander Pope, 1688–1744,
"Two or Three: A Recipe to Make
a Cuckold")

cuckold v

make a cuckold of a husband. This verb stems from the noun, defined above. A variant is **cuckle**. **Cuckoldry** is the state of being cuckolded.

cuckold the parson is an 18th-century British colloquialism meaning have sexual intercourse with one's future spouse (that is, before being married by the parson).

cuckoo n British

penis. This obsolete 19th-century usage derives from the penis's ability to **cuckold**.
cuckoo's nest is a corresponding term for vagina.

cucumber n

penis. This common colloquial 20th-century food term stems from the resemblance in shape. See also **banana**, **carrot**, and **pickle**.

cuddle v

copulate. This 19th-century euphemism is based on the standard meaning, namely, to caress and hug.
cuddle and kiss is an early 20th-century Cockney rhyming slang term for a girl or young woman. It is based on the rhyme with miss and the sexual intent of a cuddle and a kiss.

cull n British

prostitute's client. This 17th-century term, now obsolete, was probably derived from "cullian," meaning rascal, which was probably a euphemism for a prostitute's client. See also **john**.

cullions n pl

testicles. This obsolete coinage derives from the Latin culleus, meaning "bag." It was standard English usage from the 14th through the 17th century.
culls, a shortened version, was a colloquialism for testicles, and is now obsolete. Ben Johnson, quoted in Farmer and Henley's Dictionary of Slang and Its Analogues, 1890, wrote: "Claw a churl [beggar] by the culls, and he'll shite in your fist."

cundum n

See **condom**.

cunnicle n British

vagina. This 19th-century term sounds like a diminutive of **cunt**. The standard English sense means an underground passage.

cunnikin n British

vagina. The suffix "-kin" in this 19th-century word makes it a diminutive of **cunt** or **cunny**.

cunnilingus n

oral stimulation of the female genitals. This standard English term derives from the Latin cunnus, meaning "vulva," and lingere, meaning "lick." The term was first used in the late 19th century. The earliest quote in the Oxford English Dictionary is from L.C. Smithers's translation of Manual of Classical Erotology, 1887: "A man who is in the habit of putting out his tongue for the obscene act of cunnilinging."
cunnilinguist or **cunnilingist** are terms for one who performs cunnilingus.

cunning n

female genitals. This Elizabethan euphemism contains a pun on shrewdness and the sound of the first syllable, which is suggestive of **cunt**.

cunnus n

vulva or female genitals. This is the Latin formal term.

cunny n British

female genitals. This 17th-century word probably derives from **cony**, meaning a rabbit, though it may have been influenced by the Latin cunnus, meaning "vulva."
• "All my delight is a cunny in the night,
When she turns up her silver hair."
(Thomas D'Urfey, Wit and Mirth, 1719)

cunny burrow, a variant of **cunny,** emphasizes the container metaphor.
cunny-catcher is an 18th-century British term for penis.
cunny-skin is an 18th-century British expression for female pubic hair, since a rabbit has furry skin.
cunny-warren is an 18th-century British term for brothel, since rabbits live in a warren.

cunt n

1. female genitals or vagina. According to Hugh Rawson in *Wicked Words,* 1989, it was the "most heavily tabooed of all English words." John Wilmot, the earl of Rochester, 1648–1680, was one of the last writers to use the term openly. Having just described a premature ejaculation in "The Imperfect Enjoyment," he writes: "A touch from any part of her had done't: / Her hand, her foot, her very look's a cunt." Between 1700 and 1960 cunt was regarded as an obscenity and therefore a legal offense if printed in full. The *Oxford English Dictionary* omitted the term, although the 1972 *Supplement* cites its first use in 1230. The word appeared in the name of a 13th-century London lane—Gropecuntelane—apparently a dark passageway, as well as in street names in York, Oxford, and other English towns. Chaucer used a version of the word in "The Miller's Tale," 1383: "Full prively he caught her by the queinte. . . ." Though cunt was a standard term until the 16th century, it then became regarded as so vulgar as to be taboo through the 20th century, thus explaining the phenomenal number of euphemisms for it. Grose's *Dictionary of the Vulgar Tongue,* 1811, placed asterisks between the "c" and "t" and defined it as "a nasty name for a nasty thing." Only when the word began to be used by writers such as D.H. Lawrence and James Joyce did the taboo begin to crumble. The word may derive from Middle High German or Old Norse terms and the Latin *cunnus,* meaning "vulva," though the acquisition of the "t" at the end has long puzzled etymologists. Its Anglo-Saxon origins, together with some of the metaphors for the female sex, are expressed in the anonymous "Ode to Those Four-Letter Words":

It's a cavern of joy you are thinking
　of now
A warm, tender field just awaiting
　the plow.
It's a quivering pigeon caressing
　your hand
Or that sweet little pussy that
　makes a man stand
Or perhaps it's a flower, a grotto, a
　well,
The hope of the world, or a velvety
　hell.
But friend, heed this warning,
　beware the affront
Of aping a Saxon: don't call it a
　cunt.

cunt curtain is a 19th-century expression for female pubic hair.
cunt itch is 18th-century British terminology for sexual arousal in women. *See also* **itch.**
cuntkin and **cuntlet** are 18th-century British terms that are diminutives of **cunt.**
cunt-lapper is a 20th-century term for a cunnilinguist.
cunt-pensioner is a British term for a man who lives off the earnings, through prostitution, of his wife, mistress, or daughter.
cunt stand is a 19th-century British expression for sexual arousal in women, fashioned to contrast with **cockstand** (under **cock**).
cunt-struck is an 18th-century British term describing a man with a sexual fascination for a particular woman or women in general.
cunt-teaser is a 20th-century term for a man who stimulates a woman sexually but refuses to copulate. *See also* **cockteaser** (under **cock**).

2. woman considered as a sex object. This meaning is always derogatory.
- "Two cunts sail in—Americans." (Henry Miller, *Tropic of Cancer*, 1934)

3. buttocks. This is 20th-century male homosexual usage.

Cupid n

Roman god of love, especially physical love. The term is used in many sexual expressions, mainly as a euphemism.
Cupid's alley is a 19th-century British term for vagina. *See also* **alley**.
Cupid's arbor is a 19th-century British euphemism for female pubic hair. *See also* **garden**.
Cupid's archery is a 19th-century euphemism for sexual intercourse. *See also* **arrow** and **bull's-eye**.
Cupid's arms and **Cupid's hotel** are 19th-century euphemisms for the vagina. *See also* **hotel**.
Cupid's cave, **Cupid's cloister**, and **Cupid's corner** are 19th-century British euphemisms for female genitals. *See also* **cave** and **corner**.
Cupid's itch is a 20th-century American euphemism for venereal disease. *See also* **itch**.
Cupid's kettledrums is an 18th-century British euphemism for breasts. *See also* **kettledrums**.
Cupid's torch is a 19th-century British euphemism for the penis.

cups n pl

breasts. This 20th-century colloquialism is based on shape. Brassieres come in cup sizes.

cure the horn v phrase

copulate. This 19th-century expression is usually said of women. It is based on **horn** meaning an erection.

curlies, curls, curly hairs n pl British

pubic hair. These 20th-century colloquial terms are found in expressions such as "To have by the short and curlies," which means to hold by the short pubic hairs or to have someone in so tight a spot that escape can be achieved only painfully.
- "Oh, there was fuckin' in the kitchen,
      and fuckin' on the stairs;
  You couldn't see the carpets for
      The cunts and curly hairs."
(Anonymous ribald song, "The Ball at Kerremuir")

the curse, the curse of Eve n phrase

menstruation. These 19th-century expressions are based on Eve's curse in the garden of Eden for the introduction of human sexuality. However, the terms could have been influenced by **course**, a common euphemism for menstruation.

curtains n

uncircumcised foreskin. This 20th-century gay term alludes to the foreskin being drawn over the glans like a curtain. *See also* **drapes**.

cush n

1. *American* copulation. This is a 20th-century term.
2. *British* female genitals. This military usage derives from **cushion**.

cushion n

1. female genitals. This 19th-century term stems from the expression **cushion for pushing**, which from the male perspective is descriptive of the female genitals.
2. buttocks. This 20th-century usage refers to the fact that both are sat upon.

cut n

1. female genitals. This usage dates to the 18th century. *See also* **gash**, **slit**, and **wound**.

cut and come again is a British expression for the female genitals based on the standard meaning of having a second helping of **meat**.

2. *British* prostitute. This is an 18th-century term.

cut adj

1. castrated. This standard English meaning is usually said of animals; it dates back to the 15th century.

2. referring to a circumcised penis. This is a 20th-century colloquialism.

- "He's not particular about color or size, cut or uncut, he says— he's just 'so happy to have a dick to hold in these troubled times.' " (Burt Supree, "Jerk off for Jesse," in *The Village Voice*, January 7, 1992)

cut cock is a derogatory term for a Jew, based on the Jewish practice of infant circumcision.

cut out to be a man/gentleman is a jocular British phrase meaning circumcised.

cut v American

copulate. This is 20th-century usage.

cutlass n British

penis. This 19th-century term is based on the standard meaning of **sword** or knife, and is reinforced by the separate syllables in the word, **cut** and "lass," meaning girl.

cuzzy n American

1. copulation. This early 20th-century term may be related to **cooze**.

2. female genitals.

Cyclops n

penis. This obsolete 19th-century literary euphemism is based on the classical mythological race of one-eyed giants described in Homer's *Odyssey*. *See also* **one-eyed milkman**, **one-eyed worm**, and **Polyphemus**.

cylinder n Australian

vagina. This usage dates back to the early part of the 20th century, and was perhaps influenced by piston and cylinder engineering. *See also* **machine**.

Cyprian n

prostitute. This 16th-century literary euphemism is based on the ancient orgiastic worship of Aphrodite, the goddess of love and beauty, on the island of Cyprus. In 1795 *The Ranger's Magazine* of London, a precursor to magazines of today such as *Screw*, contained a listing of Covent Garden Cyprians. *See also* **Covent Garden**.

Cyprus sap n

semen. This expression dates back to the 16th century. *See also* **arborvitao**.

D

daffodil n British

young male homosexual, especially an effeminate one. This mid-20th-century term derives from the standard flower sense of the word. *See also* **daisy**, **lily**, and **pansy**.

dagger n

1. penis. This British term is yet another metaphor for penis as weapon. **Throw one's dagger**, meaning copulate and said of men, is an American variation used by college students.

2. lesbian who is **butch**. This 20th-century usage stems from the masculine attribute of dagger defined above.

daily mail, daily n British

sexual intercourse. These terms are based on the rhyme with **tail**. "Have you had any daily lately?" is a typical expression. *The Daily Mail* is an English newspaper, and the term daily suggests a high frequency rate for sex.

dairy n British

breasts. This humorous usage dates back to the 18th century; it is based on the breasts' capability for milk production. Dairy also features in phrases such as **sport the dairy** and **air the dairy**, both meaning reveal the breasts. Two variants are **dairy arrangements**, dating from the early 20th century, and **dairies**.

daisy n

1. *British* female genitals. This 19th-century term is now obsolete. *See also* **flower**.

2. *American* male homosexual. *See also* **daffodil**, **lily**, and **pansy**.

daisy chain is 20th-century terminology for a male homosexual orgy, based on the standard sense of a daisy chain, interpreted here to mean men linked penis to anus in a circle. The term also has heterosexual application as an orgy.

- "They then separate to live their separate days, St. Jacques to worry about improving his teaching methods and fantasize endless daisy chains and orgasms." (Scott Baker, "The Jamesburg Incubus," in Ellen Datlow, editor, *Alien Sex*, 1990)

dame n

woman. This term dates back to the 13th century, when it was standard English for **lady** or **mistress** of a household. It derives from the Latin *domina*. In Great Britain in the 17th century, dame became a formal title for a specific rank of nobility. In the United States, in the absence of a titled aristocracy, dame became a colloquialism for a young woman. As recently as 1949, Hollywood avoided the term—a movie called *Dames Don't Talk* was renamed *Smart Girls Don't Talk*. Dame has also been used contemptuously, as when Nancy Reagan said of Raisa Gorbachev, "Who does that dame think she is?"

damsons n pl

testicles. This obsolete literary term dates back to the 16th century. Since damsons are small round **plums**, they serve as an appropriate food metaphor based on shape.

dance v

copulate. This usage dates back to the 16th century. Dance movements are rhythmic and often suggestive of sex. Indeed, Oscar Wilde defined dance as "a vertical expression of a horizontal urge."

- "Then nothing but Dancing our Fancy could please,
  We lay on the Grass and Danc'd at our ease;
  I down'd with my Breeches and off with my Whigg,
  And we fell a Dancing the Irish jigg."
  (Thomas D'Urfey, *Wit and Mirth*, 1719)

dance the beginning of the world is a 17th-century literary euphemism for sexual intercourse in which the procreative power of sex is expressed.

dance the buttocks jig, **dance the goat's jig**, and **dance the mattress jig** are all 18th- or 19th-century British phrases for copulation, now obsolete. **Buttocks** refers to a body part that plays a role in dance and sex; **goat** refers to the animal synonymous with lechery; while mattress refers to the **bed**, a place for sex. See *also* **jig**.

dance the matrimonial polka is a 19th-century British phrase for copulation, now obsolete; "matrimonial" was a euphemism for missionary, as in **missionary position**.

dance the sheets is a 17th-century literary phrase for copulation, in which **sheets** refers to the bed.

dangler n American

penis. This early 20th-century underworld term refers to the way the penis hangs. A variation is **dangle**, found especially in the term **dangle-parade**, which is a military term for an inspection of the genitals for signs of venereal disease. Eric Partridge classifies dangle-parade as New Zealand terminology. **Dang** is a rare American version of dangler, possibly influenced by **dong**.

danglers is a 19th-century British coinage for testicles.

dark meat n American

genitals of a black person. This 20th-century usage is usually considered derogatory. See *also* **light meat** and **meat**.

dart, dart of love n British

penis. These terms date back to the 16th century, but have been obsolete since the 19th century. Dart joins the many weaponlike and piercing terms for penis, such as **arrow** and **prick**; dart of love has a more endearing tone, bringing Cupid to mind.

• "Even her such wonderous courage did surprise;
She hugs the dart that wounded her, and dies."
(Richard Duke, "After the fiercest pangs of hot desire," *Poems*, 1711)

dasher n British

prostitute. This obsolete 18th-century term suggests both a dashing appearance and fast action.

dash one's doodle v

phrase

masturbate. This is a lighthearted 20th-century expression used of men. See *also* **doodle**.

date rape n

See **rape**.

daub the brush v phrase

American

copulate. This early 20th-century expression may have artistic overtones. See *also* **brush**.

daughter n

young homosexual male, especially one introduced into homosexual society by a **mother**. This is mid-20th-century gay terminology.

dead-end street n Canadian

vagina. This term plays on the metaphor of a closed-off thoroughfare. See *also* **main avenue**.

deadeye dick n American

active male homosexual. In this 1960s gay term, "deadeye" refers to the anus. See *also* **dick** and **eye**.

dead rabbit n British

penis that cannot get an erection. In this recent usage, the choice of rabbit is probably based on the rabbit's habit of frequent copulation.

dearest adj

most cherished. This word has been incorporated in various sexual expressions.

dearest bodily part is an Elizabethan phrase for the female genitals, used by Shakespeare in *Cymbeline*.

dearest member is an 18th-century Scottish euphemism for the penis, attributed to poet Robert Burns. See also **member**.

deed n

copulation. This usage has been incorporated in sexual phrases such as **deed of kind** and **deed of pleasure**, both 19th-century British euphemisms for copulation.

deflower v

deprive of virginity. This standard English term has been in use since the 14th century. It encapsulates the metaphor of a fresh unplucked flower for a virgin. See also **flower**.

delight n

sexual intercourse. This 18th-century euphemism is based on the enjoyment the act provides. See also **pleasure**.

den n

vagina. This 16th-century literary euphemism probably stems from the standard meaning of a lair or from an obsolete sense of den meaning ravine. See also **cave**.

deposit v

ejaculate. This 20th-century term puns on the financial sense of the word, since **bank** also means vagina.

derriere n

buttocks. This colloquialism derives from the French and dates back to the 18th century.

• "As he leaps through the air
With his taut derriere,
His thighs engineered
Like an ox."
(Joan Van Poznak, "Connoisseur," in John Whitworth, editor, The Faber Book of Blue Verse, 1990)

desire n

sexual desire or lust. This standard term used since the 13th century derives from the Old French désir and the verb désirer, meaning "want."

deviate n

homosexual. This 19th-century derogatory term is used mainly by heterosexuals. In the 20th century the word also encompasses those who commit sodomy or engage in so-called sexual perversions.

devil n

penis. This humorous 18th-century term is now obsolete. Its use derived from a story in Boccaccio's Decameron, 1353, in which the devil goes into **hell** (the vagina). The devil as a biblical figure has a **tail** and horns (see **horn**), both associated with male sexuality. The Devil in Miss Jones, 1973, is a pornographic film that exploits the ambiguity of the term.

diamonds n pl

testicles. This 20th-century gay term puns on the male genitals as **jewels**. See also **stones**.

dick n

penis. As a common term dating back to the 19th century, dick may be the most popular of the many names applied to the penis. The derivation may be from a contraction of "derrick," a crane that can rise up. Another possible derivation is from **dickory dock**, which is rhyming slang for **cock**.

• "You might have thought that . . . my dick would have been the last thing on my mind."
(Philip Roth, Portnoy's Complaint, 1969)

dick v American

copulate. This term derives from the noun and represents 20th-century usage. **Dicky-dunk** is a variation. See *also* **dunking**.

dickory dock n British

penis. This is Cockney rhyming slang, based on the rhyme with **cock**.

diddies n pl British

breasts. An 18th-century euphemism, this is probably a variant of **titties** (under **tit**).

diddle v

1. copulate. This 19th-century term puns on other senses of the word, meaning shake and swindle. The sexual sense is now obsolete.
2. masturbate. This usage, now obsolete, applied to both men and women.

diddly-pout n British

female genitals. This 19th-century term probably derives from **diddle** and "pout," meaning a swelling or protrusion, as of the lips.

die v

experience orgasm. As a literary euphemism, the term has been in use since the 16th century. It can apply to both sexes, and derives from the association of coming to the end of a sexual experience with death. **Fading** shows similar intent. The French refer to orgasm as *mort douce*, or "sweet death." Shakespeare wrote in *Much Ado About Nothing* of "dying in a woman's lap" and in *King Lear:* "I will die bravely like a smug bridegroom."

diesel dike (dyke) n

American

lesbian who shows very masculine characteristics. This mid-20th-century expression is suggestive of truck drivers who drive diesel engine trucks. See *also* **dyke**.

● "I go into a town, see chicks—a real obvious diesel dike. . . ." (Lenny Bruce, in John Cohen, editor, *The Essential Lenny Bruce*, 1967)

digitate v

masturbate. An obsolete 18th-century euphemism, said of women, it derives from the standard adjectival meaning of the term, which pertains to fingers.

dike n

See **dyke**.

dildo n

object used for sexual gratification in place of an erect penis. This standard English term dates back to the 16th century. It may derive from the Italian *dilètto*, meaning "delight," or from the Old English *dyderian*, meaning "cheat."

● "Curse Eunuch dildo, senseless counterfeit,
    Who sooth my fill, but never can beget."
(Tomas Nashe, "The Merrie Ballad of Nashe, His Dildo," 1601)

dildo v

caress or arouse with a dildo. This colloquialism, now obsolete, dates back to the 18th century.

dilly boy n British

young male homosexual. This early 20th-century term derives from Dilly being short for Piccadilly Circus, a place for homosexual **cruising** (under **cruise**) in London.

dimple n British

female genitals. This colloquialism, often applied to children, is based on appearance. See *also* **cleft**.

ding-dong n American

penis. This 20th-century juvenile colloquialism derives from the way the penis hangs down or dangles. *See also* **dong**.

ding-dongs is a 20th-century colloquialism for the testicles.

dingle-dangle n

penis. This 19th-century colloquialism derives from the way the penis hangs down or dangles. *See also* **dangler**.

dingus n

1. penis. This 19th-century euphemism stems from the German *ding*, meaning "thing."
2. dildo.

dinners n pl American

nipples. This 20th-century term used in the Ozarks is based on the feeding function of nipples.

dipstick n American

penis. This 20th-century humorous term relates to the **stick** that dips, and exemplifies the automobile metaphor for sexual terminology. *See also* **oil**.

dirk n

penis, especially an erect one. This 18th-century term derives from the standard sense of a type of Scottish dagger. This word joins many others that relate to weaponry, including **bayonet**, **club**, **poker**, and **sword**.

dirt n

licentious language or subject material. In *Purity and Danger*, (1966), anthropologist Mary Douglas defines the term as "matter out of place." That is as true of language and sex as of matter; language is dirty only in specific contexts. *See also* **filth**.

- "Is sex dirty? Only if it's done right."
  (Woody Allen, *Everything You Always Wanted to Know About Sex But Were Afraid to Ask*, 1972)

dirt road is mid-20th-century coinage for anus and rectum viewed as a passage for anal intercourse.

dirty old man is a mid-20th-century colloquialism for an old man who engages in lecherous behavior. The term is also derogatory American usage for an elderly male homosexual.

discharge v

ejaculate. This standard meaning has existed since the 16th century. *See also* **shoot**.

discourse n

sexual intercourse. This euphemism dates back to the 16th century. The term captures the commonality of language and sexuality as aspects of communication. *See also* **converse** and **talk**.

discussing Uganda v
phrase British

having intercourse. This euphemism was popularized by the satirical magazine *Private Eye* in the 1970s; it is said to have come from a party in which a journalist explained a sexual encounter by reporting, "We were discussing Uganda." **Ugandan affairs** is a variant.

dish n

sexually attractive woman. This 20th-century term exploits the food metaphor. The implication is that a woman is a container as well as a tasty morsel. Recently, the word has been applied by females to attractive males.

- "Myra Breckenridge is a dish, and never forget it, you

motherfuckers, as the children say nowadays."
(Gore Vidal, *Myra Breckenridge*, 1968)

disorderly n British

prostitute. This 19th-century derogatory term is now obsolete. The word clearly expresses the moral order of its time.

ditch n

vagina. This 19th-century derogatory usage is now obsolete. *See also* **drain**.

dive n American

brothel. Today this 19th-century term is used only for a disreputable place. Typically, a disreputable brothel or bar was in a basement or cellar.

dive v

perform cunnilingus. This mid-20th-century term derives from diving meaning going down, as in **go down on** (under **go**). A variation is **dive a muff**. *See also* **muff**.
diver stands for cunnilinguist, and occasionally for the penis, especially in the phrase **do a dive in the dark**.

divine monosyllable n

British

female genitals. This is a 19th-century euphemism (*see also* **monosyllable**, a euphemism for **cunt**). "Divine" also qualifies a number of other euphemisms for the female genitals, as in **divine cut**, **divine scar**, **divine slit**, and **divine wound**.

diving suit n

condom. This recent 20th-century term joins a number of protective clothing terms such as **overcoat** and **raincoat**.

do v

This verb is part of many phrases that mean copulate. The most common is **do it**, a euphemism dating back to at least the 17th century. Though primarily applied to copulation, it can refer to any sexual activity. **Do it yourself** is a 20th-century colloquialism meaning masturbate. *See also* **it**.

• "What's the difference between frustration and utter frustration?— Frustration is the first time you find you can't do it the second time. Utter frustration is the second time you find out you can't do it the first time."
(Popular male joke)

do a bottom-wetter is a 19th-century British expression meaning copulate, said of women.
do a dive in the dark is a 19th-century British coinage meaning copulate, said of men. *See also* **diver**.
do a flop means copulate. It dates back to the 19th century and is said of women, implying a flop into bed.
do a grind, meaning copulate, also goes back to the 19th century. *See also* **grind**.
do a kindness is an 18th-century British expression for copulation, said of men. Contrast **do a rudeness** below.
do an inside worry is 18th-century British terminology meaning copulate, said of men.
do a perpendicular is a 19th-century jocular expression meaning copulate while standing. *See also* **upright**.
do a push and **do a put** are 19th-century British terms meaning copulate, said of men. See also **push** and **stand a push**.
do a rudeness is 18th-century British coinage for copulate, said of men. Contrast **do a kindness** above.
do a spread, said of women, also means copulate. Its use dates back to the 19th century.

do miracles is a 17th-century euphemism for copulation, connoting the miracle of reproduction.

do over is a 19th-century term meaning copulate, punning on the overlaying of partners and the repetition of the act. In Great Britain, the expression also means to attack someone or beat someone up.

do some good for yourself is a 20th-century Australian phrase meaning copulate, said of men.

do the chores is a 20th-century American expression meaning copulate; it implies work and drudgery.

do the naughty is a 19th-century phrase meaning copulate, said of women. See also **naughty**.

do the trick is a 20th-century American phrase meaning copulate, borrowed from prostitutes' jargon. See also **trick**.

do the two-backed beast is a 16th-century colloquialism meaning copulate, based on the formation of two backs and stressing the bestial nature of the act. See also **beast with two backs**.

dock v

copulate. This 17th-century term, said of men, is now obsolete. It probably derives from the standard sense of mooring a boat or linking parts; significantly, boats have been given female names for centuries. The noun sense of the term, meaning an animal's **tail** or part of it, may also have influenced the sexual use of this word.

Doctor Johnson n

penis. This humorous appellation refers to the famous and formidable 18th-century lexicographer Samuel Johnson: It was said that no one was "willing to stand up to" him. The term is no longer used, but it joins other eponymous terms for the penis such as **John Thomas**.

dog v British

copulate on all fours, in canine fashion. This usage dates back to the 19th century.

dog fashion and **doggie fashion** are 20th-century phrases meaning sexual intercourse with entry from the rear.

dog's rig is 18th-century terminology, now obsolete, for sexual intercourse in a casual manner.

doll n

1. attractive woman. This early 20th-century colloquialism probably derives from the baby dolls that children love to dress up. The usage may stem from the 15th century, when both "doll" and "dolly" were nicknames for Dorothy and for female pets.

2. mistress. This 16th-century euphemism is now obsolete. The variant **dolly** acquired the meaning of prostitute from the 17th to 19th century. Today it is found in the British term **dolly-bird**, popularized in the 1960s, meaning a trendy, sexy young woman.

- "Drink and dance, and pipe and play,
  Kisse our dollies night and day."
  (Robert Herrick, *Hesperides*, 1648)

Donald, Donald Duck n
Australian

copulation. These recent coinages are based on the rhyme with **fuck**.

dong n American

penis. Dating back to the 1920s, and perhaps derived from the dangling nature of the penis (see also **ding-dong**), or the closeness in sound to **donkey**, long, or **schlong**, the term is used almost exclusively by males. In 1991 the word received wide exposure through the Senate hearings on Clarence Thomas's nomination to the Supreme Court. Long Dong Silver, the name of an actor in pornographic films of the late 1970s, was mentioned in evidence during the nationally televised hearings, immediately turning "dong" into a colloquialism. Long Dong Silver is an obvious pun on Long John Silver. See also **john** and **thomas**.

donkey n

large penis. This 19th-century usage derives from the male donkey's penile endowment.

donkey-rigged is a 19th-century British term applied to a man with a large or long penis. See also **hung** and **well-hung**.

doodle n

penis. This 18th-century children's term may derive from "**cock**-a-doodle-doo," the sound of a cock's crow. Doodle also sounds like "noodle," something long and limp.

- ". . . his body still palpitating with pleasure and now fingering his still swollen doodle."
  (Anonymous, My Secret Life, 1890)

doodle-case is a 19th-century British term for the vagina. See also **case**.

doodle-dasher is a 19th-century British term for a male masturbator. See also **dash one's doodle**.

doodle-sack is 19th-century British coinage for the vagina; Grose's Dictionary of the Vulgar Tongue, 1811, defines it as "a woman's private parts."

doos n South African

female genitals. Also used (much like **schmuck**) as a term of abuse for a person regarded as silly or stupid. The word derives from the Afrikaans, meaning **box**.

dork n American

penis. Possibly derived from the blend of **dick** and **fork**, this is 20th-century usage.

dork v American

copulate. Said of men, this, too, is 20th-century usage.

dose n

venereal disease. Derived from the medical sense of a quantity of something, usually unpleasant, this word dates back to the 19th century.

dot n

1. clitoris. This 19th-century term is based on appearance. See also **button**.

2. Australian anus. This meaning also is based on appearance.

dot the i is a 20th-century phrase for anal intercourse, based on the i being an ideograph for the penis and anus. See also **eye**.

do the bowling hold v

phrase

masturbate a woman. This 20th-century phrase is usually said of a man. The phrase derives from the hold of a bowling ball, in which the fingers are spread out. This is one of many sporting metaphors that express sexual meaning. See also **catcher's mitt**, **couch rugby**, and **lose the match and pocket the stakes**.

double fire, double discharge v phrase

have two ejaculations during sexual intercourse. These terms are 18th-century colloquialisms. See also **fire**, **discharge**, and **shoot**.

- "But still there was no end of his vigour: this double discharge had so far from extinguish'd his desires. . . ."
  (John Cleland, Fanny Hill: Memoirs of a Woman of Pleasure, 1749)

dove n

elderly lesbian. This mid-20th-century term is based on the bird metaphor; it is usually used as a term of endearment. The word could have been influenced by the past tense of **dive**.

downshire n British

female pubic hair. This 19th-century term is based on both standard meanings of down: feathers and the direction toward the ground and the genitals.

downy bit n British

1. young woman regarded as a sex object. This 19th-century term is now obsolete. *See also* **bit** and **fluff**.
2. female genitals. This is also a 19th-century term.

doxy n

prostitute. This 16th-century term was used until the 19th century, when it became obsolete. The term could be derived from the Dutch *docke*, meaning "doll," or from the English **dock**, which means copulate. Shakespeare wrote in *The Winter's Tale*: "When daffodils begin to peer, / With heigh! the doxy over the dale, / Why, then comes in the sweet o' the year, / For the red blood reigns in the winter's pale."

drag n

women's clothes worn by a man, who is said to be **in drag**. This 19th-century colloquial term comes from the music hall; it reflects an earlier theatrical convention in which boys and men played women's parts in dramatic productions, since only males were allowed on stage.
drag queen is 20th-century gay usage for a professional female impersonator or for a homosexual who frequently wears women's clothes. *See also* **queen**.
• "There are easier things in life than being a drag queen. But, I

ain't got no choice. Try as I may, I just can't walk in flats."
(Harvey Fierstein, *Torch Song Trilogy*, 1981)
drag show is mid-20th-century gay terminology for a show in which a male impersonates a female.

dragon n

1. *British* prostitute, usually an old one. Now obsolete, this usage dates back to the 17th century. Dragon also had the meaning of devil or Satan in Christian lore.
2. *Australian* penis. Used especially in the phrase "drain the dragon," meaning to urinate, this is 20th-century usage.

drain n

vagina. This 19th-century derogatory usage is based on drain as a passageway for dirt. The term is now obsolete. *See also* **sluice**.

drapes n

uncircumcised foreskin. This mid-20th-century gay term refers to the fact that it can be draped or pulled over the glans. *See also* **blinds**.

draw the blinds v phrase

pull back the foreskin. This is a jocular 20th-century expression. *See also* **blinds**.

dream whip n

nocturnal emission of semen. This recent term derives from **whipped cream**.

dress for sale n American

prostitute. In a case of 20th-century synecdoche, the dress stands for the person as a whole.

dress-house n

brothel. This 19th-century term is one of many incorporating "house" in a definition of brothel.

drive v

copulate. **Drive home** and **drive into** are said of men. Drive home is current 20th-century American usage, while drive into is 19th-century British terminology that is still current.

droopers n pl

breasts, usually large ones. Derived from their hanging down on the chest, this is 20th-century coinage.

drumstick n British

penis. This 19th-century usage is based on shape and the fact that one can beat or **hit** with a drumstick. See also **stick**.

dry adj

pertaining to a lack of lubrication or ejaculation.
dry bob is 18th-century British terminology for sexual intercourse without ejaculation; it derives from "bob," meaning movement. Grose's *Dictionary of the Vulgar Tongue*, 1811, defines dry bob as "copulation without emission." The phrase is now obsolete.
dry fuck is a 20th-century phrase for sexual intercourse without ejaculation. See also **fuck**. **Dry run** is a variant, though it has also been used to refer to sexual intercourse using a condom, since that prevents direct contact with female lubrication.
dry hump is 20th-century coinage for anal intercourse, since there is no natural lubrication. See also **hump**.

duchess n British

1. a woman who has sexual intercourse with her shoes on. This 18th-century term, now obsolete, may indicate social status.
2. passive male homosexual. Perhaps derived from Duchess of Fife, which is rhyming slang for wife, regarded as the passive partner; this is 20th-century prison usage.

duff n American

buttocks. Possible derived from duff meaning inferior, or from the term being a variant of dough, which is used to make **buns**, this is 19th-century coinage.

dugs n pl

nipples. This was standard English usage from the 16th through the 19th century. In the 20th century the term became derogatory usage for both nipples and breasts. It derives from the Danish *daegge*, meaning "suckle."

dumb adj British

referring to the vagina as compared to the mouth in that it is unable to speak.
dumb glutton is 18th-century coinage for the female genitals, now obsolete. Glutton refers to appetite, in this case a metaphor for sexual lust.
dumb oracle is 19th-century usage for the female genitals, playing on the irony of an oracle that cannot talk.
dumb squint is 19th-century terminology for the female genitals, based on the metaphor of the **eye**.

dumplings n pl British

breasts. Dating back to the 18th century, dumplings may be an abbreviation for **dumpling shop** an obsolete term for breasts. The food metaphor together with the shape of dumplings explains the sexual use of the term.

dunking n British

sexual intercourse. This 1970s euphemism is based on the dipping of a biscuit or doughnut in tea or coffee.

Durex n British

trademark name for a brand of condom. The term is so widespread in Great Britain as to be used generically for condom. The brand name gives the impression of durability—an essential quality in a condom. *See also* **Trojan**.

Dutch girl n

lesbian. This 20th-century euphemism derives from the association of Holland with dikes (dykes). *See also* **dyke**.

Dutch widow n

prostitute. This 17th-century term is derogatory, one of many such English terms that refer to foreigners. It is now obsolete.

dyke, dike n

1. lesbian. This is common 20th-century usage. Early in the 20th century, this was a term of abuse for any lesbian; it then began to describe a "masculine" lesbian. The term has recently been reclaimed by lesbians as a colloquial reference without negative connotation. A possible derivation for the term is from the last syllable in **hermaphrodite**. Another possible derivation is from the second definition, below.
- "But there's never been a big dike on television."
  (Lenny Bruce, in John Cohen, editor, *The Essential Lenny Bruce*, 1967)
- " 'Are you really a dyke Harriet?'
  'I rather thought of myself as the Hoover Dam.' "
  (Rita Mae Brown, *Sudden Death*, 1983)
2. *British* female genitals. Derived from a standard meaning of dyke, namely a **ditch**, this 19th-century term is now obsolete.

E

ear v

copulate. This 16th-century euphemism, said of men, is now obsolete. The term derives from the standard sense of ear meaning plough, and makes use of the agricultural metaphor of sowing seeds.

early door n British

prostitute. Derived from the rhyme with **whore**, and based on the custom of having to pay extra for early admission to the Music Hall, this 19th-century Cockney rhyming slang term is now obsolete. The metaphor of a door as a gateway or entrance reinforces the sexual sense. *See also* **gate**.

ease v

copulate, especially reach orgasm. This 19th-century British colloquialism applies to both sexes.
ease nature is a 20th-century American euphemism meaning copulate.
ease oneself is a euphemism for masturbate and is applied to both sexes.

east and west n pl American

breasts. This early 20th-century rhyming slang term is based on the rhyme with **breast** and the fact that both are a pair. The term may also have been influenced by Mae West, a well-endowed actress. *See also* **Mae West**.

easy adj

referring to ease of access to sex. This current term is used to describe a person (usually a woman) who is willing to engage in sex on the first date, as in *Earth Girls Are Easy*, the title of a 1989 movie.

easy rider is a 20th-century American colloquialism for a pimp as well as for a woman who will perform sexual intercourse on the first date.

easy virtue is an 18th-century British term for a prostitute, now obsolete.

eat v American

perform oral sex. This 20th-century term demonstrates the food/sex connection and reinforces the Freudian idea that the oral stage is a sexual stage of psychological development in the child.

eat at the Y is a recent 20th-century verb phrase meaning perform cunnilingus; it derives from the Y representing a woman's open legs.

eat out is a variant of eat, though by suggesting not eating at home, it implies extramarital sex. In jocular use, eat out usually means perform cunnilingus.

eat poundcake is a 20th-century term meaning perform anilingus; it derives from **cake**.

eel n

penis. This 17th-century term based on shape is now obsolete.

eel-skin is a 19th-century American word for condom, while **eel-skinner** is a 19th-century British word for the female genitals. See also **skin**.

eff v

fuck. Based on the first letter of the word, this is a 20th-century euphemism.

• "When I finally did get effed, of course it had nothing to do with the world of expectations we mapped . . ."
(Albert Goldbarth, "The World of Expectations," 1986)

effie n

passive male homosexual. This 20th-century derogatory term comes from "effeminate."

eggs n pl

testicles. This 20th-century term is based on shape and the reproductive nature of eggs. The Hebrew term *baitzim* means both "eggs" and "testicles." **Eggs in the basket** is a variant; *see also* **basket**.

ejaculate v

discharge semen. This standard term, dating back to the 16th century, derives from the Latin *jacere* meaning "throw." The term, as a noun, refers to semen, while **ejaculation** is the standard noun for the act of discharging semen.

elephant and castle n
British

anus. This 19th-century Cockney rhyming slang term is based on the rhyme with arse-hole (see **arse**). It derives from the name of a pub.

embrace v

caress sexually; copulate. The word dates back to the 16th century and derives from the Old French *embracier*, meaning "clasp in the arms." This term derives from the Latin *bracchia*, meaning "arms." Shakespeare wrote in *2 Henry VI*: "Here may his head lie on my throbbing breast: / But where's the body that I should embrace?"

end n

penis. This term, which dates back to the 17th century, sometimes means just the glans or head. See also **bell end**.

endless belt n Australian

prostitute. This recent coinage stems from **belt**, meaning copulate. See also **ring** and **O**.

English vice n

flagellation. This euphemism dates back to the 19th century. It may derive from the popularity of flagellation in British brothels or from the old school practice of whipping boys' buttocks as punishment. **English culture** is a variation.

enjoy *v*

copulate. This euphemism clearly reflects the pleasure of the activity. It dates back to the 16th century. Shakespeare wrote in *The Rape of Lucrece*: "... this night I must enjoy thee: /If thou deny, then force must work my way."

envelope *n British*

condom. This 19th-century euphemism is based on the common British term **French letter**.

equipment *n American*

male genitals. This is a 20th-century colloquialism. *See also* **gear** and **tool**.

erection *n*

tumescent penis. This standard English word dates back to the 15th century.
- "[to whores] ... plague all; That your activity may defeat and quell
  The source of all erection."
  (William Shakespeare, *Timon of Athens*, 1607)
- "Obscenity is whatever gives a judge an erection."
  (Anonymous, quoted in Jonathon Green, *The Cynic's Lexicon*, 1984)

erotic *adj*

pertaining to sexual desire or pleasure. This standard term, dating back to the 17th century, is derived from the Greek *erotica*, which stems from Eros, the Greek god of love. **Eroticism** is the abstract noun, while **erotica** refers to sexually explicit writing or art.
- "By the mid-20th century, 'erotica' had broadened to include

works of such numbing artistic integrity that they precluded arousal."
(Walter Kendrick, "Increasing Our Dirty-Word Power: Why Yesterday's Smut Is Today's Erotica," *The New York Times*, May 31, 1992)

erring sister *n*

prostitute. This early 20th-century term implies moral censure. *See also* **sister**.

etcetera *n*

female genitals. This euphemism dates back to the 16th century. Shakespeare used the term in the phrase "an open etcaetera" in *Romeo and Juliet*. Compare **thing**.
- "... meanwhile my

  self etcetera lay quietly
  in the deep mud et

  cetera
  (dreaming,
  et
      cetera,of
  Your smile
  eyes knees and of your Etcetera)"
  (e.e. cummings, "my sweet old etcetera," *Is 5*, 1926)

Eve *n*

symbol of womanhood. As this is the name of the first female in the Old Testament, it is understandable that many sexual terms incorporate it. **Eve's curse** is a 19th-century euphemism for menstruation derived from the curse of mortality and childbearing, supposed to have begun on Eve's leaving the Garden of Eden. *See also* **the curse**. **Eve's customhouse** is an 18th-century humorous term for the vagina. *See also* **commodity** and **ware**.

everlasting wound *n British*

female genitals. This 19th-century expression is now obsolete. The term probably reflects the Freudian male notion of females as castrated males. There is a pun in "everlasting," that is, it is always there and available; and it will never heal or close. *See also* **wound**.

exchange DNA *v phrase*
American

copulate. This 1970s college term derives from the exchange of genetic material between the sperm and the egg that takes place during fertilization.

exchange spits *v phrase*
British

kiss or copulate. The interpretation of this 19th-century term depends on whether saliva or sperm is implied. *See also* **swap spit**.

exercise the ferret *v phrase*
Australian

copulate. This expression plays on both the animal and the tunneling metaphor. *See also* **ferret**.

exhaust pipe *n*

anus. This 20th-century expression derives from the automobile analogy. Other terms using the automobile metaphor include **chassis**, **dipstick**, and **headlights**.

expectant, expecting *adj*

pregnant. These euphemisms derive from the Latin *exspectare*, meaning "look for in anticipation," and date back to the 16th century.

extracurricular activities *n pl*

adultery. This is a 20th-century euphemism. *See also* **academy** and **knowledge**.

eye *n*

1. vulva. This 16th-century euphemism is based on the anatomical similarities of an oval shape, being surrounded by lids/lips, being moist, and having hair in close proximity. **eye that weeps most when best pleased** is a 19th-century British euphemism for the vagina based on its secretions. The phrase is now obsolete.

2. anus. This is 20th-century usage. *See also* **dot the i**.

eye doctor is a 20th-century American underworld term for a sodomite.

eye-opener is 19th-century British terminology for penis, punning on the opening of an eye (either the vagina or the anus) and the standard meaning of the term, namely, a remarkable or newsworthy thing.

eyes *n pl*

breasts or nipples. This is an early 20th-century euphemism, found especially in the phrase **big brown eyes**.

F

face cream *n*

semen. This 20th-century gay term derives from the act of fellatio. *See also* **cream**.

factotum *n British*

female genitals. This 19th-century euphemism is now obsolete. A factotum is something that controls everything. *See also* **regulator**.

fading *n*

orgasm. This literary term was first used in the 16th century. It derives from the feeling of "dying" that orgasm can bring. *See also* **die**.

fag n

male homosexual, especially one considered effeminate. One possible derivation of this derogatory 20th-century term is from another meaning of fag, namely, a cigarette, as it was once considered effeminate to smoke cigarettes (men smoked only cigars or pipes). Fag may also be an abbreviation of **faggot**. In the 1973 Gay Activists Alliance and National Gay Task Force guidelines on homosexuality, fag and faggot were listed as terms of abuse. Other terms included **queer**, **homo**, **fairy**, **mary**, **pansy**, and **sissy** (under **sister**).

• "Interested parties . . . are continually proving that Leonardo da Vinci, Shakespeare, etc., were fags."
(Ernest Hemingway, *Death in the Afternoon*, 1932)

fag hag is a mid-20th-century term for a heterosexual woman who goes out with homosexual men.

fag mag is a late 20th-century American gay term for a magazine portraying male nudity.

faggot n

male homosexual. This is a 20th-century derogatory term. From the 16th through the 19th century, the term was a pejorative one for a woman, but that meaning is now obsolete.

faggotry is a derogatory term for homosexuality.

faggoty is a derogatory adjective describing a male homosexual, usually an effeminate one.

faigele n

See **faygeleh**.

fail in the furrow v phrase

copulate without ejaculation. This is a 19th-century colloquialism. *See also* **furrow**.

fair play n British

sex between unmarried partners. This is a 19th-century colloquialism. Compare **foul play**.

the fair sex n

women. This 19th-century colloquialism is still heard today.

fairy n

male homosexual, especially an effeminate one. This 20th-century derogatory term is not as pejorative as **fag**.

• "Detectives from the vice squad with weary sadistic eyes spotting fairies."
(Langston Hughes, "Cafe: 3 A.M.," *Selected Poems*, 1959)

fairy lady is 20th-century American usage for a passive lesbian.

fall v British

engage in illicit sexual activity; conceive or become pregnant. This is a 19th-century euphemism, probably influenced by the Fall in the Garden of Eden, and the introduction of Adam and Eve to sin.

fallen angel is 20th-century terminology for a male homosexual, derived from the religious meaning of having sinned. **Fallen star** is a 20th-century variation, used especially of an elderly male homosexual, also called an aging actress.

fallen woman is an early 20th-century American euphemism for a prostitute or a woman who has sinned sexually, or engaged in sex before or outside of marriage.

fall backward v phrase

consent to copulate. This phrase is said of women who easily engage in sexual activity.

fall in the furrow v phrase British

ejaculate prematurely. This is a 19th-century British jocular expression. Compare with **fail in the furrow**. See also **furrow**.

fall off the roof v phrase
American

menstruate. This is a 20th-century euphemism.

falsies n pl

padded brassiere, or pads worn inside brassiere cups. This early 20th-century colloquialism can also refer to padding for the buttocks or hips.
• "My American friends tell me that falsies are now obtainable for the other side of the female anatomy—false bottoms in fact." (J.S. Huxley, 1964, in the *Oxford English Dictionary*).

fam v

caress sexually. This 19th-century term derives from the now obsolete word *famble*, meaning "hand."

family jewels n pl American

testicles. This early 20th-century term reflects the value or worth of the testicles. Family suggests the reproductive function of testicles. Jewels is related to a cluster of terms such as **jewel case, money**, and **diamonds**. Family jewels can also mean the male genitals as a whole. See also **crown jewels**.

family organ n American

penis. This is a 20th-century euphemism. See also **organ**.

family way adj, n

pregnancy, See **in the family way** (under **in**).

fan n British

female genitals. This 19th-century term may derive from **fanny** or from the shape of an open fan, said to resemble pubic hair.

fan v Jamaican

copulate. This 20th-century usage is applied to men. It stems from the cooling off of a woman's sexual passion.

fancy bit n British

female genitals. This is a 19th-century colloquialism. See also **bit**.

fancy house n British

brothel. This usage dates back to the 19th century. See also **house**.

fancy man n

pimp. This 19th-century term is almost obsolete.
• "My little fancy man's quite as fond of me as of you . . ." (Harrison Ainsworth, *Jack Sheppard*, 1839)

fancy woman n

mistress or prostitute. This term dates back to the 19th century.

fancy work n British

male genitals. This is 19th-century usage. See also **work**.

fanny n

1. *British* female genitals. This 18th-century term is still used today. It may derive from the protagonist of John Cleland's *Fanny Hill: Memoirs of a Woman of Pleasure*, 1749.
• "It [the name Fanny] means the Fanny-Fair . . . the Divine Monosyllable, . . . 'tis the Aunt, the Arbor . . . 'Tis the Yoni o' the East Indies an' the Passion Fruit o' the West Indies . . ." (Erica Jong, *Fanny*, 1980)
2. *American* buttocks. This usage may derive from the shape of a fan; from the common female name that is an abbreviation for Frances; or from "fantail." The term dates back to the early 20th century.

fast *adj*

sexually promiscuous. This meaning, along with the term's more conventional meaning of quick, is found in a number of terms.

fast-fuck is 19th-century usage for a quick act of copulation. Farmer and Henley, in their *Dictionary of Slang and Its Analogues*, 1890, define it as: "An act of trade done standing, or at least in quick time: as opposed to trade with an all-night lodger." *See also* **quickie**.

fast-house is a 19th-century term for a brothel, now obsolete. *See also* **house**.

fast life is 20th-century American usage for prostitution.

fast woman is a 19th-century term for a prostitute.

father-confessor *n British*

penis. This 19th-century term has religious overtones.

fatherfucker *n American*

pederast. This mid-20th-century term is fashioned after **motherfucker**.

the favor *n*

copulation. This 19th-century euphemism is primarily used of women granting a favor to men.

faygeleh *n*

male homosexual. Derived from the Yiddish, meaning "little bird," this is a 20th-century term. Bird here could be connected to a **fairy** having wings. Variants include **faigele** and **feigeleh**.

feathers *n pl British*

female pubic hair. This 18th-century term may be influenced by **tail feathers**.

feed *v*

give food. This verb offers a primary metaphor for sex.

feed one's pussy is a 20th-century expression meaning copulate, said of women. *See also* **pussy**.

feed someone's monkey is 20th-century terminology meaning copulate, said of men. *See also* **monkey**.

feed the dumb glutton is a 19th-century British phrase meaning copulate, said of men. *See also* **dumb**.

feed the dummy is another 19th-century British phrase meaning copulate, said of men.

feel, feel up, feel someone up *v phrase*

caress sexually. These colloquialisms date back to the 18th century.

give a feel and **cop a feel** both mean feel someone sexually. **Get a feel** means be felt sexually.

- "You're only as old as the woman you feel."
  (Groucho Marx)
- "I like to wake up each morning feeling a new man."
  (Jean Harlow)

feel hairy *v phrase*

be sexually aroused. **Hair** has long been a sexual symbol. This term dates back to the 19th century.

feigeleh *n*

See **faygeleh**.

felch *v American*

perform anal intercourse. This 20th-century term may derive from "fecal" or "feces."

felch queen is a term for a male homosexual. *See also* **queen**.

fellatio *n*

oral stimulation of the penis. This standard English term derives from the Latin *fellare* meaning "suck." The term has been in use since the 19th century.

- "I put fellatio right up there with chocolate truffles and *Annie Hall*

and the Pacific Ocean and life's other great pleasures."
(David Feinberg, *Eighty-Sixed*, 1989)

fellate is a mid-20th-century American standard verb meaning perform fellatio.

fellator and **fellatrix** are noun forms (the latter for females only) for a performer of fellatio.

fellow n
lesbian. This 20th-century usage derives from the connection of the term with the male gender.

female n
sex opposite to that of male. This standard English term can be traced back to Middle English. It comes from the Latin *femina*, meaning "woman." Unlike many terms for women that have a pejorative connotation, female remains a neutral word.

female spendings is a 19th-century British euphemism for vaginal secretions. See also **spendings**.

female trouble is an early 20th-century euphemism for physiological problems relating to the reproductive organs. It also means menstruation.

femme n
1. woman who takes the "female" role in a lesbian relationship. Derived from the French *femme*, meaning "woman" or "female," this is a 20th-century colloquialism. **Fem** is a variant spelling. See also **butch**.

2. *American* effeminate male homosexual. This is a 20th-century term. **Fem** is a variant spelling.

femme fatale is a colloquialism for a powerful female seducer. It derives from the French meaning "fatal woman" and has been in use since the 19th century.

femoral intercourse n
intercourse between the thighs. This standard English term derives

from "femur," meaning thighbone. The term has been in use since the 19th century.

fen n British
prostitute. This obsolete 17th-century term may have been influenced by **fan**.

ferret v British
copulate. This 19th-century term puns on the furry animal and the sense of hunting or searching out.

ferry n British, Australian
prostitute. This 20th-century term probably derives from the sense of riding. See also **ride**.

fetch n British
semen. This 19th-century term may derive from **fetch mettle**, a 17th-century phrase meaning masturbate. See also **mettle**.

fetish n
object capable of arousing sexual excitement, regarded as pathological. This standard term is an extension of the sense of an object with magical powers among primitive people. **Fetishism** is the standard term for this sexual disorder.

fettle v British
copulate. Derived from the standard English sense meaning scour, this 19th-century term is now obsolete.

fiddle v British
copulate. This 19th-century usage, said of men, puns on the musical instrument and the sense meaning cheat, as in adultery. See also **screw**.

fiddle n British
female genitals. This is 19th-century usage.

- "Fiddles alone are not to blame.
  The sticks must often take the
    shame;
  Too often feeble, short or limber
    chosen.
  And often fail for lack of resin."
  ("The Question," in *New Crazy
  Tales*, 1783)

fiddle bow and **fiddle stick** are both
British terms for penis. *See also* **bow**
and **stick**.

fig n British

female genitals. This 19th-century
term may derive from an obscene ges-
ture called the fig in which the thumb
is stuck through the fingers of a fist,
suggesting copulation, or from the
fleshy fruit. The ancient Greek euphemism for vagina was fig. The forbidden fruit in the Garden of Eden
has been said to be the fig, not the
apple.

fig leaf is a 19th-century colloquialism for female pubic hair, derived
from representations in fine art of fig
leaves over the genitals. Today the
term refers to anything covering up
sexual material.

fight in armor v phrase

wear a condom in sexual intercourse. This is an 18th-century
expression. *See also* **armor**.

figure n

breasts and buttocks of a woman,
especially in terms of sex appeal. This
euphemism dates back to the 19th
century.

filly n

young woman, especially one considered attractive. Derived from the
meaning of young mare, or from the
French *fille* meaning "daughter," this
colloquialism has been in use since
the 17th century. Many horse-related
terms have been used in sexual ter-

minology, possibly because of the
sexual sense of **ride**.

filth n

1. obscene sexual material. This
term has been in use since the time
of Old English. *See also* **dirt**.

2. prostitute. This has been a derogatory term since the 15th century.

- "To general filths convert, o' the
  instant, green virginity."
  (William Shakespeare, *Timon of
  Athens*, 1609)

finger v

1. caress sexually with the fingers.
This colloquialism has been used
since the 16th century. The finger has
long been a phallic symbol. In addition, crossing the middle and index
fingers has been a sign for sexual intercourse since the ancient Egyptian
era. Today crossing of fingers is used
as a charm to ward off punishment
for lying.

2. masturbate. This 20th-century
usage is said especially of women.

finger artist is 20th-century American gay terminology for a masturbator.

finger fuck, meaning masturbate a
woman, dates back to the 18th century.

- "She mows like reek thro a' the
    week,
  But finger-fucks on Sunday, O."
  (Robert Burns, "Green Grow the
  Rashes," 1796)

fire n

sexual arousal. This term has been
used informally since the 15th century. *See also* **heat**.

- "[Sex is a] disorder too violent in
  nature to last long: the vessels . . .
  soon boil'd over, and for the time
  put out the fire."
  (John Cleland, *Fanny Hill:
  Memoirs of a Woman of Pleasure*,
  1749)

fire v

ejaculate. This early 20th-century term puns on the noun sense of passion and the standard verb meaning of **shoot**.

fire blanks is mid-20th-century American coinage for copulation without ejaculation or copulation without impregnation. *See also* **fail in the furrow**.

fire in the air is a 19th-century British euphemism meaning ejaculate outside the vagina. *See also* **shoot in the bush**.

fireworks is a jocular 19th-century term for orgasm, punning on an explosion and a great display.

firk v

fuck. This 16th-century euphemism was obsolete by the 19th century. It may have derived from the combination of **dirk** and **fuck**.

firkytoodle is a term from the 17th century meaning caress sexually. It was obsolete by the 19th century.

first game ever played n
phrase

sexual intercourse. Derived from the primacy of the sexual "game" over all other games and sports, this is a 19th-century jocular expression. *See also* **game**.

first leg of three n phrase

penis. This is a jocular 19th-century expression. *See also* **best leg of three** and **middle leg**.

fish n

1. vagina. This 19th-century term, sometimes considered derogatory, may derive from the supposed similarity in odor and wetness. The fish has long been a sexual symbol in different cultures. The Greek *delphos* means both "fish" and "womb." In Christian theology the fish is a phallic

symbol. In French the closeness of *mer* and *mère* ("sea" and "mother") illustrates the symbolic importance of fish, and perhaps explains why in many cultures fish is regarded as an aphrodisiac.

fishing rod is 19th-century British usage for penis. *See also* **rod**.

fish pond is a 20th-century American term for vagina that exemplifies the container metaphor.

fish skin is 20th-century usage for condom. *See also* **skin**.

2. women considered sexually. This usage dates back to the 17th century.

fish market is 19th-century British terminology for brothel.

3. *American* prostitute. This is 20th-century usage.

fist fuck v

1. masturbate. This 19th-century coinage is used of men. A variant is **fist it**. The noun usage refers to an act of masterbation. *See also* **finger fuck**.

2. insert the entire fist in the rectum. This is 20th century gay usage.

fit v

copulate. This is an obvious euphemism for joining together sexually.

fit end to end is a 19th-century British colloquialism also meaning copulate. **Fit ends** is a variant.

five against one n phrase

masturbation. This early 20th-century colloquialism is based on the five fingers against one penis.

fixed bayonet n

erect penis. Now obsolete, this was a 19th-century expression. *See also* **bayonet**.

fix her plumbing v phrase
American

copulate. Said of men, this is a 20th-century euphemism. *See also* **plumbing**.

fix one up v phrase American
   1. arrange a date. This is a 20th-century euphemism.
   2. copulate. This follows from the first sense.
   3. impregnate a woman. This follows from the second sense.

the flag is up n phrase British
   menstruation. This 19th-century colloquialism is based on a signal for a halt to copulation. Variations are **my flag is up** and **her flag is up**.

flame n
   lover. Since the 14th century, sexual passion has been described in terms of flame. See also **fire** and **heat**.
   • "Amelia was engaged to be married to . . . a very old flame." (William Makepeace Thackeray, *Vanity Fair*, 1846)

flaming adj
   pertaining to exaggerated male homosexuality. This is 20th-century usage, as seen in **flaming queen**. See also **queen** and **camp**.

flap n British
   female genitals. This 19th-century usage is probably based on the shape of the labia. See also **slit**.

flapdoodle n
   penis. This 17th-century term is now obsolete. It may have derived from cock-a-doodle. See also **cock** and **doodle**.

flapper n
   penis. This obsolete 19th-century usage may have derived from **flapdoodle**.

flash v
   exhibit the naked body, especially the genitals in males or breasts in females. Though the term is current,

especially in the noun form, **flasher**, it dates back to the early 19th century, when the preferred phrase was **flash it**, usually said of men. **Flash meat** is a variant. See also **meat**.
   • "God is a flasher.
      He reveals himself to some,
      but not to others."
      (Gavin Ewart, "Haiku: The Wisdom of the Streets," in John Whitworth, editor, *The Faber Book of Blue Verse*, 1990)

flash in the pan n phrase British
   sexual intercourse without ejaculation. Derived from the idiomatic sense of this phrase, meaning short-lived, this is an 18th-century expression. Today the idiomatic sense is still used, but rarely the sexual one.

flash tail n
   prostitute. This is a 19th-century term. See also **tail**.

flash the upright grin v phrase British
   exhibit the female genitals. This usage dates back to the 19th century. See also **upright grin**.

flat-cock n British
   woman considered sexually. This 18th-century term is based on the absence of a penis in women. See also **cock**.

flat fuck n
   lesbian sexual activity of rubbing the genitals together. This is a 20th-century term. See also **fuck**.

flea and louse n
   brothel. This 19th-century coinage is based on the rhyme with **whorehouse**. Flea and louse imply that a brothel is dirty.

fleece n British

female pubic hair. This 18th-century term is based on the standard sense of wool or woolly hair. *See also* **hair**.

flesh n

genitals. This common euphemism dates back to the 16th century. *See also* **meat**.

flesh cushions is a literary euphemism for buttocks used by John Cleland in *Fanny Hill: Memoirs of a Woman of Pleasure*, 1749.

flesh factory is early 20th-century American coinage for brothel. *See also* **work**.

flesh market is 19th-century terminology for brothel.

flesh peddler is 19th-century usage for pimp or prostitute.

fleshpot is an old colloquialism, for a district catering to sexual desires. The biblical "fleshpots of Egypt" are described in Exodus. Fleshpot may also refer to a brothel or a prostitute.

fleshy excrescence is an obsolete 18th-century literary expression for the clitoris, based on its appearance.

fleshy idol is 19th-century British terminology for the female genitals (*see also* **idol**). **Fleshy part** is a variant.

flesh v

copulate. This colloquialism dates back to the 16th century and derives from the noun. **Flesh it** is a variant.

flier, flyer n British

hasty act of copulation. This is 18th-century usage. *See also* **quickie**.

flip-flap n

penis. This colloquialism probably derives from the dangling sense. The term is now obsolete.

- "I might have cleft her water-gap
  And joined it close with my flip-flap."
  (François Rabelais, *Gargantua and Pantagruel*, in Sir Thomas Urquhart, translator, *The Works of François Rabelais*, 1653)

flip-flaps n pl Australian

breasts. This 20th-century usage probably stems from the way breasts bounce.

flip-flop n American

mutual oral sex. Based on the inverted positions of the partners, this is a 20th-century term. *See also* **sixty-nine**.

flip it off v phrase

masturbate. Said of men, this 20th-century phrase joins a multitude of "off" terms for masturbation such as **jerk off**, **pull off**, and **wank off** (under **wank**).

flippy adj

bisexual. This 20th-century term is based on the ability to flip one's sexual interest around.

flipside n

buttocks. This 20th-century humorous term derives from the flip (opposite) side of a phonograph record.

flog v

masturbate. This is 20th-century Australian usage. Recent, more descriptive expressions include **flog the dolphin**, **flog the lizard**, and **flog the meat**. Flog the dolphin may refer to a dolphin's jumping or leaping ability.

flog the bishop is a 19th-century British expression for masturbate, said of men. It derives from **bishop** as the glans or head of the penis.

flog the donkey is 19th-century British terminology for masturbate, said of men. It derives from **donkey** meaning penis. **Flog the dong, flog the dummy**, and **flog the log** are recent American variants.

floods n pl American

menstruation. This is a 20th-century term.

floozie, floozy, floosie, floosy n American

1. woman with loose sexual morals. This 20th-century term may derive from the South African *vlossie*, the name given to a Hercules transport plane that "carried" men. Other more probable derivations are from Flora, meaning flower, or flossy, meaning downy or silky.
• "She has her bath and sings Ave Maria just to show she ain't no floosie."
(Bruce Marshall, *All Glorious Within*, 1944)
2. prostitute. This is also 20th-century usage.

flop v

consent to copulate. Said of women, this is a 20th-century euphemism.
flop in and **flop in the hay** are 19th-century British terms for copulate, usually said of men.

flopper-stopper n Australian

brassiere. This is a jocular 20th-century term.

floral arrangement n

male homosexual orgy, with men linked penis to anus. This is a 20th-century gay expression. See *also* **daisy chain**.

flourish n

hasty sexual intercourse. This is an 18th-century euphemism. See *also* **flier** and **quickie**.

flower n

1. hymen. This literary term dates from the 16th century, but is now rarely used. Its derivation relates to the bloom of a flower.
2. virginity. See *also* **deflower**.
3. female genitals. This derives from the above senses.
4. homosexual male. This is a 20th-century term. See *also* **daffodil, daisy, lily**, and **pansy**.
flower of chivalry is a 19th-century British euphemism for the female genitals.

flowers n

menstruation. This 19th-century term puns on flow-ers (for menstrual flow). See *also* **roses**.
• ". . . the monthly flowers that women have."
(John Florio, *A Worlde of Wordes*, 1598)

flowers and frolics n pl
Irish

testicles. Based on the rhyme with **bollocks**, this is 20th-century coinage. See *also* **fun and frolics**.

flub the dub v phrase

masturbate. Said of men, this 20th-century expression derives from the sense of spoiling or wasting that flub implies. See *also* **waste time**.

fluff n

1. female pubic hair. This 19th-century usage is based on texture or appearance. See *also* **fleece**.
2. *American, Australian* young woman. This derogatory term implies a person of no substance.
3. male homosexual, especially an effeminate one. This is a 20th-century term.

flute n

penis. This 19th-century term derives from shape and the fact that one blows a flute. See *also* **blow**.

- "He took her by the middle,
And taught her by the flute."
(Thomas D'Urfey, *Wit and Mirth*,
1719)

flute player means fellator.

fluter is an early 20th-century American underworld term for a male homosexual.

flute *v*

fellate. This is 20th-century usage.

fly-by-night *n British*

1. prostitute. This early 19th-century term is now obsolete.
2. female genitals. This usage is also obsolete.

fly the red flag, fly the flag *v phrase*

menstruate. Derived from red, the color of blood, and flag meaning sanitary napkin, these are 19th-century expressions.

fly trap, fly cage *n*

vagina. These 19th-century derogatory terms imply entrapment. They are now obsolete.

fondle *v*

1. caress sexually. This standard English term used from the 17th century onward derives from fond meaning liking.
2. *British* copulate. This is a 19th-century euphemism.

fool around *v phrase*

copulate. Today this 19th-century euphemism primarily means have extramarital affairs.

foot *v*

copulate. This 16th-century euphemism derives from the French *foutre*, which means "fuck."

foot queen *n*

male homosexual who is sexually aroused by feet. This is 20th-century usage.

foraminate *v*

deflower. This formal term from the 19th century derives from "foramen," meaning an opening. The term is now obsolete.

forbidden fruit *n*

1. sex. This euphemism dates from the early 20th century and is used mainly by teenagers. The term derives from the Garden of Eden story in the Bible.
2. *American* young virgin girl. This is a 20th-century term.

force fuck *v*

perform forced anal intercourse. This is 20th-century prison usage. *See also* **fuck**.

fore *adj*

front. This directional term has many sexual applications.

fore and aft is a 19th-century British term meaning copulate, based on the rhyme with **shaft**.

forebuttocks is an 18th-century British term for breasts, based on the similarity of shape to the buttocks. The term is now obsolete.

forecastle, **forecourt**, and **forehatch** are all 19th-century British terms for vagina. Forecastle is a naval term.

forefinger is a euphemism for penis. It is found in Shakespeare's *All's Well That Ends Well*: "Tib's rush for Tom's forefinger." Tib is a pet name for Isabel, a common female name.

foreplay *n*

stimulation before sexual intercourse. This is a 20th-century standard English term. According to Merriam-Webster, this term was not used before 1929. *See also* **play**.

foreskin n

prepuce. This standard English term dates back to the 16th century. **foreskin hunter** is 19th-century British terminology for prostitute.

forest n

female pubic hair. This is a 16th-century euphemism. *See also* **bush**.
• "Give me the Country lass,
   That trips it o'er the field,
   And opes her forest to the first."
   (Thomas D'Urfey, *Wit and Mirth*, 1719)

fork v British

copulate. This 19th-century term, said of men, derives both from the stabbing motion sense and from the noun sense.

fork n

1. female genitals. This 19th-century term derives from the shape of opened legs. The term is found mainly in the expression a **bit on a fork**.
2. *Australian* prostitute. This is a 20th-century term.

fornicate v

copulate. This standard English term dates from the 16th century. It derives from the Latin *fornix*, meaning "arch," because in the 16th century cellars, which then had arches, were sometimes used as brothels. **Fornix** is an obsolete term for a brothel.
fornicator is a 19th-century British term for penis, now obsolete.
fornicator's hall is 19th-century British usage for vagina, now obsolete.

fort n British

vagina. This obsolete 17th-century usage derives from fortress, possibly punning on "fought," and implying that sex is a battle.

forty-four n American

prostitute. This 20th-century rhyming slang term is based on the rhyme with **whore**. *See also* **six-to-four** and **two by four**.

foul play n British

adultery. This is a 19th-century colloquialism. *See also* **fair play**.

fountain n

breasts. Derived from the sense of a flowing source of liquid, this is a 16th-century euphemism.
fountain of life is a 19th-century British euphemism for the female genitals, from which life flows.

four-legged frolic n

sexual intercourse. Based on the involvement of four legs, this is an obsolete 19th-century colloquialism. *See also* **beast with two backs**.

four-letter words n pl

obscene or "dirty" words. This euphemism dates from the 1930s. Prime examples are **cock**, **cunt**, and **fuck**.

foutering v

fucking. Based on the French *foutre*, meaning "fuck," this is a 16th-century euphemism.

fox n American

very attractive female. This 20th-century usage began as a black term in the 1940s, but its use is now widespread. Foxes are both furry and clever, perhaps explaining the choice of the term, though the closeness to "fucks" could have influenced the choice. *See also* **vixen**.

foxy means sexually desirable; it is usually said of women.

franger *n Australian*

condom. This 20th-century term may derive from **French letter**.

free love *n*

sexual intercourse without societal constraints, such as wedlock. This colloquialism has been in common use since the 1960s.

French *adj*

1. lewd or sexually kinky. This usage dates back to the 16th century. **French crown** is one of many terms for syphilis. The French qualifier reflects the British view that the disease is of foreign origin. Crown refers to the bald head that can result from an advanced case of syphilis. A more common term for syphilis was **French disease**. **French goods**, **French gout**, and **French pox** were all variations. *See also* **pox**.

- "Venereal disease . . . is vulgarly called the French Pox."
  (Edward Phillips, *General Dictionary*, 1658)

French letter is a 19th-century colloquialism for condom. Still popularly used, it derives from the condom's envelopment of the penis. **Frenchie** is a variant.

- "All hairs they were shorn, no frenchies were worn,
  And this suited Abdul by far;
  and he quite set his mind on a fast action grind
  To beat Ivan Skavinsky Skavar."
  (Anonymous ribald song, "Ivan Skavinsky Skavar")

French postcard is a euphemism used since the 19th century for a postcard with a pornographic picture.
French safe is early 20th-century Canadian coinage for condom. *See also* **safe**.

French tickler is mid-20th-century usage for a dildo or condom that contains surface protuberances designed to heighten vaginal and clitoral stimulation.

2. pertaining to oral sex. This usage dates back to the early 20th century.
French dressing is a term for semen, punning on the appearance of dressing and suggesting fellatio.
Frenching and **French job** are terms for the performance of fellatio or cunnilingus, derived from the association of the French with oral sex.
French kiss is a kiss in which the tongue is inserted into the partner's mouth. The practice is imputed to be French in origin, or may simply be considered sexy, like the French. It has also been used as a euphemism for oral sex.
French tricks is a colloquialism for fellatio or cunnilingus.

- "Good sex has nothing to do with expertise, how many French tricks one knew . . . No: if there was affection and enthusiasm, that was enough."
  (Martin Amis, *The Rachel Papers*, 1973)

fresh *adj American*

sexually aroused or aggressive. This is a 20th-century term.

fresh bit *n British*

virgin or young woman not yet sexually experienced. This is a 19th-century term. *See also* **bit**. **Fresh greens** is a variant. *See also* **greens**.

Friar Tuck *v British*

copulate. This 19th-century Cockney rhyming slang term is based on the rhyme with **fuck**.

fricatrix *n British*

female masturbator. This 19th-century colloquialism derives from the Latin *fricatrix*.

frig v

1. masturbate. Derived from the Latin *fricare*, meaning "rub," though also possibly influenced by the Old English *frigan*, meaning "love," it dates back to the 16th century.

- "I frigged away, he felt its effects and sighed—I frigged on and felt the big, firm wrinkled ball bag." (Anonymous, *My Secret Life*, 1890)

frigster and **frigstress** are male and female terms for masturbators.

2. fuck. This is a 19th-century euphemism.

frigid adj

incapable of sexual arousal. This term dates back to the 15th century, and originally had the meaning extremely cold. In the 17th century, it acquired a meaning of weak, cold, and impotent, and was applied to males. By the 20th century, it came to mean sexually unresponsive, and was applied exclusively to women.

frogskin n Australian

condom. Derived from "frog," which is slang for French, this is a 20th-century term. *See also* **French letter**.

front attic, front door, front parlor, front room, front window n British

female genitals. Attic, parlor, and room suggest the vagina, while door and window suggest the vulva. All these 19th-century terms reflect the "woman as house" metaphor, a subset of the container metaphor.

- "Mrs. Fubb's front-parlour is not to be mistaken for any part of any building." (Jon Bee, *Dictionary of the Turf*, 1823)

front door mat n British

female pubic hair. This 19th-century term puns on home, hair, and welcome, while also suggesting that women get stood upon.

front suspension n

Australian

brassiere. This 20th-century coinage adds to the many automobile metaphors. *See also* **chassis** and **headlights**.

froth n

semen. This 18th-century euphemism is based on appearance.

frottage n

1. lesbian sexual activity. This standard, somewhat formal, term from the 19th century derives from the French *frotter*, meaning "rub."

2. act of rubbing against someone of either sex to reach orgasm.

fruit n

1. male homosexual. This 20th-century term may derive from the second definition, below, or from another meaning of fruit, namely, a crazy person.

fruit juice is 20th-century gay terminology for semen. *See also* **juice**.

2. woman with loose morals. Possibly derived from ripe fruit, which is easy to pick, this is early 20th-century usage.

fruitful vine n British

female genitals. This 19th-century British coinage is based on the reproductive quality.

fuck v

copulate. The earliest recorded use of this taboo term was in 1503 in northern England, and though its etymology is not certain, it likely derives from Middle English *fuken* or German *ficken*, meaning "strike." The term appeared in dictionaries from the late 16th century (in John

Florio's *A Worlde of Wordes*, 1598, fuck was gaining ascendance over **swive** and **sard**). But by the 18th century, Grose's *Classical Dictionary of the Vulgar Tongue*, 1785, already had asterisks for the two middle letters. The *Oxford English Dictionary* avoided the term, as did its supplement in 1933. The new supplement, in 1972, finally included it. The first American dictionary to include the word was the *American Heritage Dictionary* in 1969. The term is still bleeped on television and radio, though the taboo has somewhat weakened. The term is now used in reference to both sexes; it is linguistically agile, allowing for verb, noun, adjectival, adverbial, and phrasal uses. It is also a key term in abusive swearing, as in the classic "go fuck yourself" and "get fucked." The word is also much used as an expletive-for-emphasis, as illustrated by Dorothy Parker, when she reportedly turned down an invitation by saying: "I'm too fucking busy, and vice versa."

fuck buttock is 19th-century British terminology for anal intercourse.

fuckish is 19th-century British usage meaning sexually aroused.

fuck off is 20th-century American usage meaning masturbate. Interestingly, the French term **fuck-off** means British tourist.

fucksome is a 19th-century British term for sexually attractive, said of a woman.

fuck the fist, and **fuck one's fist** are 20th-century terms for masturbate, said of men. *See also* **hand job**.

fuck n

1. act of copulation. This noun derives from the verb; it has been used since the 18th century.
2. person regarded as a sex partner. The phrase, "He's a good fuck," exemplifies this usage, which dates back to the 19th century.

3. semen. This usage also dates back to the 19th century.

fuck film is a 20th-century American term for pornographic film.

fuck hole is a derogatory 19th-century term for vagina. *See also* **hole**.

fucus v

fuck. This 16th-century euphemism has been obsolete since the 17th century. *See also* **firk** and **futz**.

full adj British

erect, as applied to a penis. This is a 19th-century colloquialism.

fumble v

caress sexually. Said of men, this 16th-century colloquialism derives from fumbling, meaning impotent, and is now obsolete.

fumbler's hall is a euphemism for female genitals.

fun and frolics n pl Irish

testicles. Based on the rhyme with **bollocks**, meaning balls, this is early 20th-century coinage. *See also* **flowers and frolics.**

fundament n

1. anus. This term was standard English before becoming a euphemism. It dates back to Middle English and derives from the sense of a base or bottom.
2. buttocks. This usage also began as standard English and then became a euphemism.

fun is an abbreviation for fundament, used since the 16th century. It applies to both anus and buttocks.

funny bit n British

female genitals. This 19th-century euphemism is based on funny meaning peculiar, and **bit**.

fur n

female pubic hair. This usage dates back to the 18th century. *See also* **hair**.

furbelow is a 17th-century British humorous term for female pubic hair, punning on the words fur and below and the standard meaning of furbelow, a decorative trimming on a woman's dress.

furburger is a 20th-century euphemism for the female genitals, derived from fur and **meat**. It is another example of a food metaphor.

furrow n

female genitals. This 19th-century usage derives from the groove of the vulva. *See also* **cleft** and **slit**.

furze, furze-bush n

female pubic hair. Based on the standard sense of the term meaning gorse, an evergreen shrub, these 19th-century terms were almost certainly influenced by **fuzz**.

futter v British

fuck. This euphemism dates back to the 16th century and is probably a variation on the French *foutre*, meaning "fuck."

- "... eating and drinking and futtering for a year of full twelve months."
  (Richard Burton, *A Thousand Nights and a Night*, 1885)

future n American

testicles. This 20th-century jocular term is based on the generative capability of the testicles and is usually said of young boys.

futz v American

fuck. This 19th-century euphemism derives from the Yiddish, meaning "fidget."

futz n American

female genitals. This is a 20th-century term.

fuzz n

female pubic hair. Derived from the meaning of hair that is especially short and curly, this 17th-century usage is still current.

G

gadget n American

penis. This is a 20th-century term. *See also* **instrument** and **tool**.

gal n

prostitute. This is a 19th-century euphemism. *See also* **girl**.

gallantry n British

sexual intercourse. This 17th-century euphemism is now obsolete.

gallop the antelope, gallop the maggot v
phrase British

masturbate. Said of men, both phrases derive from "hand-gallop," meaning in horsemanship an easy gallop. Antelope reinforces the association with **horn**, while maggot has an informal meaning of **whim**.

gam v

fellate. This 19th-century term is an abbreviation of **gamahuche**.

gamahuche v

perform fellatio or cunnilingus. This 19th-century term probably derives from the French *gamahucher*, though the Japanese *gamaguchi*, meaning "purse," has also been suggested. Variants include **gamaruche** and **gamarucher**. One performing oral sex is called a **gamahucher** or **gamarucher**.

- "She was laying with eyes closed and said that what I had done was nicer than anything. I had gamahuched her till she spent." (Anonymous, *My Secret Life*, 1890)

game n British
women considered as sexual prey or willing to copulate. Both the sporting and hunting metaphors are illustrated in this 17th-century usage. *See also* **sport** and **venery**.
the game is 17th-century terminology for prostitution, still current, especially in Great Britain in the phrase **on the game**.
gamester is an Elizabethan colloquialism for prostitute.

- "She's impudent, my lord, and was a common gamester." (William Shakespeare, *All's Well That Ends Well*, 1598)

gander n
active male homosexual. Derived from **goose**, this is a 20th-century gay term. Gander also means married man in Great Britain.

gang bang n American
group sex in which several men successively copulate with one woman, usually in a rape situation. Variations of this 20th-century coinage include **gang shag** and **gang fuck**. *See also* **bang**.

Ganymede n
homosexual boy. This literary euphemism derives from the Greek myth concerning a sexual abduction by Zeus of a youth called Ganymede. The term **catamite** derives from Catamitus, Latin for Ganymede.

- "Women are kept for nothing but the breed;
For pleasure we must have a Ganymede,
A fine, fresh Hylas, a delicious boy,
To serve our purposes of beastly joy."
(Charles Churchill, *Poems*, 1764)

gap n
vagina. Dating back to the 18th century, this term is rarely used today. *See also* **hole**.

gape n British
female genitals. This 19th-century term is possibly influenced by **gap**, by a man's supposed desire to gape at a woman's genitals, or by the connection to **eye**. A variant is **gaper**.

garbonzos n pl American
breasts, usually small ones. This recent term derives from the Spanish, meaning "chickpeas." **Garbanzos** is an alternative spelling.

garden n
female genitals. Dating back to the 16th century, this literary term could derive from **Garden of Eden**, which was a **paradise** and the place where sex began. Garden could also derive from **Covent Garden**, in London, which was a **red-light district** (under **red**). Garden is a fruitful metaphor, since **seeds** (under **seed**) are sown in a garden. There is also the pun on **greens**, a term for sexual intercourse.
garden engine is 19th-century British coinage for penis, since it waters the garden. **Gardener** is a variant.
garden gate is 19th-century British usage for vagina. *See also* **gate**.
garden goddess is 19th-century terminology for prostitute.
garden gout is an 18th-century term for syphilis.

garden hedge is 19th-century British usage for female pubic hair.
garden house is 17th-century coinage for brothel. *See also* **house**.

gash n

vulva. This 18th-century term, still current, is based on shape or appearance. *See also* **cut, slit,** and **wound.**
gash eater is a 20th-century term for **cunnilinguist** (under **cunnilingus**). *See also* **eat.**

gasp and grunt v phrase
British

copulate. This early 20th-century Cockney rhyming slang term is based on the rhyme with **cunt** and reflects the sounds of copulation.

gate n

female genitals. This 19th-century term comes from association with the domestic entrance. *See also* **garden gate.**

gate swinger n American

bisexual person. This 20th-century term puns on **swing** and means lively and moving in both directions.

gay adj, n

1. female prostitute or pertaining to a sexually loose woman. Dating back to the 14th century, this term became obsolete by the mid-20th century because of the rise of the second meaning of gay, below. The term probably derived from the supposed lively, merry adjectival sense that dates back to the 13th century.
gay bit is a 19th-century term for prostitute, now obsolete. *See also* **bit.**
gay girl is 19th-century British terminology for prostitute. *See also* **girl.**
gay house is 19th-century British usage for brothel. *See also* **house.**
gaying it is a 19th-century phrase that means copulate, now obsolete.

gaying instrument is 19th-century British coinage for penis. *See also* **instrument.**
gay man is a 19th-century British term for whoremonger, a man who seeks prostitutes. It is now obsolete.
gay wench is an early 20th-century American term for prostitute. *See also* **wench.**
gay woman is 19th-century British terminology for prostitute.
2. homosexual. In the 1920s homosexuals began to call themselves gays. It is only since the 1970s, however, that gay has been fully accepted into the language and passed from being a slang term to a standard one, preferred by the gay community.
gay bar is a mid-20th-century term for a bar that caters to homosexuals, usually male.
gay boy is 20th-century usage for a homosexual male.
gay lib, short for gay liberation, and linguistically patterned after women's lib, is an early 1970s term for the political movement for homosexual rights.

gazongas n pl American

breasts. This is a 20th-century euphemism. A variant spelling is **gazungas.** *See also* **bazooms,** and its variants **bazoongas** and **bazongas.**

gear n

genitals. Applied to both sexes, this was standard English from the 16th to the 18th century. By the 19th century the term had become slang. It derives from the sense of sexual **equipment** or apparatus. *See also* **instrument** and **tool.**

gear v British

copulate. Said of men, this is a 19th-century term.
geared or **geared up** is a 20th-century colloquialism meaning lusty, or ready for sex.

gender *v*

copulate, procreate. This euphemism was used from the 15th century to the 19th century.

- "Thou shalt not let thy cattle gender with a diverse kind." (Leviticus 19:19)

gender *n*

sex. This euphemism is most often used to describe sexual differences, but can also be used to denote sexual preferences.

discover one's gender is a gay phrase meaning come out and openly experience one's sexual preference.

feminine gender is a euphemism for the female genitals.

gender bender means a person who has a transsexual image; its use is found mainly in pop culture. The term dates back to the early 1980s.

generating place *n British*

vagina. Derived from its reproductive role, this is a 19th-century euphemism. **Generating tool** is a 19th-century euphemism meaning penis. See *also* **tool**.

genitals *n pl*

male or female organs of reproduction. This is a standard English term. It derives from the Latin *genitalis*, meaning "birth," hence the Latin plural *genitalia*, which is mainly a medical term. **Genital** is also a standard adjective applied in such phrases as **genital area**, **genital stage**, and **genital zone**.

- "My natural resources consist of two joints of marijuana millions of
  genitals an unpublishable private literature . . ."
  (Allen Ginsberg, "America," 1956)

gentleman of the back door *n phrase*

male homosexual, especially the insertor. This is an 18th-century euphemism. See *also* **back door**.

gentleman's pleasure garden *n phrase British*

female genitals. This is a 19th-century euphemism. See *also* **garden**.

gentoo *n South African*

prostitute. This word derives from the name of a U.S. ship, the *Gentoo*, that was shipwrecked off the South African coast in 1846. Survivors included a number of "servant girls" who then set up **gentoo houses** (brothels). The term is mainly used by Cape Malay people in South Africa.

geography *n British*

female genitals. This early 20th-century humorous term is based on the sense of physical exploration. See *also* **cliff**, **happy valley**, **mound of Venus**, and **peculiar river**.

German helmet *n*

glans or head of the penis. This 20th-century usage is based on appearance or shape.

germen *n*

semen. This 16th-century literary word derives from germ meaning the initial or simple form of something; it is now obsolete.

get *v*

copulate. This 19th-century euphemism is said of women, who may get pregnant.

get a bellyful of marrow, get a bellyful of pudding, are 19th-century British expressions meaning copulate, said of women. See *also* **marrow** and **pudding**.

get about her is a 19th-century British colloquialism meaning copulate, said of men.

get a facial is 20th-century terminology meaning be fellated, based on **face cream**.

get any? is a mid-20th-century American colloquialism, usually said by men, questioning whether a man had sex with a specific woman or with women in general.

get blown is 20th-century American coinage meaning be fellated. *See also* **blow**.

get down is 20th-century American usage for perform fellatio or cunnilingus.

get home is a 20th-century term for copulate, said of men. It can also mean copulate to orgasm.

get into and **get into her pants** mean copulate, said of men.

get it off is a 20th-century American expression meaning copulate or ejaculate, said of men.

get it on is mid-20th-century American terminology for get sexually aroused, have an erection, or copulate, said of men.

get it up is mid-20th-century American coinage for have an erection. *See also* **up**.

get layed (or **laid**) is a 20th-century expression meaning copulate. It was first applied to women, but currently is said of both sexes. It is now more informal than slang. *See also* **lay** and **laid**.

get one's ashes hauled is an early 20th-century phrase meaning copulate, said of men, based on the heat and fire of sex.

get one's balls off, **get one's nuts cracked**, and **get one's rocks off** are all 20th-century expressions meaning reach orgasm, said of men. *See also* **balls**, **nuts**, and **rocks**.

get one's chimney swept (out) is an 18th-century British phrase for copulate, said of women.

get one's greens is a 19th-century British term meaning copulate. *See also* **greens**.

get one's leather stretched is 19th-century British coinage for copulate, said of women. *See also* **leather**.

get one's oats is an expression dating back to the 16th century meaning copulate, said of men. This began as a standard expression before becoming colloquial English. It reflects the view that sex is as necessary as food, since oats were a staple. *See also* **have one's oats** (under **have**).

get one's oil changed is a mid-20th-century American phrase for copulation, said of men, derived from the automobile metaphor. It implies that semen will be removed and replenished. *See also* **oil**.

get out at Gateshead is a 20th-century British phrase for coitus interruptus. Gateshead is a railway stop before Newcastle-upon-Tyne.

get some action is a mid-20th-century American colloquialism for having sex. *See also* **act**.

get some ass is a mid-20th-century American term for having sexual intercourse. *See also* **ass**.

get there is a 19th-century colloquialism meaning copulate, usually said of men. It derives from the sense of success associated with reaching orgasm.

get the sugar stick is an 18th-century expression meaning copulate, said of women. The term is now obsolete. *See also* **sugar stick**.

get (someone) with child is an old euphemism dating back to the 16th century and means impregnate a woman.

gherkin *n American*

penis. One of several food terms, this 19th-century usage is based on shape. *See also* **banana**, **carrot**, and **cucumber**.

giblets *n pl*

genitals of either sex. This 18th-century term was used especially in the phrase **join giblets**, meaning copulate. The sexual sense is now obsolete.

gig n

1. loose woman or mistress. Chaucer used the term in *The House of Fame*, 1373, but it was obsolete by the 17th century.

2. female genitals. Used from the 17th through the 19th century, this connotation is now obsolete. It probably derived from the first sense of gig, above, though it may have been influenced by **jig**. A variant spelling is **gigg**.

giggle-stick n American

penis. This 20th-century word is based on the rhyme with **prick**. See *also* **gig** and **stick**.

gigolo n

male prostitute. This early 20th-century standard term is also sometimes used for a pimp. It derives from the French *giguer*, meaning "dance."

Gillette blade n

bisexual woman. This recent 20th-century lesbian term derives in part from the shaving blade that is double-edged, that is, it can cut both ways, and from the term **blade** itself.

ginger beer n British

homosexual. This Cockney rhyming slang term is based on the rhyme with **queer**.

girl n

1. prostitute or mistress. In the 13th century, girl meant a child of either sex. By the 16th century, it meant a female child only. Since the late 16th century the term also has been used to mean prostitute.

girlery is a 19th-century British word for brothel.

girlie, which means a sexually provocative girl or woman, began as an endearing term, acquired pejorative meaning in the early 20th century, especially when used in such terms as **girlie magazine** and **girlie pictures**.

girl kisser is a 20th-century term for a lesbian.

girlometer is obsolete 19th-century British coinage for penis, that is, one that "measures" girls.

girl-shop is obsolete 19th-century usage for brothel, derived from the trade in girls.

2. male homosexual. This is 20th-century gay usage.

gism, gissum, jism, jizz n

semen. Possibly derived from the Latin *jacere*, meaning "throw," this term dates from the early 20th century.

give v

This word, meaning offer or grant to, appears in many sexual expressions.

give a woman a shot is a 19th-century British term for copulate, said of men. See *also* **shoot**.

give hard for soft is a 19th-century British expression meaning copulate, said of men.

give head is 20th-century coinage for perform fellatio or cunnilingus, since it is done with the head (mouth). With fellatio there is the added pun in that **head** means glans. See *also* **serve head**.

• "After they give me head I want them to stick it inside of me." (Madonna, interview in *Rolling Stone*, June 13, 1991)

give juice for jelly is a 19th-century British phrase for copulate, said of women. See *also* **juice** and **jelly**.

give oneself is a colloquialism meaning copulate, said of women. It dates back to the 17th century.

give one's gravy is a 19th-century British phrase meaning copulate, said of women. See *also* **gravy**.

give standing room for one is a 19th-century British jocular expression meaning copulate, said of women, punning on **stand** meaning an erection.

give the old man his supper is a 19th-century British phrase for copulate, said of women. It implies that sex, like food, is a daily necessity.

give way is a 19th-century British colloquialism meaning copulate, said of women.

glands n pl

1. testicles. This mid-20th-century euphemism derives from the standard anatomical use of the term.

2. breasts. This euphemism is based on the anatomical sense of the term.

glans n

penis. This standard term derives from the Latin *glans*, meaning "acorn," because of its shape. The word has been used in this sense since the 17th century.

globes n pl

1. breasts. This euphemism has been used since the 18th century. It is based on shape.

• "... and presented to the touch something like what one would imagine of animated ivory, especially in those ruby-nippled globes...."
(John Cleland, *Fanny Hill: Memoirs of a Woman of Pleasure*, 1749)

2. testicles. This euphemism is based on appearance. This usage is now obsolete.

glory hole n American

hole in a wall in a public bathroom through which men may spy on other men's genitals or perform fellatio. This is mid-20th-century gay coinage.

glove n

condom. This 19th-century colloquialism is based on the expression "fit like a glove."

• "No glove, no love."
(John Irving, *The World According to Garp*, 1978)

glue n British

1. gonorrhea. This 19th-century term derives from the secretions that the illness causes.

2. semen. This 19th-century usage is based on appearance.

go v

copulate. This 19th-century, mainly British usage is said of men.

go all the way (See **all the way**.)

go buttocking is a 19th-century British phrase meaning copulate, said of men.

go down, **go down on**, and **go south** are all 19th-century American expressions meaning perform fellatio or cunnilingus.

goer is a 20th-century British euphemism for one who copulates.

go it alone is a 20th-century colloquialism meaning masturbate, based on masturbation usually being a solitary activity.

go to bed with is a popular euphemism for copulate with dating back to the 16th century. The **bed** symbolizes the activity that takes place in it.

go tromboning is a 19th-century phrase meaning copulate, said of men. It puns on the **bone** in trombone, meaning an erection, and the sliding **in and out** (under **in**) of the **trombone**.

goalkeeper n

clitoris. This recent jocular term suggests, as the soccer metaphor implies, that scoring involves getting past the goalkeeper. See *also* **score**.

goat n

1. lecher. This connotation dates back to the 16th century; it derives from the goat's supposed sexual prowess and from its horns, the goat being a symbol of the devil and sin.

• "By temperament, which is the *real* law of God, many men are goats and can't help committing adultery when they get a chance."
(Mark Twain, in Bernard DeVoto, *Letters from the Earth*, 1962)

goat house is 19th-century British terminology for brothel. See *also* **house**.

goat's jig is 19th-century British usage for copulation. See *also* **jig**.

goat-milker is a 19th-century word for prostitute and, by extension, vagina. See *also* **milk**.

2. penis. This sense, unlike the first, is now obsolete.

gobble v

perform fellatio. This 19th-century term derives from the standard sense of eat with haste.

• "Norman had told me the other night about a girl who used to like gobbling him so much that they found it convenient to sleep one-up one-down, her feet on his pillow."
(Martin Amis, *The Rachel Papers*, 1973)

gobbler is a 20th-century term for fellator.

godemiche n

dildo. This 19th-century literary term derives from the French word for dildo, which in turn may derive from the French *miche*, meaning "prostitute's customer."

golden shower n

act of urination as part of sexual activity. This expression, which can be traced back to the 16th century,

derives from the color of urine. See *also* **water sports**.

golden shower boy and **golden shower queen** are mid-20th-century gay terms for male homosexuals who enjoy being urinated upon.

gongs n pl

testicles. This colloquial 20th-century term may derive from **ding-dongs**.

gonorrhea n

highly infectious venereal disease. This is a standard medical term that has been used since the 16th century. It derives from the Greek meaning of flow of semen. *Gonos* means "seed" in Greek.

goo n

semen. This colloquial 20th-century term is based on appearance. See *also* **glue**.

goober n American

penis. Derived from it being the name of a peanut (made up from pee, as in **peepee**, and **nut**) this is 20th-century usage.

gook n American

prostitute. This 19th-century derogatory usage has been obsolete since it also became a derogatory term for an Asian person in the mid-20th century.

goolies n pl British

testicles. Possibly derived from goolies being children's **marbles**, this is 19th-century coinage.

goose v

1. *British* copulate. This 19th-century Cockney rhyming slang term, said of men, is based on **goose and duck** rhyming with **fuck**. The long neck of the goose is also suggestive of an erect penis.

2. *American* prod in the buttocks or anus. This 20th-century usage probably derives from the jabbing action of a goose with its beak.

- "As she was bending over her work-table . . . a playful lab assistant goosed her." (Max Shulman, *Barefoot Boy with Cheek*, 1943)

3. *American* perform anal intercourse. This is 20th-century underworld usage.

goose n *British*

woman regarded as a sex object; prostitute. This is 19th-century terminology.
gooseberry bush is a 19th-century term for female pubic hair. See *also* **bush**.

gooseberries n pl *British*

testicles. Derived from shape, this is an 18th-century term.

gooser n

1. *British* penis. This is 19th-century usage.
2. *American* pederast. This is a 20th-century term.

goose's neck n *British*

penis. Based on its phallic shape, this is a 19th-century term.

gorilla salad n

thick pubic hair. This mid-20th-century expression is based on the hairy nature of the gorilla; salad implies eating, hence oral sex.

goytoy n *American*

uncircumcised penis. Derived from the Yiddish *goy*, meaning "gentile," the Jewish practice of circumcision, and **toy** meaning penis, this is a 20th-century coinage.

grafting n

sexual intercourse. This 17th-century euphemism, now obsolete, is based on the pun on joining and uniting.

grant the favor v *phrase*

copulate. This 18th-century euphemism, said of women, implies that sex is a gift that a woman bestows upon a man.

grapefruits n pl *American*

breasts. This 20th-century euphemism is based on shape. It is one of many fruit terms, including **apples**, **lemons**, and **melons**.

gravy n *British*

semen. This 18th-century usage is based on appearance. The term was also used to mean female sexual secretions. In both cases the term ties in with **meat**.

- "He cam atween my thie,
  An' creeshed it weel wi' gravy."
(Robert Burns, *Merry Muses*, 1796)
gravy-giver is 19th-century terminology for both the penis and the vagina, in that both of them secrete gravy. **Gravy-maker** is a variant, though more often applied to the penis.

grease the wheel v *phrase*

copulate. This 19th-century expression is used of men. It derives from the lubrication of the **wheel**, meaning vulva, in sexual intercourse.

Greek n

active male homosexual. Derived from the homosexual practices of ancient Greece, this is early 20th-century usage. See *also* **Turk**.
Greek love is a euphemism for anal intercourse. **Greek way** is a variant.

greek *v American*
perform anal intercourse. This is mid-20th-century usage.

green goods, green goose *n British*
prostitute who is new in the business. This is 19th-century terminology, based on green meaning inexperienced.

green grocery *n British*
female genitals. This is 19th-century usage. *See also* **garden** and **greens**.

green grove, green meadow *n British*
female genitals and pubic hair. These expressions date back to the 19th century. *See also* **garden** and **greens**.

greens *n British*
sexual intercourse. Probably derived from green vegetables as a necessary food source, or from the Old Scots grene, meaning "long for," this is an 18th-century term. Greens is most often found in the expressions **get one's greens** or **have one's greens**, said of either sex.
• "It's like how Satan would be after two thousand million years of going without his greens, misering his sperms, and then one day out with his weapon big as a space ship with a pearly warhead and working himself off both-handed."
(Paul West, *Bela Lugosi's White Christmas*, 1972)

grind *v*
1. copulate. This colloquialism dates back to the 16th century. The sexual term is based on the notion of friction and hard work. Significantly,

one grinds a **tool**, though grind in the sexual sense is applied to both sexes.
• "Like an old tart grinding to her climax."
(Joe Orton, *Entertaining Mr Sloane*, 1964)
grinding house is a 19th-century British colloquialism for brothel.
grinding tool is a 19th-century British colloquialism for penis. *See also* **tool**.
2. masturbate. This usage dates back to the 19th century.

grind *n*
1. copulation or an act of copulation. This colloquialism dates back to the 19th century.
2. sexual partner. This usage dates back to the 19th century.
grindstone is a 19th-century British colloquialism for vagina. **Grinding mill** is a variant.

gristle *n*
penis. Derived from the standard sense of sinew, this is a 17th-century term. It is now almost obsolete, though a rock group called Throbbing Gristle, formed in 1976, clearly recalls this usage.

groan and grunt *v phrase*
copulate. This early 20th-century rhyming slang term is based on the rhyme with **cunt**. It refers to some of the sounds of sexual activity. *See also* **grumble and grunt**.

groceries *n pl*
male genitals. This 20th-century term may be based on the fact that the genitals are carried in the scrotum, a kind of **basket**. Oral sex is implied in this food-related term.

groin *n*
genital area. This 20th-century euphemism is usually used of a male.

- ". . . Elvis alerted America to the fact that it had a groin with imperatives that had been stifled."
(Lester Bangs, *Village Voice*, August 29, 1977)

groove v
copulate. Punning on the groove of the vulva, and "being in the groove," meaning being in the mood, this is 1960s usage.

grope v
fondle or caress sexually. This standard English term, dating back to the 14th century, is based on the more general sense of feel about blindly or uncertainly. *See also* **paw**.

grotto n British
vagina. This connotation goes back to the 19th century. *See also* **cave**.

- "It's a quivering pigeon caressing your hand,
Or that sweet little pussy that makes a man stand.
Or perhaps it's a flower, a grotto, a well,
The hope of the world, or a velvety hell."
(Anonymous ribald poem, "Those Four-Letter Words")

ground rations n pl
sexual intercourse. This 19th-century usage is based on the sense of necessity and of rationing.

group-grope n American
orgy or a group of people engaged in sexual activity. This is a mid-20th-century expression.

group sex n
any sexual activity that more than two people engage in together. This is a standard English term, dating from the 20th century.

groupie n
follower, usually female, of a band of musicians, who is sexually available to the band. This term dates back to the 1960s. *See also* **star-fucker**.

- "His defense described the sisters as 'groupies,' girls who deliberately provoke sexual relations with pop stars."
(London *Times*, September 15, 1970)

growl, growl and grunt n
British
female genitals. These 19th-century rhyming slang terms are based on the rhyme with **cunt**. *See also* **groan and grunt**.
growlbite, dating from the 19th century, means perform cunnilingus.

grumble and grunt n
British
female genitals. Based on the rhyme with **cunt**, the sound elements in this 20th-century rhyming slang term imply sexual activity. *See also* **groan and grunt** and **growl and grunt**.

G-spot n
erogenous area in the vagina, supposedly the source of female orgasm. The term was first used in the early 1980s and was named for Ernst Grafenberg (1881–1957), a gynecologist, who first put forth this theory.

G-string n
narrow strip of cloth worn by strip-teasers to cover their pubic area. The term probably derives from the loin-cloth worn by American Indians, also called a G-string or gee-string; the "g" could stand for groin.

- "What I know about politics you could put in a chorus girl's G-string and it wouldn't raise a lump."
(Irwin Shaw, *The Troubled Air*, 1951)

gully, gully hole n

vagina. These 19th-century terms refer to a trench caused by erosion. See also **furrow** and **hole**.

gun n

1. penis. This is an early 20th-century term. See also **shoot** and **weapon**.
• "Is that a gun in your pocket, or are you just glad to see me?" (Mae West, quoted in Joseph Weintraub, *Peel Me a Grape*, 1975)
2. gonorrhea. Probably derived from an abbreviation of the term, this usage dates back to the 19th century and is now obsolete.

gusset n British

female genitals. Derived from the garment or clothing sense, this 17th-century term was also applied to women considered as sex objects. It is now obsolete. See also **muslin**.

gut n

This colloquialism for bowels or belly dates back to Old English usage. It also means a narrow passage inside the body. Both meanings have supplied sexual terminology.
gut entrance is 19th-century coinage for vagina.
gutfucker, from the 19th century, means pederast.
gutstick, also from the 19th century, means penis. See also **stick**.

gutter n British

vagina. This 19th-century derogatory term suggests dirt. See also **drain**.
gutter slut is early 20th-century derogatory American usage for poor prostitute.

gymnasium n

vagina. This obsolete 19th-century colloquialism derives from the Greek term meaning "naked exercise."

H

hackney n British

prostitute. This 16th-century term derives from the standard meaning of a horse or mount that is for rent. **Hack** is an 18th-century abbreviation. See also **mount** and **ride**.

hair n

1. female pubic hair. This meaning derives from hair being a signifier for women, and dates back to the 16th century.
hairburger is a 20th-century American term for female genitals. **Hair pie** is a variant. Both terms suggest cunnilingus. See also **meat**.
hair court is a 19th-century British term for female genitals or, by extension, copulation.
hair-divider and **hair-splitter** are 19th-century British terms for penis.
2. woman considered as a sex object. This connotation stems from the first sense.
3. *British* copulation. This is 19th-century usage.

hairy adj

sexually aroused. Said of women, this is 19th-century usage. During the 20th century in the United States, the term began to be applied to men as well.
hairy oracle is 19th-century terminology for female genitals. See also **dumb oracle**.
hairy wheel is a 19th-century Australian term for female genitals. See also **wheel**.

half adj, adv, n

Meaning one of a pair or less than whole, this word is found in these sexual terms:

half-and-half is a 20th-century colloquialism for bisexual.

half-bent is 20th-century usage for bisexual. *See also* **bent**.

half-hard, half-mast are early 20th-century colloquialisms for a half-erect penis. Half-mast, based on the lowering of a flag, usually on a sad occasion or death, more specifically applies to the detumescing penis.

half-moon is an early 17th-century British term for female genitals, now obsolete.

hambone n *American*
penis. This is an early 20th-century connotation. *See also* **bone**.

hammer n *Australian, Canadian*
penis. Dating to the early 20th century, the term reflects an aggressive view of male sexuality. *See also* **hit** and **nail**.

Hampton Wick n *British*
penis. This 19th-century Cockney rhyming slang term is based on the rhyme with **prick**. *See also* **wick**.

hand job n
masturbation, especially on another person. This is common 20th-century usage.

handstaff n *British*
penis. This is a 19th-century colloquialism since it is a **rod** held by the hand.

handle v
1. caress sexually. This is a 16th-century colloquialism.
2. masturbate. Usually said of men, this is 19th-century usage.

handle n *American*
penis. This is a 20th-century term. *See also* **handstaff**.

hand-warmers n pl
Australian
breasts. Based on the male's desire to fondle them, this is a 20th-century colloquialism.

handy-dandy n
copulation. This euphemism, now obsolete, dates back to the 15th century.

hanky-panky n
sex or illicit sexual activity, such as adultery. This common colloquialism goes back to the 19th century. The term probably derives from hoky-poky or hocus-pocus, meaning trickery or deceit.
• " 'Hanky-panky—hetero and homo—is a problem,' says Charles Moskos, a military sociologist at Northwestern University."
(Alecia Swasy, "Navy Babies," *The Wall Street Journal*, October 3, 1991)

hanging johnny n *British*
flaccid penis. This is a 19th-century term. *See also* **johnny** (under **john**).

happy adj
homosexual. This 20th-century gay term is based on the synonym **gay**. It is now obsolete.

happy hunting grounds n
British
female genitals. This 19th-century term was clearly created by men. *See also* **target**.

happy valley n *British*
female genitals. This is an early 20th-century euphemism. *See also* **geography**.

hard adj
erect (referring to the penis). This connotation dates back to the 16th century.

hard bit is a 19th-century British colloquialism for an erect penis, contrasting with **bit**.

hard-core is a mid-20th-century colloquialism meaning pornographic, probably based on the presence of an erect penis in such pornography or the ability of the pornography to stimulate an erection. *Compare* **soft-core**.

hard-on is a colloquialism for an erect penis, used since the 19th century and common today.

• "He tells me how he makes love to them. Then lying on his back with a hard-on, he raises his legs over his head and sucks himself off."
(Jerzy Kosinski, *Cockpit*, 1975)

hare n

prostitute. Punning on **hair** and **rabbit**, the animal known for its copulatory prowess, this is a 16th-century term.

harlot n

prostitute. This has been a standard term since the 16th century. In Middle English the word originally meant a vagabond or rascal. Like many English terms that originally applied to both sexes or to males only, harlot became a pejorative term applied to women only. Today harlot is not as commonly used, or as demeaning, as **whore**.

• "Tho harlots paint their talk as well as face
With colours of the heart that are not theirs."
(Alfred, Lord Tennyson, *Vivien*, 1859)

hat n

1. female genitals. This is an 18th-century term.

old hat also refers to the female genitals. It was common British usage between the 18th and 19th centuries.

2. *British* prostitute. This usage is now obsolete.

3. *American* homosexual. This 20th-century term may derive from 2., above, or from the idiom "wearing a different hat," meaning being different.

hatchway n British

vagina. This is a 19th-century colloquialism, based on it being an entrance, and suggesting a birth canal.

have v

possess sexually. This sense has been in use since the 16th century. Have also serves as a lead-in for many sexual expressions.

have a bit is a 19th-century term for copulate, said of men. *See also* **bit**.

have connection is a 19th-century British euphemism for copulation.

have it and **have it off** are both 19th-century colloquialisms meaning copulate.

have lead in one's pencil is a 20th-century colloquialism for have an erection or be sexually virile.

have one's ashes hauled is a 19th-century Canadian expression meaning copulate.

have one's banana peeled is a 19th-century expression meaning copulate, said of men. *See also* **banana**.

have one's nuts cracked is a 19th-century expression meaning copulate, said of men. *See also* **nuts**.

have one's oats is a colloquialism meaning have sexual intercourse, said of either sex. It dates back to the 18th century and derives from **sow one's wild oats**, said of men, meaning be sexually promiscuous before settling down in marriage. *See also* **get one's oats**.

have sex is perhaps the most common euphemism since the 1960s, meaning have sexual intercourse, though it can also mean engage in any sexual activity.

have the horn is an 18th-century British colloquialism meaning have an erection. *See also* **horn**.

have the hots (for) is a 20th-century American colloquialism for being sexually turned on by someone. *See also* **hot**.

have one's aunt with one *v phrase*

menstruate. British variations of this euphemism include **have one's grandmother with one** and **have a friend with one**, from the 19th century. The 16th-century expression **have the flowers** puns on the menstrual flow. A 20th-century American expression is **have the rag on**, referring to the object (formerly rags) worn to absorb the flow. *See also* **on the rag**.

hawk it *v phrase British*

solicit sex. This 19th-century phrase is used of prostitutes. **Hawk the fork** is a current British expression meaning work as a prostitute. *See also* **fork**.

head *n*

1. glans of the penis. This 20th-century term is based on the glans being at the top end.
head job is a 20th-century American colloquialism meaning fellatio or cunnilingus; see **give head**.
2. hymen. This 17th-century euphemism derives from a shortening of **maidenhead**.
headhunter is a 20th-century term for a male hunter of maidenheads that is, virgins. It also refers simply to a lecherous male.

headlights *n American, Australian*

breasts, especially prominent ones. This 20th-century term is based on the shape of early automobile headlights, which were raised and very prominent. **Headlamps** is a variant.

head over heels *n phrase*

mutual oral sex. This 20th-century expression puns on the position of head over heels and on the colloquial expression meaning "to the extreme," as in "head over heels in love."

heart *n*

glans of the penis. This 20th-century term is based on similarity of shape. The term may also be influenced by the closeness to **hard**, as in **hard-on**, and by heart as a symbol of love.

heat *n*

sexual arousal in female mammals. This term has applied to both men and women as a colloquialism; it dates back to the early 20th century. In the United States, it is used in the phrase **in heat**, while in Great Britain the phrase is **on heat**. *See also* **hot** and **fire**.

heaven *n British*

vagina. This 19th-century jocular term is based on the vagina being thought of as a **paradise**. Heaven's opposite, **hell**, is also a term for the vagina, as is **limbo**.

heavers *n pl*

breasts. This informal term is based on the breasts' up-and-down movement with breathing. The term dates back to the 17th century, but it is rarely used today.

hedge *n*

female pubic hair. This is an obsolete 18th-century term. *See also* **bush**.
hedge on the dyke is an obsolete 19th-century British term for female pubic hair. *See also* **dyke**.
hedgewhore is a 16th-century British term for a beggarly prostitute,

based on the notion that a poor prostitute might work under a hedge. The term is now obsolete.

he-haw n American

homosexual male. This mid-20th-century usage puns on **he-whore** and hee-haw, the sound of a donkey, renowned for its big genitals.

hell n British

vagina. This 18th-century jocular term is based on Boccaccio's *The Decameron*, in which "putting the devil in hell" means putting the penis into the vagina. Hell suggests the sinfulness of sex. See also **devil** and **heaven**.

hemispheres n pl

breasts. This 19th-century colloquialism is based on shape. See also **globes** and **world**.

hen n

woman. This has been a colloquialism since the 17th century. It derives from Indo-European, in which the root "kan-" meant sing. Originally, hen applied to all domestic fowl, male and female. Today hen is used mainly in the context of female domesticity. **Hen-pecked** refers to a man who is dominated at home by his wife. See also **bird**, **chick**, and **cock**.

hermaphrodite n

1. a person with both male and female sex organs. The term has been standard English since the 15th century and is a blend of "Hermes" and "Aphrodite," who in Greek mythology had a child called Hermaphroditos.
2. homosexual male. This euphemistic term, dating back to the 18th century, is no longer used today.

hermit n British

penis. This 19th-century term is used mainly in the phrase **bald-headed hermit**.

Hershey bar n American

male homosexual. This 20th-century term refers to the color of feces, as Hershey is a major U.S. brand of chocolate, and suggests anal intercourse.

Hershey highway n
American

anus, as used for anal intercourse. This 20th-century term refers to the color of feces, as Hershey is a major U.S. brand of chocolate. See also **Cadbury canal**.

he-she n American

homosexual male or lesbian. This is a mid-20th-century colloquialism.

heterosexual n, adj

person attracted to the opposite sex. This standard English term derives from the Greek *heteros*, meaning "other." However, its usage is relatively recent. It was first used in the 19th century, in translation from German. In Richard Krafft-Ebing's *Psychopathis Sexualis*, 1889, heterosexual was distinguished from **homosexual**. In the 1930s the colloquial abbreviation **hetero** was first used. In 1979 Lillian Faderman coined the term **heterocentric**, questioning the assumptions of the heterosexual paradigm. **Heterosexism**, which also dates back to the late 1970s, is defined by the *Oxford Dictionary of New Words* as: "Discrimination or prejudice in favour of heterosexuals (and, by implication, against homosexuals); the view that heterosexuality is the only acceptable sexual orientation."

he-whore n American

homosexual male or male prostitute. This mid-20th-century derogatory term puns on "hee-haw," the sound of a donkey, renowned for its large genitals. See also **he-haw**.

hickey n American

penis. This 20th-century children's colloquialism may derive from the standard meaning, a mark on the skin from a love bite. It may also come from "do-hickey," meaning thingamajig.

hide n American

1. prostitute. This early 20th-century underworld usage puns on skin and secret.

2. catamite or young homosexual male. This is a mid-20th-century term.

hide the ferret v phrase
Australian

copulate. The **ferret** is both a burrowing animal and a furry one. This is a 20th-century expression.

hide the sausage v phrase

copulate. This is a 20th-century expression. An American variant is **hide the salami**. See *also* **sausage** and **salami**.

• "Nookie, rumpy-pumpy, a little game of hide-the-sausage—those kids just couldn't wait to get their teeth into it."
(*Punch*, Winter 1989)

higher Malthusianism n
British

sodomy. This 19th-century jocular term refers to the work on population control by Thomas Malthus (1766–1834). See *also* **Malthusianism**.

hilltop drive n

upturned buttocks. This 20th-century gay expression is based on appearance. See *also* **drive**.

hind n American

buttocks. This is a 19th-century colloquialism. See *also* **behind**. **Hind end** is a variant.

hinder end is a British variant dating from the 19th century.

hinder entrance is a 19th-century British colloquialism for buttocks or anus.

hinder parts is a euphemism for buttocks dating back to the 17th century.

hinterland n

buttocks. This euphemism dates back to the 19th century and suggests exploration. See *also* **geography**.

hit v

copulate. Said of men, this usage dates back to the 16th century. See *also* **bang** and **thump**.

hit and miss is an American phrase meaning **kiss**, punning on hit, miss, and the hard-to-determine outcome of erotic adventure.

hit it off is a 20th-century American euphemism for copulate; it implies compatibility and success.

hit on the tail is a 16th-century expression for copulate, said of men. See *also* **tail**.

hive n British

female genitals. This 19th-century term is based on a hive being a place for **honey** (semen).

hive it is a 19th-century British term for copulate or ejaculate, said of men.

HIV roulette n

sexual intercourse unprotected against **AIDS**. This is a 1980s expression. HIV refers to the human immunodeficiency virus. See *also* **Vatican roulette**.

ho, hoe n American

whore. This 20th-century usage derives from the variant pronunciation and is used primarily by blacks. See *also* **weekend ho**.

• "There is, for instance, the group Hoes Wit Attitude, whose first rap

album was the scene setter,
'Livin' in a Hoe House.' "
(Meg Cox, "Female Rappers Sing
of Smut and Spice and Nothing
Nice," *The Wall Street Journal*,
April 11, 1991)

hobbyhorse n
prostitute. This 16th-century colloquialism puns on **horse** and **ride**.

hog v British
copulate. Said of men, this is a
19th-century term. Hog joins many
farm animals in supplying sexual terminology, including **bull**, **cock**, **horse**,
ram, and **tom**.

hog eye n American
female genitals. This is mid-20th-
century terminology. See *also* **eye**.

hoist v
copulate. This 19th-century usage
can be found in **do a hoist**, **have a
hoist**, and **be in hoist**, said of men.
These phrases derive from the standard naval sense of raising up.

hold a bowling ball v
phrase
masturbate a woman with the fingers spread as in bowling. This is
20th-century usage.

hole n
1. anus. An abbreviation of **asshole**
(under **ass**), this sense has been in use
since the 14th century.
2. vagina. This meaning dates back
to the 16th century.
hole in one is a 19th-century colloquialism for sexual intercourse, pun-
ning on **hole**, **club**, **hit**, and the golfing
ambition of a hole in one.
hole of content and **hole of holes**
are old euphemisms for vagina. Hole
of content dates back to the 16th century, while hole of holes is from the

19th century and puns on "holy of
holies."
hole to hide it in is a 19th-century
British phrase for vagina. See *also* **it**.

hole v
copulate. This is 19th-century
usage, said of men.

Holland n
buttocks. This 16th-century term is
based on Holland (see **Netherlands**
under **nether**) being one of the Low
Countries. See *also* **low countries**.

holloway n British
vagina. This 19th-century term derives from the London place name
and the implication of a hollow way.

holy poker n British
penis. This is 19th-century terminology. See *also* **poker** and **hole**.

holy week n
menstruation. This 19th-century
colloquialism suggests the religious
practice of sexual abstinence during
periods of holy obligation.

home v British
copulate. This 19th-century term
also means reach orgasm or impregnate.

home run n American
sexual intercourse. This recent colloquialism refers to a baseball **score**.

home sweet home n British
female genitals. This 19th-century
expression connects domesticity and
female sexuality.

homo n
homosexual, especially male. This
derogatory word derives from an abbreviation of **homosexual**. It dates
back to the early 20th century.

- "I became one of the stately homos of England."
(Quentin Crisp, *The Naked Civil Servant*, 1968)

homosexual n

a person who is attracted to someone of the same sex. Dating back to the 19th century, this standard English word comes from the Greek *homos*, meaning "the same." The word was coined together with **heterosexual**. Havelock Ellis, in *Studies in Psychology*, 1897, wrote: " 'Homosexual' is a barbarously hybrid word and I claim no responsibility for it." Today, except in formal contexts, the word has been superseded by **gay**. **Homosexuality**, which continues to be the standard abstract noun, also dates back to the late 19th century.

hone n British

female genitals. This 18th-century term is based on the standard sense of hone, meaning a whetstone used to sharpen tools. *See also* **tool**.

honey n

semen. Based on appearance, and perhaps strengthened by the sense of sweetness, this is of 18th-century origin.
- "... and the honey running between her legs."
(J.P. Donleavy, *The Beastly Beatitudes of Balthazar B*, 1968)

honeydew melons n pl
American

large breasts. This term is of 20th-century origin. *See also* **melons**.

honeyfuck v

copulate. This term dates back to the 19th century. *See also* **fuck**.

honeypot n British

vagina. This 18th-century term is still in use today. *See also* **pot**.

hooker n

prostitute. Dating back to the 16th century, this word may derive from the sense of hooking or catching a customer. **Hook** is a 19th-century American abbreviation.
hook-shop is a 19th-century term for brothel, punning on hock shop.

hoop n British

vulva. Based on appearance, this is a 19th-century term. *See also* **circle** and **ring**.

hooters n pl American

breasts. Perhaps based on the British hooter, meaning car horn, which used to be round and which one squeezed, or on the breasts being something men hoot about, this term is of mid-20th-century origin.

hoover v British

perform oral sex. This recent usage refers to the Hoover vacuum cleaner, which sucks in dirt. *See also* **suck**.

hop on v phrase

copulate. Said of men, this is a 20th-century colloquialism.

horizontalize v

copulate. This 19th-century euphemism brings to mind **lay**. It is a spatial metaphor for sex, along the lines of **study astronomy**, said of women. Variations include **horizontal bop**, **horizontal dancing**, **horizontal refreshment**, and **horizontal rumble**.

horn n

erect penis; erection. This term, used since the 15th century, is based on appearance and hardness. It is found in expressions such as **have a horn** and **get a horn**. Other connotations include the horn as a symbol of cuckoldry, and the musical horn, which is blown. Rhinoceros horns are believed to be an aphrodisiac.

- "No horn could be stiffer; yet no velvet more smooth or delicious to the touch."
(John Cleland, *Fanny Hill: Memoirs of a Woman of Pleasure,* 1749)

hornification is 19th-century British usage for an erection, usually of the penis, but also applicable to the clitoris.

old hornington is a 19th-century British term for penis, usually an erect one.

horn *v*

become sexually aroused or cuckold (someone). Based on the noun sense above, both meanings date back to the 15th century.

horny dates back to the 19th century. It means lusty or sexually aroused, and is usually said of men. Today the term is considered a colloquialism rather than slang.

horse *v British*

copulate. Said of men, this 17th-century term is based on the metaphor of riding. *See also* **mount** and **ride.**

- "Thou shalt have a leap presently, I'll horse thee myself else."
(Ben Jonson, *Bartholomew Fair,* 1614)

horsemanship is a 16th-century euphemism for copulation, usually from the male's point of view. *See also* **mount, ride,** and **vault.**

horse and trap *n British*

gonorrhea. This 19th-century usage is based on the rhyme with **clap,** and strongly influenced by **horse** and **trap.**

horse collar *n British*

female genitals, especially the labia majora. This 19th-century term is based on appearance.

horseshoe, a variant, is based on a shape that was sacred in the ancient world, for it symbolized the female genitals. Even today it is a symbol of good luck and is placed over doorways.

horsewoman *n British*

masculine lesbian. This 19th-century term may derive from the "superior" or "masculine" position in riding.

hose *n American*

penis. This 19th-century euphemism is based on shape and function.

hose *v American*

copulate. This is a 19th-century term, said of men. **Hosing** is a euphemism for copulation.

hot *adj*

lusty. Based on sexual heat, this colloquialism has been used since Chaucer's day.

hot-assed or **hot-arsed** also means lusty. It is said of women and dates back to the 17th century.

hot beef, hot meat, and **hot mutton** are 19th-century terms for prostitute. These terms have also been applied to the female genitals, which are seen as dishes to be eaten. *See also* **beef, meat,** and **mutton.**

hot dog is 20th-century usage for penis, based on shape. *See also* **sausage.**

hot juice is a 20th-century term for semen. *See also* **juice.**

hot lips is a 19th-century term for the female genitals, punning on the labia and sexual passion.

hot milk is 19th-century British usage for semen. *See also* **milk.**

hot nuts is a 20th-century American term for a lusty or horny man. *See also* **nuts.**

hot pants, in 20th-century American usage, means sexual arousal, usually in women.

hot pudding for supper is a 19th-century expression meaning sexual intercourse, said of women, based on **pudding** meaning the penis and **supper** meaning the female genitals.

hot rod is 20th-century American usage for penis; to hot rod means masturbate, said of men. *See also* **rod.**

hot roll with cream is a 19th-century British phrase for sexual intercourse, punning on **roll** meaning copulate and penis, and **cream** meaning semen.

hot stuff is a 20th-century American colloquialism for a sexually attractive female.

the hots is a mid-20th-century American colloquialism meaning sexually aroused, as in "She's got the hots for him." The term can be applied to either sex. *See also* **heat.**

hotel n

vagina. This 19th-century euphemism is based on a hotel being a place that provides lodging. There may also be a pun on inn/in. *See also* **accommodation** (under **accommodate**) and **lodge.**

house n

brothel. This has been a common euphemism since the 18th century. There are many synonyms ending in "-house" such as **accommodation house, bawdy house,** and **cathouse.** Phrases include **house of all nations, house of assignation, house of call, house of ill repute, house of fame,** and **house of pleasure.**

housekeeper and **housemother** are early 20th-century American terms for a madam in a brothel.

house under the hill n
phrase British

vagina. This 19th-century term is based on the house (container) under the hill, that is, the **mons pubis.**

housewife n British

female genitals. This is 19th-century usage.

huddle v

copulate. This 18th-century euphemism is based on the closeness of a huddle.

huffle v British

copulate. This is a 19th-century British euphemism.

hug v

embrace sexually. This colloquialism dates back to the 17th century, and can also be a euphemism meaning copulate.

hump v

copulate. Dating back to the 18th century, this term is based on the forming of a hump in certain copulatory positions. "Hump the Hostess" is a party game suggested by a character in Edward Albee's play *Who's Afraid of Virginia Woolf,* 1962.

humpy is a mid-20th-century American colloquialism meaning sexually aroused.

hump n American

1. copulation. This is a mid-20th-century term.

2. prostitute, or a woman considered as a sex object. This is also a mid-20th-century term.

hung adj

referring to the relative size of the male genitals. This colloquialism dates back to the 17th century. A common usage is in **well-hung.**

hung like a bull and **hung like a chicken** are both American gay expressions from the 1950s referring to large and small male genitals respectively.

hunger n
lust or sexual appetite. This 16th-century literary term exemplifies the food metaphor in describing sexual states.

hunk n
1. *American* sexually attractive person, usually a male. This is a 20th-century term.
2. act of copulation. This is mid-20th-century usage.
hunky is 1950s American usage for sexually aroused.

husbandry n
sexual intercourse. This 16th-century literary term, said of men, is based on the farming activities of plowing and planting seeds. It also puns on the role of a husband.

husker n *American*
male masturbator. This late 19th-century term refers to the similarity of hand action between husking corn and masturbation.

hussy n
lewd woman, wench, or prostitute. This abbreviation of housewife (originally *husewif* in Middle English) meant mistress of the house from the 16th century onward. However, by the 18th century the term had become derogatory.

hustle v *American*
copulate. This 19th-century term, usually said of prostitutes, is based on the standard sense, meaning push or obtain through force or persuasion.

hustler n *American.*
1. prostitute. This 20th-century usage applies to women and male homosexuals.
2. pimp. This is also 20th-century usage.

3. Sexually successful male. *See also* **score** and **win**.

hymen
membrane at the entrance to the vagina. This standard English term dates back to the 17th century. It derives from the Greek term meaning membrane. Hymen is also the Greek and Roman god of marriage.

hymie n *American*
copulation. Probably based on **hymen**, this 20th-century usage is now obsolete.

I

IBM n
small penis. This recent acronym for itty bitty meat is ironic, since IBM (International Business Machines) is one of the largest computer companies in the world. Perhaps it is no coincidence that both **business** and **machine** are also sexual terms. *See also* **meat**.

ice palace n *American*
fancy brothel. This 20th-century underworld term is based on ice meaning cut glass.

icing expert n
fellator. This mid-20th-century term is based on the similarity of icing to semen. *See also* **cream** and **dream whip**.

idol n
penis. This obsolete 18th-century usage refers to both worship and a fetish. Idol represents the metaphor

of religion, which accounts for a number of sexual terms, including **angel**, **devil**, **heaven**, **hell**, **kneel at the altar**, and **religious observances**.

impale v

copulate. This 19th-century usage reflects an aggressive view of sex. *See also* **bayonet** and **fork**.

impotent adj

unable to copulate. This standard English term is used of men. It dates back to the 14th century and derives from the Latin meaning "not potent." **Impotence** is the noun form.

impudence n

penis. This 18th-century colloquialism is based on the meaning "without shame," derived from the Latin, and said especially by women. It contrasts with the euphemistic **pudenda**, derived from the Latin *pudere*, meaning "be ashamed," which stands for the genitals, especially the female ones.

in prep

This word indicating inclusion, location, or position, acts as a lead-in to many sexual phrases. **Play at in-and-in**, **play at in-and-out**, and **in-and-in** and **in-and-out** are colloquial phrases for sexual intercourse dating back to the 17th century. Most are obsolete today.

- "They are sure fair gamesters . . . especially at in-and-in."
  (Henry Glapthorne, *The Hollander*, 1635)

in an interesting condition has been a euphemism for pregnant since the 18th century.

- "Mrs. Leuville was in an interesting condition."
  (Charles Dickens, *Nicholas Nickleby*, 1838)

in between is a 20th-century colloquialism meaning bisexual.

in cock alley is 18th-century terminology for sexual intercourse, said of men. *See also* **cock** and **alley**. **In Cupid's alley** is a 19th-century variation.

in full fig means with an erect penis. This 19th-century expression may derive from **fig** meaning vagina, or from "full fig," meaning fully clothed or armed.

in love lane is a 19th-century colloquialism for sexual intercourse, said of men, based on **love lane** meaning vagina.

in one's Sunday best or **in one's Sunday clothes** is a 19th-century jocular expression meaning having an erect penis. It derives from the starched clothes worn on Sunday for church, and suggests stiffness. This is another use of religious metaphor.

in pod is a 19th-century colloquialism meaning pregnant, based on the reproduction of peas in a pod.

in season is a 19th-century euphemism meaning lusty or **in heat** (under **heat**), based on the natural estrous cycle.

in the club is a 20th-century colloquialism meaning pregnant, based on having joined a new group.

in the familiar way is a 19th-century euphemism meaning pregnant; it puns on familiar and on family way. **In the family way** is a variant.

- "This stuff is the male seed, and impregnates the woman, or as it is called in simple language, gets her in the family way."
  (Anonymous, *My Secret Life*, 1890)

in the saddle is a colloquialism for menstruating, based on saddle meaning a sanitary napkin. This phrase dates back to the 19th century.

in trouble is a 19th-century colloquialism meaning pregnant; it is used mostly to describe girls or young women who do not want to be pregnant.

incognita n

prostitute. This 18th-century euphemism, now obsolete, is based on the Latin meaning "not recognized."

India n *British*

female genitals. This early 17th-century usage may be based on the idea of discovery and exploration.
* "And sailing towards her India in that way
  Shall at her fair Atlantic navel stay."
  (John Donne, *Elegy*, XVIII, 1613)

ineffable n *British*

female genitals. This 19th-century colloquialism derives from the standard sense of the term, meaning utterly inexpressible.

infanticide n

masturbation. This is a 19th-century jocular term, said of men, since masturbation effectively prevents conception.

ingle-nook n *British*

female genitals. This is 19th-century coinage. *See also* **nooky**.

insertee n

male homosexual who receives a penis in his anus or mouth. This is a 20th-century colloquialism. *See also* **catch**.

insertor n

male homosexual who places his penis in the anus or mouth of a male sex partner. This is a 20th-century colloquialism. *See also* **pitch**.

inspector of manholes n
phrase British

pederast. This early 20th-century expression puns on **manhole**, meaning the anus.

instrument n

penis. This is a 17th-century euphemism. *See also* **tool**.

intemperance n

lust or extreme sexual desire. This is a 17th-century literary euphemism.

intercourse n

sexual intercourse. This term derives from the Latin *intercursus*, meaning "running between." It dates back to the 15th century, when it meant connection, exchange, or commerce of any kind. Today the term can hardly be used except in the sexual sense. *See also* **sexual intercourse**.

intimacy n

sexual intercourse. This 17th-century euphemism is based on the standard meaning of closeness, both physically and emotionally.
be intimate with means copulate with. This euphemism dates back to the 17th century.

introduce Charley
(Charlie) v *phrase British*

copulate. This 19th-century colloquialism, said of men, is based on **Charley** being a common male name. In addition, Charley means vagina and **Charley Hunt** is rhyming slang for **cunt**. Introduce is meant in the physical sense.

invade v

copulate. This 17th-century term, said of men, is typical of the many warlike terms used in sexual slang. *See also* **charge**, **hit**, **impale**, and **fort**.
* "... invade and grubble one another's punk."
  (John Dryden, *The Disappointment*, 1684)

invert n

homosexual. This late 19th-century euphemism is based on the idea that homosexuals turn inward to their own sex rather than outward to the opposite sex. The term is obsolete.

Irish fortune n British

female genitals. This derogatory 19th-century expression alludes to prostitution.

Irish root n British

penis. This 19th-century terminology is considered derogatory. See also **root**.

Irish toothache n British

erection. This derogatory expression dates back to the 19th century.

iron hoof n British

male homosexual. This early 20th-century rhyming slang term is based on the rhyme with **poof**.

irrumation n

fellatio. This formal term derives from the Latin *irrumare*, meaning "suck" or "perform fellatio," and dates back to the late 19th century. See also **suck**.

it pron

1. sexual intercourse. This common euphemism dates back to the 15th century. See also **do it** (under **do**).

2. male or female genitals. This euphemism dates back to the 15th century. See also **affair** and **thing**.

Italian fashion n

anal intercourse. This highly derogatory euphemism, based on the supposed habit of Italians, dates back to the 19th century. A variant is **Italian way**, a term D. H. Lawrence used

in *Lady Chatterley's Lover*, 1928. See also **Greek** and **Turk**.

itch n

lust. This colloquialism dates back to the 17th century.
* "Why then to cure thy itching, Jove, thou art now going a bitching."
(Charles Cotton, *Burlesque upon Burlesque*, 1675)
itcher is 19th-century usage for female genitals.
itching jenny is also 19th-century usage for female genitals, based on Jenny, a common name, meaning a female.

ivory gate n British

female genitals. Ivory probably refers to skin color in this 19th-century term. See also **gate**.

ivory pearl n British

woman regarded as a sex object. Based on the rhyme with **girl**, this 20th-century term is now obsolete. Ivory pearl is also an item of value.

J

jack n

1. penis or an erect penis. Derived from either the common male name or from the lifting device, this is a 19th-century term.
jack-in-the-box is 19th-century terminology for penis, especially an erect one, since the jack-in-the-box springs up erect. Jack-in-the-box is also 19th-century usage for syphilis, based on the rhyme with **pox** and the pun on jack meaning penis and **box** meaning vagina.

Jack Robinson is a 19th-century term for penis. It may be based on the phrase "Before one can say Jack Robinson," which may imply premature ejaculation.

2. prostitute's customer. This is 20th-century usage, with jack being a variant of **john**.

jack v

copulate. This is a 19th-century term.

jack off is early 20th-century American usage for masturbate, said of men. It may derive from the Latin *jacere*, meaning "throw," or be influenced by **jerk off**.

jack-and-jill-off party is recent terminology for a safe-sex party, without intercourse. *See also* **jill off**.

• "Jack-and-Jill-off parties are safe sex playpens of the highest order."
(Carol Queen and David Steinberg, "The Jack-and-Jill-Off Parties,"*The Realist*, Number 115, January–February 1991)

Jacob n British

penis. This obsolete 19th-century term may derive from **jack** or from **Jacob's ladder**, below.

Jacob's ladder is a 19th-century British term for vagina. It alludes to the biblical story of Jacob's ladder leading to **heaven**. Climbing is also a common Freudian symbol for copulation. *See also* **climb**.

jag n American

male homosexual prostitute. This mid-20th-century gay term probably derives from the standard sense of the word, meaning a spree or exhilarating experience.

jag house is a brothel for male homosexuals.

jag off means masturbate. *See also* **jack off**.

jam n British

1. female genitals. Punning on jam meaning a sweet-tasting spread and jam meaning a squeeze, this is of 19th-century origin.

2. semen. This 19th-century usage is based on appearance. *See also* **jelly**.

jam pot is 19th-century usage for vagina, based on it being a container for jam. *See also* **pot**.

jam v American

copulate. Based on the sense of blocking or wedging something, and probably influenced by "jam session," a **jazz** term for an improvised performance dating back to the 1930s, this term is of black origin

Jane Shore, Jane Shaw n British

prostitute. This 19th-century rhyming slang term is based on the rhyme with **whore**. Jane is also a term for women in general, while shore implies a naval origin, that is, when sailors came ashore, they often searched for a Jane Shore. Jane Shore was the mistress of King Edward IV in the 15th century, offering another possible derivation.

janey n

1. vagina. This is 20th-century lesbian usage.

2. lesbian. Possibly derived from the first sense, above, and from the common name Jane meaning woman, this is 20th-century coinage.

jang n American

penis. This mid-20th-century term is a variant of **yang**.

janney v American

copulate. Based on the railroad term meaning to **couple**, this is early 20th-century usage.

jape v

copulate. This term, dating back to the 14th century, is probably based on its standard meaning, to amuse or make fun.

J. Arthur Rank v British

masturbate. This 20th-century rhyming slang term is based on the rhyme with **wank**. It derives from the film producer's name and suggests the portrayal of sexuality in movies.

jaw queen n

fellator. This 20th-century gay coinage uses jaw to suggest oral sex. See also **mouth music**, and **queen**.

jazz n American

sexual intercourse. This 19th-century usage may derive from "jasm," a variant of **gism**, semen. As a derivative of sexual intercourse, jazz has also been used to mean the female genitals and semen. As America's most innovative music form, jazz in the music sense has, over time, made the sexual meanings of jazz obsolescent, at least since the second half of the 20th century, even though the sexual senses are fairly commonly understood.

jazz v

copulate. This verb usage dates back to the 19th century. **Jazz it** is a variant. The titles of many jazz songs, such as "Jazz Me Blues" by Thomas Delancy, have clear sexual messages.

• "My sister was being jazzed by half the neighborhood cats by the time she was fifteen."
(H. MacClennan, Precipice, 1949)
jazz oneself is a 19th-century term for masturbate.

jeff off v phrase

masturbate. This 20th-century euphemism is said of men. See also **jerk off** and **jack off**.

jelly n

1. semen. Dating back to the 17th century, this usage is based on appearance.
• "Give her cold jelly,
   To take up her belly,
   And once a day swinge her again."
(John Fletcher, The Beggar's Bush, 1622)
jelly bag is British usage for vagina, also dating back to the 17th century. This term also meant scrotum, a container of jelly. See also **bag**.
2. buxom girl or woman. This 19th-century meaning also appears in **jelly on springs**, which refers to bouncing breasts and buttocks. The term can also apply to males.
3. American female genitals. **Jelly roll** is a variant of this 20th-century usage. The term can also refer to a lover.
• "She's got a sweet jelly, my woman's got a sweet jelly roll, ... It takes her jelly to satisfy my soul"
(Blues lyrics, quoted in Thomas Kochman, Black and White Styles in Conflict, 1981)

jerker n British

1. masturbator. This 19th-century usage, said of men, is based on the jerking motions typical of masturbation.
2. prostitute. This usage is also of 19th-century origin.

jerk off v phrase

masturbate oneself or another, usually a male. This expression dates back to the 18th century.
• "They say love thy neighbor as thyself. What am I supposed to do—jerk him off too?"
(Rodney Dangerfield, No Respect, 1980)

jerk one's gherkin v phrase
American

masturbate. Said of men, and derived from **gherkin** meaning a penis, based on shape, this is a 20th-century expression. See also **cucumber** and **pickle**.

Jersey Cities n pl American

breasts. This early 20th-century rhyming slang term is based on the rhyme with **titties** (under **tit**). See also **Bristol City** and **Manchester City**.

Jerusalem artichoke n

See **artichoke**.

jet one's juice v phrase
British

ejaculate. This 19th-century expression, said of men, is based on **juice** meaning semen.

jet stream n American

semen. This term is recent coinage.

jewel n

virginity, the hymen, or the female genitals. This colloquialism dates back to the 18th century. The sense of item of great value applies in each of the following terms.
jewel case is an 18th-century colloquialism for vagina, since it is the container of a jewel, meaning the hymen or virginity. See also **case**.
jewelry is 20th-century American usage for male or female genitals.
jewels is a 20th-century colloquialism for the male genitals, especially the testicles. See also **family jewels**.

Jezebel n British

penis. This obsolete 19th-century term is unusual in that it is a female name. It probably derives from the biblical story in which Jezebel promoted idolatry (See **idol**). Another explanation is that a jezebel means an

impudent woman, and **impudence** is an old term for penis.

jig, jig-a-jig, jig-jig v

copulate. These 19th-century terms are based on the standard senses of movement and dance of the word jig. See also **dance**.

jig, jig-jig n

1. copulation. This is 19th-century terminology.
• "He couldn't have been without any jig-jig all summer or he'd be showing it now."
  (Connie Willis, "All My Darling Daughters," 1985, in Ellen Datlow, editor, Alien Sex, 1990)
2. female genitals or penis.
jigger is 19th-century usage for vagina or penis.

jiggle v

1. copulate. This 19th-century usage comes from the association with jerky movement. See also **jig**.
2. actively display one's breasts. This 20th-century term is found especially in the term **jiggle shows**, referring to television programs that show women displaying their breasts.

jiggling bone n British

penis. This expression dates back to the 19th century. See also **bone**.

jiggumbobs n pl British

testicles. This 18th-century term is based on the pendulous appearance of the testicles. See also **bobbles**.

jill off v phrase

masturbate. This is a 20th-century lesbian expression. See also **jack off**.

jilt n British

prostitute. This 17th-century term suggests the standard sense of the term, meaning to drop a lover un-feelingly.

jing-jang n American
1. male or female genitals. This 20th-century coinage may be based on the term **ying-yang**.
2. copulation. This is also 20th-century coinage.

jism n
See **gism**.

jive v American
copulate. Like **jazz**, this primarily 20th-century music and dance term has sexual implications.

jizz n
See **gism**.

job v
copulate. This 16th-century collo-quialism derives from the standard sense meaning to work, though it could be influenced by "jab." Al-though this usage is now obsolete, the noun sense is in common use, espe-cially in such phrases as **on the job**, colloquial for engaging in sexual in-tercourse, as well as in the suffix "-job," found in **blow job**, **head job** (under **head**), etc.

jo-bag n American
condom. This 20th-century mili-tary coinage possibly derives from **joy-bag**. See also **bag**.

jock n
penis. This 18th-century term is based on the common Scottish name for Jack (see **jack**) or on an abbrevi-ation of **jockey**. The term is now ob-solete, though it survives in **jock-strap**, an early 20th-century coinage for athletic supporter.

jocker is an early 20th-century American underworld term for a ped-erast.

jock v British
copulate. This 17th-century term, used of men, probably derives from **jockey**.

jockey n American
1. pederast. This is an early 20th-century underworld term. See also **mount** and **ride**.
2. lesbian who assumes the mas-culine role, based on the position in riding.

Jodrell Bank v British
masturbate. This 20th-century Cockney rhyming slang term is based on the rhyme with **wank**. Jodrell Bank is a famous astronomical ob-servatory. See also **bank**.

Joe Buck v Australian
copulate. This early 20th-century rhyming slang term is based on the rhyme with **fuck**.

Joe Hunt n British
vagina. Based on the rhyme with **cunt**, this early 20th-century term is mainly used in a derogatory way.

jog v British
copulate. Based on jog meaning jerky movement, this 16th-century term is now obsolete.

john n
1. prostitute's customer. This early 20th-century usage probably derives from the common name John.
• "The old stereotypes of johns—husbands seeking relief once the family is big enough, traveling businessmen, people with sexual fetishes, servicemen, men eager to enjoy sexual practices

supposedly objectionable to their wives—are still valid."
(Katie Leishman, "Heterosexuals and AIDS," *The Atlantic Monthly*, February 1987)

2. penis. This 20th-century colloquialism is probably a truncation of **John Thomas**, defined below.

johnnie and **johnny** are informal 20th-century terms for penis or condom.

johnny rollicks is 19th-century British rhyming slang meaning testicles, based on the rhyme with **bollocks**.

Johnson is 19th-century usage for penis. This term exemplifies personification of the penis; however, unlike other common names for penis, such as **peter** and **dick**, Johnson is a surname. See also **Doctor Johnson**.

John Thomas also uses personification in referring to the penis. D.H. Lawrence employs the term in *Lady Chatterley's Lover*. This colloquialism dates back to the 19th century.

joint n

1. brothel. Dating back to the 18th century, this meaning is now obsolete. Today joint usually means merely a disreputable place.

2. penis. This early 20th-century American usage may derive from the penis being joined to the body.

jointess n

clitoris. This jocular 20th-century term probably is based on adding the feminine suffix "-ess" to **joint**.

jollies n pl American

sexual pleasure or thrills. Used in expressions such as "get one's jollies," this is 20th-century coinage.

jolly n

homosexual. This 20th-century gay euphemism is based on the synonym for **gay**. See also **happy**.

jolt v British

copulate. This 19th-century usage is based on the standard sense of sudden movement. See also **jog**.

jones n American

penis. Jones is early 20th-century black usage. It may be a variant of **john** or **Johnson**.

joy v

copulate. This is an obsolete 17th-century colloquialism. See also **enjoy**.

joy-bag is a 20th-century British military term for condom. See also **bag**.

joy boy is a 20th-century term for a homosexual male. See also **boy**.

joy house is an early 20th-century term for a brothel. See also **house**.

joy sister is early 20th-century American usage for prostitute. See also **sister**.

joystick is a 19th-century term for penis, still current today. See also **stick**.

- "An hour before dawn, he awoke. Piss call. His joystick was as upright and as hard as that in the Spud XIII he'd flown fifty-nine years ago."
(Philip Jose Farmer, *The Henry Miller Dawn Patrol*, 1977)

jubes n pl

breasts. This 20th-century term probably derives from jujubes, a type of gumdrop. It could also be rhyming slang for **boobs**.

judy n British

prostitute. This early 19th-century coinage is probably based on Judy being a common female name. See also **crack a judy**.

juggle v

copulate. This 16th-century literary term derives from the Latin *joculari*, meaning jest. See also **play**.

jugs n pl

breasts. This 20th-century term is based on the container metaphor, as in **milk jugs** (under **milk**).

• "Sweet darling Elspeth. No jugs to speak of, but courageous nipples." (Morris Lurie, *Seven Books for Grossman*, 1983)

juice n

1. semen. This colloquialism, based on appearance, dates back to the 19th century. *See also* **oil**.

2. vaginal lubrication. This is 19th-century coinage. *See also* **wet**.

juice v

arouse a woman sexually. This is a 20th-century term.

juicy, meaning lusty or sexually aroused, is said especially of women. Juicy also pertains to anything that is lewd or sexually arousing, for example, a juicy novel. The term dates back to the 17th century. *See also* **saucy** (under **sauce**).

juke v American, Caribbean

copulate. This is a 20th-century dialectal term. Juke means disorderly in Gullah.

juke house is early 20th-century usage for brothel. *See also* **house**.

jumble v

copulate. By the 18th century this 16th-century euphemism was obsolete.

jump v

copulate. This term dates back to the 16th century. Shakespeare used the term in *The Winter's Tale*, and it is still in use today.

jungle meat n

penis of a black man. This is a 20th-century derogatory expression. *See also* **meat**.

jutland n British

buttocks. This 18th-century jocular usage is based on the jutting out of the buttocks. Jutland is the name of a peninsula projecting into the North Sea and comprising the mainland of Denmark.

K

kanakas n pl Australian

testicles. Derived from the Hawaiian term *kanaka*, meaning man, and reinforced by its closeness to **knackers**, this is 20th-century terminology.

kate n

prostitute. This 20th-century underworld term is based on kate being a colloquialism for a loose woman. *See also* **judy**.

kazoo n

anus or vagina. This usage may derive from **cooze**, or from kazoo meaning mouth. *See also* **bazoo** and **wazoo**.

keel n

buttocks. This 19th-century colloquialism derives from the naval sense meaning bottom of a ship. *See also* **stern**.

keen adj

lusty. This has been a colloquial term since the 16th century. It probably derives from "ken," meaning **knowledge**.

keep the census down v phrase

masturbate. This jocular 19th-century expression, now obsolete, was said of men. It is based on masturbation as a form of birth control. There may be intended irony in the word "down," since masturbation implies first getting the penis **up**. A related British term is **infanticide**. A literary version is **higher Malthusianism**. The phrase also means have an abortion.

keister n American

buttocks or anus. This mid-20th-century colloquialism derives from the German *kiste*, meaning "box." Spelling variations include **keester**, **kiester**, and **kister**.

kettle n British

vagina. Punning on heat and the container metaphor, this colloquialism is of 18th-century origin. *See also* **pan** and **pot**.
• "The tinker too with Mettle,
Said he would mend her Kettle,
And stop up every Leak."
(Thomas D'Urfey, *Wit and Mirth*, 1719)
kettledrums is 18th-century British coinage for breasts, based on their roundness. It adds to the many musical terms that have sexual connotations, such as **fiddle**, **flute**, **organ**, and **trombone**.

key n British

penis. This is 18th-century usage. *See also* **lock**.
keyhole stands for vagina. *See also* **hole**.

Khyber Pass n British

anus or buttocks. This 19th-century Cockney rhyming slang term is based on the rhyme with **arse**. As with many rhyming terms, the rhyming word is dropped, so **Khyber** alone also stands for arse. The Khyber Pass is a narrow path in the mountains between Pakistan and Afghanistan.

• "If we sit on our Khybers, we will miss out on all the things that make our lives the richer." (*Crescendo*, January 6, 1968)

kid leather n British

young prostitute. This is a 19th-century expression. *See also* **leather**.

kife n American

catamite, fellator, or prostitute. This early 20th-century underworld term may derive from the Arabic *kayf*, *kif*, or *kef*, meaning a state of tranquility, usually drug induced.

kindness n

sexual intercourse. This 18th-century euphemism can be found in the expression **do a kindness**, referring to sex granted as a favor. *See also* **rudeness**.

King Lear n British

homosexual. Based on the rhyme with **queer**, and perhaps punning on leer and king/**queen**, this is early 20th-century usage.

kink n

one who is considered sexually deviant in any way. This is a mid-20th-century term.
kinky means sexually deviant, especially in the expression **kinky sex**. *See also* **bent** and **twisty**.

kip n

brothel. Derived from the colloquial sense meaning sleep, this is 18th-century usage. **Kip-shop** is a variant. Both terms are now obsolete.

kiss v British

copulate. This is an 18th-century euphemism.
• "Ten times I carnally have—kist her." (Allan Ramsay, *Fables & Tales*, 1730)

kiss it is 20th-century usage meaning perform fellatio or cunnilingus. *See also* **it**.

kit n

male genitals. This 19th-century term suggests a tool kit. *See also* **gear** and **tool**.

kitchen n British

female genitals. This 19th-century term is probably based on the **oven** located there and reinforced by the Victorian assumption that a woman's place is in the kitchen.
kitchen cleaner is a mid-20th-century gay usage for one who performs anilingus.

kitten's ear n

female pubic hair. This obsolete 19th-century expression is based on softness and shape. *See also* **cat** and **puss**.

kitty n British

female genitals. This is 19th-century usage. *See also* **cat** and **puss**.

knack n

penis. This term is obsolete. *See also* **knick-knack**.

knackers n pl British

testicles. This colloquialism dates back to the 19th century. Knacker is British for a buyer of animal carcasses, or soon-to-be-dead animals. This, however, does not explain the sexual term. It probably derives from the obsolete sense of **knack**, meaning penis, from the current sense, meaning trick, or from knackered, meaning exhausted.

kneel at the altar v phrase
American

fellate or receive anal intercourse. This 20th-century underworld expression derives from being on one's knees. The religious reference, especially to the marriage ceremony, endows these sexual activities with mock sacredness or implied profanity.

knee-trembler n British

sexual intercourse while standing. This 19th-century colloquialism is based on the sensation of trembling in the knees at the time of orgasm.

knick-knack n

male or female genitals. Based on viewing the genitals as ornaments, this is a 19th-century term. *See also* **thing**.

knight n

male homosexual. This is one of few 20th-century complimentary terms for a homosexual. It probably derives from a knight's weaponry, namely his **sword** and **armor**.

knish n

vagina. This 20th-century euphemism derives from the Yiddish meaning of a soft, stuffed pastry.

knob n

1. glans or head of the penis. This 19th-century usage is based on shape.
2. penis. This is an extension of the first meaning.
knob-job is a mid-20th-century American expression for fellatio.
knob-polisher is 20th-century gay usage for fellator.

knob v American

masturbate. This is a mid-20th-century term.

knobs n pl

nipples. This 20th-century term is based on shape.

knock v

copulate. Usually said of men, this usage dates back to the 15th century. **knock-em-down** is 19th-century British usage for prostitute. The suffix "-down" suggests detumescence. **knocking joint** and **knocking shop** are both 19th-century terms for brothel. *See also* **joint**.
knock up is an American phrase meaning make pregnant. It dates back to the 19th century. **Knocked** and **knocked up** are terms for pregnant.

knock, knocking n

1. copulation. This usage dates back to the 15th century.
2. *British* penis. This is 18th-century coinage.
knocker, meaning penis, dates back to the 15th century.

knockers n pl

1. breasts. Punning on handles and the intent to enter, this is 20th-century coinage.
2. testicles. *See also* **knackers**.

knot n British

glans or head of the penis. Based on appearance, this is a 19th-century colloquialism. *See also* **knob**.

know v

copulate. This formal term, said of men, is based on the biblical meaning of having **carnal knowledge**. The term has been used since the 13th century. Lawrence Paros, in *The Erotic Tongue*, 1984, points out that "know" is used 943 times in the Old Testament, but only 15 times does it have a sexual meaning.
knowledge meaning sexual intercourse also derives from **carnal knowledge**; its use dates back to the 14th century.

kosher dill n

circumcised penis. This 20th-century colloquialism derives from dill meaning **pickle**, and the standard sense of kosher meaning "clean," from Jewish dietary law. The expression is applied to Jewish males, who are customarily circumcised during infancy. A variant is **kosher meat**.

KS v

perform anilingus. This 20th-century coinage is based on KS being the abbreviation for "kiss shit."

kwela n South African

sexual intercourse. This 20th-century usage derives from the African Nguni term meaning "mount." Kwela is a form of township **jazz** music.

KY cowboy, KY queen n

male homosexual. These recent terms are based on the brand name lubricant KY Jelly, used to aid sexual penetration. The jocular colloquialism **JY Kelly** is a variant.

L

labia n pl

folds or lips of the vulva. The word derives from the Latin plural of *labium* meaning "lip," and has been used in standard English since the early 17th century. The term is an anatomical one, especially when further qualified into **labia majora** and **labia minora**, referring to the outer and inner vulval folds, respectively.
• "[He] lunged headlong toward her, burying his hump between Candy's legs as she hunched wildly, pulling open her little

labias [sic] in an absurd effort to get it in her."
(Terry Southern and Mason Hoffenberg, *Candy*, 1958)

labonza n American
buttocks. This mid-20th-century term may have been influenced by **buns**.

labor leather v phrase
copulate. Said of men, this is 16th-century usage. *See also* **leather**.

laborer of nature n
penis. This is a 17th-century literary term. *See also* **nature**.

lace curtains n pl
uncircumcised foreskin. This is a 20th-century gay expression. *See also* **blinds** and **drapes**.

laced mutton n British
prostitute. This expression dates back to the 14th century. *See also* **mutton**.
• "Cupid hath got me a stomacke, and I long for lac'd mutton."
(Thomas Middleton, *Blurt Master Constable*, 1602)

ladder n
vagina. Based on the sexual symbolism of climbing, this is an 18th-century term. *See also* **climb**.

lady n
classy prostitute. This term can be traced back to 9th-century Old English, when it meant mistress of the house or housewife. By 1000 lady corresponded in meaning to lord. By the 16th century, however, lady had become a euphemism, taking the pejorative path that **madam** and **mistress** also took. Lady, however, has kept the connotation of high status; hence, even with the derogation of the term,

lady is a 20th-century American colloquialism for high-class prostitute.
ladies' college is an 18th-century euphemism for brothel, punning on school, **knowledge**, and **seminary**. *See also* **academy**.
ladies' delight is a 19th-century British colloquialism for penis, based on its ability to provide enjoyment for women.
ladies' friend is a 19th-century euphemism for dildo. *See also* **widow's comforter**.
ladies' lollipop is a 19th-century British colloquialism for penis, implying fellatio. *See also* **lollypop**.
ladies' tailoring is a 19th-century British colloquialism for sexual intercourse. *See also* **stitch**.
ladies' treasure is a 19th-century British colloquialism for penis.
lady feast is a mid-17th-century British colloquialism for sexual intercourse, especially when much indulged in. *See also* **beanfeast**.
lady flower is a 19th-century literary term for female genitals. It was used by Walt Whitman in *Leaves of Grass*, 1855. *See also* **flower**.
Lady Jane is a 19th-century British euphemism for female genitals, based on Jane being a common name for a woman. It was used by D.H. Lawrence in *Lady Chatterley's Lover*, 1928.
lady lover is early 20th-century American usage for lesbian.
lady of easy virtue is a euphemism for prostitute that dates back to the 18th century. Variations of this expression include **lady of pleasure**, dating back to the 17th century; **lady of expansive sensibility**, a 19th-century British euphemism that puns on the spreading of the legs; and **lady of leisure** and **lady of the evening**, 20th-century American expressions for prostitute.
ladyware is a 16th-century euphemism for male genitals, presented as goods for a lady. *See also* **ware**.

laid, layed v

having had sexual intercourse. This 20th-century term, as a passive or intransitive verb, originally applied to females only, but it now applies to both sexes. *See also* **lay**.

get laid is a popular mid-20th-century colloquialism meaning have sex. As recently as 1987, *The New York Times* could not bring itself to publish the full title of the British film *Sammy and Rosie Get Laid*, printing instead *Sammy and Rosie*.

- "Everybody wants to get laid 'twixt twelve and twenty, thinks about it round the clock...."
  (Lester Bangs, *Creem*, October 1972)

lamb n American

young, passive male homosexual. This is an early 20th-century underworld term. *See also* **chicken** and **wolf**.

lame duck n British

sexual intercourse. This early 20th-century Cockney rhyming slang term is based on the rhyme with **fuck**. Lame adds an ironic sense, perhaps hinting at men's postcoital lameness.

lamp of life n phrase British

penis. This 19th-century phrase is a variant of **lamp of love**, meaning the female genitals. *See also* **tree of life**.

lance n

penis. Dating back to the 15th century, lance joins the many warlike penile terms such as **club**, **dagger**, and **sword**. **Lance of love** is a variation.

- "And Mankind must in darkness languish
  Whilst he his bawdy launce does brandish."
  (Charles Cotton, *Burlesque upon Burlesque*, 1675)

lap n

female genitals. This euphemism dates back to the 16th century. Lap puns on the licking sense and uses bodily displacement, from the thigh to the genitals.

- "Lady, shall I lie in your lap?
  Ophelia: No, my lord.
  Hamlet: I mean my head upon your lap."
  (William Shakespeare, *Hamlet*, 1600)

lapland is a 19th-century British jocular term for female genitals.

laplover is 20th-century coinage for cunnilinguist.

lapper is 20th-century American underworld usage for one who performs oral sex.

lard v British

copulate. This is 19th-century usage. Larding in standard English refers to the insertion of fat in meats before roasting. *See also* **meat**.

lark v British

1. masturbate. This 19th-century usage probably derives from lark meaning frolic.

2. perform oral sex, usually cunnilingus. **Larking** is the noun form of this 18th-century usage. Grose's *Classical Dictionary of the Vulgar Tongue*, 1785, defines larking as "A lascivious practice that will not bear explanation."

lascivious adj

lustful. This standard English term, derived from the Latin, *lascivia* has been in widespread use since the 15th century. Shakespeare referred to "lascivious Edward" in *Henry VI*, and the "lascivious pleasing of a lute" in *Richard III*.

last act n

sexual intercourse. This 18th-century euphemism derives from the association of orgasm with death. **Last liberties** and **last favor** are variants. See also **act** and **ultimate favor**.

latex n American

condom. This is a 20th-century euphemism. Many condoms are made from latex rubber. See also **rubber**.

lather n

1. natural secretion of the vagina. This 19th-century term is based on function and appearance.
lather-maker is a 19th-century term for vagina.
2. semen. This usage is also based on appearance. See also **soap**.

latter end n

buttocks. This is a 19th-century colloquialism. See also **caboose** and **end**.

lavender boy n American

homosexual male. This is an early 20th-century underworld term. The color lavender, or purple, has been associated with homosexuality because of its association with profanity. See also **purple** and **scarlet**.

lay v

copulate. This common 20th-century meaning comes from the standard sense of causing someone to lie down. Although originally used by males, the term has been used by both sexes since the 1960s. See also **laid**.
lay down means allow copulation, said of women.
lay off with is a 20th-century Australian expression meaning have sexual intercourse.
lay out is 19th-century British usage for copulate. This phrase is expanded on in the African-American expressions **lay pipe** and **lay some pipe**, dating back to the mid-20th-century. See also **pipe**.

lay the hip is an early 20th-century American colloquialism for copulate; the hip is a euphemistic displacement from the genitals. **Lay the leg** is a variant.

lay n

1. a person considered as a sex partner. This is widespread 20th-century usage.

- " 'Do you like him?' he finally asked.
  She shrugged. 'He's a good lay.' "
  (Judith Rossner, Looking for Mr. Goodbar, 1975)

2. copulation. This colloquialism dates back to the early 20th century.

- "Sometimes he felt the need to have a woman underneath him who wasn't his equal. . . . No intellectual meeting of the minds. Just a lay."
  (Jackie Collins, Hollywood Wives, 1983)

layed v

See **laid**.

leading article n British

female genitals. This is 19th-century coinage. See also **article**.

leak n

female genitals. This early 18th-century meaning may have been influenced by menstruation.

- ". . . her coats rose high, her master saw . . . [t]he leak through which my wine has past."
  (John Gay, Tales, 1720)

leap v

copulate. This usage dates back to the 16th century. See also **jump**.

- "Till I know who leaps my sister, I'll not stir."
  (John Webster, The Duchess of Malfi, 1623)

leaping-house, meaning brothel, is now obsolete. See also **house**.

leather n

1. female genitals. Dating back to the 16th century, this usage is based on the sense of skin and the suggestion of animality. *See also* **labor leather**.

- "If they once do come together,
  He'll find that Dido's reaching
    leather."
  (Charles Cotton, *Virgile Travestie*, 1664)

leather-lane is an 18th-century term for vagina.

leather-stretcher is 18th-century usage for penis.

2. sexual activity involving leather. This 20th-century meaning often refers to sadistic, sometimes homosexual acts.

leather-queen is a 20th-century homosexual term for a sadistic homosexual who wears leather. *See also* **queen**.

lecher n

lewd man. This standard English word derives from the Old French *lecher*, meaning "lick," and dates back to the 12th century.

lech (or **letch**) derives from lecher. It can mean a lecher or a lecherous thought or urge. To lech is a 20th-century colloquialism meaning ogle someone sexually, usually said of men, as in "He leches after young chicks."

lecherous means lewd, lustful, or smutty. Its use dates back to the 14th century. **Lechery** dates back to the 13th century.

letchwater (or **lechwater**) is an 18th-century term for the natural secretions of the vagina as well as for semen.

left-handed adj American

homosexual. This mid-20th-century colloquialism is based on the other colloquial sense of the term, meaning crooked or counterfeit.

left-handed wife n

mistress or common-law wife. This 17th-century colloquialism is based on the notion that left-handedness is inferior to right-handedness and the fact that a wife was traditionally accorded the "honorable" position on her husband's right-hand side. *See also* **wife in watercolors**.

leg n

1. *American* copulation. This is mid-20th-century usage, heard especially in the phrase **get some leg**. Leg is a euphemistic displacement from the genitals.

leg business is a 19th-century British euphemism for sexual intercourse. *See also* **business**.

leggins is of 20th-century origin. It is a euphemism for intercourse between the thighs, and probably derives from "in the legs."

legover is recent British coinage for copulation. **Legover situation** is commonly used by the British satirical magazine *Private Eye* to refer to copulation.

2. woman considered as a sex object. This is also mid-20th-century usage.

lemons n pl American, Australian

breasts, especially small ones. Based on shape, this is 20th-century usage.

- "Please let me squeeze your
    lemons
      While I'm in your lonesome
      town
  Now, let me squeeze your
    lemons, baby
      Until my loves comes down."
  (Charlie Pickett, "Let Me Squeeze Your Lemons," early 20th century)

les n

lesbian. This is a 20th-century colloquial abbreviation. *See also* **lez**.

lesbian n

female homosexual. This standard English word derives from the Greek isle of Lesbos, home of the Greek poetess Sappho. *See also* **sapphism**.

- "I've certainly had fantasies of fucking women, but I'm not a lesbian."
(Madonna, interview in *Rolling Stone*, June 13, 1991)

lesbo n

lesbian. This is a 20th-century colloquial variant of the term. See also **lez**.

let go v *phrase British*

ejaculate. This is a 20th-century colloquialism.

let in v *phrase*

copulate, said of women. This colloquialism dates back to the 16th century.

letch n

See **lech**.

letter n *British*

condom. This 19th-century colloquialism is an abbreviation of **French letter**.

Levy and Frank v *British*

masturbate. This late 19th-century rhyming slang term is based on the rhyme with **wank**. Levy and Frank was a company that ran pubs and restaurants.

lewd *adj*

sexually obscene or lusty. This standard English word derives from the Old English *loēwede*, meaning "ignorant." It dates back to the 14th century.
lewd infusion is a 19th-century British term for semen.

lewdness, apart from being the abstract noun derived from lewd, also means prostitute and copulation, as in **do a lewdness**.

Lewis & Witties n *pl*

Australian

breasts. This 20th-century rhyming slang term is based on the rhyme with **titties** (under **tit**). Lewis & Witties is the name of a Melbourne trading store no longer in existence.

lez n

lesbian. This is a variant of **les** and a colloquial abbreviation of **lesbian**. Versions include **lezz**, **lezzie**, and **lezzy**.

- "Don't worry, Arabel, if we have to go lezzy again, you know you're my first choice."
(Connie Willis, "All My Darling Daughters," 1985, in Ellen Datlow, editor, *Alien Sex*, 1990)

lib v *British*

copulate. This 17th-century usage is now obsolete. The term may have derived from **lip**, or from the Latin *libido*, meaning "desire."

libido n

sexual desire, lust, or sexual drive stemming from instinct. This standard English word derives from the Latin *libido*, meaning "desire," which in turn derives from *libere*, meaning "to please." The term was first used in 1909 in A.A. Brill's translation of Sigmund Freud's *Selected Papers on Hysteria*. It was soon used outside the psychoanalytic world as well.

- "The libido in search of expression will find, or if necessary construct, what it must have, and weave the most elaborate masturbatory scenarios

around the scantiest and least probable suggestions."
(Peter Gay, *The Bourgeois Experience*, 1984)
libidinous and **libidinal** are both standard adjectives, meaning of or relating to the libido.

licentious *adj*

lusty or lacking in sexual restraint. This standard English term derives from the Latin *licentia*, meaning "license" or "liberty." It dates back to the 16th century.

lick *v*

perform oral sex. This usage is based on the action of the tongue.
lickety-split is a mid-20th-century American term for cunnilingus, punning on performing at great speed and **split**, meaning the vulva.
lick-twat means cunnilinguist. This word dates back to the 17th century. *See also* **twat**.

lickerish *adj*

lusty, lewd, or lechorous. This is a 17th-century term.

lie in state *v phrase*

copulate in bed with two women. This 18th-century jocular expression, said of men, puns on the great status of the deceased and a man having two women in bed at the same time. The notion of death in orgasm is also implied.

lie on one's back *v phrase*

copulate. This phrase is said of women.

lie with *v phrase*

copulate. This euphemism dates back to the 16th century.

life preserver *n British*

penis. This 19th-century jocular term refers to the reproductive ability of the penis.

lift one's leg *v phrase British*

copulate. This is an 18th-century euphemism. A colloquial variant, also from the 18th century, is **play at lift leg**. These expressions are euphemistic since they focus on the leg's activity, a displacement from the genitals.

lift-skirts *n British*

prostitute. This is a 19th-century colloquialism. *See also* **skirt**.

lift up *v phrase*

get an erection. This is a 19th-century euphemism. *See also* **up**.

light meat *n*

genitals of a white person. This is a 20th-century expression. *See also* **meat**, **dark meat**, and **white meat**.

light the lamp *v phrase British*

copulate. This 19th-century euphemism puns on ignition and heat.

lily *n*

effeminate male homosexual. Based on the common female name, as well as the name of a flower, this is of mid-20th-century origin. *See also* **daffodil**, **daisy**, and **pansy**.

limbo *n British*

female genitals. This 19th-century usage joins **heaven** and **hell** as terms for the female genitals. The usage could also have been influenced by limb, since **leg** is sometimes used as a euphemism for the genitals.

the limit *n American*

copulation. This construction probably results from seeing copulation as going to the limit, or **all the way**.

limp-wrist n

effeminate male homosexual. In this 20th-century usage, limp also suggests soft, that is, not hard or erect. *See also* **bent wrist**.

line v

copulate. This 17th-century term is now obsolete. The term originally applied to dogs before it was applied to people.

ling n

1. vagina. Derived from ling being a type of **fish**, this is of 19th-century origin.

2. female pubic hair. This 16th-century euphemism is based on the Scottish sense meaning heather.

lingam n

penis. This 18th-century literary term derives from the Sanskrit *lingam*. Lingam is a phallus, symbolizing the Hindu god Siva. It was introduced to the English-speaking world through the *Kama Sutra*, a treatise on sexual love. *See also* **yoni**.

linguist n

fellator or cunnilinguist. This 20th-century jocular term derives from the Latin *lingua*, meaning "tongue." Linguist is an abbreviation of **cunnilinguist**.
linguistic exercise means mutual oral sex.

lioness n

prostitute. This late 16th-century usage is now obsolete. The word belongs to a large group of animal sexual terms and probably was used to convey the predatory nature of prostitution. *See also* **cat**.

lipstick n

penis. Punning on how the stick emerges from its container, and the sticking of the penis between lips, this is 20th-century usage.

lipwork n

sexual intercourse. This is a 20th-century euphemism. *See also* **kiss** and **work**.

little bit n

copulation. This is a 20th-century expression. *See also* **bit**.

little boy in the boat, little man in the boat n

phrase
See **boy in the boat**.

little brother n

penis. This 19th-century term suggests family membership. See *also* **big brother**.

little death n

orgasm. A direct translation of the French term for orgasm *petite mort*, this is a 19th-century literary euphemism.

little finger n

penis. This euphemism dates back to the 16th century. The term is now obsolete.

little Mary n American

female genitals. This 20th-century expression reflects the tendency to name the genitals. *See also* **mary jane** (under **mary**).

little ploughman n British

clitoris. This 19th-century euphemism suggests an object in a furrow. Ploughman suggests that the clitoris is a masculine organ.

little shame tongue n

phrase
clitoris. Derived from German, this is a 19th-century euphemism. See *also* **pudenda** and **tongue**.

little sister n

female genitals. This euphemism dates back to the 19th century.
little sister is here, **little visitor is here**, and **little friend is here** are all 19th-century euphemisms for menstruation.

little white mouse n British

tampon. This is current usage. *See also* **Mickey Mouse mattress** (under **Mickey Mouse**).

live in sin v phrase

live together and have sexual intercourse without being married. This colloquialism dates back to the 16th century.

live rabbit n British

penis. This is 19th-century usage. *See also* **rabbit**.

live wire n

erect penis. This 20th-century term puns on live wire meaning dangerous and shockable.

living fountain n phrase
British

female genitals. This is a 17th-century euphemism based on the female genitals being the source of life.

lizard n American

penis. Based on shape, this is mid-20th-century collegiate usage. *See also* **snake**.

lizzie, lizzy n

lesbian. These abbreviations pun on the common nickname for Elizabeth. *See also* **les** and **lez**.

load n

semen. This usage dates back to the 16th century. *See also* **shoot one's load** (under **shoot**).

• "There was a young idler named
    Blood,
Made a fortune performing at
    stud,
        With a fifteen-inch peter,
        A double-beat metre,
And a load like the Biblical
    Flood."
(Gershon Legman, editor, *The Limerick*, 1964)

lob n British

semierect penis. Probably derived from the Middle Low German *lubbe*, meaning "dangling," this is of 18th-century origin.
lob-cock is 19th-century coinage for a large semierect penis; **lob-prick** is a variant.

lobster n

1. penis. This 18th-century usage is based on **lob**.
lobster-pot, from the 18th century, stands for vagina. *See also* **pot**.
? vagina. This 18th-century usage may stem from the feminine suffix "-ster".

lock n

vagina. Based on **key**, meaning penis, and possibly punning on the chastity belt, this is an 18th-century term. A variant is **locker**.

lodge n

vagina. This 16th-century euphemism puns on an inn for accommodation, and on the verbal sense of lodge, meaning implant. *See also* **hotel**.

loins n pl

genitals. This standard English word dates back to the 14th century. Today the term is used euphemistically.

lollypop, lollipop n British

penis. Based on it being a **stick** and something to be sucked, this is a 19th-century colloquialism.

- "The blushing globe that crowned my lollipop had reached proportions quite magnificent as my manual attentions grew in speed and vigor."
  (Gilbert Sorrentino, *Mulligan Stew*, 1980)

long eye n British

vulva. Based on similarity of shape, this is 19th-century usage. *See also* **eye**.

long John n American

penis, especially a large one. This is a 20th-century euphemism. *See also* **john**.

long Tom n British

penis. Like **long John**, this term exemplifies the personification of the penis.

look babies in the eyes n phrase

look amorously at another. This was used by Shakespeare and others. *See also* **baby**.

- "She clung about his neck, gave him ten kisses,
  Toy'd with his locks,
  Look babies in his eyes."
  (Thomas Heywood, *Love's Mistress*, 1636)

loop-de-loop v American

mutual oral sex. This is mid-20th-century jocular coinage. *See also* **head over heels** and **sixty-nine**.

loose adj

sexually promiscuous or lewd. Usually applied to females, this has been a colloquial term since the 15th century.

loose fish is 19th-century British usage for prostitute. *See also* **fish**.
loose in the rump, **loose-ended**, and **loose-legged** are 19th-century expressions for promiscuous or lewd, said of females.

Lord knows what n phrase

female genitals. This is an 18th-century euphemism. *See also* **ineffable**, **it**, **know**, and **thing**.

lose the match and pocket the stakes v phrase

copulate. This 19th-century jocular expression is said of women. As a billiards or snooker metaphor, it puns on losing by being taken, but winning by taking the penis. *See also* **loss**, **match**, **pocket**, and **stake**.

loss n

ejaculation. Said of men, this 16th-century literary euphemism refers to the loss of semen. *See also* **die** and **spend**.

lot n British

male genitals. This is a 19th-century euphemism. *See also* **gear** and **luggage**.

love n

copulation. This common euphemism dates back to the 16th century. Since the latter part of the 20th century, **make love** has probably been the most common euphemism for having sexual intercourse. Make love used to mean court someone or flirt with him or her.
love apples is 19th-century British usage for testicles; **love blobs** is a recent variant.
love bubbles is an early 20th-century euphemism for breasts. **Love bumps** is a more recent variant, as is **love lumps**.
love bud is recent usage for clitoris. *See also* **bud**.

love juice is 19th-century coinage for either semen or natural vaginal secretion. *See also* **juice**.

love lane is 19th-century British usage for vagina. Lane puns on lain, a past tense of **lay**. Variants include **love chamber**, **love channel**, **love's fountain**, **love's harbor**, and **love's paradise**.

love muscle is a 20th-century African-American euphemism for penis. *See also* **muscle**.

love nuts is a 20th-century American colloquialism for pain in the testicles due to prolonged arousal. *See also* **nuts** and **blue balls**.

lovers' knot is a colloquial 19th-century term for sexual intercourse, punning on joining together in a knot and the sexual sense of **knot**, meaning glans of the penis.

love work, a euphemism for sexual intercourse, dates back to the 13th century. *See also* **work**.

low countries n pl British

female genitals. This 16th century term puns on the sound of "cunt" in countries and the fact that the genitals are in the lower part of the body. Low also brings with it the connotations of dirt, immorality, and hell. In standard English, the Low Countries refer to the Netherlands, Belgium, and Luxembourg. The slang term can also apply to the anus and buttocks. *See also* **Holland**, **lowlands**, and **Netherlands**.

lower wig n British

female pubic hair. This is a 19th-century euphemism. *See also* **wig**.

lowlands n pl

female genitals. This 18th-century jocular term is one of many geographical euphemisms for the genitals. *See also* **Holland**, **low countries**, and **Netherlands**.

lubricate v British

copulate. Alluding to the natural lubrication that occurs during copulation, this is an 18th-century euphemism.

lubie is mid-20th-century coinage for a lubricated condom.

lubricious adj

lecherous. This standard English term, dating from the late 16th century, means lecherous, and derives from the Latin *lubricus*, meaning "slippery." **Lubricity** is the noun form.

- "Women's magazines are not embarrassed to advise their readers regularly on erotic techniques of stunning lubricity." (Irma Kurtz, *Mantalk*, 1986)

lucky bag n British

vagina. This 19th-century euphemism is used by males. *See also* **bag**.

luggage n British

male genitals. This usage dates back to the 19th century. *See also* **basket**, **equipment**, and **gear**.

lullaby n

penis. This jocular 19th-century term may be based on the notion of copulating as a prelude to going to sleep.

lulus n pl American

breasts, especially very attractive ones. This 20th-century term may derive from the actress Gina Lollobrigida, or from loolopaloosa or lallapaloosa, meaning something outstanding.

lungs n pl

breasts. This 20th-century jocular euphemism reflects bodily displacement to avoid explicit sexuality. The term is used in expressions such as

"She has a nice pair of lungs." *See also* **tonsils**.

lusher *n American*

prostitute. This early 20th-century underworld term connects alcoholism and prostitution.

lust *n*

sexual desire. This standard English word dates back to the 11th century. The term derives from an Old English word meaning pleasure.

M

machine *n British*

1. penis. This is a 19th-century term. *See also* **tool**.
- "The table now hid her hand and his machine, tho I knew she had it in her hand . . ."
(Anonymous, *My Secret Life*, 1890)
2. female genitals. This term is of 19th-century origin.
3. condom. This 19th-century term is no longer in use.

mack *n*

pimp. This is an abbreviation of **mackerel**, which has meant pimp since the 15th century. It derives from the French *maquereau*. **Mac** is a variant spelling, used since the 19th century. **Mack man** is an African-American variation.
mack on (someone) is current usage for sexually seduce.

madam *n*

1. female brothel keeper. This term dates back to the 18th century and derives from the meaning of mis-tress of the house or woman in charge of the household. *See also* **abbess**. **Madame** is a variant spelling, especially British. Both versions stem from French *ma dame*, meaning "my lady."
2. elderly male homosexual. This is 20th-century gay usage.

madge *n*

1. female genitals. This 18th-century word stems from the common Scottish female name. *See also* **janey** and **mary jane**.
2. *American* prostitute. This is 19th-century Californian dialectal usage.
3. male homosexual. This is a 20th-century gay term. *See also* **mary**.

mad mick *n Australian*

penis. This expression is based on the rhyme with **prick**. *See also* **stormy dick**.

Mae West *n*

breast. This 20th-century rhyming term, no longer used, derives from the famous buxom film star. *See also* **east and west**.

magazines *n pl*

testicles. This obsolete 19th-century usage comes from the standard sense of cartridge or firearm. *See also* **bullets**.

magic wand *n*

penis, especially an erect one. This early 20th-century colloquial term is based on the suggestion that the penis can perform tricks. *See also* **wand**.

magnet *n British*

female genitals. This 18th-century usage comes from the sense of ability to attract. The term was mainly used by males. A pun was probably intended in that a magnet is attracted to the poles. *See also* **pole**.

magpie's nest n British

vagina. This is 18th-century coinage. The magpie is characterized by indiscriminate acquiring behavior, providing a pejorative meaning to this sexual term.

maidenhead n

hymen, virginity. This is a standard English term; both definitions date back to the 14th century. Since the 19th century the term has also been applied to a virgin anus.

- "This present morning early she
  Forsooth came to my bed,
  And gratis there she offered me
  Her high-priced maidenhead."
  (Sir John Suckling, 1609–1642,
  "Proffered Love Rejected")

main avenue n British

vagina. This is 19th-century usage. **Main vein** is a variant. See also **dead end street** and **love lane**.

main queen n American

male homosexual who is a receiver or insertee. This is mid-20th-century usage. See also **queen**.

make v

copulate. This was a standard 17th-century term used of wolves.
make a milkshake is a 20th-century phrase for masturbate, said of men. See also **milk** and **shake**.
make a settlement in tail is a 19th-century British jocular phrase meaning copulate, said of men. It is based on **tail** meaning genitals. In standard English, the phrase is a legal term referring to inheritance law.
make babies is a 20th-century euphemism meaning copulate, based on the reproductive consequences; **make faces** is an 18th-century British euphemism with the same meaning.
make ends meet is a jocular 19th-century colloquialism meaning copulate, punning on joining and surviving. See also **end**.
make feet for children's shoes/ stockings is an obsolete 19th-century euphemism meaning copulate. It suggests the reproductive consequences of copulation.
make it is a 20th-century American colloquialism for have sexual intercourse (see also **it**). **Make out** is a variant.
make love has been a euphemism for copulate since the 16th century; today it is one of the most common euphemisms.
make piggies is a 20th-century term for copulate.
make scissors is 20th-century usage meaning masturbate a woman with the fingers apart. See also **hold a bowling ball**.
make the chimney smoke is a 19th-century British colloquialism meaning make a woman reach orgasm. See also **smoke**.
make the scene is a 20th-century colloquialism meaning have sexual intercourse.
make whoopee means copulate, based on the standard sense of whoopee, meaning excitement and fun, dating back to the 19th century.

make n American

copulation. This term is found especially in the phrase **on the make**, meaning seeking to have sex.

malady of France n

syphilis. This 16th-century literary slur is probably based on the (British) assumption that syphilis came from France to England. See also **French crown** and **French disease**.

male catcher n

female genitals. This is 18th-century coinage. See also **mantrap**.

male member n

penis. This euphemism is a direct translation of the Latin *membrum virile*. *See also* **member**.

malkin n *Scottish*

female genitals. This 16th-century word derives from the Scottish term meaning cat or hare. *See also* **cat** and **bunny**.

mallee root n *Australian*

prostitute. This 20th-century expression rhymes with prostitute. Mallee is the name of a eucalyptus bush. *See also* **root**.

Malthusianism n

1. masturbation. This jocular 19th-century term is based on the notion that masturbation leads to population control. *See also* **higher Malthusianism**.
2. sodomy. This 19th-century usage is based on the same reasoning as usage 1, above.

mammary glands n *pl*

breasts. Dating back to the early 19th century, and derived from the Latin *mamma*, meaning "breast," this is an anatomical term.
mammaries is a 20th-century colloquialism for breasts.
mammets is a 16th-century literary term for breasts, now obsolete.
• ". . . this is no world
   To play with mammets and to tilt
      with lips."
   (William Shakespeare, *Henry IV: Part 1*, 1598)

man v

copulate. This 16th-century euphemism, said of men, is still used today.

man n *American*

masculine lesbian. This is 20th-century usage.

Manchester City n *British*

breast. This 19th-century rhyming slang term is based on the rhyme with **titty** (under **tit**). Manchester City is the name of a football club. The term is reinforced by "chest" in Manchester. **Manchesters** refers to breasts. *See also* **Bristol City**.

man-eater n *American*

fellator. This is a 20th-century term. *See also* **eat**.

mangle n *British*

female genitals. This is a 19th-century term. In standard English, a mangle was a machine that ironed laundry by passing it between rollers.

Manhattan eel n *American*

condom. This is a recent euphemism. *See also* **eel-skin** (under **eel**).

manhole n

vagina. This is 19th-century usage. It is also a gay term for anus. **Manhole cover** is a jocular 20th-century term for sanitary napkin. *See also* **hole**.

manhood n

penis. This is an 18th-century euphemism.

man in the boat n *phrase*

See **boy in the boat**.

manny n

lesbian. This 20th-century coinage is based on the maleness of the name.

man oil n *American*

semen. Possibly influenced by **sperm** oil from the sperm whale, this term is of 20th-century origin. *See also* **oil**.

manometer n

female genitals. Although a manometer is an instrument for measuring the pressure of gases, this 20th-century colloquial usage is based on the analogy with speedometer and odometer, employing the automobile metaphor for sexual terms.

man-root n

penis. This is a 19th-century literary term used by Walt Whitman in *Leaves of Grass*, 1855. The reference is to the mandrake plant, which was called the "phallus of the field" because of its appearance.

mantrap n

1. vagina. This is 18th-century usage.
2. prostitute. This usage dates back to the 19th century. *See also* **trap**.

map of Tasmania n phrase Australian

female pubic hair. This jocular expression is based on Tasmania's resemblance in shape to a triangular pubic patch.

maracas n pl American

breasts. This is a 20th-century usage. Maracas are round percussion instruments used in Latin music.

Marble Arch n British

female genitals. This 19th-century term refers to the famous London monument and place-name. The arch represents a crotch and female legs.

marbles n pl

testicles. This 19th-century usage refers to shape. *See also* **balls**.

market-dame n British

prostitute. This 18th-century coinage is based on the marketplace and the **business** of prostitution. *See also* **commerce**.

mark of the beast n phrase British

female genitals. This 18th-century colloquialism alludes to humankind's animal nature. *See also* **beast with two backs**.

married to Mary Fist v phrase American

habituated to masturbation. This is mid-20th-century prison slang.

marrow n

semen. This 16th-century literary term is based on semen's appearance and its emission from a **bone**.
marrowbone is a 19th-century British term for penis.

marshmallows n pl American

1. breasts. This mid-20th-century term is based on shape and softness.
2. testicles. This usage also stems from mid-20th-century usage.

martini n British

promiscuous female. This recent colloquialism is based on an advertisement claiming that the drink can be enjoyed "any time, any place, any where."

mary n

male homosexual. This 20th-century term is based on the common female name and perhaps on the rhyme with **fairy**.

mary jane n

female genitals. This 19th-century usage is based on two common female names.

masochism n

practice of deriving sexual pleasure from being hurt or humiliated. Named after the German novelist Leopold von Sacher-Masoch (1836–

1895), who wrote about such practices, this is a standard term. *See also* **sadism** and **S and M**.

mason *n*
1. pederast. This 20th-century term is based on a mason being a man who lays bricks or stones. *See also* **lay**.
2. lesbian, especially a masculine one. Possibly derived from Freemasons, a group with male members only, this is a 20th-century term.

massage parlor *n*
brothel. This is an early 20th-century euphemism.
• " 'Massage parlor' prostitution is considered by many to be 'glamorous' therapy."
(*Publishers Weekly*, April 29, 1974)

masterpiece *n*
1. female genitals. The emphasis is on **piece** in this 18th-century term.
2. penis. Also dating back to the 18th century, the allusion here is to the master's own piece.

master of ceremonies *n*
phrase British
penis. Sexual intercourse is an implied ritual in this 19th-century euphemism. *See also* **religious observances**.

masturbate *v*
manually stimulate the genitals. This standard English term dates back to the 17th century. It may derive from the Latin *manu-stuprare*, meaning "defile with the hand." **Masturbation**, the noun form, also has been standard English since the 17th century.
• "Don't knock masturbation. It's sex with someone I love."
(Woody Allen, *Annie Hall*, 1977)

mat *n*
1. female pubic hair. This is 19th-century usage. *See also* **front door mat**.
2. *American* prostitute. This mid-20th-century underworld term may derive from "mattress."

Mata Hari *n*
female pubic hair. This 20th-century jocular usage is probably based on the closeness in sound to **mat** and hairy. Mata Hari was the name of a seductive female spy during World War I. *See also* **hair**.

match *n American*
1. female genitals. This is a 19th-century euphemism, possibly based on the sense of opposition.
2. penis. This 19th-century usage may be based on the appearance of a match, which is long and thin with a knob at the end, and the sense of striking. *See also* **strike**.

mate *n American*
genitals of either sex. This 19th-century Californian dialectal term personifies the genitals.

mate *v*
copulate. This colloquialism dates back to the 17th century. The term is standard English when applied to animals.

matinee *n*
sexual activity in the afternoon. Based on the standard sense of matinee, meaning an afternoon performance, this is 20th-century usage.

matrimonial peacemaker, peacemaker *n British*
penis. This 18th-century expression puns both on **piece** and **make**. Grose's *Dictionary of the Vulgar*

Tongue, 1811, defines the term as "The sugar stick or arbor vitae."

maud *n British*

male prostitute. This mid-20th-century coinage is based on the female name.

mavis *n South African*

effeminate male homosexual. Based on the female name, this is 20th-century gay usage. *See also* **moffie**.

mayonnaise *n*

semen. This 20th-century gay term is based on appearance, with an allusion to oral sex, since mayonnaise is a foodstuff.

Mazola party *n*

party in which guests cover their naked bodies with cooking oil and perform sundry sexual activities. Mazola is a brand of cooking oil. *See also* **Wesson party**.

measles *n*

syphilis. This early 20th-century euphemism refers to the skin sores that result from the disease.

meat *n*

1. genitals of either sex. This usage dates back to the 16th century. Since meat has long been a slang term for the body, its application to the genitals was probably inevitable. *See also* **flesh**.
• "Feeling with the hand the naked meat of his own body."
(Walt Whitman, *Leaves of Grass,* 1861)
2. women considered as sex objects. This derogatory usage also dates back to the 16th century.
3. *American* men seen as sex objects. This is a 20th-century derogatory gay term.

meat and two vegetables is a British 20th-century jocular term for male genitals, in which meat refers to the penis and two vegetables to the testicles. Since meat and two vegetables were once regarded as the basics of a solid meal, the expression implies that male genitals are basic fare. *See also* **greens**.
meat-flasher is 19th-century British usage for male exhibitionist.
meat-grinder is a 20th-century American expression for female genitals. *See also* **grind**.
meat-house is a 19th-century word for brothel. *See also* **house**.
meat market is a 19th-century term for female breasts, female genitals, or a group of prostitutes. All three meanings operate on the notion of meat being on display; in the third sense, the notion of meat for sale is prominent. A further meaning, used especially of male homosexuals and dating to the 20th century, is an area or place, such as a bar, where people go to meet and select sexual partners.

meddle *v*

copulate. This 16th-century colloquialism is based on the standard sense of interfere with. The term is often found in the expression **meddle with someone** a genteel term for sexual abuse or rape.

medicine *n British*

sexual intercourse. This 19th-century jocular usage puns on the notion that medicine is both something that is good for you and something that must be taken.

melons *n pl*

breasts, especially large ones. This common 20th-century term is based on shape. *See also* **apples** and **grapefruits**.

melt v

reach orgasm, ejaculate. This colloquialism dates back to the 16th century. The term also suggests sexual **fire**.

- "In whose sweet embraces I,
  May melt myself to lust and die."
  (Thomas Carew, *Poems*, 1629)

melted butter is 18th-century British usage for semen, based on appearance. *See also* **butter**.

melting pot is a 19th-century colloquialism for vagina. *See also* **pot**.

member n

penis. This standard term dates back to the 13th century. It is a shortening of **male member**. In Middle English, member meant limb or organ, while in Latin *membrum* was a euphemism for *membrum virile*, meaning "penis." *Membrum muliebre*, meaning "female member," was the Latin term for clitoris, based on analogy.

member for Cockshire is a 19th-century British jocular expression for penis, punning on **member**, **cock**, and member of Parliament.

- "Whilst Tunewell pump'd away with his Member-for-Cockshire (as the Saying goes)..."
  (Erica Jong, *Fanny*, 1980)

memories n pl

breasts. This humorous 20th-century usage puns on **mammaries** and something memorable.

ménage à trois n

sexual threesome. This is a 20th-century literary borrowing from the French. Literally translated, the French means "household of three."

- "This happy *ménage-à-trois*—the errant wife, the lover and the unsuspecting husband."
  (London *Times*, December 28, 1959)

menstruation n

cyclical, usually monthly, discharge of blood and tissue from the uterus of nonpregnant fertile women. This standard word derives from the Latin *mensis*, meaning "month." **Menstrual period**, **menses**, and **period** are other standard terms.

- "Menstruation would become an enviable, boast-worthy event [if men menstruated]. Men would brag about how long and how much. Boys would mark the onset of the menses, that longed-for proof of manhood, with religious rituals and stag parties."
  (Gloria Steinem, *Ms.*, October 1978)

merchandise n

1. female genitals. This is 20th-century usage. *See also* **commodity**.
2. male prostitute. This meaning is of 20th-century origin.

meretrix, meretrice n

prostitute. This 16th-century literary euphemism derives from the Italian and from the Latin *merere*, meaning "earn."

merkin n British

1. female genitals, including the pubic hair. Possibly derived from the French *mère*, meaning "mother," with the suffix "-kin" denoting a diminutive, this is of 17th-century origin.
2. female pubic hair. This also dates back to the 17th century.
3. artificial pubic hair. This term stems from the 18th century. Nathan Bailey's *English Dictionary*, 1721, defines a merkin as "...counterfeit hair for the privities of women." Merkins were also worn to disguise the effects of syphilis. *See also* **lower wig** and **toupee**.

- "His penis squashed invisible under a flesh-colored leather jockstrap, over which he wears a false cunt and merkin of sable." (Thomas Pynchon, *Gravity's Rainbow*, 1973)

mermaid *n*
prostitute. This 16th-century euphemism may have been influenced by **fish** and by the purported longing for prostitutes by sailors.

merry *adj*
sexually free and adventuresome. This euphemism dates back to the 17th century.
merry bout is an 18th-century euphemism for sexual intercourse.
merryland is a 19th-century euphemism for vagina. *See also* **happy valley**.
merrylegs is a 19th-century British euphemism for prostitute.
merrymaker is a 19th-century euphemism for penis.

mess *v*
play with sexually. This is a 20th-century colloquialism. **Mess about** and **mess around** are common phrases that imply sexual play. Mess also suggests **dirt**.

mettle *n British*
semen. This 17th-century colloquialism is based on the standard senses meaning character and stamina. The word derives from "metal."
- "I must provide her . . . broths
  That may stir mettle in her . . . I find
  Her no more fit for the business of increase
  Than I am to be a nun."
  (William Davenan, *Love & Honour*, 1649)

mickey *n*
penis. This 19th-century usage is based on the rhyme with dicky. *See also* **dick**.

Mickey Mouse is a colloquial 20th-century term for a penis, one of many that personifies this body part. It is also a colloquial mid-20th-century American term for female genitals, possibly derived from the mouse's fur or the cartoon character's endearing nature. **Mickey Mouse mattress** is a 20th-century American jocular expression for a sanitary napkin. *See also* **little white mouse**.

middle *adj British*
referring to the genitals which are in the middle of the body.
middle finger is 19th-century coinage for penis based on shape.
middle gate is late 17th-century usage for vagina. *See also* **gate**.
middle leg is a 19th-century term for penis. *See also* **best leg of three**.
middle stump is a 19th-century term for penis.

midlands *n British*
female genitals. This 19th-century colloquialism puns on the geographical area in England and the midriff. *See also* **lowlands**.

midnight cowboy *n*
American
male homosexual. This mid-20th-century expression is also the title of a movie made in 1969.

the Mile High Club *n phrase*
apocryphal club of people who have had sexual intercourse on an airplane. This is a colloquialism from the 1970s.
- "Mile High Club queens (making it in airplane johns) . . ."
  (David B. Feinberg, *Eighty-Sixed*, 1989)

milk *n*
semen or natural vaginal secretions. This 17th-century usage is

based on appearance. Milk, a source of nourishment, is analogous to genital secretions as a source of regeneration.

- "Her breath is sweet as the rose in June
  Her skin is soft as silk
  And if you tickle her in the flank
  She'll freely give down her milk."
  (John Aubrey, *Brief Lives*, 1696)

milker is a 19th-century colloquialism for female genitals as well as a term for masturbator.

milk jug is 18th-century British usage for vagina, based on the vagina being a receptacle for **milk**. **Milk pan** is 19th-century British coinage for vagina.

milkman is a colloquialism for masturbator or penis. It is of 19th-century origin.

milk v

cause a male to ejaculate through copulation or masturbation. This colloquialism dates back to the 17th century. **Milk the chicken** and **milk the lizard** are recent American expressions for masturbation.

milking pail is a 19th-century British term for vagina, based on the vagina being a receptacle for milk. *See also* **milk jug** and **milk pan** (both under the noun **milk**).

milk bottles n pl

breasts. This 20th-century colloquialism is based on breasts being containers for milk.

milkshakes is 19th-century usage for breasts based on the food metaphor. *See also* **shake**.

milk shop is a 17th-century jocular term for breasts, now obsolete.

milky way is a 17th-century literary expression for breasts, punning on **heaven**.

mill n British

female genitals. This early 18th-century euphemism alludes to the grinding of grain. *See also* **grind**.

- "For Peggy is a bonny lass,
  and grinds well her mill,
  For she will be Occupied
  When others they lie still."
  (Thomas D'Urfey, *Wit and Mirth*, 1719)

milliner's shop n British

female genitals. This 19th-century expression refers back to the standard meaning of a shop that sells hats, since **hat** means female genitals. The word "milliner" derives from Milan, which has exported women's clothing since the 16th century.

milt n British

semen. This 19th-century usage is based on the standard sense of the term, meaning the male reproductive organs of fish and their secretions. *See also* **roe**.

milt-market and **milt-shop** are 19th-century terms for female genitals.

mine n

vagina. Since a mine is a hole in the ground and the earth is often regarded as female (as in "Mother Earth"), the symbolism here is natural. *See also* **cave**.

miner n

active male homosexual. This 20th-century gay usage is based on the sense of digging or drilling associated with anal intercourse.

minge n British

female genitals. This 19th-century underworld term may derive from Romany or from the Latin *mingere*, meaning "urinate." During World War II, minge was used derogatorily by servicemen to refer to women collectively.

minx n

woman regarded as a sex object. This 16th-century derogatory usage is now obsolete. The term may derive from the obsolete sense meaning a pet dog, or from the Dutch *minneken*, meaning "little love." By extension, minx is also 16th-century slang for prostitute, now obsolete. A surviving sense of minx, since the 16th century, is a pert or saucy female.

misfit n

homosexual. This 20th-century derogatory term is based on the notion of deviation and not fitting in with heterosexual society. The term is now obsolete. *See also* **deviate**.

miss n British

prostitute, especially a high-class one. This is an 18th-century euphemism. In the 15th century miss was the standard English abbreviation for **mistress**, meaning head of the house. By the 18th century the Miss/Mrs. distinction evolved for identifying marital status. By the mid-20th century Ms. was introduced; it has found more acceptance in the United States than in Great Britain. Miss is found in a number of sexual terms, especially names that personify the female genitals.
Miss Brown is an 18th-century term for female genitals. *See also* **brown madam**.
Miss Horner is 19th-century usage for female genitals, based on **horn** meaning erection, and suggesting **corner**.
Miss Laycock is an 18th-century jocular term for female genitals, punning on **lay** and **cock**.
Miss Molly is an 18th-century term for a male homosexual or an effeminate man or boy. *See also* **moll**.

missionary position n

sexual intercourse with the couple facing each other and the man on top of the woman. This jocular term dates back to the 19th century, but remains current today. It derives from the position allegedly favored by European missionaries in newly explored lands, as opposed to those of the indigenous peoples they encountered, who performed sexual intercourse in other ways. *See also* **reverse Western**.

- "The face-to-face 'missionary position' (so called because it is virtually unknown in primitive races) is actually said to have been invented by Roman courtesans to hinder conception." (*Vogue*, November 1971)

Mister Tom n American

penis. This mid-20th-century black expression is based on personification. *See also* **long Tom**.

mistress n

woman having a sexual relationship with a man, who may in return provide for her financially. This standard term dates back to the 15th century. In the 12th century, mistress simply meant the woman at the head of a household.

mitten queen n

homosexual with a penchant for masturbating other homosexual males. This is 20th-century gay usage. *See also* **queen**.

mo n

homosexual, especially a male one. This 20th-century colloquialism is based on the abbreviation of **homo** or **homosexual**.

model n

male or female prostitute. This 20th-century euphemism alludes to physical attractiveness.

modesty n

female genitals. Based on the standard sense of chastity or decency, this is a 16th-century euphemism.

moffie, moff n South African

male homosexual, especially an effeminate one or a transvestite. This 20th-century derogatory term may derive from hermaphrodite. See also **mophy**.

- "He disappears into ladies' bars. . . . Where women flash their thighs at you and drink beside the men, and sits with moffies and piepiejollers and primps his nice long hair."
(*Crux*, October 1986)

mole n British

penis. This 19th-century usage refers to the animal's proclivity for burrowing.
mole-catcher is a 19th-century euphemism for vagina.

molehills n American

small breasts. This is a 20th-century term. See also **mountains**.

moll, molly n

prostitute. This is a 17th-century term. It was first applied to any girl, being a pet name for Mary. By the early 19th century, the meaning became companion of a criminal. Jon Bee's *Dictionary of the Turf*, 1823, defines moll as "The female companions of low thieves, at bed, board, and business."
moll-shop is early 20th-century British coinage for brothel.
molly dike is a 20th-century term for a passive lesbian. See also **bull dike**.

moll v

perform anal intercourse. This meaning dates back to the 18th century. See also **Miss Molly** (under **miss**).

mollies n

breasts. This is 20th-century gay usage.

money n British

female genitals. This late 18th-century colloquialism is usually said to or by children, especially in the phrase "Don't show your money." See also **purse** and **spend**.
money box is a 19th-century term for female genitals. See also **box**.

monkey n

vagina. This 19th-century term may derive from "monkey business," or from the hair of the animal.
monkey-house is 20th-century American underworld usage for brothel. See also **house**.

monosyllable n British

vagina. This early 19th-century euphemism refers to the taboo word **cunt**, which is monosyllabic. The extreme nature of the taboo in Victorian society prompted naming it *the* monosyllable; no other monosyllabic word in English, including **fuck**, has such verbal power.

mons pubis, mons veneris n

fleshy cushion that covers the pubic bone of women. These formal, Latin-based terms date back to the 17th century. *Mons* means "hill." *Pubis* has the same root as "puberty," while *veneris* means "of Venus," the goddess of love. See also **mound of Venus**.

months n pl

menstruation. This early 17th-century euphemism is based on the monthly cycle.
monthlies and **monthly flowers** are 19th-century euphemisms for menstrual periods. See also **flower**.
monthly rag is a 19th-century euphemism for sanitary napkin. See also **manhole cover** (under **manhole**).
monthly terms is a 17th-century euphemism for menstrual period.

moonlighter n British

prostitute. This 19th-century term is based on a prostitute being most likely to work at night.

moon v

show one's naked buttocks, especially in public. See also **moons.**

moons n pl

buttocks. This 20th-century term is based on shape.

moonshot v

perform anal intercourse. This is 20th-century coinage.

mophrodite n American

homosexual male. This 20th-century underworld term may derive from **hermaphrodite.**

mophy n

effeminate young male. Probably derived from **hermaphrodite**, this term is obsolete. See also **moffie.**

morning pride n British

erection on waking in the morning. This is a 19th-century colloquialism. **Morning glory** is a more recent variant. See also **piss-proud.**

mort n

woman considered as a sex object. This 17th-century term also means death and may be an abbreviation of mortal.

mortar n British

vagina. Based on mortar meaning a vessel and suggesting **pestle** meaning penis, this usage dates back to the 19th century. See also **grind.**

mosquito bites n pl

American

very small female breasts. This is a recent colloquialism.

moss n British

female pubic hair. This 19th-century term is based on appearance. **moss-rose** is a 19th-century word for female genitals. A variant is **moss-cell.** See also **rose.**

mot, mott, motte n

vagina. This 18th-century word may derive from the French mot, meaning "word," that is, the word **cunt**, or the French motte, meaning "mound." See also **monosyllable.**

• "... spending my sperm on her thighs or on the crisp hair of her motte."
(Anonymous, My Secret Life, 1890)

mot-carpet is 19th-century British usage for female pubic hair.

mother n

1. madam of a brothel. This meaning originated in the 17th century. **Mother abbess** is a synonym. See also **madam** and **abbess.**

2. male homosexual. This is 20th-century gay usage. See also **daughter.** **mother of all saints** and **mother of all souls** are 18th-century British and Irish terms, respectively, for female genitals, based on their reproductive capability.

motherfucker n

despicable person. This mid-20th-century derogatory term is based on the taboo of incest. Perhaps because of the power of this taboo, the term has strong emotional force. The derogatory sense was unambiguous in the 1960s, but by the 1980s the term had also come to be used to indicate excellence, especially in identifying a person or thing as the motherfucker, as opposed to a motherfucker, which continues usually to denote a despicable person or thing.

mound of Venus, mount of Venus n

fleshy cushion that covers the pubic bone of women. These phrases are direct translations of the Latin *mons veneris* and are common in Oriental literature. *See also* **mons pubis**.

• "Where do you want to go, my sting,
  walking across the Mount of Venus?
  He seeks himself a cave
  while he pushes the grass aside!"
  (Anonymous poem, quoted in Paul Tabori, *The Humor and Technology of Sex*, 1969)

mount v

copulate. This 16th-century standard word, said especially of men, is based on the sense of climbing onto a horse to **ride**. Shakespeare wrote in *Cymbeline*: "He will not manage her, although he mount her." The term has now become more colloquial than standard.

mount the corporal and four fingers is an 18th-century expression meaning masturbate, said of men. *See also* **finger**.

mount n British

act of sexual intercourse. This is a 19th-century colloquialism.

mount pleasant n

female genitals. This 19th-century jocular term is based on **mons pubis**.

mountains n pl American

breasts, especially large ones. This is a 20th-century colloquialism. *See also* **melons** and **molehills**.

mouse n British

1. penis. This is 19th-century usage. It may be based on shape and the fact that the animal burrows.

2. female genitals. Possibly based on the animal's fur, or derived from **cat** and mouse, this, too, is 19th-century usage.

mouser is a 19th-century British term for vagina. It is also 20th-century usage for a male homosexual, especially one who performs fellatio. The term is based on the closeness to "mouther."

mousetrap is 19th-century British usage for vagina, based on the first definition above. *See also* **trap**.

mouth music n

fellatio and/or cunnilingus. This is a 20th-century phrase. The music part probably refers to the flute, since **play the flute** is a common euphemism for fellatio.

mouth thankless n Scottish

vagina. This 15th-century colloquialism is perhaps based on the inability of the vagina to speak or thank. *See also* **dumb oracle** and **mute**.

mouth that cannot bite n phrase British

vagina. This is an 18th-century euphemism. *See also* **bite** and **vagina dentata**.

mouth-whore n British

prostitute who performs fellatio. This is a 19th-century derogatory term.

mow v Scottish

copulate. Probably derived from the Scottish meaning of mouth, this is of 16th-century origin.

• "I am no meat for his mowing."
  (Thomas Haughton, *A Woman Will Have Her Will*, 1598)

muck about v phrase British

fondle a woman's genitals. This late 19th-century colloquialism is based on muck's sense of **dirt**, and its closeness in sound to **fuck**. This term also has a nonsexual meaning of fool around or play about.

muddle *v Scottish*
copulate. Probably influenced by **meddle**, this is 19th-century usage.

muff *n*
female genitals. This 17th-century term derives from the softness and warmth of muff meaning mitten or hand warmer.
• "I heard the merry wagg protest, / The muff between her haunches, / Resembled most a Mag-pies nest, / Between two lofty branches." (*Ballad*, circa 1720, quoted in Farmer & Henley's *Dictionary of Slang and Its Analogues*, 1890).
muff dive is a 20th-century American expression meaning perform cunnilingus. *See also* **dive**. **Muff diver** and **muff diving** refer to cunnilinguist and cunnilingus, respectively.

muffins *n pl*
breasts, especially small ones. This usage is based on the shape of muffins, and dates back to the 18th century.

multiplication *n*
sexual intercourse. This 19th-century euphemism refers to reproduction. *See also* **addition**.

mump *v British*
copulate. This is obsolete 19th-century coinage. *See also* **hump**.

munch *v American*
perform fellatio or cunnilingus. This is a mid-20th-century term. *See also* **eat**.
munch the bearded clam means perform cunnilingus. Bearded clam refers to the female genitals in this 20th-century phrase. *See also* **beard**.

murphies *n pl American*
breasts. This early 20th-century underworld term is based on the shape of a murphy, which is an Irish potato.

muscle *n*
penis, especially an erect one. This is 20th-century usage. **Love muscle** and **muscle of love** are variants.

mushroom *n*
female genitals. Possibly influenced by "mush," suggesting softness and wetness, and "room" (a container term), and mushroom being a food, this is an obsolete 19th-century term.

muslin *n British*
1. woman considered as a sex object. This 19th-century usage is based on the standard sense of the term as a fabric for women's clothing.
• "That was a pretty bit of muslin hanging on your arm—who was she?" (William Thackeray, *The History of Pendennis*, 1849)
2. female genitals. This usage also dates back to the 19th century.

mustard *adj*
sexually attractive. This 20th-century term refers to mustard being **hot**. It may also be influenced by the phrase "Cut the mustard," meaning succeed or make it.
mustard and cress is 19th-century British usage for female pubic hair, based on the appearance of the salad greens.
mustard pot is a 19th-century term for vagina and 20th-century gay usage for anus. *See also* **pot**.

mute *n British*
vagina. This 20th-century gay term is based on the vagina being a silent mouth. *See also* **dumb oracle** and **mouth thankless**.

mutton n

1. female genitals. This meaning dates back to the 16th century. *See also* **meat**.

2. prostitute, group of prostitutes, or women considered sexually. These meanings also date back to the 16th century.

3. sexual intercourse. This is 17th-century usage.

in her mutton is a 19th-century British expression for an act of sexual intercourse with a woman.

mutton-dagger is a 20th-century expression for penis. *See also* **bayonet**, **pike**, and **sword**.

myrtle n Australian

sexual intercourse. This 20th-century term derives from myrtle as a Greek synonym for the female genitals and a symbol of fertility and marriage in Roman times. The myrtle berry, or *myrton* in Greek, was associated with the clitoris.

mysteries of love, mysteries of Venus n

phrase

sexual intercourse. These 18th-century literary expressions refer to **Venus**, the Roman goddess of love, secret rites, and the mystery and wonder of sexuality.

N

nads n pl

testicles. This recent term is an abbreviation of gonads. A gonad is a reproductive gland of either sex.

naff n British

vagina. This 19th-century term may stem from a backward reading of "fan," itself an abbreviation of **fanny**, another word for vagina.

naff v British

copulate. This current euphemism for **fuck** is usually used in nonsexual contexts, as in "Naff off."

nafkeh, nafka n American

prostitute. This early 20th-century usage derives from the Yiddish, and prior to that, from the Aramaic *nafka*, meaning **streetwalker**.

nag n

1. penis. This 17th-century term is based on the standard sense of **horse**. **nags** is 19th-century British usage for testicles. *See also* **nads**.

2. prostitute. This 16th-century term may be based on the sense meaning a horse that one can **ride**, or on the sense meaning to bother someone, for example, in propositioning someone.

nail v American

copulate. This 20th-century usage, said of men, suggests similar terms, such as **hammer**, **hit**, and **screw**. It may have derived from the 17th-century Scottish expression **nail two bellies together**, meaning copulate.

naked adj

not covered by clothes, especially as applied to the genital region. This has been standard English since the time of Old English usage.

nakedness is a 17th-century euphemism for the female genitals.

naked seeing self is a 16th-century literary expression for the female genitals. *See also* **eye**.

name it not v phrase British

female genitals. This is a 19th-century euphemism. *See also* **monosyllable**.

nance n American

effeminate male homosexual. This
19th-century term is based on the female name Nancy. **Nancy** and **nancy
boy** are variations more commonly
used in Great Britain.

• "When Lord St. Clancy became a
    nancy
   It did not please the family
    fancy . . ."
  (Anonymous, in Harold Hart,
  editor, *The Complete Immortalia*,
  1971)

nanny n British

prostitute. Probably based on the
standard English meanings of a female goat (symbolizing lechery) and
a nursemaid, this is 18th-century
usage.
nanny-house is an 18th-century
British term for brothel. *See also*
house.

nards n pl American

testicles. This 20th-century usage
probably derives from **nuts** or **nads**.

nasty adj

smutty, or pertaining to "naughty"
sex. This 17th-century usage reflects
moral judgment on sexuality. As a
noun, especially as **the nasty**, it
means copulation or the sex organs
of either sex. *See also* **the naughty**.

national indoor game n

sexual intercourse. This 19th-cen-
tury jocular expression is based on
the act's nationwide and worldwide
popularity. *See also* **game** and **sport**.

natural n British

prostitute. This 17th-century euphemism implies that the activities
performed are a part of nature.

nature n

1. genitals of either sex. This 16th-
century euphemism refers to the gen-

itals being necessary for the contin-
uation of life.
natural member is a 17th-century
euphemism for penis. *See also* **member**.
naturals is a 17th-century euphemism for genitals.
nature's duty is a 17th-century British euphemism for sexual intercourse.
2. menstruation. This is a 19th-
century euphemism.

nature's fonts n pl British

breasts. This is a 19th-century euphemism. *See also* **fountain**.

nature's veil n

female pubic hair. This is a 19th-
century euphemism.

naughty adj

smutty or sexually titillating. This
euphemism dates back to the 16th
century.
naughty bits is a recent British euphemism for the genitals of either
sex, popularized by the BBC's Monty
Python television shows in the early
1970s.
naughty-house is a 16th-century euphemism for brothel. *See also* **house**.

the naughty n

1. female genitals. This 19th-cen-
tury euphemism puns on the meaning indecent or smutty, and naught
meaning nothing. *See also* **nothing**.
2. *Australian* sexual intercourse.
This is 20th-century usage.
• "I get a lot of knock backs but I
   get a lot of naughties."
  (F. Hardy, *Legends from Benson's
  Valley*, 1963)

nautch n

vagina. Possibly derived from the
Sanskrit meaning "dance," or a variation of **notch**, this 18th-century
term is now obsolete.

nautch-joint is an early 20th-century American coinage for brothel. *See also* **joint**.

navel engagement n
Canadian

sexual intercourse. This jocular term puns on naval engagement.

Neapolitan disease n

syphilis. This 17th-century euphemism is based on Naples being the alleged source of the disease. **Neapolitan favor** is a variation, with favor punning on fever.

Nebuchadnezzar n *British*

penis. Based on the Bible, and found in the expression **take Nebuchadnezzar out to grass**, meaning copulate, this 19th-century usage is no longer employed.

necessaries n pl *British*

male genitals. This 19th-century euphemism implies an indispensable nature.

neck n

breasts. This 16th-century literary euphemism is based on bodily displacement. *See also* **big brown eyes** and **lungs**.

neck v *American*

hug, kiss, and caress amorously; pet. This early 20th-century colloquialism is probably based on the twining of necks.
- "The best behaved teenager necks."
(Germaine Greer, *The Female Eunuch*, 1970)

neddy n *British*

buttocks. This 17th-century colloquialism is based on the children's term meaning donkey or **ass**.

needle n *British*

penis. This 17th-century term may stem from the sexual sense of **stitch**, meaning copulate. The term is now obsolete. *See also* **pin** and **prick**.
- "The seaman's needle nimbly points the pole;
  But thine still turns to ev'ry craving hole."
(John Wilmot, the earl of Rochester, *Poems*, late 17th century)

needle-book is a 19th-century term for female genitals.

needle-case is 19th-century usage for vagina, based on the container sense of the term. *See also* **case**.

needle-woman is 19th-century coinage for prostitute.

nelly n *American*

1. lesbian. Based on the female name, this is mid-19th-century usage.

2. male homosexual. This usage dates back to the 19th century.

nephew n *American*

young male homosexual, especially one submitting to anal intercourse or performing fellatio. This term particularly applies to one looked after by an older homosexual male or **aunt**. This is an early 20th-century underworld term.

nether adj

situated below or down. This standard English word is used in a number of sexual expressions.

nether end is 18th-century British usage for female genitals.

nether eye dates back to the 14th century and refers to the female genitals. *See also* **eye**.

nether eyebrow is 19th-century British usage for female pubic hair. Variations include **nether eyelashes** and **nether whiskers**.

Netherlands is a 16th-century jocular term for the genitals of either sex, based on the Netherlands being one of the Low countries. See also **Holland**, **low countries**, and **lowlands**.

nether lips is a 19th-century British colloquialism for the **labia majora** (under **labia**), or outer lips of the female genitals.

nether mouth is 19th-century coinage for vagina.

• ". . . my nether mouth, as full as it could hold . . . the morsel that deliciously ingorged it."
(John Cleland, *Fanny Hill: Memoirs of a Woman of Pleasure*, 1749)

nether throat is 20th-century usage for anus, since it is at the opposite or nether end of the digestive tract from the throat.

the never out n phrase British
female genitals. This 19th-century colloquialism is based on the supposition that, unlike the male genitals, the female genitals are always ready for sexual intercourse.

nibble, have a nibble v, v phrase British
copulate. These are 19th-century colloquialisms. See also **bite** and **taste**.

nick n
female genitals. This is an 18th-century term. **Nick-nack** is a British variation. See also **cut** and **crack**.

• "And as one guides me to the nick,
The other cries—Put up thy prick."
(Robertson of Struan, *Poems*, early 18th century)

nick v British
copulate. This is 18th-century usage.

nick-nacks n pl
1. testicles. This is 18th-century usage.
2. breasts. This is 20th-century usage.

nidge v British
copulate. This 19th-century meaning is now obsolete. It is based on the standard sense meaning shake.

nifty n British
sexual intercourse. This 19th-century term is used especially in the phrase **a bit of nifty**. It is probably based on the standard sense of nifty meaning good, clever, or attractive.

nig v British
copulate. This 18th-century term is an abbreviation of **niggle**.

niggle v
copulate. This 16th-century term is based on the standard meaning of trifle.

night baseball n American
copulation. This is a recent euphemism.

nightcap n American
condom. This is a recent euphemism based on the pun of something one takes before going to bed.

nighthawk n Australian
prostitute. Besides the bird sense, another standard sense of the term is a person who is active at night. This is an early 20th-century term.

nightingale n British
prostitute. This 19th-century term puns on the bird, the night, and possibly the kindness of Florence Nightingale, the famous nurse.

night physic n

sexual intercourse. This 16th-century euphemism is based on the obsolete sense of physic meaning medicine. See also **ointment** and **physic**.

night-piece n

prostitute. This is 19th-century coinage. See also **piece**.

nightstick n

penis. This usage dates back to the 19th century. See also **stick**.

nightwalker n

prostitute. This 17th-century colloquialism was obsolete by the 19th century.

night work n

sexual intercourse. This is a 16th-century euphemism. See also **work**.

nimrod n British

penis. This 19th-century colloquialism puns on the biblical Nimrod the hunter and the **rod** in his name.

ninnies n pl

nipples or breasts. This is 20th-century usage. See also **boobs**.

nipped in the bud v phrase

circumcised as an infant. This 20th-century colloquialism is based on the standard sense of being cut while very young.

nipple n

projection that provides an outlet for milk at the center of the female breast. This standard word derives from "nib," meaning point, and dates back to the 16th century. **Nips** is a 20th-century colloquial abbreviation.

nock n

female genitals. This 16th-century usage may derive from **notch** or from **knock**.

nockstress is a 19th-century British term for prostitute.

nock v

copulate. This is 16th-century coinage. See also **knock**.

nodge v Scottish

copulate. This is an 18th-century colloquialism. See also **nidge** and **nudge, nudge**.

nonesuch n British

female genitals. This 18th-century colloquialism is based on the standard sense of unrivaled best. See also **best**.

nonny-nonny n British

female genitals. This 18th-century euphemism is used especially in the phrase **a hey nonny-nonny**, which is also a euphemism for female genitals. The term is also used for anything considered vulgar.

no-nuts n

lesbian. This jocular, sometimes derogatory, 20th-century term, used by men, is based on **nuts** meaning testicles.

nooky, nookie n

1. female genitals. This 20th-century term probably derives from nook meaning corner and may be influenced by **nick** and **nug**.
2. sexual intercourse. This is a 20th-century colloquialism.
• "It's not the actual bit of nooky I find so devastatingly fascinating. It's the dynamics of human relationships, and sex is part of that."
(Rose Boyt, People, June 1990)
3. women considered as sex objects. This is 20th-century usage. See also **pussy**.
nookie bookie is 20th-century coinage for pimp, based on bookie mean-

ing bookmaker, the one who takes in the money.

noose n

vagina. This 20th-century derogatory term puns on its circular shape and a sense of entrapment. "The noose" is a 20th-century colloquialism for marriage.

norgs, norks n pl Australian

breasts. This mid-20th-century coinage derives from Norco butter, a brand that displays a picture of a cow's udder on the package.

Norma Snokkers n British

woman with large breasts. This recent jocular term is based on "(e)normous knockers."

North Pole n British

anus. This 19th-century rhyming slang term is based on the rhyme with **hole**. North may suggest **nether**.

nose n

penis. This 16th-century literary euphemism may be based on appearance as well as the ability to emit mucus, which resembles semen.
• "If you were but an inch of fortune better than I, where would you choose it? Not in my husband's nose."
(William Shakespeare, *Antony and Cleopatra*, 1607)

not alone adj phrase

pregnant. This is a 20th-century jocular expression.

notch n

female genitals. This 18th-century term derives from the standard sense meaning **cleft**, **cut**, or **nick**.
notch-girl is early 20th-century coinage for prostitute.

notch-house is early 20th-century usage for brothel. *See also* **house**.

nothing n

female genitals, especially the vulva. This 17th-century literary euphemism is based on the shape of the numeral zero and on the absence of a **thing**, where thing means penis. *See also* **O** and **vacuum**.

no toothpaste in the tube adj phrase American

impotent. This is a recent jocular expression. *See also* **have lead in one's pencil** (under **pencil**).

the novelty n

female genitals. This 18th-century jocular euphemism is based on women's genitals being interesting from the male point of view.

nubbies n pl Australian

breasts. This early 20th-century term derives from **nub** or **knob** meaning a protuberance.

nudge, nudge n British

sexual intercourse. Sometimes followed by "wink, wink," this is a 1970s euphemism made famous by a BBC Monty Python sketch. To nudge is to push gently, while to wink is to deliberately hint at something. *See also* **nidge** and **nodge**.

nug v

copulate. Possibly derived from the standard sense of nudge, meaning to push gently, this is of 17th-century origin.
nugging is 18th-century British usage for sexual intercourse.

number n American

1. sexually attractive woman or girl. Used especially in the phrases

hot number or **cute number**, this is 20th-century usage.

• "No matter what life you lead the virgin is a lovely number." (Anne Sexton, "Snow White and the Seven Dwarfs," 1971)

2. prostitute's customer. This 20th-century term may derive from the number one takes when lining up for service at a deli counter, bakery, post office, etc.

number three n

ejaculation. This 20th-century euphemism extends the traditional nursery numbering system wherein number one stands for urination and number two for defecation.

nums n pl

nipples. This 20th-century colloquialism is based on the colloquial sense of num-num, applied to children, meaning to eat.

nunnery n

brothel. This is a 16th-century euphemism. When Hamlet says to Ophelia, "Get thee to a nunnery," Shakespeare may well be using nunnery in this sense. *See also* **abbess**.

• "The Abbess of this open-thighed nunnery . . ." (Anonymous, *My Secret Life*, 1890)

nun is a euphemism for prostitute.

nursery n British

female genitals. This 19th-century colloquialism refers to reproductive capacity.

nutmegs n pl British

testicles. Based on appearance, this usage is of 17th-century origin. *See also* **nuts**.

nuts n pl

testicles. A colloquialism since the 18th century, this term is still com-

monly used. It derives from both the shape of nuts and their function as seeds from which new plants grow.

nymph, nymphet n

young woman or girl who is sexually attractive. This 20th-century term derives from the Latin *nympha*, meaning "bride." *Nymphae*, the plural, also means the inner lips of the vulva.

• "Between the age limits of nine and fourteen there occur maidens who, to certain bewitched travellers . . . reveal their true nature which is not human, but nymphic . . . and these chosen creatures I propose to designate 'nymphets.'" (Vladimir Nabokov, *Lolita*, 1955)

nympho n

woman with extreme or excessive sexual desires. This is a 20th-century shortening of **nymphomaniac**, a standard word that dates back to the 18th century.

nymph of darkness n

prostitute. This is a 19th-century euphemism. **Nymph of the pavement** is a variant. *See also* **bat**, **nightwalker**, and **streetwalker**.

nymphomania n

extreme sexual desire in women. This standard term has been used since the 18th century.

O n

female genitals, especially the vulva. This 17th-century literary euphemism is based on shape. *See also* **nothing**.

oats *n pl*

See **have one's oats** and **sow one's wild oats**.

oblige *v*

copulate. This 17th-century euphemism, used of women, alludes to men's insistence on the act.

obscene *adj*

pertaining to something sexually depraved. This standard English word also has the sense of something that is disgusting to the senses.
obscenity is the standard term for something that incites lustful thoughts or acts or is sexually depraved or repulsive. It dates back to the 17th century.
* "Obscenity is whatever gives a judge an erection."
  (Anonymous, quoted in Jonathon Green, *The Cynic's Lexicon*, 1984)

occupy *v*

copulate. This 15th-century term, used of men, is based on the sense of possessing or taking a woman. By the 17th century the term was no longer slang; today, though rarely used, it is a euphemism. *See also* **possess** and **take**.
occupant is a 16th-century term for prostitute.
occupying-house is 18th-century British coinage for brothel. *See also* **house**.

odd *n*

a homosexual, usually a male. This 19th-century colloquialism is obsolete.
oddball is a mid-20th-century American derogatory term for a male homosexual. The word also means a very eccentric person.

oil *n British*

semen. This is a 19th-century abbreviation of **man oil**. *See also* **juice**.
* "Too hasty zeal my hopes did spoil,
  Pressing to feed her lamp, I spilt my oil."
  (John Wilmot, the earl of Rochester, "The Imperfect Enjoyment," 1680)
oil change is a recent American colloquialism for an act of sexual intercourse employing the automotive metaphor.

ointment *n British*

semen. Probably based on its appearance, and reinforced by the medicinal sense of ointment, this is 18th-century usage. *See also* **medicine** and **night physic**.

old Adam *n*

penis. This 19th-century colloquialism brings to mind the first man and hence the first penis.

oldest profession *n*

prostitution. This is a common euphemism.

old girl *n*

elderly male homosexual. This is 20th-century gay usage. **Old hen** is a variant. *See also* **hen**.

old horny, old Hornington *n British*

penis. These are 18th-century terms. *See also* **horn**.

old man *n British*

penis. This is a 19th-century euphemism.

old thing *n*

female genitals. This is 19th-century usage. *See also* **thing**.

old timer n American

skilled prostitute. This 20th-century term is used especially by prostitutes.

omega n

See **alpha and omega**.

on prep

sexually aroused. This 19th-century colloquialism is said of either sex. **Turned on** is a 20th-century colloquialism with the same sense.
on the bonk and **on the honk** are both 20th-century colloquialisms, mainly British, for having an erection. Honk suggests **horn**, while **bonk** suggests craziness, as in "bonkers."

onanism n

1. coitus interruptus. This standard term, which dates back to the 18th century, derives from the Old Testament story of Onan and his brother Er. After Er died, God told Onan to "go in unto" his brother's wife, which he did, but he "spilled his seed on the ground," suggesting coitus interruptus.
2. masterbation. This euphemism dates back to the 19th century. Today onanist almost always means masturbator.

one-eyed milkman n
British

penis. This is a 19th-century jocular term. See also **milk**.

one-eyed worm n American

penis. This is a mid-20th-century derogatory term. Other versions are **one-eyed monster, one-eyed pants mouse, one-eyed trouser snake, one-eyed wonder,** and **one-eyed zipper snake.** See also **worm, mouse,** and **snake**.

one-finger exercise n

stimulation of the clitoris, said of women. This is 20th-century coinage.

one in the box adj phrase

pregnant. This is a 19th-century colloquialism. See also **box**.

one in the bush is worth two in the hand phrase
Australian

sexual intercourse is superior to masturbation. Said of men, this 20th-century expression puns on the saying "A bird in the hand is worth two in the bush."

one-night stand n

one-time sexual encounter. This is a 20th-century colloquial expression.

one of the boys n phrase

effeminate male homosexual or lesbian. This is a 20th-century colloquialism.

one of those n phrase

homosexual. Said by heterosexuals, this 20th-century term is often derogatory.

one-way street n phrase

heterosexual who will not engage in any homosexual acts, specifically anal intercourse. This is mid-20th-century gay usage.

onion n

1. glans or head of the penis. Based on similarity of shape, this is a 20th-century euphemism. See also **acorn** and **radish**.
onion skin is 20th-century usage for foreskin.
2. Australian a woman engaged in group sex. Probably based on an onion having many layers, this is also a 20th-century term. See also **lay**.

on the bash *adj phrase British*
engaged in prostitution. This is an early 20th-century military term.

on the game *adj phrase British*
engaged in prostitution. This is 19th-century coinage. *See also* **game** and **on the bottle** (under **bottle**).

on the make *adj phrase*
on the lookout for sex. See also **make**.

on the rag, OTR *adj phrase*
having a menstrual period. This is a 20th-century colloquialism. Rag means sanitary napkin.

Oom Paul *n British, South African*
cunnilinguist. This early 20th-century term refers to Oom Paul Kruger (Stephanus Johannes Paulus Kruger, 1825–1904), who was president of the Transvaal (a Boer republic in South Africa) and who had a bushy beard. In performing cunnilingus, a man may seem to have a bushy beard. *See also* **beard**.

open-arse *n British*
a woman who is ready for sexual intercourse, or a woman regarded as especially lecherous. This is 17th-century usage.

open C *n British*
female genitals. This is 19th-century coinage. C stands for **cunt**. The shape of the letter C suggests openness.

open up the ass (arse) *v phrase*
perform anal intercourse. This is 20th-century gay usage.

opposite sex *n*
man from a woman's perspective, or woman from a man's perspective. This is a standard term.

oracle *n*
female genitals. Derived from the Latin *orare*, meaning "request," this is a 19th-century euphemism. *See also* **dumb oracle**.

oral intercourse *n*
genital-oral intercourse. This shortened term is often abbreviated further to **oral sex**.

orange *n British*
female genitals. This 18th-century literary euphemism may be based on the juiciness of an orange. *See also* **fig** and **plum**.

oranges *n pl American*
breasts. Based on shape, and adding to the substantial fruit category of sexual terms, this is 20th-century usage. *See also* **apples, grapefruits, lemons, melons,** and **peaches**.

orbs *n pl*
1. breasts. This 18th-century colloquialism is based on shape.
• "And now gently lifting up those two bright orbs . . ."
(Henry Fielding, *Tom Jones*, 1749)
2. testicles. Based on shape, this is a 20th-century colloquialism.

orchard *n*
female genitals. This 16th-century literary euphemism refers to fruitfulness.

orchestra *n*
1. *British* testicles. This 19th-century rhyming slang term is based on **orchestra stalls**, which is implied, and the rhyme with **balls**. **Orks** is a variation.

2. *American* male homosexual prepared to perform any sexual act. Suggested by the full range of an orchestra, this is a mid-20th-century jocular term.

orchids *n pl*

testicles. This 19th-century literary euphemism derives from the Greek *orchis*, meaning "testicle." Orchids have long been used in love potions.

organ *n*

penis. This 19th-century euphemism derives from the Greek *organon*, meaning "tool." It remains a common euphemism and is often used humorously. *See also* **tool**.
organ grinder means vagina. *See also* **grind**.
• "I shoved old Pete right through
    the sheet
    And up her organ grinder.
    The white of an egg ran down her
    leg,
    But the rest remained inside her."
    (Variation of "The Girl I Left
    Behind Me," British military song
    of the mid-18th century)

orgasm *n*

peak of sexual excitement. This standard term dates back to the mid-18th century. The word derives from the Greek *orgasmos*, meaning "grow and swell," and is related to the Greek *ergon*, meaning "work."
• "I knew very little about Algren's
    sex life. . . . I subsequently
    learned . . . that he helped Miss
    de Beauvoir achieve her first
    orgasm. (The only person I ever
    helped achieve a first orgasm was
    good old me.)"
    (Kurt Vonnegut, *Fates Worse
    Than Death*, 1991)

orgy *n*

group sexual activity. This has been a standard English term since

the 16th century. It derives from the Greek *ergon*, meaning "work."

orifice *n*

female genitals. This colloquial term dates back to the 16th century, and is based on the standard sense of anatomical opening. It derives from the Latin *os*, meaning "mouth." *See also* **hole**.

ornament *n British*

female genitals. This is a 19th-century euphemism. *See also* **thing**.

ornaments *n pl*

testicles. This is a 19th-century term.

oscar *n British*

male homosexual. This late 19th-century term refers to Oscar Wilde, a well-known writer of that period and a homosexual.
oscarize is 19th-century British coinage for perform anal intercourse.

the other *n*

sexual intercourse. This euphemism may derive from the expression "This, that, and the other."

other parts *n pl British*

breasts. This is a 17th-century euphemism. Compare **private parts**.

other sex *n*

homosexual. This is a 19th-century colloquialism. *See also* **third sex**.

OTR *abbrev American*

See **on the rag**.

oven *n British*

vagina. This 18th-century term is based on both the container and production senses and on the notion of **heat**, meaning sexual passion. *See also* **bun in the oven**.

• "But if my Oven be over-hot
I dare not thrust it in, Sir;
For burning of my Wriggling-Pole,
My skill's not worth a Pin, Sir."
(Thomas D'Urfey, *Wit and Mirth*,
1719)

overcoat n British

condom. This 20th-century jocular
term derives from a French expression, *capote anglaise*, that translates
into "English overcoat." **Raincoat** is
a variation. These terms, together
with **skin** and **armor**, allude to the
protective function of a condom.

overnight bag n American

prostitute. This is early 20th-cen-
tury derogatory usage. See also **bag**.

over the shoulder boulder holder n phrase
American

brassiere. This is a jocular mid-
20th-century expression. See also
boulders.

owl n

prostitute. This 19th-century term
is based on the bird's nocturnal hab-
its. See also **bat** and **nightingale**.

oyster n

1. female genitals. This 19th-cen-
tury term is based on appearance,
texture, and delicacy. See also **whelk**.
2. *British* semen. Probably based
on the similarity to another sense of
the term, meaning a gob of phlegm,
this term dates back to the 19th century. See also **catch an oyster**.
oyster-catcher is 19th-century British coinage for female genitals.

P

pack n British

prostitute. Now obsolete, this 17th-
century term may be based on the
meaning of a hunting pack.

package n American

sexually attractive woman or girl.
This is a 20th-century term. See also
piece.

paddle v

caress sexually. This 16th-century
colloquialism may refer to the fact
that one can paddle with one's hands.
See also **handle**.
paddle one's pickle is a 20th-cen-
tury colloquialism meaning masturbate, said of men. See also **pickle**.

padlock n

vagina. Punning on the chastity
belt and its **lock** and **key**, this is 18th-
century usage.

paedophile n British

See **pedophile**.

pagan n

prostitute. This 17th-century literary term is based on the practice of
ritual prostitution in pagan Greece.
See also **abbess** and **nun** (under **nunnery**).

pagan adj

referring to sexual intercourse in
positions other than the **missionary
position**. This is a 20th-century colloquialism.

page three adj British

referring to photographs of women
with exposed breasts. This recent eu-

phemism refers to the *Sun* newspaper, which has had photographs of topless women on page three daily since the mid-1970s. Page three, by extension, refers to anyone or anything lascivious.
- "The page 3 cutie pinned on the locker room door inspires the same sort of automatic reverence as religious medals on the dashboards of Greek taxi drivers."
(Irma Kurtz, *Mantalk*, 1986)

painted lady n American
prostitute. This early 20th-century colloquialism refers to the use of makeup. **Painted cat** is a variant. *See also* **lady** and **cat**.

pair n
1. breasts, especially beautiful or attractive ones. This is a 20th-century colloquialism.
2. sexual pair usually consisting of male and female. This is common usage.

pan n American
female genitals. This 20th-century colloquialism may refer to flatness and the container metaphor. *See also* **pot**.

pancake n
1. woman considered as a sex object. This is 20th-century usage. *See also* **cake**.
2. *British* female genitals. This 19th-century term may refer to flatness. *See also* **flat-cock**.

pander n
procurer or pimp. This standard word dates back to the 16th century. In Shakespeare's *Troilus and Cressida*, circa 1609, Pandarus was Cressida's uncle and procured her for Troilus. The term is rarely used to-

day, though the verb form, meaning gratify another's desires, is commonly used. **Panderer** has been used for pimp since the 15th century.

pansy n
male homosexual, especially an effeminate one. This is early 20th-century usage. *See also* **flower**.

panters n pl British
breasts. This 19th-century term is based on the notion that female breasts either allow in women, or cause in men, deep breathing. *See also* **lungs**.

pantry shelves n pl British
breasts. This 19th-century colloquialism alludes to the fact that female breasts contain food (milk). The term is now obsolete.

papaya n
vagina. This 20th-century usage may refer to the fruit's shape when cut or to its juiciness. *See also* **cabbage** and **orange**.

paps n pl
nipples. Derived from the Latin *papilla*, meaning "nipple," and dating back to the 14th century, this formal term is not commonly used.
- "Ay, that left pap,
Where heart doth hop."
(William Shakespeare, *A Midsummer Night's Dream*, 1592)

paradise n British
female genitals. This is a 17th-century euphemism. *See also* **Abraham's bosom**, **heaven**, and **promised land**.
- "His daring Hand that Altar seiz'd,
Where Gods of Love do Sacrifice:
That Awful Throne, the Paradise."
(Aphra Behn, *Poems*, circa 1697)

parallel parking n

copulation. This jocular 20th-century expression makes use of the automobile metaphor.

park v American

neck or pet in a parked car. This is a mid-20th-century colloquialism.

parley v

copulate. Based on the standard meaning of communicate or converse, this is a 16th-century euphemism. See also **talk**.

parlor-house n

brothel. This usage dates back to the 19th century. See also **house**.

parlor room n

vagina. This is 19th-century coinage. See also **front room** (under **front attic**).

parsley n

female pubic hair. This 16th-century term is based on appearance.
parsley-bed means vagina. An 18th-century children's myth held that female babies come from a parsley-bed while male babies come from a nettle-bed. See also **bed**.

part v

spread legs, lips, or cheeks in sexual activity. This is standard usage.
part someone's cheeks is a colloquialism for perform anal intercourse. **Cheeks** refers to the buttocks in this 20th-century expression.

parts n pl

genitals of either sex. This euphemism is an abbreviation of **private parts**. It is also used in the singular.
• "But whilst her busy hand would guide that part

Which should convey my soul up to her heart . . ."
(John Wilmot, the earl of Rochester, "The Imperfect Enjoyment," 1680).
parts below is a euphemism for the genitals of either sex. This usage dates back to the 17th century.
parts of shame is a 19th-century British expression for female genitals.

parts behind n pl British

buttocks. This is a 19th-century euphemism.

party v American

engage in sexual activity. Based on the standard sense of party meaning celebration, this is 20th-century usage.
party hat is a recent American euphemism for condom. The term originated on college campuses.

passage n

vagina. This is an early 20th-century euphemism. See also **love lane** and **main avenue**.

passion n

sexual lust. This literary term dates back to the 16th century. Passion derives from the Old French and church Latin passio, meaning "suffering."
passionflower is a mid-20th-century American term for a sexually passionate person, especially a woman.

Pat and Mick n phrase British

penis. This 19th-century rhyming slang is based on the rhyme with **prick**. The term illustrates personification. See also **dick**.

patch n British

female genitals. This 19th-century usage refers to the appearance of the pubic patch.

patha-patha n South African

sexual intercourse. Derived from the African term meaning touch-touch, this is a 20th-century colloquialism. Patha-patha is a form of African music with sexual or romantic overtones. It was popularized by Miriam Makeba in the 1960s. See also **jazz**.

pavement princess n American

prostitute. This is a mid-20th-century colloquialism. See also **streetwalker**.

paw v American

fondle or grope someone sexually against his or her will. This is a mid-20th-century colloquialism. See also **finger**, **grope**, and **handle**.

peacemaker n British

penis. See **matrimonial peacemaker**.

peaches n pl American

breasts. This is mid-20th-century usage. It joins many other breast/food metaphors, such as **apples** and **melons**.

pearl dive v

perform cunnilingus. This 20th-century term derives from a pearl being in an **oyster**, which stands for the female genitals. Aphrodite's **pearly gates** are a symbol of the female genitals. See also **dive**.

pearl necklace n American

semen spilling from a fellator's mouth down onto the neck. This is 20th-century gay usage.

pebbles n pl British

testicles. This is a 19th-century term. See also **stone**.

pecker n American

penis. This common term dates back to the 19th century. It puns on other senses of the term such as appetite and courage.

• "I never trust a man unless I got his pecker in my pocket." (Lyndon B. Johnson)

pecker checker is a 20th-century military colloquialism for a doctor who does examinations for signs of venereal disease.

peculiar river n

vagina. This 17th-century literary term stems from the obsolete sense of peculiar, meaning a mistress or something private. See also **fish**.

• "Groping for trouts in a peculiar river." (William Shakespeare, Measure for Measure, 1603)

pederast n

man who performs anal intercourse with other men or boys. This standard word dates back to the early 18th century. **Pederasty** is the standard term for the practice.

• "Throughout the two centuries (from the early sixth to the early fourth, B.C.) during which pederasty flourished, the Greeks staunchly maintained that it was a branch of higher education." (Reay Tannahill, Sex in History, 1979)

pedophile, paedophile n

one who seeks children as preferred sex objects. This standard English term dates back to the early 20th century.

peel one's best end v phrase British

have sexual intercourse. Said of a man with an uncircumcised penis, this is a 19th-century expression. See *also* **have one's banana peeled** (under **have**).

peepee, peewee n

penis. This informal 19th-century children's term is based on pee meaning urine. **Pee hole** is a child's term for vagina.

peep v

be a voyeur. This term is based on the standard sense of peek, from which it derives.
peep show is a colloquial term, dating back to the mid-19th century, for any kind of act in which naked women are displayed or revealed.

peeping sentinel n

clitoris. This 19th-century term, one of the very few for clitoris, is based on the clitoris peeping out of the vulva. It may also pun on "pee." Sentinel suggests standing guard over the vagina.

peewee n

See **peepee**.

peg n

penis. This likely abbreviation of **pego** dates back to the 18th century.
peg-boy is a 20th-century American term for a catamite. One theory of origin is that a peg can be kept in a boy's anus in preparation for pederasty.
peg-house is American underworld usage for a male brothel. It dates back to the mid-20th century.

pego n British

penis. This early 18th-century term may derive from the Greek, meaning "fountain."
• "... I kept my pego quiet up her for a time before I thrust ..." (Anonymous, *My Secret Life*, 1890)

pen n

1. penis. This 16th-century term derives from the Latin *penna*, meaning "feather" or "quill."
2. vagina. Based on the standard sense of pen meaning an enclosure, this is a 19th-century term.

pencil n

penis. Based on shape, this 19th-century term is used especially in the phrase **have lead in one's pencil**, meaning have an erection.

pendulum n

penis. This 19th-century usage refers to the penis's propensity to hang down and sway.

penilingus n

fellatio. This 20th-century coinage is standard English.

penis n

male copulatory organ. This standard English term derives from the Latin *penis*, meaning "tail," and has been in use since the late 17th century.
penis envy is a standard term that dates back to the early 20th century. It refers to the supposed envy that girls and women have of the penis, allegedly leading to feelings of inferiority.
penis muliebris is a 17th-century medical term for the clitoris, derived from the Latin, meaning "woman's penis." This term reflects the view of the clitoris as a homologue of the penis.

perch n

penis. Possibly alluding to a bird's perch resembling an erect penis, this is mid-20th-century gay usage.

percy n

penis. This 20th-century term is an example of personification. It is used especially in the expressions **punish percy in the palm** (masturbate) and "point percy at the porcelain" (urinate).

perfect lady n

prostitute. This 19th-century expression may imply irony or delight in perfection. See also **lady**.

perforate v British

deflower or copulate. This 19th-century colloquialism is based on the standard sense of make a hole.

perform v

1. copulate. This is 19th-century colloquial usage. See also **act** and **do it** (under **do**).
2. do any sexual act, especially fellatio or cunnilingus. This is 20th-century usage.

perineum n

area between the vulva and the anus in females, and the scrotum and anus in males. This standard medical term dates back to the early 17th century.

period n

menstrual period. This common colloquialism has been in use since the 19th century.

periwinkle n British

female genitals. This 19th-century term may derive from **winkle**, meaning penis, and the prefix "peri-", meaning around. In standard usage, periwinkle is the name of a seafood and a flowering plant; see **fish** and **flower**.

pervert n

person exhibiting sexual behavior regarded as socially unacceptable. This 19th-century colloquialism is usually based on a predilection for sexual acts other than intercourse.

perversion is a standard noun applied to any sexual act regarded as abnormal.

- "Sadism and masochism occupy a special position among the perversions."
  (Sigmund Freud, Three Essays on the Theory of Sexuality, 1905)

perv, or **perve**, is 20th-century derogatory usage for a male homosexual. To **perv** means to perform anal intercourse.

pervy is early 20th-century American underworld coinage for anus.

pestle n

penis. This is 19th-century usage. See also **mortar**.

pestle v

copulate. Said of men, this is 19th-century usage.

pet v

caress sexually. This common 20th-century colloquialism may derive from the noun meaning of one's favorite.

petal n

effeminate male homosexual. This is a 20th-century term. See also **daisy**, **lily**, and **pansy**.

peter n

penis. Derived from the Greek petros, meaning "rock," this is a 19th-century colloquialism. It is another example of personification. See also **dick** and **Pat and Mick**.

- "The women, they are sweeter,
  Every year;
  There is more demand for Peter,
  Every year;
  But mine, it gets no bigger,
  And it's slower on the trigger,

And cuts less and less a figure
Every year."
(Anonymous, "I'm Getting Older,"
in Harold Hart, editor, *The
Complete Immortalia*, 1971)
peter cheater is a recent American
jocular term for sanitary napkin.
peter eater is 20th-century usage for
fellator. **Peter puffer** is a more recent
version. *See also* **eat**.
peter pansy is mid-20th-century
American coinage for homosexual
male. *See also* **pansy**.

petticoat n
woman considered sexually. This
colloquialism dates back to the 17th
century. *See also* **skirt**.

phallus n
symbol or representation of a penis
or a penis itself. This standard term
derives from the Greek *phallos* and
has been in use since the 17th century. **Phallic** is the standard adjective.
phallicize is 19th-century British
coinage for copulate.
phallic thimble is an early 20th-cen-
tury British jocular term for condom,
punning on phallic symbol.

phone sex, telephone sex n
service in which the caller listens
to or discusses explicit sexual topics
or fantasies. This type of business began in New York in the early 1980s.

physic n
copulation. This early 17th-cen-
tury euphemism, based on the then-
standard meaning of medicine, is
used especially in the phrase **night
physic**. The term is now obsolete. *See
also* **medicine**.
• "... her young doctor, Who
ministers physic to her on her
back ..."
(Philip Massinger, *The Bond-man,
an Ancient Storie*, 1623)

piccolo n American
penis. This is a 20th-century term.
See also **flute**.
piccolo player is 20th-century
American usage for fellator.

pick v
pierce or penetrate. This word is
etymologically akin to **prick**.
pick her cherry is a mid-20th-cen-
tury American expression, said of
men, meaning deflower a woman.
picklock is an 18th-century obsolete
term for penis, based on the metaphor
of opening a **lock** with a **key**.
pick the lock is a 16th-century literary expression meaning deflower,
punning on **lock** meaning vagina and
chastity belt.

pick fruit v phrase American
seek out male homosexuals. This is
a mid-20th-century underworld
expression. *See also* **fruit**.

pickup n
sexually available man or woman.
This 19th-century colloquialism is
still common today.
• "The big teashops ... were
always crowded with girls and
always offered a chance of a pick-
up."
(J.B. Priestley, *Angel Pavement*,
1930)

pick up v phrase
find someone, usually a stranger, to
have sex with. This is a common colloquialism.

pickle n
penis. This 20th-century term is
based on shape. It is used especially
in phrases such as **paddle one's pickle**
and **pump one's pickle** (under **pump**).
Pickle also suggests **prickle**. *See also*
cucumber and **gherkin**.

picnic n

orgy. This 20th-century term uses the metaphor of eating or feasting. *See also* **beanfeast**.

picnic v

perform fellatio or cunnilingus. This 20th-century usage is based on the eating metaphor.

pie n American

woman considered sexually. This is a 20th-century colloquialism. *See also* **biscuit**, **cake**, and **tart**.

piece n

woman considered as a sex object. This often derogatory term dates back to the 14th century and is still commonly used today. *See also* **bit**.

- "She seems a handsome piece.
  That opportunity Would play the Bawd a little!"
  (Thomas Nabbes, *Totenham-Court*, 1633)

piece of ass is 20th-century coinage for vagina. It also means an act of copulation. *See also* **ass**.

piece of mutton is 17th-century British usage for a woman considered sexually. *See also* **mutton**.

piece of tail is a mid-20th-century term for a woman considered sexually. It also stands for an act of copulation. *See also* **tail**.

piece of trade is a 20th-century American expression for prostitute. *See also* **trade**.

pig n American

woman regarded as competition for a male homosexual. In Greek, a term for the female genitals is *choiros*, which also means "pig." This is a recent gay term.

piggies n

breasts or nipples. This 20th-century usage is possibly based on color.

pig pile n

homosexual orgy. This is 20th-century gay coinage.

pig's knockers n American

testicles. This is an early 20th-century rural dialectal term. *See also* **knockers**.

pike n

penis. This literary term dates back to the 16th century and is representative of a metaphor of aggression. *See also* **bayonet**, **dagger**, **lance**, and **weapon**.

- "... you must put in the pikes with a vice; and they are dangerous weapons for maids."
  (William Shakespeare, *Much Ado About Nothing*, 1598)

pile v American

copulate. This is 20th-century black usage.

pile-driver n

penis. Based on the standard sense of a tool that performs repeated hammering, this is a 19th-century term. *See also* **drive**.

the pill n

birth control pill. This is a mid-20th-century colloquialism.

- "Emily knew all about the Bomb and the Pill."
  (Jennie Melville, *Murderers's Houses*, 1964)

pillicock, pillcock n

penis. This is a 16th-century literary term.

- "Methink my pillock will nocht ly doun."
  (Sir David Lyndesay, *Ane Satyre of the Thrie Estaits*, 1540)

pillicock-hill refers to the female genitals, where hill means the **mons pubis**.

pillow-mate n

one's female sexual partner. This 19th-century colloquialism is said of men. See also **bed** and **sheets**.

pills n pl British

testicles. This 19th-century rhyming slang term is an abbreviation of **Beecham's pills**.

pimp n

male procurer. This standard term dates back to the 17th century.

pimp v

live off the earnings of prostitutes. This is a standard term.

pimple n

1. American pimp. This is early 20th-century usage.
2. British baby boy's penis. This is a 19th-century colloquialism.
3. syphilitic pustule. This euphemism originated in the 20th century.

pin n

penis. This is a 17th-century term. See also **prick**.
• "Her Belly a soft Cushion where
    no sinner
  But her true love must dare stick
    a pin in her."
  (Henry Glapthorne, *The Lady
  Mother*, 1635)
pin-case and **pin-cushion** are 17th-century British colloquialisms for vagina. See also **case**.

pinch-bottom n British

lecher. This is 19th-century coinage. **Pinch-buttock** and **pinch-cunt** are variants.

pinch-prick n British

prostitute. This term dates back to the 19th century.

pink n

photographs of female genitals in pornographic magazines. This is late 20th-century usage.

pink-pants n American

homosexual boy or catamite. In this mid-20th-century term, the color pink symbolizes homosexuality. See also **lavender boy** and **purple**.

pintle n

penis. This term, dating back to the 12th century when it was standard, applied to the penis of both animals and humans.
• "A pintle like a rolling-pin."
  (Robert Burns, *Merry Muses*, late 18th century)

pinup girl, pinup n

woman who poses appealingly in posters or pictures. These terms are mid-20th-century colloquialisms.
• "She had a figure like the
  quintessence of all pinup girls."
  (Edmund Crispin, *Buried for
  Pleasure*, 1948)

pipe n

1. vagina. This 19th-century usage puns on the sense of tube and the device one smokes.
2. penis. This usage, based on shape, also dates back to the 19th century. See also **lay pipe** (under **lay**).
pipe-cleaner is 19th-century usage for vagina.
pipe-job is a mid-20th-century term for fellatio. See also **blow job** (under **blow**).

pipkin n

female genitals. This 17th-century colloquialism is based on the standard term meaning a small **pot**, and also alludes to pip, a small seed (egg) for reproduction. The term has been obsolete since the 19th century.

• "He became one of her earliest suitors, and was very importunate with her to have the cracking of her pipkin."
(Edward Ward, *London Spy*, 1699)

pisser n
penis or female genitals. This 19th-century colloquialism refers to the urinary function associated with each.

piss-proud n
morning erection sometimes caused by the need to urinate. This is a 19th-century colloquialism. *See also* **pride of the morning** and **proud**.

pistol n
penis. This 16th-century literary term is one of many warlike words for penis.
• "... a Switzer in the duchess' bed-chamber ... with a pistol in his great cod-piece."
(John Webster, *The Duchess of Malfi*, 1623)

piston, piston rod n
penis. These 20th-century terms refer to the movement of a piston and are reinforced by the sound of "piss." *See also* **rod**.

pit n British
vagina. This 17th-century term is based on the sense meaning cavity. It is now obsolete. **Pit of darkness** is a literary variant. *See also* **cave**.

pit job n
sexual intercourse in the armpit. This is 20th-century usage. *See also* **bagpipe** and **job**.

pitch n American
pederast or inserter. This is mid-20th-century underworld usage. *See also* **catch**.

pitcher n
vagina. Based on the container sense of the term, and found especially in the phrase **crack a pitcher**, this is a 17th-century term.
• "She is resolved never more to venture her pitcher to the well."
(William Wycherley, *Love in a Wood*, 1672)

pity fuck n American
sexual intercourse engaged in because one partner feels pity for the other. This is a recent expression, usually said of a woman.

pizzle n
penis. This 17th-century standard term for a bull's penis is applied colloquially to the human penis.

place of sixpence sinfulness n phrase British
brothel. This 17th-century euphemism reflects the price of "sin" at the time.
• "Go sail with the rest of your bawdy-traffickers to the place of sixpenny sinfulness."
(Thomas Dekker, *Westward Hoe*, 1607)

placket n
1. woman considered as a sex object. Placket was a standard term in the 17th century for **skirt** or **petticoat**. The sexual usage is obsolete.
2. vagina. Placket also meant a slit at the waist of a petticoat. **Placket-hole** is a variant. *See also* **hole** and **slit**.
• "Keep thy foot out of brothels, thy hands out of plackets."
(William Shakespeare, *King Lear*, 1605)
placket-racket is a 17th-century term for penis.

plague, the plague n

American

syphilis or gonorrhea. This is mid-20th-century usage. *See also* **clap** and **pox**.

plank n

penis, especially an erect one. This is a 20th-century colloquialism. *See also* **pole**.

plank v

copulate. This term is used of men.

plate v, *British*

fellate. This 20th-century Cockney rhyming slang term is influenced by the licking of a plate.

plate of ham, a 20th-century Cockney rhyming slang term meaning fellatio, is based on the rhyme with **gam**.

play v

engage in sexual activity. This euphemism has been employed since the 14th century.

play around is a recent expression meaning copulate, usually illicitly.

play at all fours is a 19th-century British expression meaning copulate.

play at in and out is a 17th-century British euphemism for copulate. *See also* **in-and-out** (under **in**).

play at lift leg is an 18th-century British euphemism meaning copulate. *See also* **lift one's leg**.

play doctor is a 20th-century euphemism for sex, based on children's use of the phrase to describe their playful examination of one another.

playground is 19th-century British usage for female genitals and 20th-century American usage for breasts, from the male point of view.

play hanky-panky is a 19th-century colloquialism for copulate, punning on foolishness and cheating. *See also* **hanky-panky**.

play house is an early 20th-century American colloquialism for copulate.

play one's ace is a 19th-century expression for copulate, said of women, since **ace** means the female genitals and puns on the highest card or winning play.

play solitaire is a 19th-century euphemism for masturbate, based on the card game played alone.

play the flute and **play the horn** are 20th-century expressions meaning fellate, since **flute** and **horn** are terms for penis and both instruments are blown.

play the national indoor game is a 20th-century jocular expression meaning copulate. The phrase extends the sports metaphor and confirms the national popularity of sex. *See also* **national indoor game** and **sport**.

play the organ is an early 20th-century colloquialism meaning copulate. *See also* **organ**.

play the piano is 20th-century jocular gay usage meaning perform anilingus, based on the Russian pianist Rimsky-Korsakov; the first syllable of his name provides the term **rim**.

play the trombone is a 19th-century term for copulate, said of men, based on the sliding in and out of the trombone; it is reinforced by the **bone** in trombone.

plaything is a colloquialism for the penis or the vagina dating back to the 19th century. *See also* **thing**.

play with oneself is a 19th-century euphemism meaning masturbate, still commonly used today.

please v

copulate. This is a 17th-century euphemism.

pleasure n

1. orgasm. This euphemism refers to the feeling an orgasm generates. It dates back to the 16th century.

2. sexual intercourse. This euphemism is found in the expressions **act of pleasure** and **deed of pleasure**.

pleasure boat is a 19th-century term for female genitals, since **boat** provides an image of the vulva.

pleasure garden is a 17th-century colloquialism for female genitals, as is **pleasure ground**. *See also* **garden** and **playground**.

pleasure lady is a 17th-century British euphemism for prostitute. *See also* **lady**.

plonker n British

penis. This coinage dates back to the early 20th century.

- "If she's game and wants your plonker, wear a Jiffi so you can bonk her."
(Slogan for Jiffi brand condoms, 1988)

plow, plough v

copulate. This literary term, said of men, dates back to the 17th century. It suggests both working in a groove and sowing seeds.

- "Royal Wench!
She made great Caesar lay his
    sword to bed:
He plough'd her and she
    cropp'd."
(William Shakespeare, *Antony and Cleopatra*, 1607)

pluck v British

1. deflower. This is a 17th-century euphemism. *See also* **flower**.
2. copulate. This is possibly a euphemism for **fuck**.

plug v

copulate. Said of men, and derived from the standard sense of the term, meaning insert and fill, this usage dates back to the 18th century.

- "Three hours with him had passed, the frigging seemed useless, . . . so I began to think of letting him go, and plugging Sarah to finish."
(Anonymous, *My Secret Life*, 1890)

plug tail is 18th-century coinage for penis. *See also* **tail**.

plum, plum-tree n

female genitals. These 16th-century literary terms are probably based on a plum being a juicy fruit and having a characteristic groove on its side.

plums n pl American

testicles. Based on shape, this is 20th-century usage.

plumbing n

male genitals. This 20th-century colloquialism refers to piping and waterworks.

plunger n American

penis. This recent colloquialism extends the plumbing metaphor.

plush n

female pubic hair. This 19th-century term alludes to soft pile. *See also* **fur**.

pocket n

vagina. This 19th-century usage, now obsolete, is an example of a container term.

pocketbook is another term for the vagina, but beyond its container sense it refers to the value contained in a pocketbook, specifically **money**, a euphemism for vagina. *See also* **book** and **purse**.

pocket pool n

male masturbation through a trouser pocket. This 20th-century expression puns on the parlor game that uses **sticks** and **balls**. **Pocket billiards** is an English variation.

pocket the red v phrase British

copulate. This obsolete 19th-century expression relies on the sports metaphor of billiards, where red puns on the red ball and on a red, engorged, penis. *See also* **lose the match and pocket the stakes**.

point n

penis or glans. This is a 17th-century colloquialism. *See also* **end**.
pointer is a 19th-century colloquialism for penis, based on a pointer being a **rod** or measuring **stick**.

points n pl American

nipples. This is a 20th-century colloquialism.

poke v

copulate. Said of men, and based on the standard sense, meaning jab or make a **hole**, this dates back to the 18th century. *See also* **prod**.

poke n

1. act of copulation. This is a 19th-century colloquialism. **A poke in the bush is worth two in the hand**, a spoof of a maxim, attests to the superiority of copulation over masturbation. *See also* **bush**.
- "BLOKE NEEDS POKE/SEND PICS/BOX 6/"
  (Kit Wright, "Personal Advertisement," *Poems 1974–1983*)

poke-hole is 19th-century British usage for vagina. *See also* **hole**.
poke party is a 20th-century gay expression for a male homosexual orgy.
2. woman considered as a sex object. This derogatory term dates back to the 19th century.

poker n

penis, especially an erect one. This is a 19th-century term. *See also* **red-hot poker**.

pole n

erect penis. This 19th-century term is based on shape.
- "My pole is shivering stiff between my legs."
  (J.P. Donleavy, *The Beastly Beatitudes of Balthazar B.*, 1968)

polecat is a 17th-century word for prostitute. *See also* **cat**.
pole-work is 19th-century British coinage for copulation. *See also* **work**.

polish one's ass (arse) on the top sheet v phrase

copulate. This 19th-century jocular expression, said of men, assumes that the man is on top of the woman and underneath the top sheet. *See also* **sheets**.

polish the knob v phrase

fellate. This is a 20th-century expression. *See also* **knob**.

poll-axe n

penis. This term dates back to the 16th century. *See also* **club**, **pike**, and **weapon**.

pollute v

masturbate. This 17th-century euphemism is based on the standard sense meaning defile or make dirty.

Polyphemus n

penis. This obsolete 19th-century literary term refers to Polyphemus, a one-eyed creature in Greek mythology. *See also* **Cyclops**.

pom-poms n pl

breasts. Possibly derived from the standard sense meaning a ship's guns mounted in pairs, or from the sense of the fluffy balls used by cheerleaders and often held in front of the chest, this is 20th-century usage.

ponce n

1. pimp. This term, possibly derived from "pounce," dates back to the 19th century.
2. young male who is the lover of an older woman. This is a 20th-century underworld term.

pond n

vagina. This 17th-century literary term is based on the vagina being a container and wet.

poof, pouf, poove, pooftah, poofter, poufter n

effeminate male homosexual. These 20th-century derogatory terms, mainly Australian and British, derive from the French *pouffe*, meaning "puff" or "stuffed seat."
• "He made a feeble attempt to mock my accent. 'You all talk like poufs.' "
(Graham Greene, *The Quiet American*, 1955)

poontang n

1. sexual intercourse. This 19th-century word may derive from the French *putain*, meaning "prostitute." In the 19th and early 20th centuries, it was used especially to indicate copulation with a black woman. **Poon** is a variant.
• ". . . perennial playboy, forever talking about poon. He had no other topic. Poon was his major and all else besides."
(Morris Lurie, *Seven Books for Grossman*, 1983)
2. vagina. **Poonoo** is a Caribbean variant of this 19th-century term.

poonts n pl British

breasts. Possibly influenced by **poontang** or derived from **points**, this is a 19th-century term.

poop n

buttocks. Dating back to the 17th century, and based on the poop being the back of a ship, this is a colloquialism.
poop-hole, meaning anus, dates back to the 17th century.

poop v British

copulate. This is an obsolete 17th-century usage. The word is now used strictly to mean defecate.

poove n

See **poof**.

pop v American

copulate. Said of men, and used especially in the phrase **pop it in**, this is mid-20th-century usage.

poperine pear n

penis or penis and scrotum. This literary term, based on shape, puns on "pop her in" or "pop it in."
• "Oh Romeo! That she were, oh, that she were
An open arse, thou a poperin pear!"
(William Shakespeare, *Romeo and Juliet*, 1595)

poppa n

lesbian. Based on poppa meaning father, this is 20th-century usage.

pork v

copulate. This term, said of men, and dating back to the 19th century, suggests animality and food. It also rhymes with **dork** and **fork**.
pork-sword is a 20th-century term for penis. See *also* **sword**.

porn n

pornography. This colloquial abbreviation dates back to the 1960s. **Pornography**, a standard term dating back to the mid-19th century, is de-

fined as material or behavior that is intended to excite one sexually. The term stems from the Greek *porne*, meaning "prostitute."
- "Porn is altogether pragmatic. It exists to stimulate and satisfy an appetite just the way cookbooks do, except the porn reader always has his ingredients to hand."
(Irma Kurtz, *Mantalk*, 1986)

porno, another colloquial abbreviation, is used as a noun and an adjective.

porthole n
1. anus. This usage dates back to the 17th century. It is based on portholes being small round holes or windows on ships.
2. vagina. *See also* **hole**.

Port Said garter n British
condom. Dating back to World War II, when the British were in North Africa and Egypt, this is military usage. Port Said is a town at the north end of the Suez Canal.

Portuguese pump n British
masturbation. This 19th-century nautical expression is an example of the attribution of "unnatural" sexual practices to foreigners. *See also* **Italian fashion**.

possess v
copulate with. Dating back to the 15th century, this word is said especially of men. Though standard in centuries past, it is now considered a formal term, especially in the expression **possess someone carnally**. *See also* **occupy** and **take**.

post a letter v phrase British
copulate. This 19th-century colloquialism refers to putting something into a letter **box**. It may also have been influenced by **letter**, meaning condom.

posteriors n
buttocks. This standard term, based on position relative to the face, dates back to the late 16th century.
- "Her posteriors, plump, smooth and prominent . . . that splendidly filled the eye . . ."
(John Cleland, *Fanny Hill: Memoirs of a Woman of Pleasure*, 1749)

pot n
1. *British* female genitals. This 17th-century usage is based on the sense of container. *See also* **kettle** and **pan**.
- "In love I'm not so simple,
  But to observe she has a Dimple.
  And such a one, as who would not
  Put all his Flesh into the Pot?"
(Charles Cotton, *Burlesque upon Burlesque, or the Scoffer Scofft*, 1675)
2. lesbian. Possibly based on the obsolete sense of pot, meaning a woman, this is a 20th-century term.

potato finger n
1. penis. This obsolete 17th-century expression is based on shape.
2. dildo. This usage follows from the above definition.

pouf, poufter n
See **poof**.

poultry n pl British
women considered as sex objects. This is a 17th-century derogatory term. *See also* **chick**, **hen**, and **quail**.

pound v American
copulate. This late 19th-century term ties in with other aggressive terms such as **hammer**, **hit**, and **nail**. **pound off** and **pound one's meat** are 20th-century expressions for masturbate, said of men. *See also* **meat**.

poundcake queen n

homosexual male who becomes sexually excited from being defecated upon. This is a mid-20th-century gay expression. See also **poundcakes** and **queen**.

poundcakes n

buttocks. This is 20th-century usage. See also **cake**.

pounders n

testicles. This 17th-century colloquialism is possibly based on the assumed weight of the testicles.

pouter n British

vagina or vulva. Based on the labia as lips, this is a 19th-century term.

powder puff n American

effeminate male homosexual. This is early 20th-century usage. See also **poof**.

pox n

syphilis. This was a standard term from the 16th through the 18th century; by the 19th century it had become slang. It derives from the plural of "pock," a mark or pustule on the skin that is a possible sign of the disease. See also **clap**.

prack n American

male genitals. This late 19th-century southern dialectal word may have been influenced by **prick**.

practice in the milky way v phrase British

fondle a woman's breasts. This is an early 17th-century jocular expression. See also **milky way** (under **milk bottles**).

prang v British

copulate. This is early 20th-century coinage. Since the mid-20th century, the term has meant crash, as in an automobile accident. Perhaps this collision sense was influenced by the sexual sense, for which the origin is unknown.

pranny n British

female genitals. This 19th-century colloquialism may have been influenced by **fanny**.

prat n

1. buttocks. Dating back to the 16th century, this term could derive from "prate," an obsolete word for idleness.
- "I'm a shmo about tennis, so if I fall on my prat a time or two you have to bear with me."
(David Delman, *Sudden Death*, 1972)
2. British vagina. This 19th-century usage is obsolete.

pray with the knees upwards v phrase British

copulate. This jocular 18th-century expression, said of women, implies that the woman is on her back, knees upward, in the act of copulation. The equating of sex with religion is fairly common, since there are sacred and profane aspects to sexuality in all human cultures. See also **kneel at the altar** and **religious observances**.

pregnant adj

carrying a fetus in the womb. This has been a standard English term since the 15th century. It derives from the Latin *prae* + *gnas*, meaning "prebirth." *Gnas* is related to *gignere*, meaning "produce." Though an innocuous term today, from Victorian times through World War II the word was taboo. **Preggers** is a 20th-century British colloquial abbreviation.

premises n British

vagina. This 19th-century usage is an example of the metaphor of vagina as container. See also **occupy**.

prepuce n

1. foreskin. This anatomical term dates back to the 15th century.
2. fold of skin covering the clitoris. This is also an anatomical term.

pretty n

1. British female genitals. This is 19th-century usage. See also **ugly**.
2. young boy unfamiliar with homosexuality. This is a 20th-century gay term.

priapus n

penis. This literary term has been in use since the 17th century. It derives from the Greek *Priapos*, god of gardens.

- "Priapus squeez'd, one Snowball did emit."
  (John Wilmot, the earl of
  Rochester, *Works*, 1600)

priapism is a literary term for an erect penis that dates back to the 18th century. It is also a medical term for a condition in which the penis is constantly erect. Lastly, it is an 18th-century British euphemism for pornography.

the price of greens n

phrase British

cost of a prostitute. This is a 19th-century euphemism. See also **greens**.

prick n

penis. This usage was standard English from the 16th through the 17th century; it derives from the verb sense meaning pierce. Prick was once a term of endearment, but since the 18th century it has been used in its slang sense. It is also a common term for an obnoxious or foolish male.

- "I would wish all young maids,
    before they be sick,
  To enquire for a young man that
    has a good prick."
  (Thomas Heywood, *The Rape of
  Lucrece*, 1608)
- "When the prick stands up, the brain gets buried in the ground!"
  (Philip Roth, *Portnoy's Complaint*, 1969)

prick-juice is 20th-century coinage for semen. See also **juice**.

prick parade is a 20th-century British military colloquialism for venereal inspection.

prick pocket is 20th-century usage for vagina, punning on pickpocket. See also **pocket**.

prick pride, meaning an erection, dates back to the 16th century. See also **morning pride**.

prick-teaser is a mid-20th-century American expression for a woman who teases a man sexually without permitting sexual intercourse. See also **cockteaser** (under **cock**).

prickle n

penis. This literary term dates back to the 17th century and is now obsolete.

- "And taking in hand my prickle, firm to the utmost of its height, she nailed it into her coynte."
  (Sir Richard Burton, *Arabian Nights*, 1885–1888)

pride n

sexual appetite or interest. This euphemism dates back to the 15th century.

in pride, meaning sexually aroused, was a British colloquialism from the 17th to the 19th century.

pride and joy is a 20th-century colloquialism for penis.

pride of the morning is a 19th-century British colloquialism for an erection. See also **morning pride** and **piss-proud**.

prides is a 19th-century colloquialism for the genitals of either sex.

prig v British

copulate. This 17th-century term may have been influenced by **frig** and **prick**.

princess of the pavement n phrase Australian

prostitute. This is a 20th-century expression. See also **streetwalker**.

privateer n British

independent prostitute. This is a 19th-century euphemism.

private parts, privities, privates, parts n pl

genitals. These euphemisms date back to the 16th century.

• "It had ever been the custom of the family . . . that the eldest son of it should have free ingress, egress and regress into foreign parts before marriage—not only for the sake of bettering his own private parts . . . but simply for the mere delectation of his fancy. . . ."
(Laurence Sterne, The Life and Opinions of Tristram Shandy, 1759–1767)

private property is a 19th-century colloquialism for the genitals, based on private ownership.

privy-hole is a 19th-century British euphemism for vagina. See also **hole**.

privy member is a 17th-century British euphemism for penis. See also **member**.

prize n

sexual intercourse. This 16th-century literary term puns on prize meaning something valuable that is won and the verb sense of force open.

pro n

prostitute. This early 20th-century euphemism is an abbreviation of professional.

• "Even now, in countries where there is no disgrace attached, almost every adult male who can afford it will have his innings with a pro."
(Irma Kurtz, Mantalk, 1986)

procurer n

pimp. This standard term, dating back to the 16th century, derives from the Latin procurare, meaning "take care of" a person.

prod v

copulate. This 19th-century term is used of men. See also **nudge, nudge** and **poke**.

promiscuous adj

having many sexual partners. This standard English term derives from the Latin pro + miscere, meaning "mix together," and dates back to the early 17th century. **Promiscuity** is the standard noun.

• "[A promiscuous person is] someone who is getting more sex than you are."
(Victor Lownes, quoted in N. Mackwood, In and Out: Debrett 1980–81, 1981)

promised land n

female genitals. This 19th-century euphemism derives from the biblical term for the homeland promised to the Children of Israel. See also **heaven** and **paradise**.

• "She took the taller by the arm, 'I'll guide you with my hand.' Alas! the lad shot off before He reached the Promised Land!"
(Anonymous, "Two Virgin Lads," in Harold Hart, editor, The Complete Immortalia, 1971)

prong n

penis. This is a mid-20th-century term. *See also* **fork**, **prick**, and **stick**.

prophylactic n

contraceptive device, especially a condom. This standard term is based on the meaning of anything that protects one from disease. It dates back to the 17th century and derives from the Greek *phylax*, meaning "guard." **propho** is early 20th-century American military usage for condom.

prostitute n

person, especially a woman, who offers to have sex for money. This standard term dates back to the early 17th century. It stems from the Latin *statuere*, meaning "station." In Noah Webster's bowdlerized Bible, **whore** was changed to the more acceptable prostitute. The verb usage, namely, to prostitute, predates the noun usage by a century. The noun **prostitution** dates back to the mid-16th century. **Pross, prosso, prossy,** and **prosser** are all abbreviations. Prosso is Australian usage from the 20th century, while the others are all 19th-century terms.

protein n

semen. This recent 20th-century usage alludes to protein being necessary for the creation of life. *See also* **vitamins**.
protein queen is a 20th-century gay term for a male homosexual fellator. *See also* **queen**.

proud adj

sexually excited. This has been a colloquialism since the 16th century. *See also* **piss-proud**.
proud below the navel is a British expression for lascivious, dating back to the 17th century.

pruney adj American

sexually aroused. This is a 20th-century dialectal term from the Ozark region.

pubes n

pubic hair or the pubic region. This standard anatomical English word dates back to the 16th century. It derives from the Latin *puber*, meaning "pubescent." **Pubic hair** is standard English dating back to the 19th century.

public ledger n British

prostitute. Based on the pun of being open to all for inspection, this is 18th-century usage. *See also* **receiver general**.

pudding n

1. penis. Dating back to the 17th century, this usage alludes to a sausage-shaped pudding. *See also* **sausage**.
pud is a 20th-century term for penis. It is an abbreviation of pudding or **pudenda**.
2. sexual intercourse. Based on the food and eating metaphor, this is a 17th-century term.
3. semen. This late 17th-century usage may derive from the appearance of certain puddings such as rice pudding.

pudenda n

genitals, especially female. This formal euphemism derives from the Latin *pudere*, meaning "be ashamed." It is the plural of **pudendum** and dates back to the 14th century.
• "Sanskrit manuscripts show Indian women with shaved pudenda."
(Eric Trimmer, *The Visual Dictionary of Sex*, 1977)

pull a train *v phrase American*

copulate. Said of a woman who copulates with many men in succession, this is a mid-20th-century expression.

pull off, pull one's peter, pull one's pudding *v*
phrase

masturbate. These 19th-century expressions are used of men. *See also* **peter** and **pudding**.

pull-over *n American*

man who is regarded as easy to persuade to copulate. This is a mid-20th-century colloquialism. *See also* **push-over** (under **push**).

pull wire *v phrase*

masturbate. This 20th-century expression is said of men. *See also* **wire**.

pulpit *n*

female genitals. This obsolete 17th-century literary term implying worship exemplifies a religion metaphor. *See also* **kneel at the altar** and **religious observances**.

pulse *n*

1. vagina. Dating back to the 16th century, this term is probably based on the throb of a pulse or on pulse meaning a leguminous seed.
2. erect penis. Based on the throbbing of engorged blood in the erect penis, this is 19th-century usage.

pump *v American*

copulate. Said of men, and based on the action of a pump, this usage dates back to the 18th century.
pumped is 20th-century American usage for pregnant, as is **pumped up**.
pump off is a 19th-century term for masturbate.

pump one's pickle is a 20th-century expression for masturbate, said of men. *See also* **pickle**.
pump one's python is a 20th-century American expression for masturbate, said of men. *See also* **python**.

pump *n*

1. vagina. This 17th-century usage refers to the vagina as a container.
2. penis. Based on a pump having a handle, this is 17th-century usage.
pump-handle is an early 18th-century British term for penis.

pumpkin *n American*

female genitals. "Kin" means little, thus pumpkin means little **pump** in this 19th-century usage.

pumps *n American*

breasts. This early 20th-century American term is based on the breasts as pumps for milk.

punch *v*

1. copulate. Based on the standard sense meaning **hit**, this is 18th-century usage.
2. deflower. This is based on an obsolete sense meaning stab.

puncture *v British*

deflower. Based on the standard sense of make a **hole**, this usage originated in the 19th century.

punish percy in the palm *v phrase*

masturbate. This jocular 20th-century expression is said of men. Punish suggests self-abuse, while **percy** personifies the penis.

punk *n*

1. prostitute. Dating back to the 16th century, this term may derive from **puncture**.

2. male homosexual. This is 19th-century usage.

punk-kid is a mid-20th-century expression for a homosexual boy or catamite.

punk v British

pimp. This usage dates back to the 17th century.

punse n

female genitals. This 19th-century coinage stems from the Yiddish term meaning to **punch**.

pup n American

penis. This mid-20th-century term is used especially in the phrase **beat the pup**, meaning masturbate.

puppies n pl

nipples. This is a 20th-century gay term. See also **paps**.

purple adj American

extremely pornographic. This colloquialism indicates a grade more extreme than **blue**, and dates back to the early 20th century.

purse n

vagina. Dating back to the 17th century, this container term suggests the contents, namely, **money**. See also **wallet**.

push v British

copulate. This usage dates back to the 17th century. Variations include **do a push**, said of men, and **stand a push**, said of women.

a push in the bush is worth two in the hand is a jocular 19th-century British expression stating that one act of copulation is worth two acts of masturbation. It puns on the maxim "A bird in the hand is worth two in the bush." See also **bush** and **hand**.

push on is a colloquial 18th-century expression meaning copulate.

push-over is an early 20th-century American colloquialism for a woman who is regarded as easy to persuade to copulate. See also **pull-over**.

puss n

female genitals. The **cat** has long been associated with women, especially as sexual beings. By the 17th century, puss became a term of endearment for a woman. By the mid-17th century, it was applied to the female genitals.

• "Aeneas, here's a Health to thee,
  To Pusse and to good company."
  (Charles Cotton, *Virgile Travestie*, 1664)

pussy n

1. female genitals. This usage dates back to the 17th century.

pussy-bumping is mid-20th-century coinage for lesbian activity. See also **bumper to bumper** (under **bump**).

2. woman considered as a sex object.

pussy-struck is a 20th-century colloquialism meaning obsessed with women sexually. An Ozark dialectal variant is **pussy-simple**. See also **cunt-struck**.

pussy-whipped is a mid-20th-century colloquialism for henpecked.

• "The word pussie is now used of a woman."
  (Philip Stubbes, *The Anatomie of Abuses*, 1583)

3. American sexual intercourse. This early 20th-century usage reflects a man's perspective.

• "Papa's in jail!
  Mama's on bail!
  The baby's on the corner
  Shouting pussy for sale!"
  (Lyrics from "Mr. Jelly Roll," early 20th century)

pussy posse is 20th-century usage for a police squad, or vice squad, dealing with prostitution.

4. anus. This is mid-20th-century male homosexual usage.

put and take v phrase British

copulate. This is a 20th-century expression.

put four corners on the spit v phrase

copulate. This 19th-century expression now obsolete, is based on the spreading of the legs in copulation and conjures up the image of roasting **meat**. **Spit**, also obsolete, means copulate or ejaculate.

put it to her v phrase American

copulate. Said of men, this is a 20th-century expression. See also **it**.

put lipstick on his dipstick v phrase American

fellate. This is mid-20th-century usage. See also **dipstick** and **lipstick**.

put the boots to v phrase American

copulate. Based on the use of the expression in horse riding, this is an early 20th-century expression. See also **mount** and **ride**.

putter n

erect penis. Possibly based on the standard sense of a golf stick, and punning on put and **hit**, this is a 20th-century euphemism.

puttock n British

prostitute. This obsolete 16th-century term was probably influenced by put and **buttock**.

putz n

penis. Dating back to the 19th century, this word derives from the Yiddish meaning of "an ornament." Like

schmuck, the term is derogatory when applied to a person.

python n

penis. Found especially in the phrases **pump one's python**, meaning masturbate, and "syphon the python," meaning urinate, this is 20th-century usage.

quagmire n

vagina. This 16th-century literary term refers to a quagmire as a soft, wet place as well as a place of entrapment. See also **trap**.

quail n

prostitute. Commonly used throughout the 17th and 18th centuries, this usage is based on a quail being a game bird. The term has more recently been applied to females regarded as sex objects. See also **chick** and **hen**.

quaint n

female genitals. Dating back to the 14th century, this word is a version of **cunt**. It derives from the Old French coint, meaning "pleasant" or "dainty." Since the 17th century, quaint has been dialectal usage in northern Great Britain.

qualify v British

succeed in copulating. This is 19th-century jocular usage. See also **score**.

quarry n

vagina. This 18th-century colloquialism puns on the two standard meanings of the term, namely, a **mine** or excavation and prey or game that is hunted. *See also* **venery**.

queen n

male homosexual. This usage derives from quean, an obsolete term for prostitute. Quean, in turn, stems from the Old English *cwene*, meaning "woman." From this neutral meaning came the sense of both female monarch and prostitute. As a common term for male homosexual, the word dates back to the late 19th century.
• "Boy George is all England needs—another queen who can't dress."
(Joan Rivers)

queen of holes n

vagina. This 17th-century literary euphemism refers to the vagina as the most important female **hole**.

queer n, adj

male homosexual. This is early 20th-century derogatory usage. Since the mid-20th century the term has also been applied to lesbians.
• "America I'm putting my queer shoulder to the wheel."
(Allen Ginsberg, "America," 1956)

quickie, quicky n American

brief or hurried sexual act. This colloquialism dates back to the mid-20th century. *See also* **snatch**.
• "A romp and a quickie,
is all little dickie
means when he speaks of
romance."
(Cole Porter, "Most Gentlemen Don't Like Love," 1938)

quid n British

female genitals. This 19th-century usage may have been influenced by **quim** or by another British meaning of the term, namely, a pound sterling. *See also* **money**.

quiff n

female genitals. This 18th-century term may have derived from **quim**. In standard English, quiff means a forelock of hair or a clever trick; both can be seen as connected in meaning to the female genitals, but both are late 19th-century coinage.

quiff v

copulate. This is an 18th-century colloquialism.
• "By quiffing with Cullies three pound she had got."
(Thomas D'Urfey, *Wit and Mirth*, 1719)

quim n

female genitals. This common term dates back to the 16th century and may derive from the Celtic *cwm*, meaning "valley" or "cleft." The *Oxford English Dictionary* relates the word to queme, an obsolete English term meaning fitting or suitable. Grose, in his *Dictionary of the Vulgar Tongue*, 1811, defines quim as "The private parts of a woman; perhaps from the Spanish *quemar*, to burn."
• "On her quim and herself she depends for support."
(Broadside ballad, "The Harlot Unmask'd," circa 1707)

quim bush, **quim whiskers**, and **quim wig** are all 19th-century British terms for female pubic hair. *See also* **bush**, **whisker**, and **wig**.

quimming is a 19th-century British term for copulating or pursuing women for the purposes of copulation, as in **go quimming**.

quimsby, **quimmy**, and **quimsy** are all 19th-century British variants of quim.

quim-stake and **quim-wedge** are 19th-century British terms for penis. *See also* **stake** and **wedge**.

quiver n

vagina. This 16th-century literary euphemism puns on a case for **arrows** and the verb meaning **shake**.

• "Since strangers lodge their
arrows in thy quiver,
Dear dame, I pray you yet the
cause deliver. . . ."
(Sir John Harington, "Of an
Heroical Answer of a Great
Roman Lady to her Husband,"
1591)

quoit n Australian
anus. This 20th-century colloquialism is based on a quoit being a **ring**.
quoits is a colloquialism for buttocks.

R

rabbit v British
copulate. This 19th-century meaning stems from the rabbit's propensity
for frequent copulation. See also **live
rabbit**.
rabbit pie is 19th-century British
usage for prostitute. See also **pie**.

racks n pl American
breasts. This 20th-century coinage
is based on the notion of meat racks
and of racks being well-stacked.

radish n
glans or head of the penis. This
20th-century usage is based on shape.
See also **acorn** and **onion**.

rag n American
sanitary napkin. This is a 20th-cen-
tury colloquialism
on the rag is a mid-20th-century colloquialism meaning to be menstruating.
rag-time is a euphemism for menstruation.

rail n British
erection. This 20th-century term
refers to a rail's firmness.

rails n pl British
labia. This recent term is used especially by men.

raincoat n
condom. This 20th-century jocular
euphemism alludes to the sense of
protection. See also **diving suit** and
overcoat.

rake n
sexually promiscuous man. This
colloquialism, common since the
17th century, is an abbreviation of
rakehell, meaning lecher or libertine.
Rakery means lechery.
• "He . . . instructed his lordship in
all the rakery and intrigues of the
lewd town."
(Roger North, The Life of Francis
North, Baron of Guildford, 1734)
rake out is 19th-century usage for
copulate, said of men, based on a
rakehell and on the movement of rak-
ing.

ram v
1. copulate. This 19th-century
term refers back to the horned animal
and the standard meaning to push. A
ram caught in a thicket has long been
a metaphor for copulation in the Middle East.
rammer is 19th-century coinage for
penis. **Battering ram** is a variant.
ramrod is a colloquial term for penis
that dates back to the 17th century.
See also **rod**.
2. perform anal intercourse. This
is 20th-century usage.
ram-job is a mid-20th-century
American term meaning an act of
anal intercourse.

randy *adj*

lustful or lecherous. Derived from "rand," meaning rave or rant, this word dates back to the 18th century. Only since the 1960s has the word become colloquial and acceptable in conversation.

• "She'll be randy directly her belly is filled."
(Anonymous, *My Secret Life*, 1890)

ranger *n*

penis. This 18th-century usage may allude to a ranger being a rover, that is, sexually promiscuous.

rape *n, v*

forcible sexual intercourse without the consent of one party. This standard term dates back to the 15th century. Perhaps because rape is a serious crime, few euphemisms have evolved.
date rape is a recent term for a rape committed by an acquaintance of the victim.

rasp *n British*

female genitals. This obsolete 19th-century usage refers to something that rasps or is rubbed.

rasp *v British*

copulate. Usually said of men, this is an obsolete 19th-century term.

raspberries *n pl American*

nipples, especially erect ones. This is a recent colloquialism, based on shape. *See also* **strawberries**.

rattlesnake *n Australian*

prostitute. The perils of prostitution, from the male perspective, are strongly expressed in this 20th-century term.

raunchy *adj*

smutty or obscene. The etymology of this 20th-century colloquialism is uncertain, though it may have been influenced by **randy** or derived from the Italian *rancio*, meaning "rotten" or "overripe."

• "At the raunchy end of the spectrum are [computer game] programs like Sexxcapades, which is a sort of kinky Monopoly, and MacPlaymate."
("Erotic Electronic Encounters," *Time*, September 23, 1991)

raw meat *n*

penis. This expression dates back to the 18th century. *See also* **meat**.

read braille *v phrase*

caress sexually. This jocular 20th-century expression refers to fingering.

ready *adj*

sexually willing or prepared. This colloquialism dates back to the 19th century.
ready to spit is a 20th-century British phrase meaning ready to ejaculate. *See also* **spit**.

real thing *n*

vagina. This is a 19th-century euphemism. *See also* **thing**.

ream *v*

1. perform anilingus. This is 20th-century usage. *See also* **rim**.
2. perform anal intercourse. This 20th-century usage is based on the standard sense of widening a **hole**.
reamer is an early 20th-century American underworld term for penis.

receive holy communion *v phrase*

fellate. This 20th-century jocular expression alludes to kneeling while receiving holy communion. *See also* **kneel at the altar** and **religious observances**.

receiver *n American*

1. catamite. This is a 20th-century gay term. *See also* **catch, insertee,** and **insertor**.
2. fellator.

receiver general *n*

prostitute. This obsolete 19th-century expression is based on the sense of taking anyone. *See also* **public ledger**.

receiving set *n American*

female genitals. This is a 20th-century colloquialism.

red *adj*

suggesting sexual heat or passion, crimson color, or blood.
red ace is 19th-century usage for reddish female pubic hair. *See also* **ace**.
red-cap and **red-end** are 20th-century British terms for penis. They refer to the sometimes reddish glans at the tip. *See also* **end**.
red-hot poker is 19th-century British usage for penis. *See also* **hot** and **poker**.
red house, red lamp, and **red light** are all euphemisms for brothel. Red lights have signified brothels since the 19th century. **Red-light district** stands for an area that contains brothels as well as adult video stores and bookstores, peep shows, strip joints, and the like.
red onion is 20th-century American usage for female genitals. *See also* **cabbage**.
red sails in the sunset is a jocular 20th-century expression for menstruation.
red sister is early 20th-century American coinage for prostitute. *See also* **sister**.

red wings is a humorous award given to Hell's Angels who perform cunnilingus on a menstruating partner. *See also* **brown wings**.

regulator *n British*

female genitals. This obsolete 18th-century euphemism refers to the female genitals as regulators of men's sexual activity. *See also* **controlling part**.

relations, sexual relations *n pl*

sexual intercourse. These are 20th-century euphemisms.

relieve *v*

1. copulate. This 19th-century euphemism refers to the relief from sexual desire that follows copulation.
2. ejaculate. Derived from the sense above, this euphemism is said of men.
relieve oneself is a euphemism meaning masturbate.

religious observances *n pl*

sexual intercourse. This 20th-century humorous expression puns on religious seriousness and ritual, and suggests a devotion to having sex. *See also* **kneel at the altar, pray with the knees upward,** and **receive holy communion**.

relish *n British*

sexual intercourse. This obsolete 19th-century usage puns on **appetite** and enjoyment.

rest and be thankful *n phrase British*

female genitals. This obsolete 19th-century euphemism may be based on the postcoital male attitude of gratitude and the need for rest.

return naked to the womb v phrase

engage in incest (a man with his mother). This expression was used by Thomas Dekker in *The Shoemaker's Holiday*, 1600.

reverse western n

sexual intercourse with the woman on top of the man. This is a 20th century prostitutes' term for a position contrary to western custom. *See also* **missionary position** and **ride Saint George** (under **ride**).

rhubarb n

penis. This 19th-century usage is based on shape.

rhythm method n

contraception based on abstention from intercourse during the woman's presumed fertile period. This is a 20th-century colloquialism. *See also* **Vatican roulette**.

ribald n British

1. sexually promiscuous or lecherous man. Though rare today, this standard term has been in use since the 14th century. It derives from Middle English and originally meant a rascal.

2. pimp. This obsolete term dates back to the 14th century.

3. prostitute. This usage is obsolete.

ribald adj

sexually crude and lusty. This has been standard English usage since the 16th century.

rice pudding n

semen. This 20th-century expression is based on similarity of appearance. *See also* **pudding**.

ride v

copulate. This common colloquialism is based on the similarity between being atop an animal and swaying, especially on a horse, and sexual intercourse. From the 14th through the 18th century, ride was standard English usage. From the 19th century on, the term became more informal. *See also* **horse** and **mount**.

ride a bicycle is a 20th-century expression for be bisexual, based on the "bi" in bicycle, and reinforced by ride.

ride bareback is a 20th-century expression for copulate without a condom, since bareback (no saddle) implies direct skin contact.

ride Saint George and **ride the dragon upon Saint George** are early 17th-century literary expressions for sexual intercourse with the woman on top of the man. The expressions derive from *The Mad Lover*, 1617, a play by John Fletcher. *See also* **reverse Western**.

ride the deck is an early 20th-century American expression for performing sodomy, where deck implies the buttocks.

ride n

act of copulation. This colloquialism dates back to the 16th century.

ride the rag, ride a white horse v phrase

have a menstrual period. These are 20th-century euphemisms. **Rag** and white horse both refer to a sanitary napkin.

rifle v British

copulate. This obsolete 17th-century term is said of men. The word's original meaning was to ransack or cut spiral grooves.

rim *v American*

perform anilingus. Based on the standard noun sense of an edge of a **hole**, this is 20th-century usage. *See also* **ream**.

• "As for rimming, even the thought of it was beyond the pale."
(David Feinberg, *Eighty-Sixed*, 1989)

rimadonna is a 20th-century American jocular term, punning on "prima donna," for a male homosexual who enjoys anilingus.

rim-job is a 20th-century term for an act of anilingus.

ring *n*

1. vagina. This colloquialism puns on circular shape and wedding ring. It dates back to the 16th century. *See also* **Carvel's ring**.

• "Never fail to have continually the ring of thy wife's Commodity upon thy finger."
(François Rabelais, *Gargantua and Pantagruel*, 1534)

2. anus. This is derived from the Latin *anus*, meaning "ring."

ring around the rosey is 20th-century gay usage for a male homosexual orgy, with men linked penis to anus. *See also* **rosey** and **daisy chain**.

ring the bell *v phrase*

American

manually stimulate the clitoris. This is a 20th-century euphemism. *See also* **bell**.

rip off *v phrase*

copulate. This 20th-century prostitute's jargon refers to another sense meaning exploit.

rise *v*

have or get an erection. This colloquialism dates back to the 17th century. A recent variation is **rise to the occasion**.

road *n*

female genitals. This term, in use since the 16th century, suggests a journey and a passageway. **Road to heaven** and **road to paradise** are variations.

road up for repairs is a jocular British colloquialism for menstruation.

rock *v*

copulate. This mid-20th-century usage is based on the reference to movement.

rock python *n British*

erect penis. This is a mid-20th-century term. *See also* **python** and **snake**.

rocks *n pl*

testicles. This is 20th-century usage. *See also* **pebbles** and **stones**.

get one's rocks off is a colloquialism for have sexual intercourse, said mainly of men.

rod *n*

penis. This colloquialism is based on shape. It dates back to the 18th century. A fuller version is **Aaron's rod**, based on the biblical story in which the rod performs miracles. *See also* **angle**, **handstaff**, **stick**, and **wand**.

roe *n*

semen. This colloquialism is based on the standard English word for the eggs or testes of fish and dates back to the 19th century. *See also* **milt**.

roger *n*

penis. Dating back to the 17th century, this example of personification possibly derives from the name frequently given to a bull.

roger *v*

copulate. This 18th-century term, used today mainly in Great Britain, is said in reference to men. The term is also applied to bulls copulating with cows.

- "Should not a Half-pay Officer roger for sixpence?" (James Boswell, *London Journal*, 1762)

roll *v*

copulate. This early 20th-century colloquialism is based on movement. *See also* **rock**, **shake**, and **jelly roll** (under **jelly**).

roller *n*

prostitute. This usage, based on **roll**, originated in the 19th century.

roller skate *v American*

copulate. This is a mid-20th-century expression. *See also* **roll**.

rolling-pin *n*

penis. This colloquial term goes back to the 19th century. *See also* **pin**.

roll in the hay *n phrase*

act of copulation. This is an early 20th-century colloquialism.

rolls *n pl*

buttocks. Based on shape, this is a 20th-century colloquialism.

roly-poly *n*

penis. Dating back to the 19th century, this term comes from the sense of a sweet or pudding made from rolled dough and filled with **jam** or **jelly**.

Roman night *n*

male homosexual orgy. This 20th-century gay usage refers back to Roman orgies.

romp *n*

1. prostitute. This is obsolete 17th-century coinage.

2. act of copulation. Derived from the verb, below, this is a modern colloquialism. *See also* **rump**.

romp *v*

copulate. This 19th-century colloquialism is based on the standard senses of be boisterous, move freely, and win easily.

rompworthy is a 20th-century colloquialism for sexually desirable.

rooster *n*

1. *American* penis. This obsolete 19th-century euphemism is based on the synonym **cock**.

2. *British* female genitals. This 19th-century euphemism refers to the place where the cock roosts.

root *n*

penis. Dating back to the 17th century, this word puns on shape and origin or source.

- "The gals up Rainy Creek they are full grown,
  They'll jump on a root like a dog on a bone." (Vance Randolph and George P. Wilson, *Down in the Holler*, 1953)

root *v Australian*

copulate. Probably based on the noun sense and on the standard verb sense of root and **rootle**, meaning poke about, this usage dates back to the 19th century *See also* **poke**.

rooty is a colloquialism for lustful.

rootle *v British*

copulate. This 19th-century meaning derives from the standard sense of poke about.

Rory O'More *n British*

prostitute. Based on the rhyme with **whore**, and probably influenced by the "more" in the name, this is 19th-century rhyming slang. Note also the derogatory imputation of prostitution to the Irish through the name.

rose n British
1. female genitals. This 18th-century literary usage is based on the appearance of the flower and the shape of the petals. Rose is one of a number of horticultural terms for the female genitals, such as **daisy**, **flower**, and **garden**.
rosebush stands for female pubic hair. See also **bush**.
• "There was something about her eloquence at that moment and the way she thrust that rosebush under my nose which remains unforgettable."
(Henry Miller, *Tropic of Cancer*, 1934)
2. virginity. This is an 18th-century colloquialism. *La rose* is French for "maidenhead."

rosebud n
anus. This 20th-century gay term is based on appearance.

rosebuds n pl
nipples. Based on similarity of shape, this is 20th-century usage. See also **buds of beauty**.

rosey, rosy n
buttocks. These 20th-century terms are based on reddish **cheeks**.

roses n British
menstruation. This is a 19th-century euphemism. See also **flowers**.

rosy n
See **rosey**.

rough trade n
cruel or sadistic sexual behavior with a male homosexual. This gay euphemism dates back to the 1930s.

round the world v phrase
See **around the world**.

rounders n pl
buttocks. This 20th-century colloquialism refers to the roundness of buttocks.

roust v British
copulate. This 16th-century usage is related to the word "arouse."

rout v American
copulate. This mid-20th-century term is said of men. The standard sense means **poke** about. See also **root**.

rub v
masturbate. This meaning has applied since the 16th century. It refers equally to males and females.
rub off is a 17th-century colloquialism for copulate. Since the 19th century it has also come to mean masturbate.
rub one's radish is a 20th-century expression for masturbate, said of men. See also **radish**.
rub up is 17th-century British usage for masturbate or copulate.

rubber n American
condom. This 20th-century colloquialism refers to the usual material from which a condom is made. (This term can give rise to cross-Atlantic embarrassments, since in Britain rubber means pencil eraser.)

rubber fetishist, rubber man, rubber woman, rubber queen n
one whose sexual activities include dressing in rubber. These are mid-20th-century euphemisms.

rubbins n
intercourse between the thighs. This is 20th-century coinage.

rubigo n Scottish

penis. This 16th-century word derives from the Latin *ruber*, meaning "red," and suggests **rub**.

rudder n British

penis. This 17th-century usage probably alludes to a rudder cutting a path through water, with water representing vaginal lubrication.

rudeness n Jamaican

sexual intercourse. This 20th-century term, which suggests that sex is dirty or impolite, is heard especially in the phrase **do a rudeness**. *See also* **kindness**.

rug n American

pubic hair, especially of females. This is a 20th-century colloquialism. *See also* **mat**.

rug muncher, implying cunnilinguists, is a recent derogatory term for a lesbian.

ruin v British

deflower. This 17th-century euphemism is based on the presumed ruin of a woman's or girl's reputation once deflowered.

rule of three n phrase British

male genitals. This 18th-century jocular expression refers to the penis and two testicles. Rule here not only means control or guidance, but also a measure.

rummage v

copulate. This 19th-century colloquialism may be based on the sense of searching, or on the obsolete noun sense of rummage, meaning energetic activity.

rump n

1. buttocks. This standard term derives from the Dutch *romp*, meaning "stump." It has been in use since the 15th century.

2. female genitals. This mainly British usage dates back to the mid-17th century.

• "Robin he chast me about the stack,
Robin laid me on my back,
Robin he made my rump to crack."
(Broadside ballad, "Scotch Moggy's Misfortune," circa 1635)

rump v British

copulate, especially from behind. This is 18th-century usage.

rumper is 19th-century usage for prostitute or **whoremonger** (under **whore**).

rump splitter is a mid-17th-century term for penis.

rump work is a 19th-century expression for sexual intercourse. *See also* **work**. **Rumpo**, **rumpy-pumpy**, and **rumpty-tumpty** are more recent variations.

run one's tail v phrase British

prostitute oneself. This is a 19th-century colloquialism. *See also* **tail**.

Russian duck v British

copulate. This early 20th-century rhyming slang term is based on the rhyme with **fuck**.

rut v

copulate. This 17th-century colloquialism derives from the sense meaning copulation of deer, dating back to the 15th century. Rut is also a standard term for **furrow**.

have the rut or **be in rut** refers to sexual excitement among males.

rutter is a 17th-century colloquialism for a person who is sexually aroused.

Ruttish is the adjective meaning sexually aroused or lustful.

rutting means copulation.

- "What with some Goddess he'd
  have bin
  Playing, belike, at In-and-In,
  And would be at the rutting-
  sport."
  (Charles Cotton, *Burlesque upon
  Burlesque, or the Scoffer Scofft,*
  1675)

S

sacking n
prostitution. This 16th-century derogatory term is based on the standard sense of material for a **bag**.

saddle n
1. *British* female genitals. This
17th-century usage is based on the
connection with **horse, mount,** and
ride.
- "The adulterer sleeping now was
  riding on his master's saddle."
  (Robert Burton, *The Anatomy of
  Melancholy,* 1621)
2. *American* condom. Based on the
contrast with **ride bareback** (under
ride), this is 20th-century black
usage.

sadism n
practices involving hurting and/or
humiliating a person in order to derive sexual pleasure. This standard
English word was named after the
Marquis de Sade (1740–1814). **Sadist**
and **sadistic** date back to the late 19th
century, while **sadomasochism** and
sadomasochist are early 20th-cen-
tury terms. **Sadie-masie** is a recent
colloquialism for sadomasochist. *See
also* **masochism** and **S and M**.

safe n
condom. This late 19th-century
colloquialism refers to protection
against conception.
safety is a mid-20th-century American colloquialism for condom, short
for **safety-sheaths**.

safe sex n
sexual intercourse using a condom,
primarily to guard against AIDS. This
is a mid-1980s colloquialism. In the
early 1990s the term was qualified to
safer sex, since all sex is risky to
some degree.
- "Safe sex has actually made sex
  more enjoyable, that's the new
  party line. We enjoy the stability,
  safety, ... the "new equality" of
  jack-off clubs, phone sex and
  anonymous sexual encounters. At
  least that's what we say."
  (William Hayes, "To be young
  and gay and living in the '90s,"
  Utne Reader, March/April 1991)

sailor's bait n American
prostitute. This early 20th-century
term regards a prostitute as bait to
hook a sailor. **Sailor's delight** is a variant.

Saint Peter n British
penis. This 19th-century expression adds a religious dimension to the
common term **peter**.

saint's delight n
vagina. This 19th-century colloquialism is suggestive of **heaven**. *See
also* **delight**.

salami n American
penis. This 20th-century usage is
based on shape. The term is found
most often in the phrase **hide the salami**, meaning copulate. *See also* **pudding, sausage,** and **meat**.

saleslady n
prostitute. This early 20th-century euphemism refers to **commerce**. See also **lady**.

sally n South African
fellatio. Based on the sense meaning **suck**, which may derive from "salivate," this is a 20th-century gay term.

salt v
copulate. This 17th-century term, now obsolete, puns on the standard noun senses of a substance necessary for survival, a flavoring, and an experienced sailor.

salt n
lust. This is a 16th-century literary term. See also **flavor**.
saltcellar is a 19th-century term for vagina, based on both being containers.

Sam n
masculinity. This 20th-century term is used especially among homosexuals. It stems from "Samson," a classic and strong-sounding male name.

sample v
1. copulate. This is a 19th-century colloquialism. See also **taste**.
2. fondle sexually. This is a 19th-century colloquialism.
sample of sin is an 18th-century British euphemism for prostitute.
• "That delicate sample of sin, who depends on her wantonness for her attractions."
(Tobias Smollett, The Adventures of Gil Blas, 1749)
sampler is a 19th-century British term for female genitals.

S and M n phrase
sadism and masochism as forms of sexual pleasure. This abbreviation

dates back to the early 20th century. See also **masochism** and **sadism**.

sandwich n
sexual threesome. Based on the three layers of food, this is 19th-century coinage. See also **club sandwich**.

sapphism n
lesbianism. This literary term refers to Sappho, a famous female Greek poet born on the island of Lesbos, who wrote lyrical poetry that included lesbian themes. It dates back to the 19th century. **Sapphic** is the adjective.

sard v
copulate. Possibly derived from the Latin, meaning "fish," the word was used from the 10th through the 17th century, thereafter becoming obsolete.

sardine n American
prostitute. This is early 20th-century usage, possibly derived from **sard**. See also **fish**.

satchel n American
female genitals. This Ozark dialectal term dates back to the early 20th century and may derive from the standard container sense. See also **bag** and **case**.

sauce n British
venereal disease. This late 17th-century usage may refer to the discharge from gonorrhea.
• "I hope your punks will give you sauce to your mutton."
(John Vanbrugh, The Provok'd Wife, 1697)

sauce v British
copulate. This is a recent euphemism.

saucy is a colloquialism for lusty. *See also* **juicy**.

sausage n

penis. Based on shape, and found especially in the phrase **hide the sausage**, this term dates back to the 17th century. *See also* **baloney, pudding, meat, salami,** and **wiener**.
sausage-grinder means vagina or prostitute. *See also* **grind**.

saw off a chunk, saw off a piece v phrase Canadian

copulate. These early 20th-century expressions probably refer to the **in-and-out** (under **in**) movement of sawing.

say high mass v phrase

fellate. This 20th-century gay expression alludes to kneeling in worship. *See also* **kneel at the altar**.

scale v British

copulate. This 17th-century literary term is used of men. *See also* **jump, leap,** and **mount**.

scarf up v phrase

perform fellatio or cunnilingus. Based on the slang sense of scarf meaning **eat**, this is 20th-century usage.

scarlet adj

pertaining to or characterized by sexual immorality. The origin of this usage is found in Revelations: "I saw a woman sit upon a scarlet coloured beast, full of names of blasphemy...."
scarlet sister is an early 20th-century American euphemism for prostitute.
scarlet woman is a euphemism for prostitute that dates back to the 16th century. **Scarlet lady** is a variant. In Nathaniel Hawthorne's *The Scarlet Letter*, 1850, the scarlet "A" stood for adultery.

scepter, sceptre n

penis. This usage dates back to the 17th century. *See also* **staff**.

schlang, schlange, schlong n

penis. This 19th-century term derives from the Yiddish and German words meaning **snake**.

schmuck, schmock n

penis. This derogatory early 20th-century term derives from the Yiddish word meaning "ornament." It is now more commonly applied to a person—one regarded as silly or stupid—than to the sexual organ. *See also* **prick** and **putz**.

schwanz, schwantz n

penis. This 19th-century term derives from the Yiddish and German words meaning **tail**.

scoff v American

perform oral sex. This is mid-20th-century coinage. *See also* **scarf up**.

score v

copulate. Said especially of men, and based on the colloquial sense meaning succeed, this is a 20th-century colloquialism. *See also* **qualify**.
score between the posts is a jocular Australian expression meaning copulate, said of men, using rugby or football as the metaphor, with "posts" punning on goalposts and bedposts.

scratch n

female genitals. This 20th-century term may derive from **itch**.

screaming fairy n American

blatant or camp male homosexual. This is a mid-20th-century derogatory term. A British variant is **screamer**. Both terms are rarely used today. See also **fairy**.

screw v

copulate. This common term dates back to the 18th century. The sexual meaning stems from the standard sense of rotate into something. Though originally said only of males, the term has been applied to females since the mid-20th century.

• "Christ says, Don't consider yourself better than someone else because one guy screws a whole bunch of women while the other guy is loyal to his wife." (Jimmy Carter, *Playboy* interview, November 1976)

screw n

1. act of sexual intercourse. This use dates back to the 18th century.
2. person considered as a sex partner. This usage originated in the 19th century.

• "As a matter of fact, he's not such a great screw, but at least he isn't a nag." (Milton Machlin, *Pipeline*, 1976)

screwdriver is 20th-century usage for penis. See also **hammer**.

screw off is a mid-20th-century American expression meaning masturbate.

screw some ass is 20th-century coinage for copulate or perform anal intercourse.

scrotum n

external sac that contains the testicles. This standard English word derives from the Latin *scrautum*, meaning "sheath for arrows." It dates back to the late 16th century.

• "The snotgreen sea. The scrotum-tightening sea." (James Joyce, *Ulysses*, 1922)

scuffer n American

prostitute. This mid-20th-century usage may be based on "scuff" meaning to walk. See also **streetwalker**.

scum n

semen. This 20th-century derogatory term stems from the standard sense meaning dirt or dirty liquid. See also **slime**.

scum bag is mid-20th-century American usage for condom. It is highly derogatory when applied to a person.

scupper n American

prostitute. Based on the standard sense, meaning the opening that drains the deck of a ship, this is a 20th-century term. See also **drain**.

scut n

1. female pubic hair. This obsolete usage dates back to the 16th century. The word is still the standard term for the furry tail of an animal, especially a rabbit. See also **brush**.
2. female genitals. This term also dates back to the 16th century. See also **tail**.

• "I rumpl'd her Feathers, and tickl'd her scutt." (Broadside song, "Gee Ho Dobbin," 1730)

scuttle v British

1. deflower. Based on the standard nautical sense, meaning make a hole in a boat, this is 19th-century usage.
2. *American* copulate. This usage dates from the mid-20th century.

scuttle n British

vagina. This 19th-century meaning stems from the standard nautical sense of a trapdoor or hatchway in a ship's deck. See also **trap**.

seafood n American

sailor considered as a sex object by a homosexual male. This underworld and gay term dates from the mid-20th century.

seal v British

make pregnant. This is a 19th-century colloquialism.

seals n pl British

testicles. This 19th-century colloquialism refers to a seal as an assurance that something is authentic and to the seals (wax-impressing insignia used to seal letters) that men used to wear attached to their watch chains. See also **testicle** and **watch and seals**.

seat n

buttocks. This is a 20th-century colloquialism.
seat-cover is mid-20th-century American citizens band radio usage for an attractive female driver.

secret parts n pl

female genitals. This euphemism dates back to the 16th century. Shakespeare illustrated this usage in *Hamlet*: "Then you live about her waist . . . / In the secret parts of Fortune?" **Secret places** is a variant. See also **parts** and **private parts**.
• "He laid his hand close and firm over her secret places, in a kind of close greeting."
(D.H. Lawrence, *Lady Chatterley's Lover*, 1928)

secrets n pl

genitals of either sex. This is a 19th-century euphemism. **Secret works** is a mid-20th-century American variant.

secret services n pl British

sexual intercourse. This 18th-century euphemism has religious overtones. See also **religious observances**.

secret vice n

masturbation. This is a 19th-century euphemism. See also **vice**.

see v British

copulate. In this 19th-century euphemism, see is a homonym for the letter C, the first letter of **cunt**. See also **eye**.

seed n

1. semen. This standard term dates back to 13th-century Old English. Today its usage is more formal or literary.
2. testicle. This is a mid-20th-century colloquialism used especially in the plural, **seeds**.

seed plot n

vagina. Based on the metaphor of Mother Earth and reproduction, this colloquialism originated in the 19th century.

see madam(e) thumb and her four daughters v phrase

masturbate. Said of men, this 19th-century expression is based on the use of fingers.

seen more ass than a toilet seat adj phrase American

sexually promiscuous. This recent jocular expression is said of men. See also **ass**.

seen more pricks than a dartboard adj phrase British

sexually promiscuous. This recent expression is said of women. See also **prick**.

see one's aunt, see one's auntie, see one's friend v phrase

menstruate. These 19th-century euphemisms refer to the sense of being unavailable for sexual intercourse.

see stars lying on one's back *v phrase*

copulate. Said of women, and punning on lying back, looking upward, and being knocked out, this is a 19th-century jocular expression. *See also* **study astonomy**.

self-abuse *n*

masturbation. This early 18th-century euphemism is based on the concept that masturbation is unhealthy and sinful.

sell one's bacon, sell one's flesh *v phrase American*

prostitute oneself. These are mid-20th-century euphemisms.

semen *n*

whitish testicular liquid containing spermatozoa. This standard English word derives from the Latin *serere*, meaning "sow." It dates back to the 14th century.
- "From the days of Aristotle until the seventeenth century, there was no doubt in any Western mind that semen was the active ingredient in conception."
(Reay Tannahill, *Sex in History*, 1979)

seminary *n British*

female genitals. This 19th-century jocular term puns on **semen** and **ladies' college** (under **lady**).

semiglobes *n pl*

breasts. This 19th-century colloquialism is based on shape. *See also* **globes**, **hemispheres**, and **world**.

sensitive plant, sensitive truncheon *n British*

penis. These are 19th-century euphemisms. *See also* **stalk** and **club**.

sensitive spot *n*

clitoris. This is a 19th-century colloquialism. *See also* **spot**.

sergeant *n American*

lesbian. Based on the masculine image of a sergeant, this is mid-20th-century usage.

serve *v*

copulate. Originally said of a stallion, this is a 16th-century euphemism.
serve head is a mid-20th-century gay American expression for perform fellatio. *See also* **give head** and **head**.

service *v*

1. copulate. This 19th-century euphemism is often said of prostitutes.
- "She is acutely humiliated, thinking that this means she is dependent on men for 'having sex,' for 'being serviced,' for 'being satisfied.' "
(Doris Lessing, *The Golden Notebook*, 1962)
services is a euphemism for sexual intercourse, punning on **commerce** and religion and dating back to the 17th century. *See also* **religious observances**.
2. perform fellatio, cunnilingus, or anal intercourse. This is 20th-century gay usage.

sewer *n American*

anus. This mid-20th-century usage refers to a conduit for passing feces.

sew up *v phrase*

1. copulate. This is a 19th-century expression. *See also* **stitch**.
2. *British* make pregnant. This is 19th-century usage.

sex *n*

1. *British* genitals, especially female. This is a 19th-century euphemism.

sex glands is a 20th-century euphemism for testicles or ovaries.
2. sexual intercourse. This is a 20th-century colloquial abbreviation. **sex job** is a mid-20th-century American colloquialism for act of copulation.
3. sexual matters in general.
• "Like fleas and puns, sex gets everywhere; it crosses all frontiers, invades all zones, whether erogenous, topographical, or semantic."
(Walter Redfern, *Puns*, 1984)
sex appeal is a standard term for attractiveness, particularly to the opposite sex. This standard term dates back to the 1920s and is now understood almost anywhere in the world.
sex life is a 20th-century colloquial term for love life or sexual activity.
• "It can no longer be said that continental people have sex lives and British people have hot water bottles."
(*Time Out*, August 8, 1990)
sex machine is a recent American euphemism for an extremely sexually active male or female.
sex object is a standard English expression for an object or person that one is attracted to sexually. It derives from psychoanalytic theory. The term is also applied, often insultingly, to a person who is considered solely for the sexual gratification he or she can provide.
sexpot is a mid-20th-century American term for a sexually attractive woman.
sex symbol is a standard term for a famous person, often a movie star, who has great **sex appeal**. The term dates back to the 1960s.

sexism n
belief that one sex is superior to the other. This standard English term, usually applied to men in regard to women, dates back to the 1960s. **Sexist** is the standard adjective and noun.

sexual commerce n
copulation. This is a 19th-century euphemism. *See also* **commerce**.

sexual discharge n
semen or vaginal secretion. This euphemism dates back to the 19th century.

sexual intercourse n
copulation involving the penetration of the penis into the vagina. Though standard English, it harbors the euphemism "intercourse," derived from the Latin *intercurrus*, meaning "running between." The term dates back to the end of the 18th century.

sexual relations n pl
See **relations**.

sexual science n
sexual intercourse. This is an obsolete 19th-century euphemism that contrasts science and knowledge with the **art of pleasure** (under **art**).

sexy adj
sexually appealing or erotic. Dating back to the 1920s, this is a standard term.

seymour n
effeminate male homosexual. This is a 20th-century heterosexual term based on the supposedly sissy or effeminate sound of the name.

shad n American
prostitute. This 19th-century term may be based on a shad being a **fish**.

shaft n
erect penis. This usage derives from the Latin *scapus*, meaning **stalk**. The term has long been used in the expressions **shaft of Cupid** and **shaft of delight**.

- "It is a shaft of Cupid's cut,
  'Twill serve to Rove, to Prick, to
    Butt."
  (Thomas D'Urfey, *Wit and Mirth*,
  1719)

shaft v

copulate. This is a 19th-century term.

shaft in the bum is 20th-century British usage for perform anal intercourse. *See also* **bum**.

shag v British

1. copulate. Dating back to the 18th century, this colloquialism may derive from other senses of shag, such as hair or exhaustion. *See also* **shake**.
- "There are plenty of men who will shag anything if it's a virgin." (Colleen McCullough, *The Thorn Birds*, 1977)

shag bag is a 19th-century derogatory term for a woman considered as a sex object or for a vagina. *See also* **bag**.

2. masturbate. This is a 19th-century term.

shake v

1. copulate. Dating back to the 16th century, this usage is based on movement. The names of a number of dance forms in the latter half of the 20th century have sexual references to shaking.

shake bag is 19th-century usage for vagina. *See also* **bag**.

shake the sheets is a 17th-century British euphemistic expression for copulate.

2. masturbate. This usage, used of men, dates back to the 16th century.

shake up is 19th-century coinage for masturbate, said of men.

shake n British

prostitute. This term is of 19th-century origin.

shank n American

prostitute. This is a mid-20th-century term. *See also* **leg**.

shape n

vagina. Use of the abstract noun in this obsolete 18th-century euphemism implies that it is *the* shape, much as **cunt** is *the* **monosyllable**, from the heterosexual male perspective.

sharp and blunt n phrase British

vagina. This 19th-century Cockney rhyming slang term is based on the rhyme with **cunt**. The opposites in sharp and blunt also suggest the erect penis and the vagina.

shaving brush n

female pubic hair. This is an obsolete 19th-century euphemism. *See also* **bushy**.

she n

penis. This is 20th-century gay usage.

sheath n

1. vagina. Derived from the Latin *vagina*, meaning "sheath," this 18th-century term is obsolete.

2. condom. This colloquialism is based on shape and function. It dates back to the 19th century. Originally, it was a medical term.

sheep-herder n American

pederast. This mid-20th-century term alludes to the allegedly bestial practices of shepherds and implies that pederasty is like bestiality.

sheets n pl

place where sexual intercourse occurs. This word has long been part of euphemisms for sexual intercourse. Expressions dating back to the 17th century include **shaking of the sheets**, referring to the act of copulation; **between the sheets**, meaning in the act; and **possess a woman's sheets**, meaning copulate, said of men. See also **bed** and **polish one's ass (arse) on the top sheet**.

- "In all these places ... my
  fiddlers playing all night
  The shaking of the sheets, which
  I have danced
  Again and again with my
  cockatrice."
  (Philip Massinger, City Madam, 1659)

she-he, she-male n
effeminate male homosexual. These are mid-20th-century terms.

sheila n Australian
woman considered as a sex object. This colloquialism dates back to the 19th century. It is based on Sheila being a common female name, and reinforced by the "she" in Sheila.

shell n
female genitals. This 19th-century colloquialism refers to a shell being a container and the connection with eggs.

she-male, she-man n
lesbian. These are 20th-century heterosexual terms.

shift-work n British
copulation. This 19th-century euphemism puns on the movement of shift, the time frame of a shift, and shift meaning a woman's chemise or slip. See also **work**.

shim n
transvestite. This colloquial term, used in Singapore, derives from a contraction of "she-him."

shit n
excrement. This well-known Anglo-Saxon vulgarity finds sexual expression in a number of terms.
shit-fuck is 20th-century usage for anal intercourse.
shit-hole is a 19th-century British term for anus. See also **hole**.
shitter is a 20th-century expression for anus, based on function.

shoot v
ejaculate. This colloquialism is based on the standard sense meaning eject or discharge. The term dates back to the 19th century. See also **fire**.
shoot a bishop is a 19th-century British euphemism meaning have a **wet dream**, or nocturnal emission, based on **bishop** meaning **glans**.
shoot between wind and water is an 18th-century British expression meaning copulate, punning on the naval reference to the weak part of the hull of a ship and the vagina being positioned between the bodily areas associated with farting and urinating.
shooter's hill is a 19th-century British jocular term for female genitals; hill refers to the **mons pubis**.
shoot in the bush and **shoot over the stubble** are British colloquialisms for premature ejaculation. The first expression dates back to the 18th century, the second to the 19th century. See also **bush** and **stubble**.
shoot in the tail is a 19th-century British expression for copulate, said of men, or perform anal intercourse. See also **tail**.
shoot one's load is a 20th-century expression for ejaculate. Variations include **shoot one's milt** and **shoot one's roe**, both of 19th-century British origin, and **shoot one's wad**, a mid-20th-century American expression. See also **load**, **milt**, **roe**, and **wad**.

short and curly, short and curlies n phrase
pubic hair. These 20th-century colloquialisms are based on appearance.

short arm n

penis. This World War II expression derives from the colloquial terms **short-arm drill** and **short-arm inspection**, which refer to medical inspection for venereal disease. **Short-arm practice** is 20th-century military coinage for copulation. *See also* **small arm**.

short hairs n

pubic hair. This colloquialism dates back to the 19th century. "Have someone by the short hairs" is a common colloquial expression meaning have control by rendering that person helpless.

short strokes n

masturbation. This 20th-century colloquialism is said especially of men. *See also* **stroke**.

shove v

copulate. This colloquialism, said of men, is based on copulatory movement. It dates back to the 17th century.

shove n

act of copulation. This colloquialism dates back to the 17th century. *See also* **push**.

shower cap n American

condom or contraceptive diaphragm. This mid-20th-century colloquialism is based on shape and protective function. *See also* **raincoat**.

shrimp n

1. prostitute. This obsolete 17th-century term may be based on shrimp being a **fish** (shellfish) and a scavenger.

2. penis, especially a small one. This 20th-century usage is based on size and shape.

shrimp queen n American

male homosexual with a foot fetish. This mid-20th-century gay term is based on shrimp being similar to toes in shape. **Shrimper** is a variant.

shrine of love n phrase

vagina. This 19th-century literary euphemism has religious overtones. *See also* **idol**.

shrubbery n

female pubic hair. This is a 19th-century colloquialism. *See also* **bush**.

shtup v American

copulate. This early 20th-century term, said usually of men, derives from the Yiddish, meaning "push." *See also* **push** and **shove**.

- "As any regular reader of *Marie Claire* magazine knows, some four out of five young French women would rather shop than shtup."
  (*Elle* magazine, December 1987)

siff, siph n

See **syphilis**.

silent beard n

female pubic hair. This jocular colloquialism dates back to the 17th century. *See also* **beard**.

silent flute n

penis. This is an 18th-century jocular colloquialism. *See also* **flute**.

simple infanticide n

masturbation. This jocular 19th-century expression refers to the "killing" of future generations. *See also* **Malthusianism**.

sin n

offense against religious or moral laws. This standard term, dating back to the 12th century, has long been a euphemism for any sexual offense or vice. *See also* **live in sin**.

sinner is an early 17th-century British euphemism for prostitute.

siren n

seductive woman. This standard, mostly literary, term derives from the Greek myth concerning nymphs who lured sailors and their ships onto rocks. It dates back to the 14th century.

sister n

1. *British* prostitute. This euphemism dates back to the 17th century and makes use of the family metaphor. *See also* **aunt** and **uncle**.

sisterhood is a 19th-century euphemism for prostitution, implying some camaraderie in the profession.

sister of the night is a 19th-century euphemism for prostitute, based on **night work**.

2. *American* male homosexual, especially an effeminate one. Also abbreviated to **sis**, **siss**, and **sissy**, this is early 20th-century gay usage. Sissy is perhaps the commonest, most derogatory, and oldest variation, dating back to the 19th century.

sit on the fence v phrase

be bisexual. This 20th-century colloquialism is based on the standard sense of the phrase meaning be undecided.

sitter n American

buttocks. This 20th-century colloquialism refers to that upon which we sit. *See also* **seat**.

six-to-four n phrase British

prostitute. This early 20th-century rhyming slang term is based on the rhyme with **whore**. Six may have been chosen for its closeness to **sex**. *See also* **forty-four** and **two by four**.

sixty-nine, 69 n

mutual oral sex. This 20th-century colloquialism is based on the ideograph of 69, representing two clinched and inverted bodies facing each other. The direct French translation **soixante-neuf** is a more literary usage. *See also* **thirty-nine** and **vice versa**.

size queen n

male homosexual who is attracted to men with large penises. This is a mid-20th-century gay expression. *See also* **queen**.

skin n

1. female genitals. Dating back to the 17th century, this term is also a euphemism for the whole body viewed sexually. *See also* **flesh**.

skin-coat is a 17th-century literary term for the female genitals.

skin dive is a 20th-century term for perform cunnilingus. *See also* **dive**.

skin flick is mid-20th-century American term for pornographic movie.

skin house is a mid-20th-century American expression for pornographic movie theater.

skin mag is a mid-20th-century American coinage for pornographic magazine.

skin the cat is an African-American euphemism for copulate. *See also* **cat**.

skin-the-pizzle is 19th-century British usage for vagina, based on **pizzle** meaning penis.

2. condom. This colloquialism refers to the fact that condoms often look like skin. The term dates back to the 19th century.

3. *British* foreskin. This is a 19th-century abbreviation.

skin the live rabbit is a 20th-century colloquialism meaning fold back the foreskin of an uncircumcised penis. *See also* **live rabbit**.

skirt n

1. woman considered sexually. In the 16th century, this was a standard term, based on the clothing worn by women. By the 19th century the term had acquired negative sexual connotations. In the 20th century, the reference is usually to an attractive woman. *See also* **petticoat**.

2. prostitute. This usage dates back to the 19th century.

skull-job n American

act of cunnilingus. This mid-20th-century expression alludes to skull meaning **head**.

skull pussy n

fellator. This 20th-century term is based on skull meaning **head** and **pussy** referring to the mouth as analogous to the vagina.

slacks n

lesbian. This early 20th-century colloquialism is based on pants being regarded as primarily male clothing.

slag n British

woman of loose morals. This abusive contemporary term may derive from "slack," one who is lazy, or from the obsolete **slagger**, meaning brothel keeper, dating back to the late 19th century. *See also* **slut**.

slap and tickle n phrase

sexual intercourse. This 20th-century euphemism refers to actions considered foreplay.
• "A slap and tickle is all the fickle male has in his head."
(Cole Porter, "Most Gentleman Don't Like Love," 1938)

sleaze n

something sexually tawdry or cheap. This term dates back to the 1950s.

sleazy, meaning tawdry or pornographic, is the adjective. Sleaze is a back formation from sleazy, whose origin is unknown.

sleep around v phrase

copulate promiscuously. This euphemism dates back to the 16th century.

sleep with someone v

phrase

copulate. This common euphemism dates back to the 16th century.
• "I slept with her, and never had a more voluptuous night . . ."
(Anonymous, *My Secret Life,* 1890)

slime n British

semen. This is 19th-century derogatory usage. *See also* **scum**.
old slimy is a 19th-century British term for penis.

sling one's jelly, sling one's juice v phrase British

masturbate. These 19th-century colloquial expressions are used of men. *See also* **jelly** and **juice**.

slip a length, slip her a length v phrase

copulate. These expressions are said of men, date back to the 19th century, and are based on length meaning penis. *See also* **yard**.
slip into is a 19th-century colloquialism meaning copulate, said of men.

slit n

vulva. This colloquial euphemism is based on shape. It dates back to the 17th century. *See also* **cleft**, **crack**, **cut**, **gash**, and **placket**.
• "Good Sir, make no more cuts i'
th' outward skin,

One slit's enough to let Adultry
in."
(Robert Herrick, "Upon Scobble,"
Hesperides, 1648)

slithery n *British*

copulation. This 19th-century euphemism refers to the tactile experience created by sexual lubrication.

sloppy seconds n

an act of copulation with a woman
who has just copulated with another
man. This is a 20th-century jocular
expression. *See also* **buttered bun**.

slug n *Australian*

penis. This 20th-century military
term puns on the standard senses of
a slimy, snail-like creature and a bullet. *See also* **worm** and **bullets**.

sluice n

vagina. This obsolete 17th-century
colloquialism is based on the standard meaning of a channel or passageway. *See also* **drain**, **pipe**, and
waste pipe.
• "That whore, my wife . . . that
us'd to open her sluice . . . to
gratify her concupiscence."
(Thomas Brown, *Works*, late 17th
century)

slut n

1. sexually promiscuous female. A
slut originally meant a dirty person,
without any sexual connotation. By
the 16th century, the word was at-
tributable to females only. Today slut
is a term of abuse for a woman regarded as sexually loose. It sometimes refers to a prostitute.
• ". . . A peevish drunken flurt, a
waspish cholerick slut."
(Richard Burton, *The Anatomy of
Melancholy*, 1621)
2. *American* promiscuous male
homosexual. This is mid-20th-cen-
tury gay usage.

small arm n

penis. This is an early 20th-century
military colloquialism. *See also* **short
arm**.

smock n

woman considered as a sex object.
This usage is of 17th-century origin.
See also **skirt**.
smockage is a 17th-century British
term for copulation.

smoke v

1. copulate. Based on the heat gen-
erated and sexual fire or passion, the
term dates back to the 17th century.
It is found most often in the expression **make the chimney smoke**, meaning bring on an orgasm in a woman.
2. fellate. Based on the analogy of
smoking a cigarette, this is a 20th-
century euphemism.

smut n

pornography. This standard term
dates back to the 17th century. It derives from the Middle High German
smutzen, meaning "stain." **Smutty**,
meaning pornographic, is the adjective.

snag v *American*

1. copulate. Based on the standard
sense of capture or trap, this is a 20th-
century term.
2. rape. This is a 20th-century euphemism, one of the very few for
rape.
3. perform anal intercourse. This
is an underworld term.

snake n

penis. This 20th-century term is
based on shape. However, the sexual
symbolism of snake goes back to the
story of the Garden of Eden, where
the snake introduces sexuality to Eve
and Adam.

snake in the grass is a colloquial expression for copulation. **Grass** refers to female pubic hair.

snapper n

1. *British* penis. This is 19th-century usage, possibly based on an obsolete sense of the term meaning an accomplice.

2. *American* foreskin. This 20th-century usage refers to pliability. **Snapper flapper** is a variant, used mainly by male homosexuals.

3. *American* vagina. Possibly based on the *vagina dentata* (vagina with teeth) castration fantasy, this is mid-20th-century usage. **Snapping turtle** is a variant. *See also* **turtle**.

4. *American* sexually attractive woman. Presumably alluding to a woman a man would like to "snap up," this is a 20th-century coinage.

snatch n

1. hasty act of sexual intercourse. This usage dates back to the 17th century. *See also* **quickie**.

• "I could not abide marriage, but as a rambler I took a snatch when I could get it."
(Richard Burton, *The Anatomy of Melancholy*, 1621)

2. vagina. This usage dates back to the 19th century.

• "... his [Mick Jagger's] show, with its leers and minces has always been outrageous ..., a spastic flap-lipped tornado writhing from here to a million steaming snatches and beyond ..."
(Lester Bangs, *Creem*, November/December 1970)

piece of snatch refers to a woman, often derogatorily, as a sex object.

3. *American* buttocks. This is a 20th-century underworld term.

4. *American* catamites viewed collectively. This is mid-20th-century gay usage.

snippet n

vagina. This 19th-century term is obsolete. *See also* **bit**, **cut**, and **piece**.

snug v British

copulate. This 19th-century colloquialism may derive from **nug** and "snog," a colloquialism meaning caress or pet.

soap n British

semen. This is a 19th-century term. *See also* **lather**.

social disease n

venereal disease. Since the mention of any venereal disease, particularly syphilis and gonorrhea, was taboo for the first half of the 20th century, this euphemism and others such as "blood disease," "communicable disease," and "secret disease," were employed. Today this term is rarely used.

social evil n

prostitution. This is a 19th-century euphemism. *See also* **vice**.

sodomy n

anal intercourse with a man or woman or certain sexual practices considered perverse, including copulation with animals. This standard term dates back to the 13th century. It can extend to any sexual behavior considered nonstandard, including oral sex. The term derives from Sodom, the city mentioned in the Bible (Genesis) as an evil town.

sodomite is a standard term for a man who commits sodomy. It dates back to the 14th century. **Sodomist** is a variant. **Sod** is a 19th-century abbreviation.

sodomize is a mid-20th-century colloquial term meaning perform sodomy on someone.

• "The notion (fundamental to Sade and much pornographic art) that

one can double one's ecstasy by engaging in coitus while being at the same time deftly sodomized is sheer nonsense."
(George Steiner, *Night Words*, 1965)

soft-core *adj*

pertaining to mild pornography. Contrast this early-1970s term with **hard-core**.

- "It is soft-core pornography which represents the true degradation of sex. And also its maximum exploitation . . . because it never delivers the goods, the customers can be strung out for years . . . hoping *this* time to see a *little* more . . ."
(John Hofsess, "Misadventures in the Skin Trade," *Maclean's*, July 1974)

soixante-neuf *n*

mutual oral sex. This colloquial term is French for **sixty-nine**. It dates back to the late 19th century. As a French borrowing, it is a literary and formal term.

- "In familiar language this divine variant of pleasure is called: *faire soixante-neuf*."
(P. Perret, *Tableaux Vivants*, 1888)

soldier's joy *n*

masturbation. This obsolete 19th-century expression is used in reference to military men. See *also* **joy**.

south-end *n*

buttocks. Based on south typically being the direction downward, this is a 20th-century term.

sow one's wild oats, sow one's oats *v phrase British*

copulate in a carefree manner, especially prior to marrying. This colloquial expression, said of young men, is based on sowing meaning planting or plowing and oats referring to seeds or semen. It dates back to the 16th century. See *also* **furrow** and **seed**.

Spanish gout *n*

syphilis. This colloquial term dates back to the 16th century. **Spanish pox** is a more recent variant, dating back to the 19th century. Both terms xenophobically suggest that the disease either came from, or was prevalent in, Spain. See *also* **French crown**.

spanners *n Australian*

sexually attractive woman. This mid-20th-century jocular term is based on the notion that a spanner (wrench) tightens **nuts**, that is, testicles.

speak low Genitalese *v phrase*

perform fellatio or cunnilingus. In this 20th-century gay jocular expression, Genitalese puns on a fictitious language and implies oral-genital activity, while low puns on the genitals and on classifications for forms of language, as in low, middle, or high Dutch or German.

specialties *n pl British*

condoms. This is a 19th-century euphemism.

spend *v*

ejaculate. This usage dates back to the 16th century. Spending implies making a payment or deposit, thus tying sex with **money**. The term also suggests losing energy and becoming exhausted.

- "With such a tool I thought he'd split her . . . she held it fast, and made it stand, And spend its venom in her hand."
(Thomas Bridges, *A Burlesque Translation of Homer*, 1770)

spender is an 18th-century British term for vagina.

spend n

semen. This is 19th-century usage. **spendings** is British usage for semen or vaginal fluid; it dates back to the 16th century.

sperm n

semen or the male reproductive cells, called **spermatozoa**, that make up semen. The term derives from the Greek *sperma*, meaning "seed," and dates back to the 14th century.
* "Inside the body of the male are organs for secreting and forming a stuff called sperm, or spunk, which is whitish, partly thickish . . ." (Anonymous, *My Secret Life*, 1890)
sperm bank is a place for storing sperm that is used for articial insemination. This standard term dates back to the early 1970s.

spew v British

ejaculate. This is a 17th-century euphemism.

spice n

sexual attractiveness or sexual content, as in a story. This is a colloquial 20th-century term.

spike n British

erect penis. This is a 19th-century term. See also **nail** and **sword**.

spindle n

penis. This usage dates back to the 19th century. See also **rod**.

spinster n British

prostitute. This obsolete 17th-century usage derives from the activity of spinning that was forced on prostitutes in jail.

spit v British

copulate or ejaculate. Said of men, this usage dates back to the 16th century.
* "That makes them spit white broath, as they do." (John Lyly, *Mother Bombie*, 1594)

spit n

penis. This usage originated in the 20th century.

split v

copulate. Said of men, and based on the standard sense meaning divide, this term dates back to the 16th century.
split someone's buns is 20th-century coinage meaning perform anal intercourse. See also **buns**.

split n

1. female genitals. This 19th-century term is based on appearance. See also **slit**.
* ". . . He . . . plunged his finger into her carmine split." (Anonymous, *My Secret Life*, 1890)
split apricot is a 19th-century British colloquialism for female genitals, based on appearance.
split beaver is mid-20th-century usage for female genitals, especially in a photograph or pose. See also **beaver**.
2. *American* woman considered as a sex object. **Split-tail** is a variation.
split mutton means penis, based on what it does. See also **mutton**.

spoil a woman's shape v phrase

make a woman pregnant. This colloquialism dates back to the 17th century.

spoon v

1. caress sentimentally or engage in sexual foreplay. This colloquialism dates back to the 19th century.

2. copulate. This is a 19th-century euphemism.

3. perform cunnilingus. Possibly based on the curving of the tongue, this is a mid-20th-century term.

sporran n

pubic hair. This 19th-century euphemism, now obsolete, is based on the standard sense of a fur pouch. *See also* **fur**.

sport n

1. sexual play. This 16th-century colloquialism puns on **game**.

• "In England, if you trust report,
  Whether in country, town or
    court,
  The parson's daughters make best
    sport."
  (Thomas Bridges, *A Burlesque Translation of Homer*, 1770)

2. male prostitute. This is a 20th-century term.

sport blubber v phrase British

show one's breasts. This expression is of 19th-century origin.

sporting girl n American

prostitute. This is a 19th-century euphemism. *See also* **girl**.

sporting house n American

brothel. This euphemism originated in the 19th century. *See also* **house** and **sport**.

sport of Cupid's archery n phrase

vagina. Based on Cupid, represented with bow and arrow, being the Roman god of love, this is an obsolete 18th-century euphemism. *See also* **bull's-eye**, **Cupid**, and **target**.

spot n

female genitals. This euphemism dates back to the 18th century.

sprain one's ankle v phrase

become pregnant. This euphemism dates back to the 18th century and implies a mishap. It also exemplifies bodily displacement, from genitals to ankle.

spread v British

spread one's legs in order to copulate. Said of women, this colloquialism dates back to the 17th century. **spread beaver** is mid-20th-century American coinage for pornographic pictures of women's genitals. *See also* **beaver** and **wide-open beaver**.

spunk n British

semen. This 19th-century colloquialism is based on the standard sense of courage. *See also* **mettle**.

• "There she lay now, a large drop of his spunk on her motte . . ."
  (Anonymous, *My Secret Life*, 1890)

spunk-holders is a 19th-century British colloquialism for testicles.

square someone's circle v phrase

copulate. This recent college colloquialism is said of men. *See also* **circle**.

squeeze and a squirt n phrase British

copulation. This 19th-century colloquialism is said of men. **Squeeze 'em close** is a variation.

squint n British

female genitals. This is a 19th-century term. *See also* **eye**.

squirrel n

1. prostitute. This 18th-century term is obsolete.

2. *American* female genitals. Based on the image of **fur**, this is mid-20th-century usage.

squirt v

ejaculate. This is a 19th-century colloquialism. *See also* **spit**.

stab in the thigh v *phrase*

copulate. This 19th-century euphemism, said of men, indicates aggression and illustrates bodily displacement, from the genitals to the thigh.

stable n

erection. Dating back to the 16th century, this euphemism is based on the Latin *stabilis*, meaning "enduring" or "firm."

• "I'll keep my stables where I lodge my wife."
(William Shakespeare, *The Winter's Tale*, 1611)

stacked adj *American*

shapely. This mid-20th-century colloquialism, said of females, refers especially to having large breasts.

staff n

penis. This colloquial 17th-century term is found especially in the phrase **staff of life**. *See also* **arborvitae** and **handstaff**.

stag adj *American*

for men only. This 20th-century colloquial term derives from the noun meaning male deer. It is found in such expressions as **stag mag**, referring to a pornographic magazine for men, **stag movie**, meaning a pornographic movie shown privately to men, and **stag party**, dating back to the 19th century, meaning a men-only party, usually for a bridegroom prior to his wedding.

stake n

penis. This 17th-century term suggests both aggression and possession. *See also* **lance** and **pike**.

• "I could not help feeling the stiff stake that had been adorn'd with the trophies of my despoil'd virginity."
(John Cleland, *Fanny Hill: Memoirs of a Woman of Pleasure*, 1749)

stalk n

penis. This literary term dates back to the 16th century. It is a common Middle Eastern and Far Eastern metaphor. *See also* **root** and **stick**.
stalk-on is a recent colloquialism for an erection.

stallion n

1. male who copulates frequently or who is lascivious. Derived from the standard sense of a male horse, this usage originated in the 17th century. *See also* **bull**.
2. *British* prostitute's customer. This is 19th-century usage.
3. *British* a man kept by a woman for sexual purposes. This usage dates back to the 18th century.
4. *American* penis. This is 20th-century black usage.

stand n

erection. This colloquialism dates back to the 16th century. **Standard** and **standing** are variants. *See also* **cockstand**.

stand v

get an erection. This usage dates back to the 16th century.

• "Knowing a touch of her soft hand . . . will make him stand."
(Thomas Bridges, *A Burlesque Translation of Homer*, 1770)

stand up and cheer, stand up and shout n
phrase

reach orgasm. These 20th-century jocular expressions, said of women, pun on applause and celebration at reaching a goal or end.

stand a push v phrase British

copulate. This phrase is said of women. *See also* **push** and **do a push**.

star n

female genitals. This euphemism dates back to the 18th century. *See also* **heaven**.
• "Give me the star that shines over the garter."
(Lord Cork, *The Bumper Toast*, 18th century)
star-gazer is obsolete 18th-century usage for an erect penis. *See also* **see stars lying on one's back**.

starch n British

semen. This 19th-century term puns on the stiffness of an erection and the appearance of dried semen.

star-fucker n American

fan, usually female, who follows rock musicians and is sexually available to them. *See also* **groupie**.

stay v American

maintain an erection. This is a mid-20th-century colloquialism.

steamy adj

lusty. This 20th-century colloquialism refers to the heat of sexual passion. *See also* **hot**.

stem n

penis. This 19th-century term is based on shape. **Stemmer** is a variant. *See also* **root** and **stalk**.

stern n

buttocks. This colloquialism is based on the standard sense meaning rear of a ship. It dates back to the 16th century.

do a stern job or **perform a stern job** is a 20th-century jocular expression meaning perform anal intercourse.

stew n

1. brothel. This colloquial term is based on stew meaning bath. It dates back to the 14th century. The plural, **stews**, is also used.
• "The bawds of the stews be turned all out;
But some think they inhabit all England throughout."
(Robert Crowley, *Epigrams*, 1550)
2. prostitute. This usage is of 17th-century origin.

stick n

penis. Based on shape, this usage dates back to the 17th century. *See also* **stalk**.
stick and bangers is a 19th-century British term for penis and testicles. It derives from billiards jargon, where the phrase means cue and balls. *See also* **bangers**.

stick v British

copulate. This obsolete 19th-century usage, said of men, puns on the noun sense of a long, thin object and the verb senses of being glued together and poking. *See also* **poke**.

sticky n

semen. This 20th-century term is based on texture. *See also* **glue**.

stiff n

erect penis. Based on firmness, this usage dates back to the 17th century.
stiffeners is mid-20th-century American coinage for pornographic material.
stiffy or **stiffie** is a term for an erection, dating back to the 19th century.

sting n

penis. This 19th-century usage suggests sexual aggression. *See also* **prick**.

stinkpot n

vagina. This is a derogatory mid-20th-century term. *See also* **pot**.

stir v

caress someone sexually. This literary term dates back to the 16th century.

stir fudge, stir chocolate

v phrase

perform anal intercourse. These 20th-century expressions are based on fudge and chocolate being suggestive of feces.

stir shit v phrase British

perform anal intercourse. This is a 19th-century expression. *See also* **shit**.

stitch v

copulate. This 18th-century term is used in reference to men. *See also* **sew up** and **prick**.

stone n

testicle. This was a standard term from the 12th through the 19th century. Only in the 19th century did the term become colloquial.
stone-ache is 20th-century American dialectal usage from the Ozarks for pain in the testicles resulting from prolonged arousal. *See also* **blue balls**.

stonk, stonker, stonk-on n

British

erection. These contemporary terms may be based on the rhyme with **bonk**.

stork v American

impregnate. Based on the myth of the stork delivering babies, this is mid-20th-century usage.
storked is an early 20th-century colloquialism meaning pregnant.

stormy dick n American

penis. This 20th-century expression is based on the rhyme with **prick**. *See also* **dick**.

straight adj

heterosexual. This colloquial term dates back to the late 19th century. It is based on the standard senses meaning straightforward, honest, or proper. Compare **bent**.

strain v

copulate. This term appeared as early as the 14th century; it was used by Chaucer in *The Canterbury Tales*, 1387. It probably refers to the sense of effort.

strap v

copulate. This 17th-century usage suggests aggression. *See also* **hit**.

strap n American

penis. This is a mid-20th-century term. *See also* **belt**.

strawberries n pl

nipples. Based on color and shape, as well as the food sense, this colloquialism can be traced back to 17th-century literature. *See also* **raspberries**.

strawberry patch n

red pubic hair. This is a 20th-century expression.

street of shame, street of sin n phrase American

prostitution. These are mid-20th-century euphemisms.

street-sister n

prostitute. This euphemism originated in the 20th century. See also sister.

streetwalker n

prostitute. Based on solicitation on the street, this is a 19th-century euphemism.

stretcher n British

penis, especially a large one. This is an 18th-century colloquialism.

stretch leather v phrase

copulate. This is a 17th-century colloquial expression. See also leather.

strike v

copulate. This term, which dates back to the 17th century and is said of men, is one of many aggressive or warlike terms used as sexual metaphors. See also hit and punch.

striptease n

performance in which clothing is removed in an erotic manner. Though Webster's Ninth New Collegiate Dictionary dates the word to 1937, the act dates back at least to Roman times. The first striptease act on the English stage was seen in The Rover, 1677, a popular play by Aphra Behn; it was performed by a man. Modern striptease is an offshoot of American burlesque theater.

stroke v

1. copulate. This 18th-century usage refers to the motion typical of the act.
2. American masturbate. This is recent usage.
stroke book is a recent euphemism for a pornographic book or magazine.
• "If Vox had been published 20 years ago, it would have gone

among the "stroke books" it archly resembles."
(The New York Times Book Review, May 31, 1992)
stroker is a recent euphemism for a male masturbator.
stroke the lizard is a mid-20th-century American expression for masturbate, said of men. See also lizard.

strop one's beak v phrase British

copulate. This 19th-century colloquialism is said of men. In standard English strop means sharpen. The action of a bird sharpening its beak could be seen as similar to the male's movements during sexual intercourse. See also beak.

strum v

copulate. Said of men, and based on the playing of a musical instrument, the term dates back to the 17th century. See also fiddle.

strumpet n

prostitute. Although this is a standard term dating back to the 14th century, its etymology is unknown. Curiously, the word is made up of two syllables, strum and pet, that have sexual references. In fact, the abbreviation strum, now obsolete, was also used for prostitute.
• "As Junoes proud bird spreads the fairest taile,
So does a strumpet hoist the loftiest saile."
(Thomas Dekker, The Honest Whore, 1604)

stubble n

female pubic hair. This colloquial usage goes back to the 18th century. See also beard, hair, and shoot over the stubble (under shoot).
take a turn in the stubble means copulate.

stud n

virile man, especially a male prostitute. This colloquial term is based on the standard sense of a male animal used for breeding. It dates back to the early 20th century.

study astronomy v phrase

copulate. This jocular 20th-century expression, said especially of women, refers to looking upward during sex in the **missionary position**. See also **see stars lying on one's back**.

stuff v

copulate. This common term, said of men, is based on the standard sense of filling a space. It dates back to the 17th century.
• "Trying to stuff another man's wife, is that your idea of being a friend?"
(Brian Moore, The Luck of Ginger Coffey, 1960)

stuff n

semen. This usage originated in the 17th century.

stuffer n American

pederast. This is a mid-20th-century term.

stump n British

penis. This 17th-century term refers to shape. It is found in the expression **carnal stump**. See also **root** and **stem**.

suck v

perform fellatio or cunnilingus. Based on both being oral activities, the term dates back to the 19th century. See also **blow** and **eat**.
suck and swallow is 19th-century usage for vagina, based on the notion of its sucking the penis and swallowing semen.

suck ass or **suck asshole** is a 20th-century expression for perform anilingus.
suckathon is a 1960s American term for group oral sex that stems from the word "marathon."
sucker is 18th-century British usage for penis derived from sucker meaning lollipop (see also **ladies' lollipop**). Sucker is also an abbreviation for **cocksucker**, one who performs fellatio.
suck off is a variant of suck, with "off" suggesting performing until the recipient reaches orgasm.
suck queen is a mid-20th-century expression for a male homosexual whose preference is fellatio. See also **queen**.
suckster and **suckstress** are 19th-century British terms for a male and a female, respectively, who perform oral sex.

sugar basin n British

vagina. This 19th-century expression is based on the container sense and the idea of sweetness.

sugar stick n British

penis. This is a 19th-century euphemism. See also **stick**.

superdroopers n pl American

especially large breasts. This mid-20th-century coinage puns on "super-duper" meaning excellent or exceptional.

supper n British

female genitals. This 19th-century colloquialism equates the evening meal with having sex. It can be found in the phrase **give the old man his supper**.
warm the old man's supper, said of women, means sit before the fire with petticoats lifted.

swallow a sword v phrase

fellate. This is a 20th-century expression. See also **sword** and **eat**.

swap spit v phrase

1. perform mutual fellatio. This is mid-20th-century underworld usage.
2. kiss while inserting the tongue into the partner's mouth. This is a colloquialism. See also **French kiss**.

sweaty adj

sexually aroused or lusty. This colloquial term dates back to the 18th century. See also **steamy**.

sweet agony, sweet death n

sexual intercourse. These literary terms are from the 18th century. See also **die**.

sweet potato pie n

American

female genitals. This is a 20th-century black expression. **Sweet potatoes** is also used for breasts.

swing v

1. copulate. This 16th-century colloquialism is based on movement.
2. American swap sex partners or be promiscuous. This is a mid-20th-century colloquialism.
swing both ways is a mid-20th-century term for be bisexual.
swingers is 19th-century usage for testicles or breasts, but it is 20th-century usage for people who swap sex partners.

swinge v

copulate. Said of men, and dating back to the 16th century, the term was obsolete by the 18th century. It may derive from an obsolete sense meaning beat, but it also may have been influenced by **swing** and **swive**.

swish n American

effeminate male homosexual. This 20th-century term, somewhat derogatory, refers to a manner of walking in which the rustle of skirts is suggested.

switch v

copulate. This 18th-century term may have been influenced by **swinge**.
• "Paris had not got enough
Of trimming her bewitching buff,
But longs to switch the gypsy
   still."
(Thomas Bridges, *A Burlesque Translation of Homer*, 1770)

switch-hitter n American

bisexual person. Derived from baseball jargon meaning an **ambidextrous** hitter, this is 20th-century colloquial usage.

swive v

copulate. This was a standard term from the 14th through the 16th century. Thereafter, the word became informal before becoming obsolete by the 18th century. Swive derives from the Old English meaning of swivel or revolve.
• "But I, the most forlorn, lost man
   alive,
To show my wished obedience
   vainly strive:
I sigh, alas! and kiss, but cannot
   swive."
(John Wilmot, the earl of Rochester, "The Imperfect Enjoyment," 1680)
swiver was a 15th-century term for lecher. In the 20th century the word has been revived as a term for penis.

sword n

penis. This colloquialism dates back to the 16th century. It joins a multitude of terms related to weaponry, including **club**, **gun**, **lance**, **pike**, **poker**, and **weapon** itself.

syphilis n

contagious venereal disease. This standard term dates back to the 18th century. It is named after Syphilus, the eponymous hero of a poem by Girolamo Fracastoro, a 16th-century Italian writer. *See also* **pox**.

- "Patronage of brothels and ordinary prostitutes seems to have faltered in the early days of the sixteenth century with the epidemic spread of syphilis, a disease whose patronage remains obscure. Busily passing the buck, as always, the French called it the Neapolitan malady, the Spaniards the French disease, and the Germans the Spanish scabies."
  (Reay Tannahill, *Sex in History*, 1979)

syph, **siph**, and **siff** are 19th-century colloquial abbreviations.

- "I'll come down with the syph just from touching the ticket."
  (Philip Roth, *Portnoy's Complaint*, 1969)

T

tail n

1. buttocks. This was a standard term from the 14th through the 18th century. In this sexual sense, the derivation is from the position of the tail in animals.

tail pipe is American usage for anus, based on the automobile metaphor.

2. female genitals. This usage was standard from the 14th through the 18th century. *See also* **scut**.

tail-box is 20th-century American coinage for female genitals. *See also* **box**.

tail feathers is a 17th-century colloquialism for female pubic hair. *See also* **feathers**.

tail gap, **tail gate**, and **tail hole** are colloquial variations meaning female genitals. *See also* **gap**, **gate**, and **hole**.

tail tickling, **tail wagging**, and **tail work** are all 19th-century British colloquialisms for sexual intercourse. *See also* **tickle**, **wag**, and **work**.

3. penis. Based on shape, this is yet another standard word from the 14th through the 18th century.

- "We are all mortal men and frail, And oft are guided by the tail."
  (Thomas Bridges, *A Burlesque Translation of Homer*, 1770)

tail juice and **tail water** are 17th-century colloquialisms for semen. *See also* **juice**.

tail pike, **tail pin**, and **tail tackle** are 19th-century colloquial terms meaning penis. *See also* **pike** and **pin**.

4. prostitute or a woman considered as a sex object. This usage dates back to the early 19th century and is based on the second definition above.

- "You've got a piece of tail. I want a piece of tail too. . . ."
  (Graham Greene, *The Quiet American*, 1955)

tail v

copulate. This usage dates back to the 18th century.

- "It will be wearisome to tell how I tailed Mary one night, if I have told that I did it the same way to Fanny the night before."
  (Anonymous, *My Secret Life*, 1890)

take v

copulate with a woman. Used especially in the phrase **take someone**, this literary euphemism, said of men, is based on the sense of **possess** or **occupy**. The term dates back to the 16th century.

take a slice is 17th-century jocular usage meaning copulate; it likens a woman to a piece of **cake** or **meat**. *See also* **cut**.

take Nebuchadnezzar out to grass is a 19th-century expression meaning copulate. It is based on Nebuchadnezzar meaning penis and grass meaning **greens** or sexual intercourse; the presence of pubic hair is also suggested. Nebuchadnezzar was the name of two kings of Babylon.

take a trip to the moon *v phrase*

perform anilingus. Based on **moons** meaning buttocks, this is a 20th-century expression.

take down *v phrase*

masturbate. Said of men, this 20th-century expression refers to the postorgasmic detumescence of the penis.

take in beef, take in cream *v phrase*

copulate with a man. Said of women, these 19th-century expressions are based on **beef** meaning penis and **cream** meaning semen.

take oneself in hand *v phrase American*

masturbate. Said of men, and based on the literal meaning and the figurative sense of controlling oneself, this is a mid-20th-century expression.

take the starch out of *v phrase British*

copulate. Said of women, and based on **starch** meaning semen, this is a 19th-century expression.

take to bed *v phrase*

See **bed**.

tale of two cities *n phrase*

breasts. This 20th-century usage is based on the rhyme with **titties** (un-der **tit**). The phrase comes from the title of a novel by Charles Dickens.

talk *v*

copulate. This literary euphemism dates back to the 16th century. It is based on the concept of communication. *See also* **converse**, **discourse**, **intercourse**, and **parley**.

talk to the canoe driver *v phrase American*

perform cunnilingus. This 20th-century expression is based on the canoe driver being the clitoris. See *also* **little boy in the boat**.

talk to the mike *v phrase American*

perform fellatio. This is recent collegiate usage.

talk turkey *v phrase*

perform oral sex. Based on the turkey's proclivity to **gobble**, this is a recent expression.

tallywag, tallywacker *n*

penis. These are 18th-century colloquialisms. Tallywag is British, and probably derives from wag meaning hang. Tallywacker is American and comes from wacker meaning hitter. Tally derives from Latin *talia*, meaning "twig." See *also* **wag** and **whacker**.

tallywags is a colloquialism for testicles. It dates back to the 18th century and is based on the hanging sense of wag. **Tarrywags** and **tarriwags** are variants.

- "By gum, my arse is bare
  I wish I had a clout, or rags,
  Just to wrap up my tarriwags."
  (Edmund Beckett, *Paradise Lost*, 1838)

T and A *n phrase*

tits and ass. This abbreviation is a mid-20th-century euphemism for any exposure of breasts and buttocks in magazines, the theater, or art. **B and T** is a British variant standing for **bum** and **tit**.

- "There are certain images which come to mind when people talk about beauty queens. It's mostly what's known as t and a. . . ." (Studs Terkel, editor, *American Dreams: Lost and Found*, 1980)

tantrum n British
penis. This obsolete 17th-century term may be based on the standard sense of rage or frenzy; it may also derive from the Latin *tentum*, meaning "stretch," or from "tantrems," meaning frolics.

- "Twixt some twelve and one o'clock,
  He tilts his tantrum at my nock."
  (Charles Cotton, *Burlesque upon Burlesque*, 1675)

target n
vagina. This colloquialism dates back to the 19th century. It suggests that the vagina is something to be fired at. See also **arrow**, **bull's-eye**, and **shoot**.

tart n
1. sexually promiscuous woman. This derogatory term derived originally from the standard sense of a sweet pastry, and was a genuine term of endearment. By the late 19th century, however, the term had degenerated to its current slang meaning.
2. prostitute, female or male. This is 20th-century usage.

tassel n
child's penis. Based on the standard sense of an ornament that hangs or dangles, this is a 20th-century colloquial term.

taste v
copulate. This 16th-century literary euphemism is based on the standard sense of sampling something. See also **sample**.

taste bud n
clitoris. This current term suggests cunnilingus. See also **bud**.

tasty adj
sexually inviting. This colloquialism dates back to the 19th century.

teacups n pl American
small breasts. Based on shape and size, this is mid-20th-century usage.

teahouse, tearoom n
American
public lavatory used for male homosexual cruising. These are 20th-century gay terms.

- "The danger in rough trade, the lack of intimacy in "tea-room" sex, was not what Halliwell craved." (John Lahr, *Prick Up Your Ears*, 1978)

team-cream n American
group sex. Based on **cream** meaning semen, or to ejaculate, this is a mid-20th-century expression.

teapot n American
child's penis. Based on the spout and the association of tea with urine, this is 19th-century coinage.

tear off a piece v phrase
copulate. This 19th-century expression, said of men, is based on a food metaphor. See also **cut** and **piece**.

tearoom n
See **teahouse**.

teat n
nipple. This standard term, dating back to the 13th century, derives

from the Old French of the same meaning, *tete*. See *also* **tit**.

* "... her nearly naked teats
  throw taut shadows
  when she stretches up ..."
  (Lawrence Ferlinghetti, "Away
  Above a Harborful," *A Coney
  Island of the Mind*, 1955)

teazle n

vagina. This obsolete 19th-century term is based on teasel meaning a plant. It also puns on tease.

telephone sex n

See **phone sex**.

temple of low men n

phrase British

female genitals. This 19th-century expression puns on the temple of "high men," meaning **hymen**, with low implying the genitals. Temple carries with it religious overtones.

tender agony n

sexual intercourse. This is an 18th-century literary euphemism.

tenderloin madam n

American

prostitute or brothel keeper. This is early 20th-century usage. The first tenderloin district, or **red-light district** (under **red**), was in New York City.

tenuc n

female genitals. This 19th-century back slang is based on **cun[e]t** spelled backward.

testicle n

one of the two male reproductive glands in the scrotum. This standard English word derives from the Latin *testiculus*, the diminutive of *testis*, meaning "witness." The testicles were regarded as a witness to virility,

and in swearing an oath, men would hold their testicles, much like placing a hand on the Bible, to guarantee veracity. The term dates back to the 15th century.

testimonials n pl British

testicles. This 20th-century military term hints at the sense of witness inherent in the etymology of testicles.

that n

genitals of either sex. This is a 19th-century euphemism. See *also* **it** and **thing**.

that there is 19th-century British dialectal usage for sexual intercourse.

that way adj phrase

1. homosexual. This is a 20th-century heterosexual euphemism.

2. pregnant. This is also a 20th-century euphemism.

that way inclined adj

phrase

homosexual. This is a 20th-century heterosexual euphemism.

thatch n British

female pubic hair. This 18th-century colloquialism is based on appearance.

* "My prick rubbed the spunk drop
  on her thatch ..."
  (Anonymous, *My Secret Life*,
  1890)

thatched house is an 18th-century colloquialism for vagina, based on the container sense of house.

thatched house under the hill is an 18th-century British colloquialism for vagina, based on hill meaning **mons pubis**.

Thatcher girls n pl British

prostitutes. This 1980s expression suggests that Prime Minister Margaret Thatcher's policies caused great unemployment, leading to the growth of prostitution.

thighs, thigh sandwich n
intercourse between thighs held closely together. These are 20th-century terms.

thing n
genitals of either sex. This euphemism dates back to the 17th century. **Thingams** is a 19th-century variant. **old thing** is a 19th-century British euphemism for the female genitals. **thingamabobs** and **thingumbobs** are 18th-century euphemisms for testicles, punning on bobs or things hanging down and unnamed or unmentioned things, the standard meaning of these terms. **thingstable** is an obsolete 17th-century British literary euphemism for the female genitals, based on the association with "constable," which, in Britain, is pronounced **cunt**-ste-bill.

the thing n
menstruation. This is a 20th-century euphemism.

third leg n American
penis. This is 20th-century usage. *See also* **short arm** and **small arm**.

third sex n
homosexuals. This is a 20th-century colloquialism.

third way n
anal intercourse. This 20th-century usage is based on the first and second ways being vaginal intercourse and oral sex.

thirty-nine, 39 n
anilingus. This mid-20th-century gay expression is based on the ideograph of 3 meaning buttocks. *See also* **sixty-nine**.

thistle n
penis. This literary euphemism dates back to the 16th century. *See also* **prick**.
- "There thou prick'st her with a thistle."
(William Shakespeare, *Much Ado About Nothing*, 1599)

Thomas n British
penis. Dating back to the 17th century, this offers an example of personification of the genitals. The term may derive from **John Thomas**, though **tom** may have been an influence as well.

thorn n
penis. This literary euphemism originated in the 16th century. *See also* **prick** and **thistle**.
- "Maybe Thou lets this fleshly thorn
Buffet Thy servant e'en and morn . . ."
(Robert Burns, "Holy Willy's Prayer," late 18th century)
thorn in the flesh is a 19th-century British euphemism for penis. *See also* **flesh**.

thoroughbred n American
skilled prostitute. This 20th-century term is based on the standard sense of a thoroughbred being a good **ride**. It is used mainly by prostitutes.

thousand pities n pl
breasts. This 19th-century Cockney rhyming slang term is based on the rhyme with **titties** (under **tit**).

thread v British
copulate. Based on thread going through the eye of a needle, this usage dates back to the 19th century. *See also* **stitch**.
thread the needle also means to copulate; it is said of men. *See also* **eye**.

• "Sheila would be sorry she did not let me thread her. . . ."
(Brendan Behan, *Borstal Boy*, 1958)

three-dollar bill n American

homosexual. This 20th-century expression is used especially in the phrase **queer as a three-dollar bill**.

three-legged beaver n
American

male homosexual. This citizens band radio usage refers to **beaver**, suggesting woman, and **third leg**, meaning penis.

three-letter man n American

male homosexual. This derogatory 20th-century term alludes to the three letters in the word **fag**. More recently it has become a euphemism based on the word **gay**.

threepenny bits n pl

breasts. Based on the rhyme with **tits** (under **tit**), and reinforced by the roundness of coins, this is 20th-century usage. *See also* **tracy bits** and **tray bits**.

three-way adj

pertaining to a sexual threesome. This is a mid-20th-century colloquialism.

thrill n

orgasm. This early 20th-century colloquialism derives from the Middle English *thrillen*, meaning "pierce."

throw a leg over v phrase
British

copulate. This 18th-century colloquialism is said especially of men.

throw one a hump v phrase
American

copulate. This early 20th-century underworld expression is said of men or women. *See also* **hump**.

throw up v phrase

ejaculate. This is a 19th-century colloquialism. *See also* **spit**.

thrum v

copulate. This 16th-century term, said of men, refers to fingering an instrument and making music. *See also* **strum**.
• "Paris . . . we know you can
The wenches thrum."
(Thomas Bridges, *A Burlesque Translation of Homer*, 1770)

thrust v

copulate. This colloquialism is based on the pelvic thrusting characteristic of sexual intercourse. The sexual use of the term dates back to the 19th century.

thumb v British

copulate. This 18th-century colloquialism, said of men, refers to the similarity in shape of a thumb and a penis.
thumb of love is a 19th-century euphemism for penis.

thump v

copulate. This colloquialism, said of men, refers to the thrusting activity characteristic of sexual intercourse. It dates back to the 16th century. Shakespeare wrote in *The Winter's Tale*: ". . . jump her and thump her." *See also* **hit** and **thrust**.

tib n

prostitute. This 16th-century coinage may derive from the backward spelling of **bit**.

tickle v

1. caress sexually. This colloquialism dates back to the 14th century and derives from the Latin *titillare*, meaning "titillate."
tickle one's crack is a 19th-century British expression for masturbate, said of women.
2. copulate. This euphemism dates back to the 16th century.
tickle your fancy is a 20th-century British expression for male homosexual, based on the rhyme with **nancy**.

tickler n British

penis. This is 19th-century usage. The term is also used, though rarely, for clitoris, possibly a borrowing from other languages. *Ginter*, for example, is an Abyssinian (Ethiopian) name for clitoris, meaning "the tickler."
tickle-tail is 18th-century British coinage for both penis and prostitute. *See also* **tail**.
tickle-Thomas is a 19th-century term for vagina, based on **Thomas** meaning penis.

tick-tack n

sexual intercourse. This 16th-century colloquialism may be based on the sound or a game or sport.
• "You will to tycke-tacke, I fere Yf thou had time."
(Frederic Weaver, *Lusty Juventus*, circa 1550)

tidbit, titbit n

female genitals. These 17th-century euphemisms are based on the standard sense of a tasty piece of food. *See also* **bit** and **tit**.

tie the lover's knot v phrase

copulate. This is a 19th-century euphemism.

tie up v phrase British

make pregnant. This is a 19th-century colloquialism.

tight-assed (-arsed) adj

pertaining to an anal retentive personality. This is a 20th-century colloquialism. An even more recent meaning is attractive, firm buttocks.

till n British

female genitals. This 19th-century term is based on the container metaphor and the connection with **money**. *See also* **box**.

tillage n

sexual intercourse. This 16th-century literary euphemism, said of men, alludes to the sowing of crops.

tilting n

sexual intercourse. This 16th-century euphemism, said of men, refers to the thrusting of poles in the sport of jousting. *See also* **pole**.

tip v

copulate. This 20th-century American usage may have been influenced by **tup**.
tip the long one is a 19th-century British colloquial expression meaning copulate. Said of men, it is based on long one meaning penis.
tip the middle finger is a 19th-century British colloquial expression meaning masturbate a woman, said of men.
tip the velvet is 17th-century British usage for perform cunnilingus, punning on **velvet** meaning both tongue and vagina. It is also a 17th-century British colloquialism meaning to **French kiss**.

tit n

1. nipple. Derived from **teat**, this term dates back to the 17th century.
2. breast. This term has been in use since the 18th century. The plural, **tits**, is probably the most common

English slang expression for breasts. However, only in the 20th century did this sense of tit supersede other senses of the term, such as a filly, a bird (as in titmouse), and a young girl. *See also* **T and A**.

tit-bag and **tit-hammock** are 20th-century colloquial terms for brassiere.

titiculture is a jocular 20th-century term for breast worship.

titties is a colloquialism for breasts that dates back to the mid-18th century.

titty is 20th-century gay usage for heterosexual intercourse, based on the involvement of a female partner.

titty-oggy or **tittie-oggie** is 19th-century British coinage for fellatio, possibly based on the connection of sucking and breasts. Oggy may be back slang for "go."

   3. prostitute. This 15th-century usage is obsolete.

   4. female genitals. This 20th-century usage is rare.

titmouse is a 17th-century British term for female genitals.

titbit n
   See **tidbit**.

tivvy, tivy n British
   female genitals. This obsolete 19th-century term derives from "tantivy," meaning a full gallop.

toby n British
   1. buttocks. Dating back to the 17th century, and possibly derived from the name, this term is an example of personification.

   2. female genitals. Dating back to the 17th century, this usage is obsolete.

tochas, tokus, tooky n
American

   buttocks. Dating back to the 19th century, this word derives from the Yiddish *tochis*.

tocks n American
   buttocks. This is a 20th-century colloquial abbreviation.

token n
   female genitals. This is an early 16th-century literary euphemism. *See also* **money** and **piece**.
   • "And fell so wyde open
      That one myght see her
         token...."
      (John Skelton, "The Tunnying of
      Elynour Rummyng," *Poetical
      Works*, early 16th century)

tokus n
   See **tochas**.

tom v
   copulate. This 19th-century colloquial term, said of men, is based on the standard sense of the male of certain animals, as in "tomcat."

tom n
   lesbian. Based on it being a male name, this usage dates back to the early 20th century.

tomboy is a euphemism for lesbian, based on the standard sense of a girl who acts boyishly. The word dates back to the 16th century.

tomato n American
   1. attractive woman. This colloquial sense is reinforced by a tomato's redness and juiciness.
   • "I can rush back to that night
      club before Aarfy leaves with that
      wonderful tomato he's got
      without giving me a chance to
      ask about an aunt or friend she
      must have who's just like her."
      (Joseph Heller, *Catch-22*, 1961)
   2. prostitute. This 20th-century underworld term is based on the first meaning.

tommy n British

penis. This is 19th-century usage. See also **John Thomas**.

Tommy Rollicks is a 19th-century British rhyming slang term for testicles, based on the rhyme with **bollocks** (under **ball**).

tongue v

perform cunnilingus or fellatio. This colloquialism refers to the licking of the tongue. The term dates back to the 19th century.

• "I get my girls to tongue one
  another before my eyes."
(Paul West, *Auguste Rodin*, 1990)

tongue fuck is 20th-century gay usage for perform cunnilingus, fellatio, or anilingus. **Tongue-job** is a colloquialism for such an act.

• "The size of the Mother Superior
  Made a tongue-job as weary, nay
    wearier
  Than late Henry James,
  The Commonwealth Games
  Or an evening of opera seria."
(James Fenton and John Fuller,
Nuns, 1987)

tonsils n pl American

breasts. This jocular 20th-century term offers an example of bodily displacement; it is also suggestive of breasts, since they come in pairs and are glandular. See also **lungs**.

tooky n

See **tochas**.

tool n

penis. This still-current colloquial term was standard English from the 16th through the 18th century. It is based on the standard **instrument** sense.

tool bag is a 19th-century colloquialism for scrotum. See also **bag**.

tool chest is a 19th-century British term for vagina, based on the container metaphor.

toothache n British

erection. This is a 19th-century euphemism. See also **Irish toothache**.

top ballocks n pl British

breasts. Based on their position on the body, and being shaped somewhat like ballocks, that is, rounded, this is a 19th-century term. See also **ballocks** (under **ball**).

top buttocks n pl

breasts. Based on position and shape, this expression dates back to the 19th century.

top-heavy adj American

large-breasted. This euphemism originated in the 20th century.

topless adj

referring to exposed breasts. Said of women, this colloquialism dates back to the 1960s. The word is found in terms such as **topless bar**, **topless beach**, and **go topless**.

• "Today's broker next door can be
  found in an upscale topless joint
  . . . where women decked in
  sequins and silicone take their
  tops off at your table for $20 (and
  take home $1,000 a night)."
("Sex in the '90s," *New York*
magazine, June 8, 1992)

top-sergeant n

lesbian. Based on the masculine, even macho, role of a sergeant as being on top, this is mid-20th-century usage. See also **sergeant**.

torch of Cupid n phrase British

penis. This is a 17th-century euphemism. See also **Cupid**.

tosh n British

penis. This 19th-century term also means nonsense, much like **balls** (under **ball**).

toss in the hay *v phrase*
American

copulate. This early 20th-century expression probably has its origins in farming jargon. *See also* **roll in the hay**.

toss off *v phrase*

masturbate. Said of men, and based on the movement to completion (off), this expression dates back to the 18th century. *See also* **jerk off**.

touch *v*

copulate. This euphemism dates back to the 16th century.
touch bun for luck is defined by Grose's *Dictionary of the Vulgar Tongue, 1811*, as "... a practice observed among sailors going on a cruize." *See also* **bun**.
touch-crib is an obsolete euphemism for brothel.
touch-hole is an obsolete term for vagina. *See also* **hole**.
touch-trap is obsolete usage for penis. *See also* **trap**.
touch up is a colloquialism meaning caress sexually that dates back to the 18th century. In Japan *tatchi geimu* is a euphemism for sexual petting that derives from combining "touch" and "game." Touch up is also a colloquialism meaning masturbate, said of either sex, that dates back to the 19th century.

toupee *n*

1. female pubic hair. This jocular term dates back to the 18th century.
2. wig or artificial hair for the pubic area. This usage originated in the 18th century. *See also* **merkin**.

town bike *n*

sexually loose woman or prostitute. This expression puns on **ride** and being accessible to all. *See also* **bike** (under **bicycle**) and **woman about town**.

town bull *n*

lecherous male. This colloquial term goes back to the 16th century. It refers to bulls owned by towns and kept for breeding purposes.

town pump *n*

woman who permits copulation with any man. This is a 20th-century colloquialism. *See also* **pump**.

towns and cities *n pl British*

breasts. Based on the rhyme with **titties** (under **tit**), this rhyming slang term is 20th-century usage. *See also* **tale of two cities**.

toy *n British*

1. female genitals. Based on **play** and **game**, this is a 19th-century colloquialism. **Toy-shop** is a variant.
2. penis. This, too, is a 19th-century colloquialism. *See also* **bauble** and **trifle**.

toy *v*

caress sexually. This colloquialism originated in the early 16th century.

toyboy *n British*

older woman's young male partner. This is a colloquialism of recent origin.
- "At 48 she is like a teenage girl again—raving it up with four different lovers including a toyboy of 27!"
(*News of the World*, November 15, 1987)

tracy bits *n pl Australian*

breasts. Based on the rhyme with **tits** (under **tit**), and possibly influenced by tracy meaning three, this is a 20th-century term. *See also* **threepenny bits**, and **tray bits**.

trade n

prostitution or sexual commerce. This is a 20th-century term, said of either sex.

the trade is 20th-century American usage for prostitution.

trader is a British term for prostitute that dates back to the 17th century.

trading is a 16th-century British term for sexual intercourse, especially with a prostitute. *See also* **commerce**.

traffic n

1. prostitutes or prostitution. This literary euphemism is based on circulation. It dates back to the 16th century.

2. sexual intercourse. This euphemism also dates back to the 16th century. *See also* **commerce**.

transsexual n

person who feels that he or she belongs to the opposite sex, or one who undergoes surgery to change his or her sex. This is a 1960s standard and medical term. **Trannie** is an affectionate abbreviation in the gay community.

transvestite n

person, usually male, who dresses and often behaves like the opposite sex. This standard term dates back to the 1920s. *See also* **shim**.

trap n

vagina. This is a 17th-century term, found especially in the phrase **carnal trap** (under **carnal parts**).

trapstick is a 17th-century term for penis. *See also* **stick**.

tray bits, trey bits n pl
Australian

breasts. Based on the rhyme with **tits** (under **tit**), and derived from tray

meaning three, this is 20th-century coinage. *See also* **threepenny bits**.

tread v

copulate. This old euphemism is based on the standard sense of copulation among turtles and fowl. It dates back to the 14th century.

● "I'll hug, I'll kiss, I'll play,
And cock-like, hens I'll tread,
And sport in any way,
But in the bridal bed."
(Robert Herrick, 1591–1674, "The Poet Loves a Mistress, But Not to Marry")

treason n

illicit sexual intercourse. This is a 17th-century literary term that refers to its occurrence out of wedlock or as adultery.

● ". . . to have committed fleshly treason with her."
(Thomas Dekker, *Westward Hoe*, 1607)

treasury n

vagina. This colloquial term dates back to the 16th century and is based on the sense of value. *See also* **jewel case** and **purse**.

tree of life, tree of love n
phrase

penis. These are 19th-century euphemisms. *See also* **arborvitae**, **stalk**, and **stem**.

● "Then straight before the wondering maid,
The tree of life I gently laid."
(Richard Brinsley Sheridan, 1751–1816, "The Geranium")

trench n *British*

vagina. This late 18th-century term is based on shape. Today the term may be suggestive of aggression because of the allusion to trench warfare. *See also* **cleft**, **furrow**, and **gash**.

• "I'll give them seven wenches,
  With fists so hard they've kept
      their trenches
  From being storm'd."
  (Thomas Bridges, *A Burlesque
  Translation of Homer*, 1770)

trey bits *n pl*
See **tray bits**.

tribadism *n*
lesbianism. This standard and formal term dates back to the 17th century. It derives from the Greek *tri-
bein*, meaning "rub."
• "The dildo was used not only for
  solitary satisfaction but by
  women homosexuals, whom the
  Greeks . . . called tribads.
  Tribadism was believed by the
  Athenians to be more common in
  Sparta than in Athens. . . ."
  (Reay Tannahill, *Sex in History*,
  1979)

trick *n*
1. copulation. This usage originated in the 17th century and is probably based on the standard sense of
a mischievous act.
2. *American* prostitute's customer.
Possibly referring to the deceit of pre-
tending to be sexually turned on, this
usage dates back to the mid-20th century. *See also* **turn a trick**.
trick-babe is mid-20th-century
American usage for prostitute.
trick baby is a child born to a prostitute resulting from sex with a client.
trickster is a 20th-century American
term for prostitute.

trick *v*
copulate. This 20th-century term is
used of women, especially prostitutes.

trifle *v*
sexually caress or play with someone. This euphemism dates back to
the 19th century.

trifle *n*
penis. This is a 19th-century colloquialism. *See also* **toy**.

trigger *n*
penis. This is a 19th-century term.
See also **gun** and **shoot**.

trim *v British*
1. deflower. This is a 16th-century
term.
2. copulate. This usage dates back
to the 16th century.
• "Let him with Nell lay tit for tat,
  And trim her till I eat my hat."
  (Thomas Bridges, *A Burlesque
  Translation of Homer*, 1770)
trim and buff is 18th-century usage
for deflower or copulate.

trinket *n British*
female genitals. This is an 18th-
century euphemism. *See also* **ring**
and **jewel**.
• "Women sometimes lose more
  than they are able to pay, and . . .
  the lady may be induced to try if,
  instead of gold, the gentleman
  will accept of a trinket."
  (John Vanbrugh, *The Provok'd
  Husband*, 1728)

trip *n*
prostitute. This 19th-century term
may be based on **ride**.
trip up the Rhine is British military
usage for copulation dating to post–
World War II, when British troops
were stationed in Germany.

Trojan *n American*
condom. This 20th-century colloquialism is based on a trademarked
brand of condoms. *See also* **Durex**.

troll *v*
seek customers for prostitution.
Significantly, troll also means to fish
with a hook. *See also* **trollop**.

trolley and truck n phrase
British

copulation. This early 20th-century rhyming slang term is based on the rhyme with **fuck**. It also suggests **ride**.

trollop n

sexually promiscuous woman. This standard term derives from the German *trolle*, meaning "prostitute." It has been in use since the 17th century. The term is also applied colloquially to prostitutes. *See also* **trull**.

trombone n

penis. This 19th-century usage is based on shape and the sliding **in-and-out** (under **in**) in playing the instrument. Furthermore, the **bone** in trombone has sexual meaning. *See also* **flute** and **horn**.

trot n British

prostitute, especially an old one. This is a 16th-century derogatory term. *See also* **ride**.

trot out one's pussy v
phrase British

copulate. This 19th-century expression, said of women, may refer to trotting out a horse to get it ready for being mounted. *See also* **pussy**.

trounce v British

copulate. This 19th-century usage suggests aggressiveness. The expression may have been influenced by **bounce**. *See also* **hit**.

trout n

vagina. This 17th-century literary euphemism may be based on **fish**.

truck driver n American

male or female homosexual with strong masculine characteristics. This is a mid-20th-century gay term.

trull n

prostitute. This early 16th-century colloquialism derives from the German *trolle*, meaning "prostitute." *See also* **trollop**.

- "This is no place for such youths and their trulls."
  (John Fletcher, *The Fair Maid of the Inn*, 1625)

tube n

1. vagina. This is a 20th-century term based on shape. Like **pump**, tube serves to characterize both the vagina and the penis.
2. penis. This is also a 20th-century term based on shape.
tube-steak is mid-20th-century African American usage for penis. *See also* **meat**.
3. *American* promiscuous female. This is a derogatory 20th-century term.

tubs n pl

baths, especially public or Turkish, where homosexual men meet. This is a 20th-century term. *See also* **baths**.

tumble v

1. copulate. This 16th-century literary euphemism is based on the standard sense of fall or toss about.
- "What priest beside thyself e'er grumbl'd
  To have his daughter tightly tumbl'd."
  (Thomas Bridges, *A Burlesque Translation of Homer*, 1770)
tumble in is a 19th-century British euphemism meaning get into bed and copulate.
2. caress or fondle sexually. This usage also dates back to the 16th century.

tummy fuck v phrase
American

simulate copulation. This 20th-century gay term, applied to male homosexuals, is based on the rubbing of the penis on the partner's midriff.

tuna n American

1. women considered as sex objects. This is a 20th-century term. *See also* **fish**.
2. female genitals, especially in the phrase **have a tuna sandwich** or **eat a tuna sandwich**, meaning perform cunnilingus.

tunnel n

vagina. This euphemism embodies the classic Freudian symbolism of a train entering a tunnel, representing sexual intercourse. *See also* **cave**.

tup v British

copulate. This 19th-century colloquialism is based on the standard sense of a ram's copulation with an ewe.
• "Before our chief could tup her
  . . . send home the dame
  As good a virgin as she came."
  (Thomas Bridges, *A Burlesque Translation of Homer*, 1770)

turk n

active male homosexual. Possibly derived from the alleged practice of sodomy among Turkish soldiers in the 19th century, this is 20th-century usage. *See also* **Greek**.

Turkish medal n

undone fly. This 20th-century colloquialism is based on the showing of medals, meaning the male genitals, and may be influenced by **turk**. *See also* **X.Y.Z.**

turn n

an act of copulation. This colloquialism is based on the standard meanings of turn as a short trip out and back, as in a turn through the park, or a period of activity in a game or bout.

take a turn in the bush, take a turn in the hay and **take a turn in the stubble** are all 19th-century colloquialisms meaning copulate. Hay suggests a farm setting. *See also* **bush** and **stubble**.

turn a trick is an early 20th-century American underworld expression meaning practice prostitution or perform a homosexual act.

turn gay v phrase British

1. become a prostitute. This late 19th-century usage is now obsolete.
2. become homosexual. This newer usage, dating to the mid-20th century, has replaced the first meaning.

turn on v phrase

sexually arouse someone. This colloquialism dates back to the early 20th century and may refer to switching on a switch, as for a light. **Turn-on** is the noun.
• "Besides the sexual ennui that set in over the past twenty years, with the sight of naked flesh no longer the turn-on that it used to be, a growing disenchantment with promiscuity and recent evidence that sun exposure damages skin have conspired to cover up the body again."
  (Holly Brubach, "In Fashion," *The New Yorker*, September 2, 1991)

turnip n

glans or head of the penis. Based on shape, and reinforced by a turnip being a food, this is 20th-century usage. *See also* **acorn** and **radish**.

turnpike n

vagina. This 18th-century term puns on **gate**, **passage**, and **pike**.

turns n pl

menstruation. This 20th-century colloquialism refers to the cyclic nature of menstruation.

turrets n pl

breasts. This 16th-century literary euphemism is based on the standard sense of small, outwardly protruding towers found in fortresses. *See also* **fort**.

turtle n

1. *British* female genitals. This 19th-century usage may derive from turtledove or **snapping turtle** (under **snapper**).

2. *Australian* prostitute. This is early 20th-century usage.

tush, tushy n

buttocks. These colloquial terms derive from the Yiddish *tochis* and date back to the late 19th century. *See also* **tochas**.

• "Her tush is tight and she's got great boobs."
(George V. Higgins, *Rat on Fire*, 1981)

twang v

copulate. This obsolete 16th-century term refers to the sound of a plucked string of a musical instrument. *See also* **thrum**.

twanger is an obsolete 16th-century term for penis.

twat, twot n

female genitals. This word dates back to the mid-17th century and may derive from *twachylle*, an Old English term for "passage," or from two, as perhaps suggested by the labia.

• "A man! That was what she craved. A man with something between his legs that could tickle her, that could make her writhe in ecstasy, make her grab that bushy twat of hers with both hands and rub it joyfully."
(Henry Miller, *Tropic of Cancer*, 1934)

twatchel and **twachel** are British and American dialectal variants, respectively.

twat rug is a 19th-century British term for female pubic hair.

twat say is a 1950s camp expression for "What did you say?"

tweak n British

1. prostitute. This 16th-century colloquialism is obsolete.

2. lecher. This 18th-century colloquialism is based on the standard sense of pinch.

twiddle v British

copulate. This is 19th-century coinage. *See also* **diddle**.

twig and berries n phrase

penis and testicles. This 20th-century euphemism is said especially of young boys. *See also* **berries**.

twin n British

female genitals. Possibly derived from **twat**, this is a 20th-century euphemism.

twin lovelies n pl

breasts, especially attractive ones. This is a late 19th-century euphemism.

twins n pl American

1. testicles. This is early 20th-century usage.

2. breasts. This is also early 20th-century usage. *See also* **pair**.

twinkle toes n

effeminate male homosexual. This is a 20th-century expression. *See also* **angel** and **fairy**.

twist n

passive lesbian. This mid-20th-century gay usage may derive from the rhyming slang term **twist and twirl**, meaning a girl.

twister n

person who is considered to be sexually perverted or twisted. This is a mid-20th-century term. **Twisty** is the adjective. *See also* **bent** and **kinky**.

twit n

effeminate male homosexual. This is a 20th-century derogatory term.

twitchet n American

female genitals. This 19th-century dialectal term may derive from **twat** or **twatchel**.
twitchet-struck is a dialectal term for someone who is crazy over women, equivalent to **cunt-struck**.

twixt wind and water adj

phrase
referring to the vagina. This 17th-century jocular expression is based on the location of the vagina between the anus and the urethral opening.

twixter n British

masculine female or feminine male. This 19th-century euphemism is based on "twixt," meaning "between."

two-bit hustler n American

cheap prostitute, either male or female. This is 20th-century underworld usage. *See also* **hustler**.

two-by-four n

prostitute. Based on the rhyme with **whore**, this is a 20th-century rhyming slang term. *See also* **six-to-four**.

twofer n

prostitute. Possibly based on two-timing, that is, deceiving, this is 19th-century usage. *See also* **trick**.

two leav'd book n

See **book**.

twot n

See **twat**.

two-way baby n

bisexual. This is a 20th-century euphemism.

U

udders n pl

breasts. This sometimes derogatory term is based on the standard sense of an animal's teats. It dates back to the 18th century.

Ugandan affairs n British

sexual intercourse. This is a current euphemism. *See also* **discussing Uganda**.

ugly n American

sexual intercourse. Used especially in the expression **the ugly**, this is 20th-century southern dialectal usage. *See also* **the naughty**.

the ultimate favour n

phrase British
sexual intercourse. This is a late 17th-century euphemism. A variant is **the last favour** (under **last act**). *See also* **favor**.
• "If she ever grants me the last favour—I give her leave to cast me off for ever."
(John Crowne, *Married Beau*, 1694)

uncle n

1. penis. This colloquial term stems from uncle being a familiar and

familial term of address. In its sexual sense, the word dates back to the 19th century. *See also* **big brother**.

uncle dick is 20th-century usage for penis, based on the rhyme with **prick**, although **dick** itself is a term for penis.

2. *American* male homosexual, especially a pederast interested in young boys or an elderly homosexual. This usage dates back to the early 20th century. *See also* **aunt**.

undamaged goods n
American

female virgin. This 20th-century, often derogatory, expression exemplifies the sexual objectification of women. *See also* **commodity**, **merchandise**, and **wares**.

under adj, n, prep
referring to the genitals.

bit of under is a 1960s British colloquialism for copulation, also suggesting under the sheets.

go underpetticoating is an obsolete 17th-century expression for copulate, said of men, and based on the connection of underclothes with the genitals.

under-dimple is a 19th-century British euphemism for female genitals. *See also* **dimple**.

undergo is a 16th-century literary euphemism for copulate, said especially of women and punning on being under a man.

underpants is an obsolete 19th-century colloquialism for genitals, either male or female.

understand is a 16th-century literary euphemism meaning copulate. It is said of women and puns on **stand**, meaning an erection, and understand, meaning **know**.

undertake is a 16th-century literary euphemism meaning copulate. It is said of women and puns on the standard senses take from under and

commit to do. Consequently, **undertaker** is an obsolete British jocular term for vagina. It dates back to the 19th century and puns on the literal sense of take under and the standard sense of one who prepares the dead for burial. *See also* **bury**.

undercover man n
American

male homosexual. Punning on secrecy and being in bed, under the sheets, this is an early 20th-century term.

the unemployed n British
penis. This jocular contemporary term used by men suggests celibacy but not by choice. The terms puns on the current high rate of unemployment in Britain, hence the popular joke: "Question: Do you wear underpants in the bath? Answer: Yes, it doesn't do to look down on the unemployed."

unfortunate n
prostitute. This obsolete 19th-century euphemism alludes to a profession regarded as resulting from unfortunate circumstances. **Unfortunate woman** is a fuller version.

union n
sexual intercourse. This euphemism is based on the standard meaning of joining or coming together. It dates back to the 15th century. The word also applies to animal copulation. **United** is a euphemism for engaged in sexual intercourse. *See also* **congress**.

unit n American
penis. This 20th-century euphemism puns on singularity and on **equipment**.

unmentionable vice n

British

any sexual act considered perverted, especially sodomy. This is a 19th-century euphemism. *See also* **vice**.

unnatural *adj*

referring to any sexual act considered perverted, especially sodomy. Based on the premise that vaginal intercourse is the only natural sexual act, **unnatural connection**, **unnatural intercourse**, and **unnatural vice** are typical 19th-century euphemisms.

unruly member n *British*

penis. This 19th-century jocular euphemism relies on a parliamentary analogy. *See also* **member for Cockshire** (under **member**).

unsliced bologna n

American

uncircumcised penis. This 20th-century term refers to shape and to bologna being a **sausage**.

up *adj*

referring to an erect penis. This colloquialism dates back to the 19th century and is found in the expression **get it up**. *See also* **stand** and **stiff**.
uplifting is a 20th-century American euphemism for sexually arousing, punning on the senses of erection and of improving and inspiring.
upright grand is a 20th-century jocular expression for erect penis, punning on piano, which suggests **organ**.

up *v*

copulate. This 19th-century colloquialism is said of men.
have it up (a woman) is a 19th-century colloquialism for copulate, said of men.

upper works n pl *British*

breasts. Variants of this obsolete colloquialism are **upper decks** and **upstairs**.

upright n *British*

sexual intercourse in the standing position. This is 18th-century British usage. It is found in the expression **do an upright**. *See also* **do a perpendicular**.

upright grin, upright wink n *phrase British*

female genitals. These are obsolete 19th-century terms based on shape and position. *See also* **eye** and **yawn**.

up the duff, up the spout *adj phrase British*

pregnant. These are 20th-century colloquialisms. Spout suggests vagina, though another colloquial sense of up the spout means spoilt, giving the expression a pejorative sense. The same is true of duff, which is slang for "no good." **Up the poke**, **up the pole**, and **up the stick** are variants.

uranian n, *adj*

male homosexual. This literary term is based on the Greek *ouranios*, meaning "heavenly." It was probably strongly influenced by **anus** in the word Uranus. The term dates back to the late 19th century.
• "To have altered my life would have been to have admitted that Uranian love is ignoble." (Oscar Wilde, in R. Hart-Davis, *Letters*, 1962)

use *v*

copulate. This euphemism dates back to the 16th century.

use of the sex n *phrase*

copulation. This is a 19th-century euphemism.

usher n British

pederast. This term dates back to the late 18th century and is based on the sense of ushering in, meaning leading in or inserting.

V

vacuum n British

vagina. This is an 18th-century jocular term. *See also* **nothing** and **hole**. **vacuum cleaner** is a 20th-century term for cunnilinguist, based on the suction of a vacuum cleaner.

vagina n

female copulatory organ. This standard English term derives from the Latin word meaning "sheath." It dates back to the late 17th century. **vagina dentata** is Latin for vagina with teeth. It is a psychoanalytic term for a male castration fantasy. *See also* **bite** and **mouth that cannot bite**.

valve n

female genitals. This 19th-century usage is based on the standard sense of a device that regulates in-and-out movement. It may have been influenced by the closeness in sound to **vulva**.

varnish one's cane v

phrase Canadian

copulate. This 20th-century expression is used of men. *See also* **polish** and **stick**.

Vatican roulette n American

the rhythm method of contraception; that is, abstention from intercourse during the woman's presumed fertile period. This mid-20th-century jocular expression refers to the Catholic doctrine that forbids all artificial methods of contraception. Roulette implies that this method involves a big risk.

vault v

copulate. This late 16th-century literary term is said of men, especially when illicit activity is involved. As a term of action, vault joins similar terms with the same sexual meaning such as **jump**, **mount**, and **scale**. **vaulting school** and **vaulting house** are 17th-century British euphemisms for brothel.

• "A vaulting house . . . Where I use to spend my afternoons among superb she-gamesters . . ." (Philip Massinger, *The Unnatural Combat*, 1619)

VD n

venereal disease. This is a 20th-century colloquial abbreviation.

vegetable n

lesbian. This 20th-century gay term is based on the parallel with **fruit**, meaning a male homosexual. Contrast **meat** and **flesh**.

vegetarian n

male homosexual who will not fellate. This is 20th-century gay jocular usage. It refers to the diet of a vegetarian, who will not **eat meat**.

velcro n

lesbian. This late 1980s term refers to a brand name for fasteners that mesh together and the supposed resemblance to two female pubic areas in contact.

velvet n

vagina. This 17th-century usage is based on smoothness. The term is made more explicit in **velvet sheath**

(See also **sheath**). Velvet is also a colloquial term for tongue.

tip the velvet means perform cunnilingus. This British expression also dates back to the 17th century.

velvet orbs n pl

testicles. This expression dates from the 1960s and suggests smoothness. See also **orbs**.

venery n British

sexual sport. This literary euphemism puns on hunting and on **Venus**. It dates back to the 15th century. **Venereal** is the standard adjective, while **venereal disease**, which dates back to the mid-17th century, is the standard term for any contagious disease contracted from sexual activity.

vent n

vagina. This 20th-century usage refers to an opening. See also **gate**.

venture v

copulate. This obsolete 17th-century euphemism puns on to try and to undertake an adventure.
venturer is 19th-century British usage for prostitute.

Venus n

sex in general. The Roman goddess of love and beauty inspired this common euphemism that dates back to the 15th century.
Venus's cell is a 16th-century euphemism for vagina.
Venus's curse is a 19th-century euphemism for venereal disease.
Venus's glove is a 16th-century literary euphemism for vagina, based on glove meaning **sheath**.
Venus's highway is an 18th-century euphemism for vagina based on highway being a passage. See also **dead-end street** and **main avenue**.

Venus's honeypot is an 18th-century British euphemism for vagina. See also **honeypot**.
Venus's mark is a 19th-century euphemism for female genitals. See also **mark**.

verge n

penis. This 15th-century colloquialism is based on the Latin virga, meaning **rod**. The term is standard English for the copulatory organ of insects.

vert n

sexual pervert. This is a 19th-century colloquial abbreviation of **pervert**.

vibrator n

battery-operated dildo or vibrating device. This is a 20th-century standard term.
• "As vibrators have been mentioned, may I add that it need not be ... penis-shaped." (Germaine Greer, The Female Eunuch, 1970)

vice n

1. sexual immorality. This standard term which dates back to the 13th century, also means sinfulness in general or depravity.
2. vagina. This 16th-century literary term puns on grip and sin. **Vise** is an American variant.
3. American prostitution. This is a 20th-century euphemism.
vice sister is a 20th-century American euphemism for prostitute. See also **sister**.

vice versa n

mutual oral sex. Based on mutuality of action, and suggesting sinfulness, this is 20th-century usage. See also **sixty-nine**.

Victoria Monk n British

semen. This obsolete 19th-century rhyming slang term is based on the rhyme with **spunk**.

virgin n

person who has never had sexual intercourse. This standard term derives from the Latin and dates back to the 13th century. Though originally applied to females only, it now applies to males as well. Throughout the Victorian period, the term was taboo. In ancient Greece, the word originally applied to an unmarried woman who was free to take or reject lovers. Christianity directed the change in meaning to the current one. **virgin-head** is a 17th-century colloquialism for hymen; **virgin-knot** is a variant. See also **maidenhead**.
virgin queen is 20th-century American gay usage for a male homosexual who refuses anal intercourse until after "marriage."
virgin treasure is an early 16th-century British term for female genitals.

virile adj

potent or having masculine copulatory capability. This standard English term derives from the Latin *virilus*, meaning "manly," and dates back to the 15th century.
virile member is a euphemism for penis that dates back to the 18th century. See also **member**.
virilia is the standard Latin medical term for the male genitals.

vise n American

See **vice**.

visitors n pl

menstruation. This is an early 20th-century euphemism. See also **have one's aunt with one**.

vitals n pl

genitals of either sex. This 19th-century euphemism refers to their importance in being essential for the creation of life.

vital statistics n pl

body measurements supposedly relating to sexuality. This colloquialism usually refers to a woman's breast, waist, and hip measurements, though the term has also been applied to the size of a man's penis.

vitamins n pl

semen. This 20th-century euphemism is based on the life-giving quality of vitamins. See also **protein**.

vixen n

sexually aggressive or sexually athletic woman. From the 12th century on, vixen had a negative connotation, meaning shrew or bad-tempered woman. Today, however, it has taken on a certain positive connotation within the world of pornography. See also **fox**.
• "Passionate Patti is only one of the voluptuous vixens Leisure Suit Larry pursues." ("Erotic Electronic Encounters," Time, September 23, 1991)

voluptuous adj

sexually arousing. Derived from the Latin *voluptas*, meaning "pleasure," and dating back to the 14th century, this is a standard English term.

voyeur n

one who gains sexual gratification from observing others in sexual acts. This standard term dates back to the early 20th century. See also **peep**.

vulva n

external female genitals. Derived from the Latin term meaning uterus or matrix, this standard English word dates back to the mid-16th century. The *Oxford English Dictionary* reveals it to be primarily an anatomical term from its first use through to the 20th century.

- "Three things are insatiable: The desert, the grave, and a woman's vulva."
  (Allen Edwardes, *The Jewel in the Lotus: A Historical Survey of the Sexual Culture of the East*, 1959)

W

wad *n American*

semen. This 20th-century usage is found in expressions such as **shoot one's wad**, meaning ejaculate. The term derives from a standard sense of wad meaning a soft mass.

wag *n American*

penis, especially that of a child. This is a 20th-century euphemism. *See also* **tail**.

wag-tail *n*

prostitute. This usage dates back to the 16th century. *See also* **tail**.

waiter *n American*

male homosexual who waits in public rest rooms to meet other male homosexuals. This is mid-20th-century gay usage.

walk-up *n*

brothel. This is a 20th-century American euphemism.
walk-up fuck is a 20th-century Australian term for a woman who will have sex with any man who walks up to her and asks.

wallet *n*

vagina. This 18th-century usage is based on the container metaphor. *See also* **purse** and **money**.

wallopies *n pl American*

breasts, especially large ones. This is mid-20th-century coinage.

wallow *v American*

copulate. Based on the standard sense meaning delight or take pleasure in something, this term originated in the 20th century.

wand *n British*

penis. This 19th-century usage puns on shape and the ability to make magic, perhaps in helping a woman achieve orgasm. *See also* **magic wand** and **stick**.

wang, whang *n*

penis. This 20th-century coinage may derive from whang meaning a thong, or the sound of a strike.

- "My wang was all I really had that I could call my own."
  (Philip Roth, *Portnoy's Complaint*, 1969)

wank, whank *v British*

1. masturbate. **Wank off** is a variant. These common colloquialisms may derive from **wang**, meaning strike, or from combining whack and **yank**. The terms date back to the 19th century.

- "For screwing's always fit to spout
  And VD you can moan about,
  But wanking hasn't any clout."
  (Charles Thomson, "On the Low Status of Masturbation," in John Whitworth, editor, *The Faber Book of Blue Verse*, 1990)

wanker is a colloquialism for masturbator.

2. copulate. This 19th-century usage is obsolete.

wanton adj, n

lustful, sensual; also lewd, bawdy. This standard term dates back to the 14th century. It is also used as a noun for a lewd or lascivious person.

• "I pictured him in his office . . . some exotic olive-skinned wanton sprawled on her back across his desk, her ankles locked around his waist. . . ."
(Lewis Shiner, "Scales," in Ellen Datlow, editor, *Alien Sex*, 1990)

wap v

copulate. This 17th-century usage is based on the sense meaning to strike. It is now obsolete.
wapping-mort, also obsolete, means prostitute. *See also* **mort**.

ware n

male or female genitals. This euphemism dates back to the 15th century. *See also* **article**, **commodity**, **merchandise**, and **thing**.

wares n pl British

breasts. This is an 18th-century euphemism.

warm member n British

1. prostitute. This is 19th-century coinage.
2. lecher. This is also a 19th-century term. *See also* **member**.

warm shop n British

brothel. This is a 20th-century euphemism.

warren n

brothel. This 17th-century euphemism is based on the standard sense of a rabbit colony, with rabbit implying **cunny**, and suggests the rabbit's reputation for prolific copulation.

warts n pl

small breasts. This is a 20th-century derogatory term.

washer n

condom. This 20th-century colloquialism is based on its protective use in plumbing.

wasp n British

prostitute with venereal disease. This 19th-century term refers to a wasp's ability to inflict a painful sting.

waste pipe n British

vagina. This is 19th-century derogatory usage. *See also* **drain**, **pipe**, and **sluice**.

waste time v phrase

masturbate. This is a 20th-century euphemism.

watch and seals n phrase British

penis and testicles. This 19th-century colloquialism evolved because men used to wear their watches and seals hanging on a chain in a pocket. *See also* **seals**.

watch-queen n

voyeur. This is a mid-20th-century gay expression. *See also* **queen**.

water engine, water works n

1. urethral opening in women. These colloquialisms date back to the 19th century.
2. penis. Also dating back to the 19th century, these terms refer to the urinary function.

water mill, water-box n British

female genitals. Water mill is a 19th-century colloquialism, while water-box dates back to the 16th century. *See also* **mill** and **box**.

water sports n

urination that forms part of sexual activity. This is a 20th-century expression. *See also* **sport** and **golden shower**.

watermelons n pl American

large breasts. This 20th-century colloquialism is based on size. *See also* **melons**.

wazoo n American

any of various sexual parts, including the vagina, anus, penis, or mouth. This is a 20th-century euphemism. *See also* **bazoo** and **kazoo**.
- "A portable vacuum cleaner is most helpful for sand up the wazoo."
(David Feinberg, *Eighty-Sixed*, 1989)

weapon n

penis. This has been a standard term since the 11th century, and was commonly found in literature. Only during the 20th century did the sexual usage become a rarity. Many weaponlike terms have been used to symbolize the penis, including **bayonet**, **gun**, **lance**, **pike**, and **sword**.
- "And now . . . I saw, with wonder and surprise . . . not the plaything of a boy, not the weapon of a man, but a maypole of so enormous a standard . . . it must have belong'd to a giant."
(John Cleland, *Fanny Hill: Memoirs of a Woman of Pleasure*, 1749)

wear bifocals v phrase

be bisexual. This is a 20th-century euphemism. *See also* **bi** (under **bisexual**).

wedding-kit n British

male genitals. This is a 19th-century euphemism. **Wedding tackle** is a recent variant.

wedge n

penis. This 19th-century usage is based on shape and function.

wedge v

copulate. This usage may be Caribbean in origin.

weekend ho n American

part-time prostitute. **Ho** is a dialectal version of **whore**. **Weekend warrior** based on the colloquial term for military reservists, is a variant of this mid-20th-century black expression.

weenie n American

little boy's penis. This is a 20th-century colloquialism, often used by small children.

weewee n

1. urethral opening in a female. This euphemism dates back to the 19th century and is based on wee meaning urine.
2. penis, especially that of a little boy. This is also a euphemism.

well-bred adj

lascivious. This 20th-century colloquialism puns on frequency of acts of breeding (copulation) and good breeding.

well-developed, well-stacked adj

referring to a woman who has large breasts. These are 20th-century colloquialisms. *See also* **stacked**.

well-endowed adj

referring to a male with large genitals or a female with large breasts. This is a 20th-century euphemism.

well-hung, well-built *adj*

pertaining to a male with large genitals. These euphemisms date back to the 17th century.

- "Had she picked out, to rub her arse on,
  Some stiff-pricked clown or well-hung parson."
  (John Wilmot, the earl of Rochester, "A Ramble in St. James's Park," *Works*, 1680)

welt *n British*

large penis. This 20th-century military term is obsolete. A welt results from flogging, and thus may suggest aggressive intent.

wench *n*

1. lascivious young woman. The term dates back to the 13th century, when it meant female servant. The word derives from the Old English meaning of a child of either sex. By the 14th century the word had obtained its current meaning.
- "I am a gentiwoman, and no wenche."
  (Geoffrey Chaucer, *Canterbury Tales*, 1383)
2. prostitute. This usage also dates back to the 14th century.
- "These London Wenches are so stout,
  They care not what they do;
  They will not let you have a Bout,
  Without a Crown or two."
  (Thomas D'Urfey, *Wit and Mirth*, 1719)

wench *v*

chase or pursue prostitutes. This term dates back to the late 16th century.
- "Given he was exceedingly to wenching."
  (Philemon Holland, translator, *Pliny's Historie of the World*, 1601)

Wesson party *n American*

group sex party in which participants cover their naked bodies in cooking oil. This mid-20th-century expression refers to Wesson, a brand name of cooking oil. *See also* **Mazola party**.

western end *n*

buttocks. This obsolete 19th-century expression is based on direction. *See also* **end**.

wet *adj*

sexually aroused. This colloquial usage, said especially of women, refers to the lubrication that comes from arousal. The term dates back to the 18th century. *See also* **juicy**.
do a wet bottom means copulate. This British expression, said of women, dates back to the 19th century. A variant is **get a wet bottom**.
wet decks is a 19th-century expression for a woman who has just copulated. *See also* **buttered bun** (under **butter**).

wet dream *n*

emission of semen while asleep. This colloquialism dates back to the 19th century.

wet one's wick *v phrase American*

copulate. Said of men, this is a 20th-century expression. *See also* **wick**.

wet season *n Australian*

menstrual period. This is 20th-century usage.

whack it up *v phrase British*

copulate. Possibly based on whack meaning strike, this is a 19th-century expression. *See also* **up**.

whack off _v phrase_
masturbate. This is a 20th-century expression.

whacker _n American_
penis. This coinage originated in the 20th century.

wham bam thank you ma'am _n phrase American_
sexual intercourse characterized by the man's rapid and selfish, though polite, use of the woman. This jocular expression dates back to the late 19th century.

whang _n_
See **wang**.

whank _v_
See **wank**.

what _n British_
1. penis. This is an 18th-century euphemism.
2. female genitals. This euphemism is found especially in phrases such as **what's-its-name** and **the Lord knows what**.

what Eve did with Adam, what mother did before me _n phrase British_
copulation. These are 19th-century euphemisms. See _also_ **do**.

wheel _n_
vulva. This literary euphemism is based on shape. See _also_ **ring**.

whelk _n_
female genitals. This is a 19th-century term. See _also_ **oyster**.

where uncle's doodle goes _n phrase British_
vagina. This is a 19th-century euphemism. A Scottish variant is **where the monkey sleeps**. See _also_ **doodle** and **monkey**.

whim _n_
female genitals. Perhaps based on the standard sense of an impulsive thought or wish, and almost certainly reflecting the male viewpoint, this is an 18th-century term.
whim-wham is an early 18th-century British expression meaning the female genitals, with wham meaning **hit**, thus suggesting sexual intercourse.

whip _n_
penis. This mid-20th-century usage suggests a punitive instrument.

whip one's wire, whip one's dummy _v phrase American_
masturbate. These 20th-century expressions are said of men. See _also_ **wire**.

whipped cream _n_
semen, especially when ejaculated in an erotic dream. This is 20th-century usage. See _also_ **cream**, **dream whip**, and **wet dream**.

whirlygigs _n pl British_
testicles. This colloquial 17th-century term is probably based on the shape of a whirlygig, a type of spinning toy.

whisker _n American_
prostitute. This 20th-century usage may refer to a connection with **hair**, suggesting sexuality, **cat**, since it too is a slang term for prostitute and is associated with whiskers, or be based on the sense of whisking, that is, snatching. See _also_ **snatch**.

whistle n

penis. This colloquialism dates back to the 19th century. *See also* **flute**.

whistle v American

fellate. This is 20th-century usage. *See also* **blow**.

white honey n British

semen. Based on appearance and texture, this is late 19th-century coinage. *See also* **honey**.

white meat n

genitals of a white person, especially a woman. This is 20th-century usage, often derogatory. **Light meat** is a variant. *See also* **meat** and **dark meat**.

whitewash v American

ejaculate. This recent term is based on the similarity in appearance of semen and whitewash.

whole n

vagina. This 16th-century literary euphemism puns on **hole** and on whole meaning total or complete.

wholemeal is a mid-20th-century lesbian term for a heterosexual female, perhaps punning on **hole** meal and suggesting healthiness.

wholesale is a 16th-century literary euphemism for prostitution, punning on **hole** and sale.

whole voyage is a 16th-century euphemism for sexual intercourse, suggesting **go all the way** (under **all**).

whomp it up v phrase

fellate. Based on the sound of eating, where it means penis, this is 20th-century coinage.

whore n

1. prostitute. This standard term dates back to the 11th century. Its et-

ymology can be traced back via Old English and Old Norse to the Latin *carus*, meaning "dear." Up through the 18th century, the word was acceptable even in serious literature. By the 19th century, the word was considered vulgar and had become taboo. Noah Webster dropped every occurrence of the term in his 1833 edition of the Bible. By the 1970s the taboo had largely disappeared: In 1977, *The New York Times* printed the full title of a musical called *The Best Little Whorehouse in Texas*.

whore-bitch is early 20th-century American dialectal derogatory usage for prostitute.

whorehouse has been a standard term for brothel since the 16th century, though somewhat risqué from the Victorian period to the mid-20th century.

whoremonger is a standard term for a sexually promiscuous man, especially one who pursues prostitutes. It has been in use since the 16th century, though it is rarely used today.

whore-pipe is an obsolete 18th-century term for penis. *See also* **pipe**.

whore's milk is 20th-century usage for semen. *See also* **milk**.

2. promiscuous male homosexual. This is 20th-century gay usage.

wick n

penis. This 20th-century rhyming slang term comes from Hampton Wick, an area in London, rhyming with **prick**. The term may have been influenced by the connection of wick with **candle**. Expressions such as **bury one's wick**, **dip one's wick**, and **wet one's wick** all mean copulate.

wicket n British

female genitals. This obsolete 18th-century colloquialism is based on the standard sense meaning **gate**. The term may also have been influenced by "wicked."

wide-open beaver n

pornographic photographs of female genitals. This 20th-century usage is based on **beaver** meaning female genitals. See also **spread beaver**.

widow's comforter n

dildo. This colloquial term dates back to the 19th century.

wiener n

penis. This 20th-century usage refers to **sausage** and puns on wee meaning both urine and small. It is a term often used by children, or in reference to a small boy's penis.

wife n

"feminine" partner in a male homosexual pair. This colloquialism is based on the standard heterosexual sense of the term, which dates back to the 12th century. The homosexual usage dates back to the 19th century.

wife in watercolors n

phrase

mistress. This obsolete 18th-century colloquial expression refers to the nonbinding nature of the relationship with a mistress. See also **left-handed wife**.

wife's best friend n phrase

penis. This colloquialism is used mainly by men. It is found in the expression **shake hands with the wife's best friend**, meaning masturbate.

wig n

female pubic hair. This usage dates back to the 18th century. **Lower wig** is a variant. See also **hair** and **toupee**.

willing adj

sexually available or lusty. This has been a standard term since the 14th century.

willy, willie n British

1. penis. This 20th-century colloquialism is often used by children. See also **weewee**.
2. effeminate male homosexual. This is 20th-century derogatory heterosexual usage.

wiltshire n British

impotence. This jocular term dates back to the 1970s and is based on wilt meaning become limp. See also **cockshire** (under **cock**).

win v

copulate. This literary euphemism from the 16th century refers to success, as in a sport. See also **score**.

windmill n British

anus. This 19th-century colloquialism alludes to the outlet for wind, just as **water mill** refers to the female genitals.

window-tappery n American

brothel. This 20th-century underworld expression is based on the practice of tapping on a window to gain admission to a brothel, or a prostitute's tapping to get the attention of passersby.

windward passage n

British

anus. This late 18th-century colloquialism refers to an outlet for wind or farts. See also **windmill**.

winkle n British

penis. This 19th-century colloquialism is used mainly by children. See also **weewee**.

wire n

penis. Based on both length and the idea of pulling a wire, this is 20th-century usage. See also **pull wire**.

wired up *adj phrase*

sexually willing or lusty. Based on the notion of being connected to electricity, this 20th-century expression also means drugged up.

wolf n

1. male who chases after women. Based on the aggressive or seductive characteristics of a wolf, this is early 20th-century usage.
2. masculine lesbian. This is mid-20th-century gay usage.
3. pederast. Based on **lamb** meaning catamite, this, too, is 20th-century gay usage.

wolf v

perform anal intercourse. This is a 20th-century gay term.

woman n

1. adult female. This has been a standard term since the time of Old English. It derives from *wifman*, tho gender opposite of *weapman*, meaning "man." Though *wif* is not etymologically connected to wife, it could be related to Old English *we-fan*, meaning "weave." With the derogation of **lady**, woman is, today, the most common term for an adult female.
old woman is 19th-century British usage for female genitals.
woman about town is a 20th-century British euphemism for prostitute. *See also* **town bike**.
womanhood is a mid-20th-century American euphemism for female genitals. It is the opposite of **manhood**, meaning male genitals or male virility.
woman of easy virtue and **woman of loose morals** are euphemisms for prostitute, the first dating back to the 19th century, the second being 20th-century, mainly American usage.
woman's terms is a 17th-century literary euphemism for menstruation.

woman's home companion is a 20th-century euphemism for menstruation.
2. *American* effeminate man. This is a mid-20th-century colloquialism.

wong n *American*

penis. This is mid-20th-century coinage. *See also* **wang**.

wood n

penis, especially an erect one. This colloquialism originated in the 18th century. *See also* **bat**, **plank**, and **wedge**.

woollies n

pubic hair. This is 20th-century coinage. *See also* **curlies** and **plush**.

wop n

1. penis, especially a large one. This 20th-century colloquialism is possibly based on "whopper," meaning something large, or on the mispronunciation of the Italian *guappo*, meaning "a large handsome man."
2. *Australian* prostitute. Perhaps based on **wap**, this is a 20th-century derogatory term.

work v

perform any sexual activity, including acts of prostitution. This is a 20th-century euphemism.
working girl is a 20th-century American euphemism for prostitute. **Working woman** and **working broad** are variants. With the rise of women in the work force, these terms are obsolescent.
work off and **work it off** are colloquialisms for masturbate that date back to the 19th century. They make use of the classic suffix "off" to indicate orgasm.
work out is a mid-20th-century American expression meaning copulate, based on the athletic sense.

work the hairy oracle and **work the dumb oracle** are 19th-century British euphemisms meaning copulate, said of men. *See also* **oracle**.

work up is a 19th-century colloquialism meaning copulate, said of men.

workshop n

female genitals. This obsolete 18th-century euphemism puns on a place in which to work and a place where things (babies) are made. *See also* **gymnasium**.

world n

breast. This 16th-century literary euphemism alludes to spherical shape. It also suggests everything, which the breast is at first to an infant. *See also* **hemispheres**.

worm n

penis. Dating back to the 19th century, and based on shape, this is one of the few derogatory terms for penis, implying limpness, lowliness, and smallness. *See also* **snake**.

wormeater is 20th-century usage for fellator. *See also* **eat**.

worship at the altar v phrase

fellate. This 20th-century gay expression refers to kneeling in worship. *See also* **kneel at the altar**.

wound n

female genitals. This literary euphemism dates back to the 16th century. It may be based on appearance or on menstrual bleeding. **Everlasting wound** is a variation. *See also* **cut**, **gash**, and **nick**.

wounded in the thigh is a 16th-century literary euphemism meaning deflowered, with thigh offering bodily displacement from the genitals.

wreck a rectum v phrase

perform anal intercourse. This 20th-century coinage is based on the potential harm done to the rectum.

wren n British

prostitute. This 19th-century euphemism may be based on the **bird** sense. *See also* **quail**.

wrench off v phrase

masturbate. This 20th-century expression, said of men, alludes to the hand movements in using a wrench. *See also* **jerk off**.

wriggle v British

masturbate. This 19th-century euphemism, applied to both sexes, is based on the body movements associated with the act.

wriggle navels is a 19th-century British euphemism meaning copulate, based on movement. The expression provides bodily displacement from the genitals to the navel. *See also* **navel**.

wrinkle n

female genitals. This obsolete 20th-century term is based on appearance. *See also* **furrow**.

wrist job n

act of masturbation. This current expression is usually used of males. *See also* **hand job**.

wrong door n

anus. This is a jocular 18th-century expression juxtaposing the anus and the vagina. *See also* **back door**.

X

X-rated *adj*

referring to the rating for pornographic content in films or other material. This standard term was introduced in 1975 in the United States, but in 1991 the X rating for sexually explicit material, which was never copyrighted, was officially dropped. In Great Britain the term **X-certificate** was abandoned in the 1980s. X has long been a symbol for **kiss**, and kiss has long been a euphemism for copulate. X-rated continues to mean sexually explicit or lascivious.

- "She had the usual junk cosmetics; blond tinted hair, red nails, nothing original, except that it all came out X-rated."
(Robert Pirsig, *Lila*, 1991)

X.Y.Z. *v phrase American*

examine your zipper. This is a colloquial 20th-century abbreviation for an expression used by men to alert a man who has an open fly. *See also* **Turkish medal**.

Y

yang *n American*

penis. This mid-20th-century term is probably based on yang being the male principle in Chinese philosophy. In Chinese, yang means light, while yin means dark. The influence of Zen on American culture in the 1960s may have introduced or reinforced this term. Yang is also close in sound to **wang**.

yank *v*

masturbate. This mid-20th-century colloquialism, said of men, is applied in much the same way as **pull** and **jerk**. The term is also found in expressions such as **yank one's strap** and **yank one's yam**, which also mean masturbate. *See also* **wank**.

yard *n*

penis. This term was standard usage from the 14th century until it became obsolete in the 19th century. The term derived from the now obsolete sense of measuring rod, which preceded the current meaning of a measure of length.

yard measure is an obsolete 19th-century British euphemism for vagina.

yard *v*

copulate. This 18th-century colloquialism is now obsolete.

yawn *n*

vagina. This 20th-century term is based on the notion of an open mouth. *See also* **upright grin**.

yeast-powder biscuit *n* *American*

female genitals, especially when swollen from sexual stimulation. This is late 19th-century Californian dialectal usage. *See also* **biscuit**.

yentz *v American*

copulate. Derived from the Yiddish, meaning "that thing," this term dates back to the late 19th century. It also means cheat.

yentzer is a term for one who copulates frequently, usually said of males.

yield one's favors *v phrase* *British*

copulate. This is a 19th-century euphemism, used of women. *See also* **favor** and **grant the favor**.

ying-yang n American

penis. This is a 20th-century term. *See also* **yang**.

yodel v American

1. perform fellatio. This 20th-century underworld term is based on the use of the mouth and tongue.

2. perform cunnilingus. This usage is found especially in the phrase **yodel in the canyon of love**.

3. perform anal intercourse. This is also 20th-century underworld usage.

yogurt n American

semen. This is a recent collegiate colloquialism suggesting fellatio. *See also* **milk**.

yoni n

female genitals. This literary term is based on the Sanskrit, meaning "womb." It dates back to the 18th century, but became familiar in the West with the open publication in the 1960s of the *Kama Sutra. See also* **lingam**.

yosh n

penis. This 20th-century colloquialism may be a variant of **yard**.

you-know-what n phrase

1. female genitals. This euphemism dates back to the mid-17th century. *See also* **it**, **monosyllable**, and **thing**.

2. *British* sex. This is a current euphemism.

yummy it down v phrase

fellate. Based on the sense of eating with relish or pleasure, this is a 20th-century expression. *See also* **eat** and **scarf up**.

yum-yum n British

1. genitals. This 19th-century colloquialism views the genitals as delicious or tasty, and suggests oral sex.

2. sexual intercourse. This colloquialism also dates back to the 19th century.

- "Come, ducky, it's time for yum-yum."
(Samuel Beckett, *Stories and Texts for Nothing*, 1967)

Z

zig-zig v

copulate. This 19th-century obsolete military usage derives from the sense of movement. It is a variant of jig-jig or **jig**, which means to dance. As such it is also related to **jiggle**, another term meaning copulate based on the shaking movement.

zig-zig n

act of copulation. This is obsolete 19th-century military usage. *See also* **jig**.

zipper morals pl n American

loose sexual morals. This mid-20th-century colloquialism is applied to either sex. It refers to a willingness to unzip one's pants for sex.

zipper sex n

fellatio. This is current gay terminology. **Zipper dinner** is a variant.

zipless fuck n

sex without stress, especially between strangers. This is a recent term.

- "The zipless fuck is absolutely pure. It is free of ulterior motives. There is no power game. . . . The zipless fuck is the purest thing there is. And it is rarer than the unicorn."
(Erica Jong, *Fear of Flying*, 1974)

zoo n *American*

brothel. This early 20th-century underworld usage is based on the idea that prostitutes in a brothel often are varied in appearance or origin. The term, though jocular in intent, is derogatory.

zubrick, zoobrick n
Australian

penis. This 20th-century coinage may be based on the rhyme with **prick**, or derived from the Arabic *zubb*, meaning "prickle" or "penis."

Bibliography

The following books and articles have provided me with ideas and quotations for this book.

Arango, Ariel. *Dirty Words*. Jason Aronson, 1989.

Augarde, Tony. *Oxford Dictionary of Modern Quotations*. Oxford University Press, 1991.

Bailey, N. *Universal Etymological Dictionary*. 1721.

Barltrop, Robert, and J. Wolveridge. *The Muvver Tongue*. Journeyman, 1980.

Barnhart, Clarence L. *A Dictionary of New English*. Barnhart Books, 1973.

———. *The Second Barnhart Dictionary of New English*. Barnhart Books, 1980.

Bataille, George. *Eroticism*. City Lights, 1986.

Branford, Jean, editor. *A Dictionary of South African English*. Oxford University Press, 1980.

Bristo, A. *The Sex Life of Plants*. Barrie & Jenkins, 1978.

Bryson, Bill. *The Mother Tongue*. William Morrow, 1990.

Cassidy, Frederic G., editor. *Dictionary of American Regional English*, Vol. 1. Harvard University Press, 1985.

Chapman, Robert L., editor. *New Dictionary of American Slang*. Harper & Row, 1986.

Charney, Maurice. *Sexual Fiction*. Methuen, 1981.

Claire, Elizabeth. *Dangerous English*. Eardley, 1980.

Colman, Ernest A. M. *The Dramatic Use of Bawdy in Shakespeare*. Longman, 1974.

Comfort, Alex. *The Joy of Sex*. Crown, 1972.

Crisp, Quentin. *Quentin Crisp's Book of Quotations*. Macmillan, 1989.

Dally, Peter. *The Fantasy Game*. Avon, 1976.

Daly, Mary. *Gyn/Ecology*. Beacon, 1979.

Dickson, Paul. *Words*. Dell, 1982.

———. *Slang!* Pocket Books, 1990.

Doke, Clement M., and B.W. Vilakazi. *Zulu-English Dictionary*. Witwaterrand University Press, 1964.

Douglas, Mary. *Purity and Danger*. Routledge & Kegan Paul, 1966.

Edwardes, Allen. *The Jewel in the Lotus*. Julian Press, 1959.

Eisiminger, S. "Colorful Language," *Verbatim*, 4:1, 1979.

Farmer, John S., and William E. Henley. *Slang and Its Analogues.* Arno, 1970.

Foucault, Michel. *The History of Sexuality*, Vol. 1. Pantheon, 1978.

Franklin, Julian. *A Dictionary of Rhyming Slang.* Routledge & Kegan Paul, 1960.

Freud, Sigmund. *The Complete Psychological Works.* Norton, 1976.

Fryer, Peter. *Mrs Grundy: Studies in English Prudery.* Corgi, 1965.

———. *Private Case—Public Scandal.* Secker & Warburg, 1966.

Gay, Peter. *The Bourgeois Experience: Victoria to Freud.* Oxford University Press, 1984.

Gerber, Albert. *The Book of Sex Lists.* Ballantine, 1984.

Goldenson, Robert and Kenneth Anderson. *Sex A to Z.* World Almanac, 1989.

Green, Jonathan. *The Dictionary of Contemporary Slang.* Pan, 1984.

Grose, Francis. *Classical Dictionary of the Vulgar Tongue, 1785.* Ayer, 1963.

———. *Dictionary of the Vulgar Tongue, 1811.* Ayer, 1963.

Harrison, Fraser. *The Dark Angel.* Sheldon, 1977.

Hart, Harold H., editor. *The Complete Immortalia.* Bell, 1971.

Henke, James T. *Courtesans and Cuckolds.* Garland, 1979.

Hurwood, Bernhardt. *The Golden Age of Erotica.* Sherbourne, 1965.

Johnson, Samuel. *A Dictionary of the English Language.* Ayer, 1980.

Katz, Jonathon Ned. *Gay/Lesbian Almanac.* Harper, 1983.

Lakoff, George, and Mark Johnson. *Metaphors We Live By.* University of Chicago Press, 1980.

Landau, Sidney I. "Sexual Intercourse in American College Dictionaries," *Verbatim* 1:1, 1974.

Landy, Eugene E. *The Underground Dictionary.* Simon & Schuster, 1971.

Legman, Gershon. *Rationale of the Dirty Joke.* Grove, 1968.

———, editor. *The Limerick.* Bell, 1964.

Longman/Guardian New Words, 1986.

Loth, David. *The Erotic in Literature.* Julian Messner, 1961.

Maledicta: The International Journal of Verbal Aggression, 1977–. Maledicta Press.

Marcus, Steven. *The Other Victorians.* Norton, 1985.

McConville, Brigid, and John Shearlaw. *The Slanguage of Sex.* Futura, 1985.

Miller, Casey, and Kate Swift. *Words and Women.* Doubleday, 1977.

Mills, Jane. *Womanwords.* Virago, 1991.

Moers, Ellen. *Literary Women.* Oxford University Press, 1976.

Montagu, Ashley. *The Anatomy of Swearing.* Macmillan, 1967.

Morris, Desmond. *The Human Zoo.* Dell, 1970.

Neaman, Judith, and Carole Silver. *A Dictionary of Euphemisms.* Unwin, 1983.

Okamato, David. "The Joy of Sex in Music," *CD Review,* February 1991.

Oxford Dictionary of English Etymology. Clarendon Press, 1969.

Oxford English Dictionary, with new supplements. Oxford University Press, 1933.

Paros, Lawrence. *The Erotic Tongue.* Madrona, 1984.

Partridge, Eric. *Dictionary of Historial Slang.* Penguin, 1972.

———. *Dictionary of Slang and Unconventional English.* Macmillan, 1985.

———. *Shakespeare's Bawdy.* Routledge & Kegan Paul, 1968.

———. *Slang Today and Yesterday.* Methuen, 1970.

Phythian, B. A. *A Concise Dictionary of English Slang.* Hodder & Stoughton, 1973.

Rainbird, Evelyn. *The Illustrated Manual of Sexual Aids.* Minotaur, 1973.

Random House Dictionary, Second Unabridged Edition. Random House, 1987.

Rawson, Hugh. *A Dictionary of Euphemisms and Other Doubletalk.* MacDonald, 1981.

———. *Wicked Words.* Crown, 1989.

Richter, Alan. *The Language of Sexuality.* McFarland, 1987.

Rodgers, Bruce. *Gaytalk.* Paragon, 1972.

Rossi, William A. *The Sex Life of the Foot and Shoe.* Ballantine, 1978.

Rosten, Leo. *The Joys of Yiddish.* McGraw, 1968.

Sagarin, Edward. *The Anatomy of Dirty Words.* Lyle Stuart, 1962.

Silverstein, Charles, and Edmund White. *The Joy of Gay Sex.* Simon & Schuster, 1978.

Simons, G. L. *A Place for Pleasure.* Harwood Smart, 1975.

The Slang of Venery. Privately published, 1916.

Spears, Richard. *Slang and Euphemism.* Jonathan David, 1991.

Spender, Dale. *Man Made Language.* Methuen, 1985.

Stallworthy, Jon, editor. *A Book of Love Poetry Poetry.* Oxford University Press, 1974.

Tabori, Paul. *The Humor and Technology of Sex.* Julian, 1969.

Tannahill, Reay. *Sex in History.* Stein & Day, 1982.

Thass-Thienemann, Theodore. *The Subconscious Language.* Washington Square Press, 1967.

Thorne, Tony. *Bloomsbury Dictionary of Contemporary Slang.* Bloomsbury, 1990.

Tulloch, Sara, editor. *The Oxford Dictionary of New Words.* Oxford University Press, 1991.

Walker, Barbara G. *The Woman's Dictionary of Symbols and Sacred Objects*. Harper & Row, 1988.

Webster's Ninth Collegiate Dictionary. Merriam-Webster, 1983.

Webster's Third New International Dictionary. Merriam-Webster, 1976.

Wedeck, Harry E. *Dictionary of Erotic Literature*. Citadel, 1962.

Wentworth, Harold, and Stuart Berg Flexner. *Dictionary of American Slang*. Crowell, 1960.

Whitworth, John, editor. *The Faber Book of Blue Verse*. Faber & Faber, 1990.

Wilson, Robert. *Playboy's Book of Forbidden Words*. Playboy Press, 1972.

Winokur, Jon, editor. *The Portable Curmudgeon*. New American Library, 1987.

Young, Wayland. *Eros Denied*. Corgi, 1968.